Social Work Law, Ethics & Social Policy

Sara Miller McCune founded SAGE Publishing in 1965 to support the dissemination of usable knowledge and educate a global community. SAGE publishes more than 1000 journals and over 800 new books each year, spanning a wide range of subject areas. Our growing selection of library products includes archives, data, case studies and video. SAGE remains majority owned by our founder and after her lifetime will become owned by a charitable trust that secures the company's continued independence.

Los Angeles | London | New Delhi | Singapore | Washington DC | Melbourne

Social Work Law, Ethics & Social Policy

Muna Sabbagh
Gill Korgaonkar

Los Angeles | London | New Delhi
Singapore | Washington DC | Melbourne

Los Angeles | London | New Delhi
Singapore | Washington DC | Melbourne

SAGE Publications Ltd
1 Oliver's Yard
55 City Road
London EC1Y 1SP

SAGE Publications Inc.
2455 Teller Road
Thousand Oaks, California 91320

SAGE Publications India Pvt Ltd
B 1/I 1 Mohan Cooperative Industrial Area
Mathura Road
New Delhi 110 044

SAGE Publications Asia-Pacific Pte Ltd
3 Church Street
#10-04 Samsung Hub
Singapore 049483

Editor: Kate Keers
Senior assistant editor: Catriona McMullin
Senior project editor: Chris Marke
Marketing manager: Camille Richmond
Cover design: Wendy Scott
Typeset by: C&M Digitals (P) Ltd, Chennai, India
Printed in the UK

Library of Congress Control Number: 2021940621

British Library Cataloguing in Publication data

A catalogue record for this book is available from the British Library

ISBN 978-1-5297-2383-0
ISBN 978-1-5297-2382-3 (pbk)

At SAGE we take sustainability seriously. Most of our products are printed in the UK using responsibly sourced papers and boards. When we print overseas we ensure sustainable papers are used as measured by the PREPS grading system. We undertake an annual audit to monitor our sustainability.

Contents

About the authors

Dr Muna Sabbagh holds a PhD from Kingston University, exploring the various approaches used in the UK youth justice system and the autonomy of the family in relation to young people who offend. She worked as a law lecturer at Kingston University and the University of Hertfordshire Law School lecturing in criminal law, tort law and English legal systems and methods. Muna has also published on youth justice and restorative justice in the criminal justice system. She currently lectures in law at the University of Hertfordshire to both undergraduate and postgraduate social work students.

Gill Korgaonkar has an LLB (University of London) and an LLM (London School of Economics). Gill is a qualified social worker. She taught law at the University of Hertfordshire to both undergraduate and postgraduate law and social work students.

About the contributor

We would like to thank Professor Brian Littlechild for his contribution to the following chapters: Chapter 5 – sole author of ethics section; Chapter 10 – sole author of ethics section; Chapter 15 – contributor to policy section (the last section on over-representation of Black and Minority Ethnic patients in the MHA detention statistics) and sole author of the ethics section; Chapter 20 – sole author of the ethics section.

Professor Brian Littlechild is Social Work Research Lead at Hertfordshire University. A registered social worker, he has worked with children, young people and their families, and people with mental health challenges for over 40 years. He has long experience of teaching students and qualified social workers on the application of ethics.

List of cases

A (Capacity: Social Media and Internet Use: Best Interests) [2019] EWCOP 2

A Local Authority v *M* [2018] EWHC 870 (Fam)

A Local Authority v *M & Ors* [2017] EWFC B66

A Local Authority v *R–B* [2019] EWCA Civ 1560

Adan v *Secretary of State for the Home Department* [1999] 1 AC 293

AG v *BMBC & Anor* [2016] EWCOP 37

Ali v *Virgin Active Limited* Case Number: 2206652/2017

AM v *SLAM & Sec of State for Health* [2013] UKUT 0365 (AAC)

AM v *Wirrall MBC* (2021)

AMM and others (conflict: humanitarian crisis: returnees; and FGM) Somalia CG [2011]

An NHS Trust and Child B (2014) EWHC 3486

Armes v *Nottinghamshire County Council* [2017] UKSC 60

Attorney-General v *Guardian Newspapers Ltd* (No 2) (1990) 1 AC 109

B (A Child) (Fact Finding) [2019] EWFC B46

B (A Child) (Post-Adoption Contact) [2019] EWCA Civ 29

B and B v *A County Council* [2006] EWCA Civ 1388

B & C (Children: Child Arrangements Order) [2018] EWFC B100

B-S (Children) [2013] EWCA Civ 1146

B (by her litigation friend, the Official Solicitor) v *A Local Authority* [2019] *EWCA Civ 913*, 2019 WL 02425771

B v *UK* [2000] 1 FLR 1

Baker v *CPS* [2009] EWHC 299

Banks v *Banks (Occupation Order: Mental Health)* [1999] 1 FLR 726

Bell v *Tavistock and Portman NHS Foundation Trust* [2020] EWHC 3274 (Admin)

Birmingham City Council v *D* [2016] EWCOP 8

Y (Children) [2014] EWCA

Yemshaw v *Hounslow LBC* [2011] UKSC 3

YL v *Birmingham City Council* [2007] UKHL 27 [2008] 1 AC 95

List of Legislature and Legal Documents

Acts of Parliament

Adoption Act 1949

Adoption Act 1958

Adoption Act 1976

Adoption and Children Act 1926

Adoption and Children Act 2002

Aliens Act 1905

Anti-social Behaviour, Crime and Policing Act 2014

Asylum and Immigration Appeals Act 1993

Care Act 2014

Carers (Recognition and Services) Act 1995

Childcare Act 2006

Childcare Act 2016

Child Care Act 1980

Child Support Act 1991

Children Act 1908

Children Act 1948

Children Act 1989

Children Act 2004

Children and Adoption Act 2006

Children and Families Act 2014

Children and Social Work Act 2017

Regulations

Care and Support (Eligibility Criteria) Regulations [2015] SI No 313

Care Planning and Fostering (Miscellaneous Amendments) (England) Regulations 2015

Care Planning, Placement and Case Review Regulations 2010

Children (Private Arrangements for Fostering) Regulations [2005]

Data Protection, Privacy and Electronic Communications (Amendments etc.) (EU Exit) Regulations 2019

EU General Data Protection Regulations (GDPR) 2017

Fostering Services (England) Regulations [2011]

Health and Social Care Act 2008 (Regulated Activities) (Amendment) Regulations 2015

Health Protection (Coronavirus, Restrictions) (England) Regulations 2020/350

Health Protection (Coronavirus Restrictions) (Wales) Regulations 2020/353

National Health Service (Amendments Relating to the Provision of Primary Care Services During a Pandemic etc.) Regulations 2020/351

Police Act 1997 (Criminal Records) (Amendment) Regulations 2020/359

Social Security (Coronavirus) (Further Measures) Regulations 2020/371

Social Workers Regulations 2018

Special guardianship: Statutory guidance for local authorities on the Special Guardianship Regulations 2005 (as amended by the Special Guardianship (Amendment) Regulations 2016)

Statutory Sick Pay (Coronavirus) (Suspension of Waiting Days and General Amendment) Regulations 2020/374

Young Carers (Needs Assessments) Regulations 2015

Court Rules

Children and Families Act 2014: Safer from Sexual Crime Practice Direction 12A – Care, Supervision and other Part 4 Proceedings: Guide to Case Management (GOV. UK)

The Court of Protection Rules 2017 No. 1035 (L. 16) Mental Capacity, England and Wales

The Criminal Procedure Rules 2015

The Family Procedure Rules 2012 (PD16A Part 6) (updated January 2017)

Judicial College Youth Court Bench Book (2017)

Practice Direction 14C: Reports by the Adoption Agency or Local Authority Part 14

Tribunal Judiciary Practice: Direction Statements and Reports in Mental Health Cases: Home Office Guidance (2004) (Home Office)

Codes of Practice

Equality Act 2010: *Codes of Practice* (Equality and Human Rights Commission)

Mental Capacity Act 2005: *Code of Practice* 2007

Mental Health Act 1983: *Code of Practice* 2015

Government Papers

Adoption: A New Approach: White Paper [2000] DoH Cm. 5017

Adoption: A Vision for Change (March 2016) (DfE)

Adult Safeguarding: Statement of Government Policy (2013) (DH)

Age Assessment policy (2019) (Home Office)

Care and Support Statutory Guidance (2020) (DHSC)

Children's Social Care: Getting the Best from Complaints: Statutory guidance for local authority children's services on representations and complaints procedures (September 2006) (DfE)

Children's Social Care Services in England: House of Commons Briefing Paper (March 2021)

Dilnot Commission on Funding of Care and Support (2011)

Fostering Services: National Minimum Standards (2011) (DfE)

Homelessness (Priority Need for Accommodation) (England) Order 2002

Independent Review of Children's Social Care in England (2021) DfE

Lammy Review: An independent review into the treatment of, and outcomes for, Black, Asian and Minority Ethnic individuals in the Criminal Justice System (2017)

Law Commission's Report on Reform of Adult Social Care (Law Com No. 326) (2011)

Lord Laming: *The Victoria Climbié Inquiry*, CM 5730

Ministry of Housing, Communities & Local Government Homelessness Code of Guidance (2018)

The Munro Review of Child Protection: Final Report: A child-centred system (2011) (DfE)

National Framework for NHS Continuing Healthcare and NHS-funded Nursing Care (2018) (DH)

Putting Children First: Delivering our Vision for Excellent Children's Social Care (2016) (DfE)

Reforming the Mental Health Act White Paper (January 2021) (DHSC)

Report of the Inquiry into Child Abuse in Cleveland (1987) (HMSO)

Working Together to Safeguard Children (2018) (DfE)

European Legislature

European Convention on Human Rights (ECHR)

UN Convention on the Rights of Persons with Disabilities (UNCRPD)

United Nations Convention on the Rights of the Child

Universal Declaration of Human Rights 1948

List of Abbreviations

AA	Adoption Agencies
AA	Attendance Allowance
ACA	*Adoption and Children Act 2002*
ACMD	Advisory Council on the Misuse of Drugs
ACPO	Association of Chief Police Officers
ACR	Adoption Contact Register
ACS	Adult Care Services
AMHP	Approved Mental Health Professionals
AO	Adoption Order
ASC	Adult Social Care Team
BAME	Black, Asian and Minority Ethnic
BASW	British Association of Social Workers
BGS	British Geriatric Society
CA	*Children Act 1989/2004*
CAF	Common Assessment Framework
CAFCASS	Children and Family Court Advisory and Support Service
CAMHS	Child and Adolescent Mental Health Service
CBPM	Cannabis-based Products for Medicinal Use
CCE	Children's Commissioner for England
CCG	Clinical Commissioning Groups
CCTV	Closed Circuit Television
CEO	Chief Executive Officer
CG	Children's Guardian
CHC	Continuing Healthcare
CiN	Children in Need
COP	Court of Protection
CPAG	Child Poverty Action Group
CPC	Child Protection Conference
CPD	Continuing Professional Development
CPR	Cardiopulmonary Resuscitation
CPS	Crown Prosecution Service
CQC	Care Quality Commission
CSDPA	*Chronically Sick and Disabled Persons Act 1970*
CSEW	Crime Survey for England and Wales
CTO	Community Treatment Order
CWIG	Child Welfare Inequalities Group

CYPA	*Children and Young Person's Act 1933*
DBS	Disclosure and Barring Service
DCMS	Department for Digital, Culture, Media & Sport
DfE	Department for Education
DHSS	Department of Health and Social Security
DLA	Disability Living Allowance
DoE	Department of Education
DoH	Department of Health
DoL	Deprivation of Liberty
DHP	Discretionary Housing Payments
DHSC	Department of Health and Social Care
DPA	*Data Protection Act 2018*
DPA	Deferred Payment Agreements
DWP	Department for Work and Pensions
ECHR	European Convention on Human Rights
ECtHR	European Court of Human Rights
EEA	European Economic Area
EPA	Enduring Power of Attorney
EPO	Emergency Protection Order
EqHRC	Equality and Human Rights Commission
ESA	Employment Support Allowance
EU	European Union
FDAC	Family, Drug and Alcohol Courts
FGM	Female Genital Mutilation
FGMPO	FGM Protection Order
FMU	Forced Marriage Unit
GDPR	General Data Protection Regulations
GP	General Practitioner
HB	Housing Benefit
HCPC	Health and Care Professions Council
HMCTS	HM Courts & Tribunals Service
HMRC	HM Revenue and Customs
HRA	*Human Rights Act 1998*
ICO	Interim Care Order
ICO	Information Commissioner's Office
IFS	Institute for Fiscal Studies
IFSW	International Federation of Social Workers
IIDB	Industrial Injuries Disablement Benefit
ILR	Indefinite Leave to Remain
IMCA	Independent Mental Capacity Advocates
IOPC	Independent Office for Police Conduct
ISA	Independent Safeguarding Authority
IT	Information Technology
JRF	Joseph Rowntree Foundation

JSA	Job Seeker's Allowance
LA	Local Authority
LAC	Looked After Child
LASPO	Legal Aid, Sentencing and Punishment of Offenders
LASSA	*Local Authority Social Services Act 1970*
LGBTQ+	Lesbian, Gay, Bisexual, Transgender, Queer (or sometimes questioning), and others
LGSCO	Local Government and Social Care Ombudsman
LPA	Lasting Power of Attorney
LPS	Liberty Protections Safeguards
MA	Maternity Allowance
MCA	*Mental Capacity Act 2005*
MDA	*Misuse of Drugs Act 1971*
MHA	*Mental Health Act 1983*
MHT	Mental Health Tribunal
MOJ	Ministry of Justice
MR	Mandatory Reconsideration
NASS	National Asylum Support Service
NHS	National Health Service
NLW	National Living Wage
NRM	National Referral Mechanism
NRPF	No Recourse to Public Funds
NSPCC	National Society for the Prevention of Cruelty to Children
ONS	Office for National Statistics
OPG	Office of the Public Guardian
OSPT	Official Solicitor and Public Trustee
PCF	Professional Capabilities Framework
PHE	Public Health England
PIP	Personal Independent Payment
PO	Placement Order
PR	Parental Responsibility
PSED	Public Sector Equality Duty
RJ	Restorative Justice
RJC	Restorative Justice Council
RPR	Relevant Person's Representative
SAB	Safeguarding Adults Board
SCA	Single Competent Authority
SCR	Serious Case Review
SCR	Social Circumstances Reports
SDP	Severe Disability Premium
SEC	Socioeconomic Classification
SG	Special Guardianship
SGO	Special Guardianship Order
SI	Statutory Instrument

SIF	Single Inspection Framework
SMB	Statutory Maternity Benefit
SMI	Support for Mortgage Interest
SOAD	Second Opinion Appointed Doctor
SRP	State Retirement Pension
SSMG	Sure Start Maternity Grant
SSP	Statutory Sick Pay
SWE	Social Work England
SWET	Social Work Evidence Template
TUC	Trades Union Congress
UC	Universal Credit
UK	United Kingdom
UN	United Nations
UNCRC	United Nations Convention on the Rights of the Child
UNCRPD	UN Convention on the Rights of Persons with Disabilities
UNHCR	United Nations High Commissioner for Refugees
WHO	World Health Organization
YJB	Youth Justice Board
YJS	Youth Justice System
YOP	Youth Offending Panels
YOT	Youth Offending Teams
YRO	Youth Rehabilitation Order

Introduction

The study of law, social policy and ethics forms a key part of the curriculum of academic social work courses. This core text provides a unique approach to the study by incorporating these three significant areas of the curriculum in social work courses that are directly relevant to social work practice. Social work is regulated by a legal and regulatory framework. Social Work England (SWE) is an independent protection body that sets out the professional, education and training standards for social workers. It assesses and approves all social work education and training courses, as well as investigating complaints about fitness for practice. The *Qualifying Education and Training Standards Guidance 2021* provides guidance on the standards that SWE uses to assess and approve social work education and training courses to ensure that students who successfully complete a social work course meet their professional standards and qualify for registration. While not setting out detailed course content requirements for educational providers to follow, they do approve and monitor 'how [education providers] have achieved the required outcomes, the policies, and processes [they] have in place, and how [they] implement, review and evaluate them'.

SWE 2020 Standard 4 Curriculum and assessment states:

> Social work courses are shaped by the needs and insights of academia, employers, practitioners and people with lived experience of social work. This is to ensure a continually evolving curriculum which is evidence-informed, matches the contemporary demands of the whole sector, is delivered by appropriately qualified and experienced professionals, and produces informed, capable, prepared and motivated graduates who deliver safe and effective services.
>
> (www.socialworkengland.org.uk/media/1642/socialworkengland_
> ed-training-standards-2020_final.pdf)

The British Association of Social Workers (BASW) 'is the UK's professional membership organisation for social work'. It is the 'independent voice of social work' and helps members 'achieve the highest professional standards'. Members are required to sign a *Code of Ethics* which underpins social work practice. Its *Professional Capabilities Framework* (PCF): *Readiness for Direct Practice* sets out the following capabilities which qualified social workers must demonstrate.

1. Professionalism, which requires identifying and behaving as a professional social worker, committed to professional development.
2. Values and Ethics, which requires social workers to conduct themselves and make decisions in accordance with the Code of Ethics.
3. Diversity and Equality, which requires social workers to recognise diversity and apply anti-discriminatory and anti-oppressive principles to social work practice.
4. Rights, Justice and Economic Wellbeing, which requires social workers to 'recognise and promote the fundamental principles of human rights, social justice and economic wellbeing enshrined in national and international laws, conventions and policies'.
5. Knowledge which includes the requirement to demonstrate 'an initial understanding of the legal and policy frameworks and guidance that inform and mandate social work practice'.
6. Critical Reflection and Analysis, which requires social workers to apply critical reflection and analysis to inform and provide a rationale for professional decision-making.

(www.basw.co.uk/system/files/resources/pcf-readiness.pdf)

This book provides readers with the key legal and ethical principles and social policy considerations that all social workers must be able to understand and apply, whatever their chosen area of practice. The unique approach of this book is that it:

- draws together the law, ethical considerations and social policy relevant to social work students at the end of each section;
- provides legal, ethical academic text and social policy within the chapters that are pertinent to the topic to help the reader identify the relevant issues within the topic;
- provides links to relevant material that saves the reader time accessing the information;
- helps the reader access authoritative texts that will help consolidate understanding of the topic and references documents that are relevant to future research assessments that are required in a social work degree.

The book is divided into five parts: the first four parts include a chapter specifically dedicated to policy and ethical considerations to help develop their relevance to social work practice and the law. The first section provides an overview of the relationship between law and social work, and examines the key underpinning principles that all social workers must know and be able to apply. It sets out the overarching legal framework involved with the protection of human rights, anti-discrimination law, and privacy and confidentiality. The law in this area has profound implications for everyone, and therefore it is vital to know and understand the practical implications of those rules and be able to identify any shortcomings in the protection they provide.

Understanding the way in which the legal system operates is crucial as social workers can expect to have regular involvement with the courts, particularly when working with children and families, older people, people with disabilities, youth justice and mental health. The *Coronavirus Act 2020* was enacted very quickly in response to the Covid-19 pandemic and provides an important example of how the law can be changed by Parliament in response to an urgent challenge. Understanding how the changes in the law impact on society generally and on certain groups, including social workers and service users, is clear to see, as are the important human rights considerations involved. BASW was among the professional organisations that opposed the government's original proposal for the Act to remain in force for two years without review, particularly because of the human rights implications involved. The government subsequently agreed that the Act would be reviewed every six months (the *Coronavirus Act 2020 and Social Work Practice – A Briefing*, BASW, April 2020). This highlights the relationship between law and social policy that impacts on social work practice.

In *Medway Council* v *M & T (By Her Children's Guardian)* [2015] EWFC B164, the judge criticised both the social work and legal teams about their lack of knowledge of the law. 'What is betrayed is the most shocking misunderstanding of the law by both social work and legal teams at Medway Council, and of the proper limitations of their exercise of power over this family, compounded by an ignorant or arrogant disregard for the advice and recommendations being provided by the Looked After Child (LAC) review process and the permanency panel.'

Social workers must be advocates for change where change is necessary to improve the lives of service users. The ethical and social policy considerations are also examined, and assessment exercises are included in all the chapters to help ensure that the relevant rules are understood and how that knowledge can be applied to practice. The book also encourages the reader to critically analyse the important requirements necessary for successful completion of course assessments and recognise that additional reading (as indicated) will be needed to achieve this. The need to keep up to date must never be ignored.

The second part examines the law, ethics and social policy considerations relevant to safeguarding children, which includes child protection, adoption and fostering, and youth justice. The Crime Survey for England and Wales (CSEW, March 2019) estimated that 'one in five adults aged 18 to 74 years experienced at least one form of child abuse, whether emotional abuse, physical abuse, sexual abuse, or witnessing domestic violence or abuse, before the age of 16 years (8.5 million people)'. This is a sobering statistic and requires not only an understanding of the legal rules, but of the ethical principles and social policy implications, as well as the potential consequences for victims. The link between poverty and child neglect is also stark (Chapters 10 and 20), as is the over-representation of Black, Asian and Minority Ethnic (BAME) children in the criminal justice system.

The third part examines the law, ethics and social policy considerations of adult social care, with particular emphasis on the *Care Act 2014*, mental capacity and mental health law. Examining how a society protects adults at risk of harm is just as important as how society protects children at risk, but has not always had the same high public profile. However, the incidence of elder abuse in the UK is no less worrying than child abuse. Research by Action on Elder Abuse (WHO, n.d.) found that 'nearly 10% of older people say that they are being abused, according to a nationwide poll which has called the situation "an epidemic of elder abuse across the UK"'. It is imperative that social workers (along with all other relevant health and social care professionals) understand and know how to respond appropriately to the victims of such abuse and advocate for change where this is necessary. Covid-19 has had a disproportionate impact on older people (see, for example, the British Geriatric Society (BGS): 'Advice to older people, families, friends and carers'), and on people from BAME communities (see Public Health England (PHE): Disparities in the risk of outcomes of Covid-19 (August 2020)), as well as people with underlying health conditions: 'We must guarantee the equal rights of people with disabilities to access healthcare and lifesaving procedures during the pandemic' UN Secretary-General António Guterres at the launch of Policy Brief on Persons with Disabilities and Covid-19 (May 2020). How society responds or should respond to this evidence reflects the value that society places on people's lives and has important ethical and social policy implications. Furthermore, the pandemic has also placed a spotlight on how adult social care is funded, and the response from government will have important consequences in this area.

The fourth part examines the legal, ethical and social policy considerations relating to domestic abuse, substance abuse, immigration and asylum law, and welfare and homelessness. This part is one of the unique aspects of this core text as it incorporates these issues alongside the conventional topics taught on social work programmes. These important welfare issues impact disproportionately on service users, and understanding and responding to the human rights and other important considerations which are involved is vital. For example, in social work practice the terms 'toxic trio' and 'multiple and complex needs' are used in relation to safeguarding both children and adults at risk of harm. The terms draw together issues of substance misuse, mental health problems and domestic abuse. Furthermore, alongside these problems, a service user may experience welfare and homeless issues. This means that for a social worker to be able to help a service user they need to be able to identify other issues impacting on their lives. Throughout the book there are thought boxes and exercises for the reader to interact with, as one of the many important aspects of social work practice is to ask questions in order to establish what support an individual needs.

The fifth and final part draws together the theoretical aspects of the book and helps prepare the student for the court experience. This part provides guidance on report writing and giving evidence in court, skills that all social workers must develop both during training and beyond. One of the specific skills required of a social worker is to correctly record and articulate the findings required to support a service user. This skill begins at the social work recruitment stage. Most higher education institutions require an applicant seeking entry on a social work course to undertake a written assessment. Writing skills are developed throughout the social work course and are significant when on placement and in practice. Many placement providers will want to ensure that the student has good writing skills as well as good spoken English. One reason for this is that social workers, at some point in their career, may be required to be a witness in court. The judge will expect that their record keeping and report writing skills meet the recognised professional standards as well as their being able to answer questions coherently. These skills will continue to be developed in practice with support sessions, often with the statutory authority's legal team (see Chapter 21).

Finally, understanding the law requires reading around the subject area. Reading peer-reviewed commentary helps to understand the implications of the legislation relevant to social work practice. Peer review is the process by which work is assessed by an expert in that area to ensure the validity, quality and originality of the work. This is important for social work students as they develop their knowledge and research important topics. Articles accessed and used for assignments must be of high quality; this is achieved through the peer review process. Reading the rationale for a court's decision also helps social workers understand how and why the courts reached their decisions and the impact of the decisions in practice.

We hope you enjoy this core text as much as the authors enjoy teaching law, ethics and social policy to social work students and qualified social workers.

Part 1

The Legal Context of Social Work, Ethics and Social Policy

1

An Introduction to the English and Welsh Legal Systems

Chapter Objectives

By the end of this chapter, the reader will be able to:

- have an overview of the English and Welsh legal systems;
- understand the law-making process, social policy and ethics in relation to social work practice;
- identify the legal sources and institutions that impact on social work practice;
- understand the significance of social work practice in relation to the statutory duties of a local authority, as well as accountability.

Introduction

Understanding the law is a necessary requirement for social workers because their duties and powers are derived from the law and must be applied by all frontline practitioners. The functions of the law include the governance and maintenance of social order and upholding individuals' rights, which is a significant component that underpins social work practice.

The following overview sets out the rules that underpin the English and Welsh legal system. It begins by discussing the relationship between law, ethics and social policy within our law-making system, followed by an introduction to the rule of law, the relationship between the constitution and the separation of powers. The sources of law are discussed with relevance to social work practice and the institutions that develop and apply the law.

Law and Ethics in Social Work Practice

Social workers help individuals, children and families, and ensure that people at risk of harm are safeguarded. They do this by following the relevant professional regulations and the legislative framework that applies to their practice. A social worker will need to make a professional judgement that will impact on an individual or family's life, but this must be made in accordance with the relevant legislative framework. However, a social worker's duty may conflict with their ethical values. Social work practice must balance the statutory duties placed on it and ensure best practice through empowerment and respect for the individual they are working with. An example of the conflict can be found when working with families, adults at risk of harm and maintaining confidentiality. Ethically, the social worker wants to encourage self-determination and respect a service user's right to confidentiality unless this right conflicts with the law and the need to safeguard the service user and others (see Chapter 4).

Social workers must also comply with the additional regulations that support their decision-making process, which can also hold the social worker to account. For example, the *Children and Social Work Act 2017* made provisions for many aspects of safeguarding children (e.g. providing relationship and sex education in schools), but it also provided for the establishment of a new regulatory body for social workers in England. Social Work England (SWE) became the regulatory body for social workers in December 2019. The ethos behind this change is to raise the professional standards specific to social care and the education of social workers. SWE regulations cover the delivery of social work degrees from admission through to assessment and pastoral care for students. It ensures that degrees are academically rigorous and high standards are maintained. Furthermore, it also ensures that social work students undertake placements that expose them to social work practice. Placements introduce the student to the roles and responsibilities of practice in social care. They also introduce the student to the application of the law they have learnt – for example, a placement in children's services will give students insight into the practical implications of important provisions in the *Children Act 1989*.

Social Policy and the Legislative Procedure

Another factor to understand as a social worker is the relevance of policy to law making. New government proposals for law reform are sometimes preceded by a Green Paper, which sets out for discussion proposals that are still at a formative stage. It may then be followed by a White Paper which sets out the government's proposals for legislative change and may invite comments from particular interest groups. Following on from the consultations above, a Bill (a draft of a proposed new law) will begin its journey through Parliament, starting either in the House of Commons (which is usual) or in the House of Lords. The Bill must be scrutinised by members of both Houses of Parliament and amendments will be made if necessary. This process allows for scrutiny of the Bill from members with varying knowledge and expertise. Before a Bill is proposed, the rationale behind it may have arisen as a result of a pressure group highlighting a particular problem (e.g. pressure from Shelter, a housing charity, led to the *Housing Act 1977*) or a Commission (e.g. the Law Commission) identifying the need for law reform. The impact of policy on legislation is important for social workers to understand because of the implications for practice. For example, following the UK's exit from the European Union, the UK made changes to immigration rules that impact on social workers and their service users' rights (see Chapter 18).

There are three different types of Bills:

1. Public Bills are the most common and concern matters affecting the public; they are put forward by a government minister. A recent example of a Public Bill affecting the practice of health and social care is the Mental Capacity (Amendment) Bill 2018, which became an Act of Parliament in 2019. This is a very significant piece of legislation for health and social care workers as it amends the current safeguards in place for individuals deprived of their liberty (Chapter 14).
2. Private Members' Bills are brought before Parliament either by a member of the House of Commons or by a member of the House of Lords. As with Public Bills, these concern matters affecting the public. Very few become an Act of Parliament, usually because of lack of government support. An example of a successful Private Members Bill is the Health and Social Care (Safety and Quality) Bill 2014 which became the *Health and Social Care (Safety and Quality) Act 2015*; it included provision for information sharing between agencies about a person's direct care needs (see: www.legislation.gov.uk/ukpga/2015/28). An example of an unsuccessful Bill is the Young Offenders (Parental Responsibility) Bill 2013–14. This Bill aimed to make the parents of young offenders legally responsible for their children's actions. It was subsequently withdrawn because of lack of support.
3. A Private Bill is bought before Parliament, usually by an organisation – for example, a local authority or a private company. It is designed to affect certain groups or individuals who can petition the Bill at certain stages throughout the Bill's passage. Canterbury City Council were successful in the passage of their Bill regulating street traders in Canterbury City Centre despite the petition made against the Bill while it went through the scrutiny process.

Once a Bill has passed though the Houses of Parliament, it must receive royal assent before it becomes law (see the passage of a Bill through Parliament at: www.parliament. uk/about/how/laws/passage-bill/).

Rule of Law

The rule of law is a fundamental principle of the UK constitution. The UK has an unwritten constitution, which means that the principles and rules that determine the governance of the country are found in legal documents such as legislation and constitutional conventions (that is, informal and uncodified procedural agreements followed by the institutions of the state). The concept of the rule of law is a broad one and has been discussed by many legal theorists. The following proposition of the rule of law was provided by the nineteenth-century legal theorist and philosopher, Albert V. Dicey (1885):

- That citizens are subject to clearly defined rules determined by the state (i.e. Parliament, which is the supreme law-making body), rather than arbitrary or discretionary rules made as a result of personal whims. For example, government institutions, such as local authorities, the police and the NHS are regulated by laws made in Parliament and they must follow that law when carrying out the duties imposed on them.
- Every citizen of the state is equal under the law. This means that state institutions and people working in them are not above the law and a citizen can get redress if their rights are infringed.
- The unwritten constitution of the UK has developed from rules developed by the courts and by Parliament in contrast to rights laid down in a written constitution, which many countries have – for example, the USA.

It is important to understand the underpinning principles embodied in the rule of law when exploring the English legal system as social workers must comply with the statutory duties imposed on them and not make decisions based on their own views about what they think is right for the individual they are working with.

A further concept that protects the citizen from abuse of power by people in authority is that of the separation of powers.

Separation of Powers

The concept of the doctrine of separation of powers was initially considered in the work of the English philosopher Locke (1632–1704), followed by the French philosopher Montesquieu (1689–1755) (Kelly, 2020). Locke argued that a true government should have three distinct branches within it, each with separate powers, to protect against the abuse of power. These are: 1) the legislature, 2) the executive and 3) the judiciary.

The legislature is the UK Parliament, which is the supreme law-making body in the UK. All Acts of Parliament are made or repealed by the UK Parliament. However, within the UK's law-making system it is also necessary to consider the implications of devolution, which resulted in the establishment of separate Parliaments in Scotland,

Wales and Northern Ireland; this is discussed further in the chapter. There are also secondary law-making powers which give government ministers power to make 'secondary legislation' (see below) and local authorities can make byelaws.

The executive is the government of the day such as the prime minister, government ministers and the Crown. It also includes government bodies such as the police and local government. Both the constitution and the rule of law requires decisions made by the executive on behalf of the electorate to be based on the law and not made arbitrarily.

Finally, the role of the judiciary ensures that the law is interpreted and dispensed fairly in legal disputes. The judiciary sits in the courts and tribunals in England and Wales, the hierarchy of which is discussed below. The Supreme Court is the highest court in the UK and its ethos is based on transparency and that it is impervious to political influence. For example, judicial review, whereby a court can review the lawfulness of a decision by a public body (the executive and legislature) makes the separation of power between the judiciary and the other two bodies so distinct. See *R (on the application of Miller) (Appellant)* v *The Prime Minister (Respondent) and Cherry and others (Respondents)* v *Advocate General for Scotland (Appellant) (Scotland)* [2019] UKSC 41 where the Supreme Court held that the prime minister's advice to the Queen to suspend Parliament was unlawful.

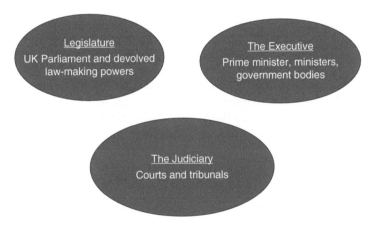

Figure 1.1   The separation of powers

Sources of Law in England and Wales

Having identified how law is introduced and scrutinised by Parliament, it is necessary to gain an understanding of the different sources of law in the UK. This knowledge helps to ensure that the important decisions made by social workers when safeguarding children and adults at risk of harm are supported by the relevant legislation, common law rules and codes of practice.

Statute Law

Statute law is legislation created by Parliament which scrutinises all proposed legislation before it becomes part of UK law. The parliamentary process highlights the principle that Parliament is the supreme law maker for the UK. However, before the UK left the European Union, the UK had to comply with any relevant law made by the EU – for example, on consumer protection and workers' rights.

Legislation as derived from Parliament is divided into the following categories:

> *Primary legislation* is an Act of Parliament that has passed through the legislative process outlined above. It can make and amend existing law. For example, the *Mental Health Act 2007* amended three Acts of Parliament, as the Explanatory Notes to the Act states:

>> The main purpose of the 2007 Act is to amend the 1983 Act. It is also being used to introduce 'deprivation of liberty safeguards' through amending the Mental Capacity Act 2005 (MCA); and to extend the rights of victims by amending the Domestic Violence, Crime and Victims Act 2004.

> *Secondary legislation* (also called delegated legislation) is law created by ministers who have been authorised under an Act of Parliament to do so. It enables greater detail to be applied to the Act of Parliament and amendments can be made to existing legislation. The Social Workers Regulations 2018 No. 893 provides an important example. The Explanatory Memorandum states:

>> Part 2 of the Children and Social Work Act 2017 establishes Social Work England as the new regulator of social workers in England, taking over from the Health and Care Professions Council (HCPC). This instrument supports the implementation of Social Work England by setting out the detail of the new regulatory framework.

These provisions are discussed below.

Another significant example relating to social work practice is section 10 of the *Human Rights Act 1998* which provides for a minister to amend primary legislation if it is found to be incompatible with the rights provided under the European Convention of Human Rights (ECHR).

It is important that social workers understand and keep up to date with primary and secondary legislation that informs their practice. Acts of Parliament can be difficult to understand; to help understand them, schedules and explanatory notes are now included within Acts of Parliament. Furthermore, some Acts have approved Codes of Practice or statutory guidelines. These resources help to understand the wording found in the legislation. For example, the *Mental Health Act 1983* has alongside it a Code of Practice that provides greater detail on how the provisions found in the Act should be applied. Although these Codes of Practice are not law, they must be followed by social workers in their practice.

Common Law

Common law derives from decisions of the judges dating as far back as 1066. Historically, it has developed from the customs that existed in different regions of England and Wales. This is also known as case law, or 'judge-made law'. This means that part of the law has been, and still is, developed by the decisions made by judges on a case-by-case basis. An example can be found in the decision in *Re A (conjoined twins)* [2001] 2 WLR 480 where the court was asked to determine whether it was lawful for doctors to separate conjoined twins without parental consent, even though they knew that surgery would result in the death of one of the twins. The court held that it was permissible in this case as the motive was to save the life of the stronger twin. If an individual wants to bring a claim against another person, or the state wants to prosecute an individual, the lawyers involved in the case will know the relevant case law with similar facts. These decisions are just as significant to our law as an Act of Parliament and the two work together, but the common law can be overridden by an Act of Parliament because Parliament is the supreme law-making body.

Judicial Precedent

Judicial precedent means that a decision of a higher court will be binding on a lower court. Not only do judges check to see if the case they are trying has similar facts to another, but lawyers will be familiar with the decisions and will prepare their arguments based on the facts of the previous case and how the law was applied. This helps them advise their client as to the likely outcome of their case.

An example of the use of precedent in a case which has important implications for social work practice can be seen in *Cheshire West and Chester Council* v *P* [2014] UKSC 19 [2014] MHLO 16 (see Chapter 14), which established the 'acid test' used for determining whether a person who lacks capacity has been deprived of their liberty. It is an example of how important judicial precedents are in the development of UK law and in interpreting the words used in Acts of Parliament.

European Union Law

The European Union (EU) began as a response to maintaining peace following the Second World War. The aim was to ensure that the countries in Europe had a common objective to prevent future wars between them, and to increase economic prosperity and remove trade barriers. Member states that have ratified the various EU treaties are bound to follow the laws that come from the EU. Following the UK's withdrawal from the EU in December 2020, the UK has retained in national law some of the law which came from the EU law; this is known as 'retained EU legislation' (see: www.legislation.gov.uk/eu-legislation-and-uk-law).

There is a clear distinction between EU law and the European Convention on Human Rights (ECHR) in that decisions made by the European Court of Justice involving the application and interpretation of EU law were binding on UK law. UK courts do not, however, always have to follow the decisions of the European Court of Human Rights 'particularly if they consider that the Court has not sufficiently appreciated or accommodated particular aspects of our domestic constitutional position' (The Supreme Court and Europe, see: www.supremecourt.uk/about/the-supreme-court-and-europe.html).

European Convention on Human Rights (ECHR)

The European Convention of Human Rights was drawn up following the horrors of the Second World War and the need to protect fundamental human rights and freedoms (see Chapter 2). Since the implementation of the *Human Rights Act 1998*, an individual's rights under the Convention are directly enforceable in the UK courts. There has been discussion about whether, following withdrawal from the EU, the UK should also withdraw from the ECHR and whether the UK should create its own Bill of Rights (see: https://commonslibrary.parliament.uk/how-might-brexit-affect-human-rights-in-the-uk/).

Devolution

Devolution in the UK means the decentralisation of governmental power by the transfer of some of the powers from Westminster to the devolved parliaments and local governments. The reason for this transfer of power is to ensure that the needs of different geographical areas are met by their own authorities which have a greater understanding of those needs than the government in Westminster. It is important for social workers studying the law to understand the concept of devolution as it impacts on social work practice in relation to the different legislative-making bodies.

Following referenda in the late 1990s, Parliament passed legislation creating the Scottish Parliament, the National Assembly for Wales and the Northern Ireland Assembly. To ensure the administration of devolved powers, extra statutory arrangements are provided. For example, even though Parliament remains supreme and may make decisions regarding devolved law, these decisions require the consent of the devolved legislature.

Health and social care are one of the main powers devolved to Scotland, Wales and Northern Ireland. For example, the Welsh equivalent of the *Care Act 2014*, which makes provision for the care of adults at risk and their carers is contained in the *Social Services and Well-being (Wales) Act 2014*. The latter Act has broader provisions as it also includes children's services (England has two separate Acts, the *Children Act 1989* and the *Care Act 2014*). The Scottish Parliament has greater legislative powers when enacting primary legislation, but any new laws passed must not conflict with those laws that the Westminster Parliament only can make.

The Northern Ireland Assembly holds the same legislative powers as Scotland in that they are still bound by reservations from Westminster when making primary legislation. Debate surrounding the devolution of powers to regions within England continues in that, of the four nations that make up the UK, three have their own significant legislative-making powers unlike England, which does not. However, there has also been some devolution at a more local level – for example, between the Treasury and Greater Manchester, which allowed the councils and NHS in Greater Manchester to have control of the region's £6 billion health and social care budget (The King's Fund, 2015).

Civil and Criminal Law

The difference between civil and criminal law is that the former concerns legal relationships between individual citizens, companies and public bodies, and the latter between the state and an individual or company. However, private prosecutions can be brought by individuals, as in the case involving the murder of Stephen Lawrence (*R v Dobson* [2011] EWCA Crim 1255).

The table below sets out some of the key differences between the two.

Civil law	Criminal law
Heard in county court and high court.	Heard in the magistrates' and Crown Court.
Individuals/companies/organisations bring the dispute to court.	The state brings the case to court in the name of the Crown.
Remedies available include compensation, injunctions and orders.	Sanctions include imprisonment and community sentences.
The standard of proof is on the balance of probabilities.	The standard of proof is beyond reasonable doubt.

Figure 1.2   Civil and criminal law comparison

Public and Private Law

The general principle is that public law administers the relationship between the person and the state, whereas private law administers the relationship between individuals. The following are public bodies listed in the *Human Rights Act 1998*:

- government departments;
- courts and tribunals;
- local authorities;
- police, prison and immigration officers;

- schools (or in Scotland, education authorities) if publicly funded;
- ombudsmen;
- public prosecutors;
- NHS trusts, health boards and hospitals.

These also include other organisations that have been set up by the law – for example, the General Medical Council and SWE.

Although private law regulates the relationship between individuals, in family law cases there can be an overlap between public and private law where there are concerns about the welfare of a child. For example, an application for a child arrangement order (a private law order) can result in the court making an order that requires the local authority to investigate safety concerns about the child. This is explored further in Chapters 6 and 7.

Courts and Tribunals

The legal institutions of the UK are made up of courts and tribunals. Both are formal processes for administering the law. Judges in the courts interpret the law and determine its effect. The tribunal process is more informal but is adjudicated by a specialist in the area being contested. For example, a Mental Health Tribunal is made up of a judge or legally qualified chairperson, a medical representative and a lay person. One of their functions is to hear applications for discharge from detention by the patient or their nearest relative (Chapters 13 and 22).

The hierarchy of the court system is significant (see the discussion above about judicial precedent). This means that the higher courts' decisions set the precedent and must be followed by the lower courts and tribunals. For example, the Supreme Court is the highest court of appeal for civil cases in the UK and for criminal cases in England and Wales. Court of Appeal decisions that are not appealed to the Supreme Court can also set precedents for the high courts and other lower courts.

On the next page is a diagram that shows the hierarchy of the court system and where tribunals sit in that system.

The legal system in the UK is based on an adversarial system. This means that legal representatives for each party in the court argue the points of law that favour their client. The judge in the proceedings is there to ensure that the law is correctly interpreted, ensure fairness throughout the proceedings and provide a judgment. The adversarial system in the UK contrasts with other European countries which use an inquisitorial system. The judge in an inquisitorial system collates the evidence for each party from the relevant agencies and from that evidence makes a judgment. Discussion has taken place over the last eight years about whether the family courts in the UK should adopt a more inquisitorial system. This is because the formality of the adversarial system can heighten the existing conflict between the parties, and affect parents and children emotionally and physically.

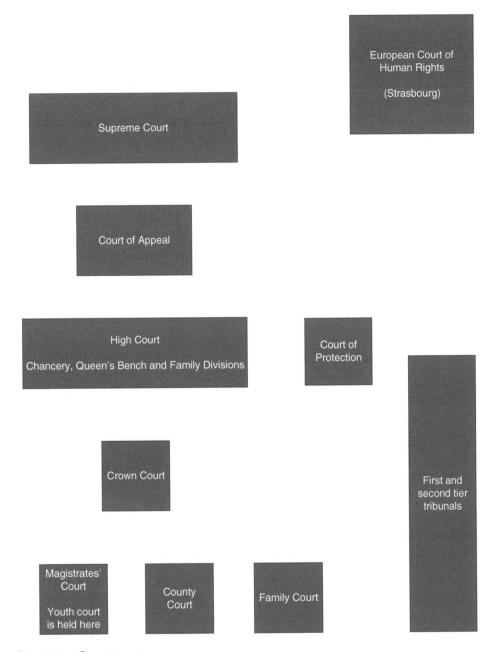

Figure 1.3   Court structure

Legal Advocates and Officials in the Courts

Understanding who the parties are in a court room can help social workers prepare to act as a witness in court proceedings. Chapters 21 and 22 develop this understanding further.

Judges

Unlike politicians, judges are unelected. Both solicitors and barristers can be appointed judges. Judges are appointed by the Judicial Appointments Commission, which selects candidates for judicial office based on their experience and their worthiness. As has already been established above, judges decide legal cases or, if the trial involves a jury, they control the proceedings and interpret the law to ensure that the jury reaches a decision using the correct processes. They also determine sentence in a criminal trial where the jury has found the defendant guilty.

Barristers

Barristers are legal advocates who specialise in a specific area of law and are experienced in representing people in the courts. They take their instructions from a solicitor, not directly from their client. In pleading the case for their client, they put legal arguments to the judges, magistrates and juries, and examine and cross-examine witnesses. Only barristers or qualified solicitor advocates may represent clients in the higher courts. Barristers are highly trained courtroom advocates and deal with the most serious and high-profile court cases.

Solicitors

Solicitors are generally the first point of contact for an individual seeking legal advice. They can specialise in a certain area of law, but generally work in many different areas of law or in law firms that offer advice in many areas. As the first point of contact, the solicitor will provide legal advice for their client and find a barrister to advocate for them in court should they need one. Some solicitors will represent their clients in the lower courts and those who specialise in a specific area of law can advocate in the higher courts.

Clerks in magistrates' courts

Clerks, who are qualified barristers or solicitors, are required in magistrates' courts to give legal advice to the magistrates, who are not (usually) legally qualified.

Ushers

Ushers carry out an important role in the courtroom as they ensure that the court process runs smoothly. Their duties are varied and include making sure that the parties involved in the case are present and well prepared. They prepare the court lists, call the witnesses into court and administer the oaths.

Local Authority Statutory Duty

Local authorities in England and Wales are bound by the duties set out in the relevant legislation (e.g. the *Children Act 1989* and *Care Act 2014*). This means that social workers, as employees of a local authority, are bound by legislation to a greater degree than a lay person because they provide a service to the public. This concept of public bodies being bound by specific legislation maintains the doctrine of the rule of law, separation of powers and devolution discussed above. Local authorities have an obligation to make decisions in accordance with the statutory duty imposed on them by Acts of Parliament. For example, the Seebohm Committee was set up to 'review the organisation and responsibilities of the social services functions of local authorities'. The recommendations in their report (published in 1969) resulted in the *Local Authority Social Services Act 1970* (LASSA) which is 'An Act to make further provision with respect to the organisation, management and administration of local authority social services'.

The above introductory text means that the Act provides a legal framework for the practice of social work and is amended when necessary to ensure that any new statutory duties which are provided for in subsequent legislation are incorporated into the LASSA. These Acts are discussed in subsequent chapters.

Judicial Review

The process of judicial review has very important implications for social work practice and needs to be understood because of the impact it can have on local authorities and their decision-making processes. Incorrect decisions can potentially have serious consequences for service users. Public bodies are obliged to carry out their functions in accordance with the law. Decisions made in circumstances where correct procedures have not been followed can be reviewed by a judge in the High Court. The court concerns itself with the legality of the decision; it does not change the decision. This means that if it is found that the public body made a mistake in their decision-making process, the courts will quash or nullify the decision and ask the public body to go through the process again following the proper procedure.

The procedure for asking the court to review a decision of a public body begins with the claimant seeking permission to bring a claim for judicial review. This is an important starting point as there may already be an alternative remedy available. For example, a remedy may be specifically provided for within the Act of Parliament. There is also recourse to a remedy through the local authority's complaints process, through the ombudsman service or the appeal process. Furthermore, there is pre-action protocol that encourages the claimant to seek alternative dispute resolution. This is because taking a claim to court is expensive and it must be seen that the parties have tried to come to an agreement without unnecessarily using the court's time and taxpayers' money.

An example of the importance of the judicial review process can be seen in the following case of *R (P, W, F, and G) v Essex County Council* [2004] EWHC 2027 (Admin) where the court stressed the following:

> that the court's function in this type of dispute was essentially one of review of the local authority's decision rather than of primary decision making. It was not the function of the court itself to come to a decision on the merits. The court

was not there to exercise a 'best interests' or 'welfare' jurisdiction and did not exist to monitor and regulate the performance of the public authorities. The Administrative Court was there solely to adjudicate upon specific challenges to discrete decisions.

The number of judicial review cases has increased since the process was made more accessible in the 1980s. However, many of the cases have been filtered through to tribunals. Remedies include a quashing order, which means that the decision is defective; a mandatory order, which means that the public body is made to carry out its duty; and finally an injunction, which is an order to make or stop a person/body doing something.

Inherent Jurisdiction of the Courts

Another term that social workers will encounter is that of the inherent jurisdiction of the courts. This is an important concept as it provides for higher courts (from the High Court and above) to deal with cases that cannot be resolved through statute or common law. Importantly, the jurisdiction allows the courts to protect vulnerable adults and children. An example can be found in wardship, whereby the court has a duty to protect a child who is at risk or has been removed from their family (see Chapters 6 and 12 for examples).

Complaints Procedures

If there is a complaint by an individual who believes that the public body has acted unlawfully, using the courts to obtain justice is an expensive way of resolving the issue for both parties and the taxpayer. Tribunals are an alternative to the courts and are less expensive and more informal than the courts. Local complaints processes are also important. Local authorities must have a complaints procedure and complaints should first be made to the local authority concerned to allow them to resolve the complaint. These are rigorous processes that the statutory body is obliged to provide and follow – for example, the complaint would initially be directed to the relevant department, which is required to respond to the complainant within a set time. If it is found that the complaint needs further investigation, the complainant should be notified of the time this will take. If it is not resolved, the complaint may go to an independent panel and if it is still not resolved at this stage, the complainant can complain to the Local Government and Social Care Ombudsman (LGSCO). The LGSCO investigates complaints by individuals personally affected by decisions made by adult and children's social care services. If the complaint is upheld, the LGSCO can award a remedy, including an apology and a payment if there is quantifiable financial loss (see: *Guidance on Good Practice: Remedies* (LGSCO, 2021)). This proce-dure also applies to non-statutory organisations such as charities where complaints should first go to the organisation before it is taken to the Charities Commission (which regulates charities in England and Wales).

Accountability

The legislative framework and regulatory bodies support the social worker in practice and hold them to account for the decisions they make. For example, The Social Workers Regulations 2018 provide detail to Part 2 of the *Children and Social Work Act 2017*. As discussed above, these regulations are statutory instruments and their purpose is to provide more detail to the Act of Parliament to ensure that the law is understood. Part 5 of the regulations provides for issues around discipline and fitness to practise and is a good example of how social workers can be held to account if their practice does not comply with the requisite standards. The link to the regulations is provided below. All social workers should be familiar with the regulations and understand how they relate to practice (see also: www.socialworkengland.org.uk).

A further example of accountability in social work practice can be found in section 75 agreements that involve inter-agency working. These agreements are made under s.75 of the *National Health Service Act 2006* between a local authority and a clinical commissioning group. Clinical Commissioning Groups (CCG) were created in the *Health and Social Care Act* in 2012. They are statutory NHS bodies with responsibilities for the commissioning of healthcare services in their area. A s.75 agreement allows local authorities and CGCs to pool resources in relation to health-related functions (see: Risk Sharing/s.75 agreement at: england.nhs.uk, which provides support materials on risk sharing).

Finally, in relation to accountability, secondment within social work is encouraged as part of continuing professional development (CPD) and highlights the importance of accountability when working in different departments and for different employers. The ethics and values surrounding accountability are discussed further in Chapter 5.

Chapter Summary

This chapter has:

- provided an overview of the English and Welsh legal systems and highlighted its significance for social work practice;
- explained the principles underpinning the UK constitution and why this is relevant for social work;
- identified the sources of the law and the institutions that impact on social work practice;
- discussed the statutory duties of a local authority and explained the importance of accountability when making decisions that impact on service users.

Exercises

1. What is judicial precedent and statute?
2. What is the relevance of judicial precedent in relation to the hierarchy of the court system?
3. What is a tribunal and how does it differ from a court?
4. What is a judicial review?

Answers can be found in the Appendix.

Further Reading

GOV.UK, Devolution of powers to Scotland, Wales and Northern Ireland:
www.gov.uk/guidance/devolution-of-powers-to-scotland-wales-and-northern-ireland
Jolly, A. (2018) No recourse to social work? Statutory neglect, social exclusion and undocumented migrant families in the UK. *Social Inclusion*, 6(3).
The Judicial System of England and Wales: A Visitor's Guide:
www.judiciary.uk/wp-content/uploads/2016/05/international-visitors-guide-10a.pdf
Judiciary for England and Wales, *The Administrative Court Judicial Review Guide 2019*: https://assets.publishing.service.gov.uk/government/uploads/system/uploads/attachment_data/file/825753/HMCTS_Admin_Court_JRG_2019_WEB.PDF
Mental Capacity (Amendment) Act 2019 (passage and debate): https://services.parliament.uk/Bills/2017-19/mentalcapacityamendment/stages.html
Seebohm Report: https://api.parliament.uk/historic-hansard/lords/1969/jan/29/social-services-the-seebohm-report
The Social Workers Regulations 2018: www.socialworkengland.org.uk/media/1502/social workers-regulations-2018.pdf

2

Human Rights

Introduction

Protection of individuals' human rights in the UK can be seen in national and international legislation that has developed since the Magna Carta which was signed in 1215 and guaranteed citizens' important liberties. Another important milestone in the history of human rights protection was the *Habeas Corpus Act 1679*, which is still in force today and gives protection against unlawful imprisonment; it was used successfully in the courts in 1771 to challenge the legality of slavery – *Somerset* v *Stewart* (1772) 98 ER 499. The expansion of national human rights legislation had its inception in the European Convention of Human Rights (ECHR) in 1950. This agreement between the member states of the European Council on Human Rights drew on the Universal Declaration of Human Rights 1948 which set out for the first time the fundamental human rights to be universally protected following the atrocities of the Second World War. The ECHR protects the basic rights and freedoms of the citizens of the 47 member states who are signatories to the treaty. It gives citizens, who claim that their rights have been infringed, the right to claim redress in the courts. The *Human Rights Act 1998* (HRA) incorporated the rights set out in the ECHR into UK law. It took 48 years for the UK to implement national legislation as it was assumed that the UK already had legislation in place to protect its citizens' rights (Hoffman and Rowe, 2003). As a result of the HRA, all proposed new legislation must have regard for and be interpreted in accordance with Convention rights.

Human Rights and Ethics in Social Work Practice

It is essential that social workers recognise and understand the legislation underpinning human rights law in the UK and ensure that it is upheld throughout social work practice. Not only is it important to know the law on human rights, but also to understand the policy decisions that developed the principles used both legally and ethically. *Social Work and Human Rights: A Practice Guide* (Harms-Smith et al., 2019) highlights the relationship between social work practice that is a social justice and human rights profession, and one that requires a holistic human rights approach to it.

An example of how human rights law and ethics needs to be balanced in practice can be seen in the human rights assessments that practitioners carry out for the purpose of determining the local authority's responsibilities to people who have no recourse to public funds (NRPF). If a person is refused welfare support because of their immigration status (see Chapters 18 and 19), it may be necessary to carry out a human rights assessment to ensure that their human rights are not being breached.

Social workers will be in situations where they may need to advocate for the rights of the individual while applying the law and maintaining the code of ethics that guides their practice. BASW released a statement of guidance for social workers with the aim of informing government policy (BASW, 2020a).

Modern-day slavery also highlights the ethical issues relevant to social work practice. The Anti-Slavery Day in 2019 led to a call for social workers to speak out against exploitation. See the commentary from The Social Work with Adults Blog about the Anti-Slavery Day on GOV.UK on the significance of social workers being aware of the impact of the exploitation and the need for education on the issue. See, too, the BASW *Code of Ethics* (Chapter 5). Social workers need to understand that the abuse and trauma that victims have suffered may make them reluctant to disclose their situation because of fear of possible reprisals. They should also use their knowledge of the law and ethics to offer appropriate support.

Human Rights and Social Policy Considerations

There has been speculation that the *Human Rights Act 1998* will be repealed and replaced with new legislation providing for the rights of individuals (Home and Maer, 2010). This speculation has increased since Britain's departure from the European Union, although signatories to the ECHR do not have to be members of the EU – for example, Norway and Switzerland. In 2020, the government called for a review of the *Human Rights Act 1998* to ensure that the rights of citizens are still being met after 20 years of the Act being in force (*Independent Human Rights Act Review*, 2020a: GOV.UK).

The review has two key themes in the terms of reference:

- the relationship between domestic courts and the European Court of Human Rights (ECtHR);
- the impact of the HRA on the relationship between the judiciary, the executive and the legislature.

The review will consider reforms in relation to the domestic courts 'taking account' of ECtHR decisions and whether there are risks of the courts being drawn into policy matters that are the responsibility of the executive (Chapter 1; see: www.gov.uk/guidance/independent-human-rights-act-review).

If the HRA is repealed, it may have important implications for the health and social care sector as human rights law underpins practice in all the health and social care professions.

Public Bodies' Duties under the *Human Rights Act 1998*

Public bodies cannot contravene the *Human Rights Act* by making decisions or acting in ways that adversely impact on a citizen's rights or freedoms. This obligation is found in s.6 of the HRA. This means that if a claim for breach of a person's right is brought before the courts, it must first be established whether the party alleged to be contravening the right is a public body. Section 6 lists what a public body is but does not define it. As a result, some private organisations or bodies can be construed by the courts as constituting a public body for the purposes of the HRA where they are found to be carrying out a public function (s. 6(3)). This is important for social workers as their practice brings them into contact with many private organisations that may be deemed a public body because they are carrying out a public function. An example can be seen in the case of *YL* v *Birmingham City Council* [2007] UKHL 27, [2008] 1 AC 95.

YL v *Birmingham City Council* [2007] UKHL 27, [2008] 1 AC 95

Y, who suffered from dementia, was a resident of a care home owned by a private company. Her placement had been arranged and part of her fees paid by the local authority in accordance with s.21 of the *National Assistance Act 1948*. A top-up fee was paid by Y's family and the nursing element of her care was funded by the NHS (see Chapter 1). Following allegations about the conduct of Y's family during their visits, a decision was taken by the home to transfer Y to a different home. Y claimed that her rights under Article 8 of the European Convention of Human Rights (see below) were infringed. The courts therefore had to determine whether the private care home was carrying out a public function under s.6 of the *Human Rights Act 1998*.

(Continued)

> The court held that the private organisation was not carrying out a public function in this case:
>
> > I am of the view that the provision of care and accommodation by Southern Cross to Mrs YL, even though it was arranged, and is being paid for, by Birmingham pursuant to ss.21–26 of the 1948 Act, does not constitute a 'function of a public nature' within s.6(3). (Lord Neuberger, p. 170)
>
> Furthermore, it was found that the care home was providing a service to Y on a commercial, contractual basis that did not fall under the ambit of a public function.

As a result of that decision, s.145 of the *Health and Social Care Act 2008* was enacted, which brought private care home providers who provide accommodation, together with nursing or personal care, in a care home for an individual into the definition of bodies 'exercising a public function' if the services are provided under statutory arrangements such as those provided or arranged by local authorities. Section 145 is no longer in effect; however, s.73 of the *Care Act 2014* now provides for HRA protection.

> ## *Care Act 2014*, explanatory notes, Part One
>
> 425. Section 73 makes explicit that registered care providers, when providing adults with either personal care in their home or accommodation with nursing or personal care, which has been arranged or funded by a public authority pursuant to specific duties and powers, are exercising a function of a public nature for the purposes of the Human Rights Act 1998. It extends to the whole of the UK.

It is therefore important to be able to identify whether a violation of a person's rights is being committed by a public body or a private organisation to establish whether the *Human Rights Act 1998* affords them protection.

Articles of the *Human Rights Act 1998* and their Restrictions

The relevant Articles in the ECHR have been incorporated into the HRA. Articles 1 and 13 of the ECHR were not incorporated because, by creating the *Human Rights Act*, the UK had secured these rights into UK law.

Restrictions to human rights

The ECHR places certain restrictions on some of the rights and freedoms it sets out. Convention rights fall into three categories: absolute, qualified and limited rights. These restrictions reflect the need to balance the rights of others and to ensure that individual rights are in accordance with other domestic law. However, absolute rights are those Convention rights that cannot be derogated (departed) from. For example, Article 2, which provides 'a right to life', allows member states to do so in times of war and, when necessary, to prevent the death of others. However, the state's actions must be a proportionate response to the situation it is being applied to.

Articles 3, 4 and 7 are also absolute rights that may not be derogated from except where specific situations allow – for example, in time of war or an emergency. Further examples of these rights are modern-day slavery and forced labour.

Limited rights protect the rights of others and in some cases safeguard the individual. For example, Article 5 is a limited right in that a deprivation of liberty may take place following a criminal conviction or if the individual needs protection under mental health or mental capacity law. However, in depriving a person of their liberty, there must be proper procedures in place to safeguard those whose liberty has been taken away and the right of appeal (see Chapter 14).

Finally, Articles 8, 9, 10, 11 and 12 are qualified rights, which means that they can be restricted in certain circumstances if the aim is legitimate. Courts can balance the rights of others and ensure that the rights are in accordance with other domestic laws. The case of *B v UK* [2000] 1 FLR 1 (see below) demonstrated the balance between B's Article 8 rights and her right to freedom of expression in Article 10.

Article 2: Right to life

This right determines the obligation of the state to preserve life and that this right can only be derogated from in certain circumstances. This means that the state must protect its citizens' right to life and that the state must refrain from taking life. However, there are circumstances where the state or its agencies can justifiably take a person's life – for example, when the police are protecting citizens from the criminal activity of a person who is threatening the life of others – e.g. in cases of threatened terrorism. Any derogation of a right to life by a state body should be investigated; the Independent Office for Police Conduct (IOPC) investigates the conduct of police officers.

An example of a case involving Article 2 and the conflict between a child's right to life, their parents' wishes and medical opinion can be seen in the following case.

> ## *Raqeeb* v *Barts NHS Foundation Trust* [2019] EWHC 2531 (Admin) and [2019] EWHC 2530 (Fam)
>
> A five-year-old child required life-sustaining treatment because she suffered from a rare condition that caused irreversible brain damage. The Trust treating her
>
> *(Continued)*

contended that it would be in the child's best interests for life-sustaining treatment to be withdrawn. Her parents objected as they wanted to take her to a hospital in Italy which had agreed to provide her with palliative care, which would still require the child to be ventilated. The court, in deciding that the parents taking her to Italy was in her best interests, considered the rights which parents derive from their having parental responsibility for the child (see Chapter 6) and the child's cultural background. The right to life under Article 2 was also considered.

> With respect to the sanctity of life . . . Tafida's right to life under Art 2 of the ECHR falls to be considered in the context of her current state. Within this context, the state, in the form of the court, should not concern itself with teleological or ontological arguments concerning the meaning of life (such as whether a life without awareness or experience is properly consistent with conceptions of being) but rather consider the quality of Tafida's current existence as measured against the principle that sanctity of life is of the highest importance. Within this context, and in circumstances where the Trust submits that Tafida derives no benefit from life and any change of circumstances for Tafida will only be negative, this is a case in which the sanctity of life is outweighed by other considerations.

The court held that the child could be transferred to a hospital in Italy and that the continuation of life-sustaining medical treatment was in the child's best interests. This highlights the state's obligations and need to protect the right to life, but the case also illustrates that there are circumstances when life-saving treatment can be withdrawn.

Thought Box

What are your thoughts on the relationship between law, ethics and values with regard to the case above? See also the judgment in the case Charlie Gard (*Gard and Others* v *UK* ECHR app. no. 39793/17): www.supremecourt.uk/cases/docs/charlie-gard-190617.pdf

Article 3: No torture, inhuman or degrading treatment

Article 3 rights cannot be derogated from. This means that the right is an absolute one; it highlights the principle of it being a fundamental human right and the requirement placed on the state and its agencies to protect this right.

A Local Authority v M [2018] EWHC 870 (Fam)

This case highlights this obligation. A local authority applied to the court for a Female Genital Mutilation Protection Order (FGMPO) (see Chapter 16) to prevent a young girl from travelling to Sudan with her mother because, they argued, it was probable that the child would be subject to female genital mutilation when she arrived there.

The court had to consider whether the family's right to be together under Article 8 (see below) were outweighed by the child's rights under Article 3. The Court found that there was a real risk that the child would be subject to FGM in Sudan, and, if she was, this would constitute inhuman and degrading treatment in breach of Article 3. The local authority's application was successful; the parents were prevented from removing the young girl from the UK.

Article 4: No slavery or forced labour

This right is also an absolute one; it ensures that people are not held in servitude – that is, the condition of being a slave or under the control or ownership of someone else. Forced labour may be defined as a person being made to work for another involuntarily with fear of reprisals if they do not. There are very limited exceptions to this right, which include work carried out while in prison or on community service.

Examples of slavery and forced labour include both sexual slavery and work slavery. It is known that people working in car washes, nail bars and begging may fall into these groups (see the investigative powers of the Gangmasters and Labour Abuse Authority, HMICFRS, 2019). Local authorities play a key role in preventing these forms of slavery and forced labour (see also the Guide on Article 4 of the European Convention on Human Rights: prohibition of slavery and forced labour; updated December 2021; see Chapter 18).

Article 5: Right to liberty

This fundamental right provides people with the freedom to conduct their lives as they wish without state interference. The right is, however, a limited one, which means that that there are circumstances when the state can interfere with a person's liberty, but only if this is prescribed by law. For example, in certain areas of the law, such as immigration, criminal justice, mental health and mental capacity, the law sets out the specific circumstances when a person can lawfully be deprived of their liberty. An example can be found in the Cheshire West case, which concerned human rights issues about equality and the deprivation of an individual's liberty.

P (by his litigation friend the Official Solicitor) (Appellant) v Cheshire West and Chester Council and another (Respondents) and P and Q (by their litigation friend, the Official Solicitor) (Appellants) v Surrey County Council (Respondent) [2014] WLR(D) 140

The two cases went to the Supreme Court where the following issues were considered:

- What constitutes a deprivation of liberty?
- Are there instances when a deprivation of liberty is permissible?

(Continued)

> - Is the fundamental right protected by Article 5 the same for everyone regardless of mental or physical ability?
>
> The Supreme Court judgment included discussion of circumstances in which people with disabilities who lacked capacity could be deprived of or have their liberty restricted. It was agreed that human rights promote equality and apply to everyone. The case defines and sets a precedent for what constitutes deprivation of liberty, which has important implications for social work practice.

For a detailed discussion of this case and the deprivation of liberty safeguards and procedures, see Chapter 14.

Article 6: Right to a fair hearing

Article 6 highlights the basis of the rule of law, discussed in Chapter 1. The ethos of this right is that anyone charged with a crime must be treated fairly by the criminal justice system and is legally entitled to a fair and impartial trial. This fundamental principle also applies to all civil cases. For example, when a local authority is considering whether to apply to the court for a care order for a child, they must give those with parental responsibility (PR – see Chapter 6) the opportunity to express their opinions and objections, as well as ensuring that they have access to the information being presented about their case. Similarly, if the LA does decide to apply to the court for a care order, the case must be conducted in accordance with Article 6 and the parties (including anyone with PR) have a right to be legally represented.

In the Matter of *R (A Child)* [2012] EWCA Civ 1783, the judge said (in a case involving allegations of sexual abuse of a child by her father):

> The father has an absolute and fundamental right to a fair trial on the issue of sexual abuse. The allegations against him and the findings sought against him are extremely serious. They depend solely on the assertions of an 8 year old child, who I rule cannot be cross-examined and, as I have been at pains to point out earlier in the judgment, the court is entitled to make findings based on such evidence but must exercise a great deal of care.

Article 7: No punishment without law

Article 7 embodies the principles of the rule law in that a punishment cannot be imposed unless the law provides for it. It also provides that the law cannot impose retrospective liability. This means that a person cannot be held liable for an action if it was not a breach of the state's law at that time. However, there is a caveat to this absolute right, which is that a person could be held liable if their action at the time contravened the law of a civilised nation. The prosecution of war crimes provides an example of this caveat.

Article 8: Right to a private and family life

Article 8 protects an individual's rights to a private and family life, and to correspondence. Social work practice may involve working with immigrants who are in breach of immigration law and asylum seekers (Chapter 18). In these instances, the UK must ensure that when considering deportation of an immigrant, their right to a family life must be considered. Article 8 is a qualified right, which means that any interference must be 'in accordance with the law' and 'necessary in a democratic society'.

The case below provides a good example of how the courts protect an individual's Article 8 rights when there are safeguarding concerns.

B (by her litigation friend, the Official Solicitor) v *A Local Authority* [2019] EWCA Civ 913, 2019 WL 02425771

B, a 31-year-old woman with learning difficulties, epilepsy and significant caring needs, was under the care of her local adult social care services and lived with her parents. B regularly used social media to communicate with strangers online such as WhatsApp, Facebook and Snapchat. Her social workers became concerned for her safety after they discovered that she had met a man in his seventies online, who had previous convictions for sexual offences and was under a sexual offences' prevention order. The local authority sought declarations from the court regarding B's mental capacity to make decisions that included wanting to live with the man and having a child with him. In the first hearing the declarations were made regarding B's residence, care, contact with others, sexual relations and social media usage. The decisions made were appealed by B's legal representative regarding her understanding of using social media and there were cross appeals by the local authority as to whether she had the capacity to decide where to live. The Court of Appeal made the following important observation:

> Cases, like the present, which concern whether or not a person has the mental capacity to make the decision which the person would like to make involve two broad principles of social policy which, depending on the facts, may not always be easy to reconcile. On the one hand, there is a recognition of the right of every individual to dignity and self-determination and, on the other hand, there is a need to protect individuals and safeguard their interests where their individual qualities or situation place them in a particularly vulnerable situation . . .

They also noted that 'the court must always be careful not to discriminate against persons suffering from a mental disability by imposing too high a test of capacity' (see, for example, *PH* v *A Local Authority* [2011] EWHC 1704 (Fam) at [16xi]).

The court allowed the local authority's appeal. The significance of this case is the court's deliberations regarding B's Article 8 rights, her capacity to make the relevant decisions and the conflict between the Article 8 right to correspondence and Article 10 right to free speech.

Article 9: Freedom of thought and religion

This article protects people's right to their thoughts and beliefs. Local authorities should ensure that their policies and procedures do not infringe this right – for example, when recruiting professional staff and considering the religion or faith of service users.

Article 10: Freedom of expression

This right provides an individual with freedom to express their thoughts and opinions. The state cannot interfere unless it conflicts with other rights. This is relevant to social work practice when deciding whether to share information between agencies or other individuals. Information sharing should always be carried out with the person's consent unless this is not possible and the disclosure achieves a legitimate aim – for example, where it is necessary to safeguard another person (see Chapter 4).

Article 11: Right to protest and freedom of association

This right provides for the right to demonstrate and counter-demonstrate, but both can be limited if it interferes with another person's right to do so. For example, in the case of *Islington* v *Wells* [2021] 1 WLUK 372, the court had to balance the rights of the local authority landowner with those protesting against the felling of mature trees to make way for a housing development. The court held in favour of the local authority on the basis that they were upholding the rights of the local authority as the freeholder over the rights of the protestors.

Article 12: Right to marry

Article 12 provides the right of those of legal age to be free to marry under national law.

You can get married or form a civil partnership in England or Wales if you are:

- 16 or over;
- not already married or in a civil partnership;
- not closely related.

GOV.UK, Marriages and civil partnerships in England and Wales: www.gov.uk/marriages-civil-partnerships

---

The state can also prevent 'sham marriages' where the relationship is not genuine, and where it is being used to gain entry into the UK (see Chapters 11 and 14 for further relevant case law).

Article 14: No discrimination

This article provides that the rights and freedoms set out in the articles of the ECHR and the *Human Rights Act 1998* must be secured without discrimination on any ground such as race, religion, sex or political opinion (see Chapter 4). This right can only be used in conjunction with a breach of one or more of the rights discussed above.

Protocols in the ECHR supplement the basic rights listed above. For example, Protocol 1, Article 2 protects a person's right to an effective education and incorporates a right to respect a parent's right to choose education for their children in accordance with their religious beliefs. This is not an absolute right as the government can regulate the provision and delivery of the education system.

Figure 2.1 is a summary of the articles within the *Human Rights Act 1998* and their limitations discussed above.

Article 2	Right to life	Absolute but at certain times a member state can derogate from it
Article 3	No torture, inhuman or degrading treatment	Absolute right
Article 4	No slavery or forced labour	Absolute right
Article 5	Right to liberty	Limited right
Article 6	Right to a fair hearing	Absolute, but in certain circumstances a member state can derogate from it
Article 7	No punishment without law	Absolute right
Article 8	Right to a private and family life	Qualified right
Article 9	Freedom of religion	Qualified right
Article 10	Freedom of expression	Qualified right
Article 11	Right to protest and freedom of association	Qualified right
Article 12	Right to marry	Subject to national laws on marriage
Article 14	No discrimination	This is not a free-standing right but is used to support a breach of any of the above rights

Figure 2.1   Articles and restrictions

Remedies Available under the HRA

The HRA enables courts to provide remedies for breach of the *Human Rights Act 1998*. Only the victim whose right has been violated can bring a claim; this includes a family member or a corporation. Once identified as a victim with a legitimate claim, the ECHR states that they 'may be entitled to a remedy for the violation'. Remedies can be in the form of:

- An award of damages, which provides monetary compensation for the violation of the rights.
- An injunction, which prevents a given act being carried out or compels a body to carry out an act.
- A judicial review of a decision made by a public authority (see Chapter 1).
- A declaration of incompatibility.

A declaration of incompatibility means that an Act of Parliament is declared to be incompatible with Convention rights. The courts cannot change the legislation, but Parliament should consider amending the Act. The case below highlights how this has happened in relation to the *Mental Health Act 1983* and highlights the complexities of Parliament amending legislation.

R (on the application of M) v Secretary of State for Health [2003]

The case concerned a woman, M, who was detained under the *Mental Health Act 1983* (MHA 1983) for treatment of a mental health condition. The Act requires that once a person is detained under the MHA 1983, their nearest relative is given certain rights that include access to their personal information and about their treatment. Under section 26 of the MHA 1983, M's adoptive father was her nearest relative, whom M accused of sexually abusing her when she was a child. He denied the allegations but the doctors treating M believed she was telling the truth. The case highlighted the lack of legislative provision for detained patients to be able to displace their nearest relative where appropriate. The courts found that M's Article 8 rights were being breached by not allowing her to displace the nearest relative. A declaration of incompatibility was made regarding s.29, MHA 1983 and the Convention rights. As a result, the MHA 2007 amended the MHA 1983 to allow a patient to apply to the court to have their nearest relative displaced on the grounds of unsuitability. The discussion in the case report also highlighted the resistance from Parliament to amend national law based on a decision by the ECHR (see Chapter 13).

Thought Box

What rights do you think conflict with each other regarding social work ethics and values?

Human rights law extends beyond the *Human Rights Act 1998* to specific areas of social work practice such as equality, information sharing and a right to a private and family life, which are discussed in the following chapters.

Chapter Summary

This chapter has:

- provided an outline of the development of human rights law in the UK, focusing on the significance of rights that underpin social work practice;
- highlighted section 6 of the *Human Rights Act 1998* and its significance as it places a duty on all public authorities to ensure that their actions are compatible with the Act;
- highlighted the implications of Brexit on social work practice.

Case study – Human rights

Consider the potential violation of human rights in the scenario below. Are there any restrictions on those rights?

J is 19 years old; she has severe learning difficulties and autism spectrum disorder. Furthermore, due to a lack of verbal capacity J is only able to communicate with people through gestures and using pictures. She was first taken into local authority care as a respite placement while her mother went on holiday for two weeks. While J was in the care home, the staff noticed bruising on her chest and, following a medical report on J's previous behaviour, it was decided that the bruises were unlikely to be self-inflicted. However, there had not been an investigation into any previous behaviour. This meant that when J's mother came to pick her up, the staff would not allow J to leave to go back to her family because of safeguarding concerns. J desperately wanted to go back to her family but, based on a mental capacity assessment, it was decided that she should be moved to another assessment centre where deprivation of liberty safeguards were put in place.

The staff did not advise J's parents that they could dispute the deprivation of liberty in the Court of Protection and they did not investigate her previous behaviour, which would have showed that prior to entering respite care J had been seen hitting herself at school. The school had recorded this, but it was not included in the subsequent investigation that separated J from her parents.

Answers can be found in the Appendix.

Further Reading

The Human rights implications post Brexit (HL Paper 88, HC 695, 2016): https://publications. parliament.uk/pa/jt201617/jtselect/jtrights/695/695.pdf

R (M) v *Secretary of State for Health* [2003] EWHC 1094 (Admin)

3

Anti-discrimination

Chapter Objectives

By the end of this chapter, readers will be able to:

- understand the development, and importance of, anti-discrimination law;
- understand the specific provisions in the *Equality Act 2010* and the implications for social work practice;
- use case law to identify types of discrimination and the protected characteristics found in the *Equality Act 2010*;
- consider the principles related to anti-discrimination law both nationally and internationally;
- discuss the impact of policy on the development of anti-discriminatory law and ethical principles.

Introduction

The Universal Declaration of Human Rights 1948 set out the protection provided for individuals' fundamental rights. Article 1 states that 'All human beings are born free and equal in dignity and rights. They are endowed with reason and conscience and should act towards one another in a spirit of brotherhood.' Following on from the discussion in Chapter 2 concerning individuals' rights found in the ECHR and the UK's *Human Rights Act 1998* (HRA), this chapter provides a more detailed discussion about the right not to be discriminated against based on an individual's specific characteristics. Article 14 ECHR (which is incorporated into the HRA) prohibits discrimination and can be used in conjunction with any other ECHR right that has been breached; it is not an article that can be used on its own.

Ethical Considerations

Important ethical principles relevant to civil rights inequalities are identified in the BASW *Code of Ethics*.

2.2 Social Justice

Principles

1. *Challenging discrimination*

   Social workers have a responsibility to challenge discrimination on the basis of characteristics such as ability, age, culture, gender or sex, marital status, socioeconomic status, political opinions, skin colour, racial or other physical characteristics, sexual orientation or spiritual beliefs.

2. *Recognising diversity*

   Social workers should recognise and respect the diversity of the societies in which they practise, taking into account individual, family, group and community differences.

3. *Distributing resources*

   Social workers should ensure that resources at their disposal are distributed fairly, according to need.

4. *Challenging unjust policies and practices*

   Social workers have a duty to bring to the attention of their employers, policy makers, politicians and the general public situations where resources are inadequate or where distribution of resources, policies and practice are oppressive, unfair, harmful or illegal.

5. *Working in solidarity*

   Social workers, individually, collectively and with others have a duty to challenge social conditions that contribute to social exclusion, stigmatisation or subjugation, and work towards an inclusive society.

Development of Legislation and Social Policy in the UK

The development of anti-discriminatory laws in the UK grew from the 1960s as the need to protect citizens' rights began to be recognised. An example is the *Sexual Offences Act 1967*, which amended the law relating to homosexuality in England and Wales by decriminalising homosexual acts between two consenting adults over the age of 21. This was a much-needed reform at the time, but there were still many restrictions for gay couples (see Steven Dryden, A short history of LGBT rights in the UK: bl.uk/lgbt-histories/articles/a-short-history-of-lgbt-rights-in-the-uk).

The anti-discriminatory legal framework in the UK was grounds based, which means that the law was developed on a case-by-case basis. Those who had experienced discrimination based on a specific characteristic had to bring their claim to court and the decision of the court would set the precedent (see Chapter 1). Moreover, individuals or groups had to lobby Parliament to have their rights protected. The *Race Relations Act 1968* made it unlawful to racially discriminate against people, specifically in education, housing and advertising. The legislation was created following the recognition that many immigrants who had moved to the UK from Commonwealth countries were being discriminated against on the grounds of colour, race, ethnic or national origins. An example of the direct discrimination experienced by immigrants can be seen in the treatment towards the Windrush Generation who came to the UK in 1948 to take up employment in sectors where there were labour shortages, such as the NHS (see Chapter 18). The reforms are also a consequence of the work of pressure groups representing individuals with specific characteristics.

Equality and Human Rights Commission

The *Equality Act 2006* provided for the establishment of the Equality and Human Rights Commission (EqHRC). This is a statutory non-departmental government body, which means that it operates outside government departments. The role of the commission is to uphold equality law in the UK by monitoring human rights and advocating for individuals affected by discrimination. It provides 'advice and guidance to individuals, employers and other organisations, reviewing the effectiveness of the law and taking legal enforcement action to clarify the law and address significant breaches of rights'. It has also produced codes of practice on employment, services and equal pay. See what its role is at: www.equalityhumanrights.com/en

The Equality Act 2010

Even with the rapid increase in anti-discriminatory law, the development has been complex and inconsistent. In 2005, a review of the effectiveness of anti-discrimination rights began. The *Equality Act 2010* was the result of many years of campaigning by organisations like trade unions, and equality and human rights non-governmental organisations.

Consultation with stakeholders informed policy and led to proposals for a single Equality Bill in 2008–9. This resulted in the *Equality Act 2010*, which drew together over 100 pieces of legislation that protected the individual from discrimination based on certain chacteristics. It incorporated the existing legislation into one Act to provide consistency and clarity to the UK's anti-discrimination legal framework and strengthened the legal provisions for disability (see below).

Nine Protected Characteristics of the *Equality Act 2010*

Discrimination is unlawful if an individual is treated differently from others based on one or more of the protected characteristics below. Section 4 of the *Equality Act 2010* determines the nine protected characteristics that have encompassed the law above.

1. Age

(1) In relation to the protected characteristic of age—

   (a) a reference to a person who has a protected characteristic is a reference to a person of a particular age group.

   (b) a reference to persons who share a protected characteristic is a reference to persons of the same age group.

(2) A reference to an age group is a reference to a group of persons defined by reference to age, whether by reference to an age or to a range of ages.

This means that people of all ages are protected under the *Equality Act 2010* rather than just certain age groups. Young people are just as likely to be discriminated against as older people are.

Mr S Kisitu v *Inclusive Care Support Ltd*: 3200241/2018

In the Employment tribunal hearing of *Mr S Kisitu* v *Inclusive Care Support Ltd*: 3200241/2018, his claim of age discrimination succeeded against the respondent, Inclusive Care Support. Mr Kisitu was 19 and he worked as a support worker. He had an altercation with his line manager who made derogatory and offensive comments relating to his age and his race.

2. Disability

The legal definition of disability in s.6 of the Act provides:

(1) A person (P) has a disability if—

   (a) P has a physical or mental impairment, and

   (b) the impairment has a substantial and long-term adverse effect on P's ability to carry out normal day-to-day activities …

Data in 2019–2020 from the UK government states the following:

- In 2019 to 2020, 14.1 million people reported a disability, an increase of 2.7 million since 2009 to 2010.
- Twenty-four per cent of females (7.8 million) reported a disability in 2019 to 2020, an increase from 19% (6.1 million) in 2009 to 2010. In comparison, reporting a disability amongst males increased from 18% (5.3 million) in 2009 to 2010 to 19% (6.3 million) in the most recent survey year.
- Among all the specific impairments, mobility, stamina (or breathing or fatigue), and mental health impairments were the three most reported categories.
  - For working-age adults, 42% reported a mental health impairment. Mobility impairment was the second most likely disability type to be reported by working-age adults, at 41%.
  - For those of State Pension age, 68% reported a mobility impairment. Stamina, breathing, fatigue were reported by 44% of State Pension age adults and one in ten people reported a mental health impairment.
  - In children, social or behavioural impairments were the most common category reported, applying to 45% of disabled children. Learning impairment was the second most prevalent for children, with 35%. A mental health impairment was reported for 31% of disabled children, making it the third most prevalent impairment type reported by this age group.

(DWP, 2021)

As can be seen from the data above, there has been a recorded increase in people with disabilities. Disabled people may experience various forms of discrimination due to their disability both in a medical and social sense. Improvements in protection against discrimination for individuals with disabilities were incorporated into the *Equality Act 2010*.

Provisions relating to disability

- extending protection against indirect discrimination to disability
- introducing the concept of 'discrimination arising from disability' to replace protection under previous legislation lost as a result of a legal judgment
- applying the detriment model to victimisation protection (aligning with the approach in employment law)
- harmonising the thresholds for the duty to make reasonable adjustments for disabled people
- extending protection against harassment of employees by third parties to all protected characteristics
- making it more difficult for disabled people to be unfairly screened out when applying for jobs, by restricting the circumstances in which employers can ask job applicants questions about disability or health.

(*Equality Act 2010*: guidance found at GOV.UK)

The following case highlights the connection between disability discrimination and human rights issues.

Mathieson v Secretary of State for Work and Pensions [2015] UKSC 47

X needed complex daily care, provided by his parents, as, soon after he was born, he was diagnosed with cystic fibrosis and Duchenne muscular dystrophy. X was admitted to hospital for over a year and during his time in hospital his parents continued to be X's primary caregivers and incurred substantial extra expense. During X's stay in hospital the Secretary of State decided to suspend payment of his Disability Living Allowance (DLA), which meant that payments to the parents ceased for four months into the hospital stay. The family continued to receive other state benefits; however, the DLA had been a valuable part of their income. Sadly, X died in October 2012.

X's father appealed that at the time the decision to remove the DLA was made X was a severely disabled child who needed lengthy in-patient hospital treatment, and that the decision discriminated against him contrary to ECHR Art.14, when taken together with Article 1 of Protocol 1 (Protection of Property, which includes money).

The court found in favour of the parents and upheld their appeal, stating that disability was a prohibited ground, and discrimination between disabled persons with different needs engaged art.14 as much as discrimination between a disabled person and an able-bodied person. The rationale also included that the courts would not interfere with the government's approach to the provision of social benefits unless the rule to be applied was manifestly without reasonable foundation.

---

3. Gender reassignment

Gender reassignment can also be known as transgender. This means that a person's gender does not correspond with that assigned at birth. The *Equality Act 2010* identifies gender reassignment as a process an individual has gone through, is going through, or is intending to go through. The process does not need to be a medical one for the gender reassignment discrimination provisions to apply. This is a significant area in social work practice and has prompted calls for development in social work training. In 2018, a report was published by the Department for Education (DfE) to identify the efficacy in social work training specifically for children and families in relation to gender identity (DoE, Transgender awareness in child and family social work education, 2018: see: www.gov.uk/government/publications/transgender-awareness-in-child-and-family-social-work).

The *Adoption and Children Act 2002* allows unmarried couples, including same-sex couples, to apply for joint adoption, as well as an individual. When assessing for adoption, the agency or local authority must consider the principles of gender identity as found in the *Equality Act 2010* (see Chapter 8).

4. Marriage and civil partnership

This characteristic protects those in a marriage or civil partnership, which includes people who have married or entered into a civil partnership either inside or outside the UK.

An example is *Hawkins* v *Atex Group Ltd* [2012] ICR 1315, whereby an employment tribunal found against the claim of a wife that she had been discriminated against when she lost her job as she was married to the CEO of the company. The CEO had been asked not to employ family members. The tribunal found against the wife as her employment had been terminated on the grounds of her close relationship with the CEO rather than her marriage to him. She was not, therefore, disadvantaged any more than anyone else in a close personal relationship.

5. Pregnancy and maternity

It is unlawful to discriminate against an individual due to pregnancy or maternity – that is, to treat a person unfairly because they are pregnant, breastfeeding or because they have recently given birth. The person must suffer a disadvantage because of the unfair treatment.

In the case of *Freear* v *Vossloh Cogifer UK Ltd* 1800747/2016, Mrs Freear was awarded £43,000 compensation because of her employer's discriminatory actions. Mrs Freear was made redundant after she had informed her employers that she was pregnant. Before then she had no reason to believe her job was at risk. The tribunal found in her favour and awarded compensation for, among other things, loss of past and future earnings and injury to her feelings.

6. Race

Race discrimination means treating a person unfavourably because of their colour, nationality (including citizenship) or their ethnic or national origins.

A recent case highlights the court's deliberations regarding the protected characteristic of race and religion.

R (on the application of Z and another) v *Hackney LBC* [2019] UKSC/0162

A mother of four children, one of whom was autistic, applied for social housing through the local authority and a housing association. The housing association was specifically set up to provide social housing for Orthodox Jews. The mother was not an Orthodox Jew but had lived in the area all her life and she and her family were in high priority for rehousing; their application was rejected because they were not part of the Orthodox Jewish community. The mother sought judicial review of the decision on the grounds of race and religious discrimination. The court found in favour of the local authority and the housing association because of the exemptions in s.158

Equality Act 2010 which allows for organisations and employers to compensate for disadvantages that it reasonably believes are faced by people who share a particular protected characteristic (here, the Orthodox Jewish community). Furthermore, s.193(2)(a) permits charities to restrict benefits to those with a protected characteristic if the restriction is 'a proportionate means of achieving a legitimate aim' and s.193(2)(b) permits charities to restrict benefits to those who share a protected characteristic 'if the restriction seeks to prevent or compensate for a disadvantage linked to the characteristic'.

7. Religion or belief

Section 10 of the *Equality Act 2010* states:

(1) Religion means any religion and a reference to religion includes a reference to a lack of religion.
(2) Belief means any religious or philosophical belief and a reference to belief includes a reference to a lack of belief.
(3) In relation to the protected characteristic of religion or belief—

    (a) a reference to a person who has a particular protected characteristic is a reference to a person of a particular religion or belief;
    (b) a reference to persons who share a protected characteristic is a reference to persons who are of the same religion or belief.

A recent example of a philosophical belief is that an employment tribunal found that veganism is a protected characteristic and people who hold that belief cannot be discriminated against (see *Casamitjana* v *The League Against Cruel Sports*, Case No: 3331129/2018).

The *Equality Act 2010, Employment Code of Practice* (EqHRC), para. 2.59 provides a five-point test to determine what is a philosophical belief.

For a philosophical belief to be protected under the Act:

1. it must be genuinely held;
2. it must be a belief and not an opinion or viewpoint based on the present state of information available;
3. it must be a belief as to a weighty and substantial aspect of human life and behaviour;
4. it must attain a certain level of cogency, seriousness, cohesion and importance;
5. it must be worthy of respect in a democratic society, not incompatible with human dignity and not conflict with the fundamental rights of others.

8.   Sex

Section 11 of the *Equality Act 2010* states:

In relation to the protected characteristic of sex—

(a) a reference to a person who has a particular protected characteristic is a reference to a man or to a woman;
(b) a reference to persons who share a protected characteristic is a reference to persons of the same sex.

There are circumstances when sex discrimination can be lawful. An example is an all-female support staff for women who have experienced domestic abuse by their partners.

9.   Sexual orientation

Sexual orientation means the gender an individual is sexually attracted to. The *Equality Act 2010* protects individual rights to relationships with members of the opposite, same or both sexes.

A well-known case that highlights the rights of those individuals listed above and those providing a service to them is the following.

Lee (Respondent) v *Ashers Baking Company Ltd and others (Appellants) (Northern Ireland)* [2018] UKSC 49

The owners of a bakery refused to put a message on a cake supporting gay marriage. They argued that due to their Christian beliefs they could not fulfil the order placed by Mr Lee, which was to celebrate an event supporting gay marriage. The bakers claimed that their religious teachings stated that the only form of marriage was between a man and a woman, which meant that their religious conscience would not allow them to fulfil the order.

Mr Lee brought a claim against the bakers for discrimination on the grounds of sexual orientation. His claim for unlawful discrimination was upheld at first instance and then again in the Court of Appeal. However, the decision was overturned by the Supreme Court who found in favour of the bakers. The court held that the bakery would have refused to supply this particular cake to anyone, whatever their personal characteristics and therefore there was no discrimination on grounds of sexual orientation.

> ## Thought Box
>
> Are there other characteristics that need to be protected and, if so, what are the arguments for and against protecting them?

The characteristics protected by law are still being updated. An example relevant to social work practice involves the rights of carers. Carers' rights are not included in the *Equality Act 2010*, although they can be discriminated against, as a recent case regarding benefit claims for unpaid carers illustrates.

> ## *Hurley & Ors* v *Secretary of State for Work and Pensions* [2015] EWHC 3382 (Admin)
>
> This case concerned the UK Government's decision to include the Carer's Allowance in the calculations for deciding the amount of benefits a person can receive. The issues considered were whether that decision discriminated unlawfully against both carers and the disabled people needing their care. The claimants argued that (1) not to exempt those caring for disabled adult family members was disproportionate and that Article 8 rights should be engaged, and (2) there was unlawful discrimination contrary to ECHR art.14 in the impact on carers and those for whom they cared.
>
> The court found in favour of the claimants because under Article 14, the enjoyment of all ECHR rights must be secured without discrimination on any ground such as sex, race, colour, language, religion, political or other opinion, national or social origin, association with national minority, property or any other status.
>
> This meant that the carers were recognised as being protected under Article 14 and that the treatment was discriminatory towards disabled people and that Article 8 was engaged. The Regulations used in the calculations would not be declared unlawful. However, consideration should be given to an amendment that exempted at least individual family carers such as the claimants, since they were very few and the cost to public funds if the cap was to be maintained was likely to significantly outweigh the cost of granting the exemption.

Forms of Discrimination

The *Equality Act 2010* not only protects individuals who hold any of the nine protected characteristics discussed above, but also provides for how the unlawful discrimination may take place.

Form of discrimination	Definition (GOV.UK)	Example	Case law
Direct discrimination	Treating someone with a protected characteristic less favourably than others.	Refusing a person access to a club due their disability.	*Bull and another* v *Hall and another* [2013] UKSC 73 B&B owners directly discriminated against two gay men.
Indirect discrimination	Putting rules or arrangements in place that apply to everyone, but that put someone with a protected characteristic at an unfair disadvantage.	Employment policies that disadvantage parents – e.g. having to travel long distances at short notice.	*Moore and Coates* v *Secretary of State for Communities and Local Government* [2015] EWHC 44 (Admin) Indirect discrimination against travellers.
Harassment	Unwanted behaviour linked to a protected characteristic that violates someone's dignity or creates an offensive environment for them.	Physical or verbal bullying in the workplace.	*Ali* v *Virgin Active Limited*, Case Number: 2206652/2017 An employment tribunal found that Mrs Ali had been forced to resign based on age discrimination.
Victimisation	Treating someone unfairly because they've complained about discrimination or harassment.	An employer threatens to dismiss an employee if they support other employees' work-related complaint.	*Jessemey* v *Rowstock Ltd & Anr* [2014] EWCA Civ 185 Employer gave a bad reference to employee after he had complained about age discrimination.
Discrimination by association	Discrimination by association occurs when a person is treated less favourably because they are linked or associated with a protected characteristic.	Being treated less favourably than others because of a protected characteristic of a friend, spouse, partner, parent or another person with whom they are associated.	*Coleman* v *EBR Attridge Law* (2008) Mother discriminated against due to her son's disability.
Discrimination by perception	Discrimination by perception happens when a person is discriminated against because they are thought to have a particular protected characteristic when in fact they do not.	Discriminating against people because it is thought they are transsexual or gay, then they will be protected even if they do not have these protected characteristics.	*Chief Constable of Norfolk* v *Coffey* [2019] EWCA Civ 1061 Norfolk police rejected candidate application due to the possibility that her hearing condition might worsen.

Figure 3.1   Forms of discrimination

Source: Authors, based in part on GOV.UK (2010) and GOV.UK: https://www.gov.uk/discrimination-your-rights/how-you-can-be-discriminated-against

Liability under the *Equality Act 2010*

The *Equality Act 2010* applies to public bodies, employers and people providing a public service to ensure that they do not discriminate against individuals or groups who fall under the nine protected characteristics discussed above. Organisations providing a public service need to ensure that they have made reasonable adjustments within their services for individuals who have a disability.

For example, in *FirstGroup Plc (Respondent)* v *Paulley (Appellant)* [2017] UKSC 4, a wheelchair user could not board a bus as a mother had taken the space used for wheelchair users with her child's buggy. The Supreme Court found that the bus company had not made reasonable adjustments to accommodate a situation such as this, and required the bus company to develop a policy and provide staff training to ensure that the needs of wheelchair passengers were catered for to the same degree as non-wheelchair users.

The *Equality Act 2010* also provides for the public body equality duty, which means that social workers and local authorities must ensure that there is no unlawful discrimination in their practice and processes (see *R (on the application of Gullu)* v *Hillingdon LBC* and *R (on the application of Ward)* v *Hillingdon LBC* [2019] EWCA Civ 692). It was argued that the LA's housing allocation policy, which prioritised people who had been resident in the local area for ten years, indirectly discriminated against certain protected groups on the grounds of race. Two challenges were brought against the local authority, the first by Irish Travellers, which was successful but the second, brought by a Kurdish refugee, was unsuccessful. However, an appeal against the second decision was successful; the court determined that the local authority had breached the public sector equality duty (PSED) in s.149 of the *Equality Act 2010*.

Local authorities must promote and foster good relations between individuals that share the protected characteristics found in the *Equality Act 2010*. As can be seen in the list above, this duty also covers protection for social workers as employees. For example, if a social worker employed by a service user is discriminated against by the service user based on one of the nine protected characteristics, employers should have policies and procedures in place that the social worker can draw upon when reporting the discrimination. These will include the need for a risk assessment regarding future provision to the service user and support for the social worker. This means that the employer has a duty to protect social workers while they carry out their duties. Furthermore, an employer can be held vicariously liable for the unlawful actions of their employees. This means that if an employee has acted in a way that harms a third party, while undertaking their duties, the employer can be held responsible for those actions.

Thought Box

- Can you think of situations when you have witnessed or experienced discrimination and what if anything was done about it?
- Knowing what you now know about anti-discrimination law, what could have been done about the situation you identified above?

Ensuring the protection of an individual's personal characteristics is complex, as a person generally has more than one, which means that for some groups or individuals the chances of being discriminated against are more acute. The concept of intersectionality (see Chapter 20) is one that is growing in relation to those who are discriminated and disadvantaged because they fall under two or more protected groups. The concept also means that institutions must ensure they are accommodating those needs to avoid individuals being discriminated against. For example, a Muslim disabled woman may experience more discrimination based on the three protected characteristics than another woman. This concept highlights the need for development in this area of the law.

Objective Justification

There are situations when discrimination can be proved to be justifiable and not considered unlawful. For example, an advertisement for a job may exclude a certain group; however, this may be justifiable in relation to carrying out the role being advertised (e.g. work with female victims of domestic abuse may justify the exclusion of male applicants). In relation to social work practice, the local authority's duty to provide personal care must be proportionate in achieving a legitimate aim for the service user. This is recognised as an objective justification, which means that if it can be shown there is an objective to the perceived discrimination, it can be found to be justifiable. For example, if an organisation needs to recruit an employee for a service aimed at people of the same race, then this could be seen as an objective justification. Furthermore, the word 'proportionality' is significant as public bodies must show that the justification claimed is a proportionate means of achieving a legitimate aim (see *Jonathan Akerman-Livingstone* v *Aster Communities Ltd* [2014] EWCA Civ 1081 regarding a claim for possession of the home of a disabled person). The court held that the proportionality of making a possession order and the suitability of the matter for summary disposal (i.e. terminating the proceedings at an early stage) could not simply be assumed.

Positive Action

Positive action allows for those with protected characteristics to be encouraged to participate in an event where they may have been disadvantaged in the past. It is lawful if the action taken follows the provisions under ss.158 and 159 of the *Equality Act 2010* which allows for underrepresented groups with one or more protected characteristics to be given a fair chance to achieve the same goals as other individuals. This can be seen in recruitment and education – for example, police forces will work with community groups to ensure that access to their recruitment process is understood to encourage people from different groups to apply for police roles.

Section 158 *Equality Act 2010*

Positive action: general

(1) This section applies if a person (P) reasonably thinks that—

  (a) persons who share a protected characteristic suffer a disadvantage connected to the characteristic,
  (b) persons who share a protected characteristic have needs that are different from the needs of persons who do not share it, or
  (c) participation in an activity by persons who share a protected characteristic is disproportionately low.

(2) This Act does not prohibit P from taking any action which is a proportionate means of achieving the aim of—

  (a) enabling or encouraging persons who share the protected characteristic to overcome or minimise that disadvantage,
  (b) meeting those needs, or
  (c) enabling or encouraging persons who share the protected characteristic to participate in that activity.

However, positive discrimination is unlawful but positive action is not. An example of unlawful positive discrimination would be when an employer wants to recruit an individual with one of the protected characteristics rather than being the best candidate for the role. This means giving a specific group preferential treatment over others.

A recent development which relates to social work practice is that of the Return to Social Work Scheme which is run in conjunction with the Government Equalities Office and Local Government Association (LGA). It enables social workers who, for varied reasons such as caring responsibilities, have had to leave the profession for a while to return to work on completion of updated training and placement requirements. This means ensuring equality for those wanting to return to the profession they have trained for (LGA: Return to Work Scheme).

International Obligations to Principles of Equality

Principles of equality can be found in Article 1 of the United Nations Charter.

Article 1

The Purposes of the United Nations Charter are:

1. To maintain international peace and security, and to that end: to take effective collective measures for the prevention and removal of threats to

(Continued)

the peace, and for the suppression of acts of aggression or other breaches of the peace, and to bring about by peaceful means, and in conformity with the principles of justice and international law, adjustment or settlement of international disputes or situations which might lead to a breach of the peace;

2. To develop friendly relations among nations based on respect for the principle of equal rights and self-determination of peoples, and to take other appropriate measures to strengthen universal peace;

3. To achieve international co-operation in solving international problems of an economic, social, cultural, or humanitarian character, and in promoting and encouraging respect for human rights and for fundamental freedoms for all without distinction as to race, sex, language, or religion; and

4. To be a centre for harmonizing the actions of nations in the attainment of these common ends.

Nations who have ratified the UN charter can evidence their obligation through their national laws that protect and enforce citizens' rights. However, nations developing the law alone cannot combat the inequalities that many individuals face. It is the work of voluntary organisations whose research papers feed into government policy documents that recognise the need to improve inequalities.

Chapter Summary

This chapter has:

- identified the development of anti-discrimination law;
- discussed the specific provisions in the *Equality Act 2010* and explained who can be liable, which includes public body liability and its relevance to social work practice;
- identified the nine protected characteristics and types of discrimination, and discussed them with reference to current case law;
- considered the policy, principles and ethical consideration in relation to social work practice.

Case study – Anti-discrimination

Yousef is a social worker working in adult social care. He has been designated to work with T and B, who are both in their eighties. T tells Yousef that he does not want help 'from someone like you' and refuses to let him in the house. T rings Yousef's manager, Carmel, and demands that he is allocated a social worker 'with the same colour skin as I have'.

T and B have a son, S, who has undergone transgender surgery, he has recently joined a gym and was told that their policy stated he must use the changing rooms assigned to his birth gender or prove his gender reassignment by showing a gender recognition certificate.

Identify what equality rights are being breached and in what form. Who is liable and what can be done if anything?

Answers can be found in the Appendix.

Further Reading

Hudson-Sharp, N. and Metcalf, H. (2016) Inequality among lesbian, gay bisexual and transgender groups in the UK: a review of evidence. National Institute of Economic and Social Research.

Malleson, K. (2018) Equality law and the protected characteristics. *Modern Law Review*, 81(4).

4

Data Protection, Confidentiality and Information Sharing

Chapter Objectives

By the end of this chapter, readers will be able to:

- understand the relevant legislation relating to data protection;
- identify the difference between confidentiality and information sharing in relation to social work practice;
- understand the rules involving consent from children regarding confidential information;
- understand the importance of e-professionalism to social work practice.

Introduction

This chapter introduces significant aspects of social work practice in relation to the law on confidentiality, the principles of information sharing and the *Data Protection Act 2018*. It also discusses the importance of gaining consent to share information when working with children and adults. Gaining and giving consent is a fundamental human right and, as the previous chapters have shown, it is important in ensuring that individuals' rights are maintained. However, in the context of information sharing, the social work practitioner needs to establish a balance between the rights of the individual and the need at times to safeguard and protect the individual without their consent to share information about them. Effective social work practice is reliant on efficient data storage and the sharing of data, which means that social workers need to ensure that they follow the law regulating the control of data they hold.

An example of the need for effective information sharing can be seen in some serious case reviews that highlight the lack of or inefficiency in communication between agencies when working with vulnerable people. Serious case reviews (SCR) are held to identify the circumstances leading up to the death or serious harm to a child, and where an adult at risk of harm has died where abuse or neglect is suspected. Since September 2019, local authority safeguarding panels are now responsible for conducting their own reviews. Their purpose is to gather the facts and ensure that the same circumstances do not happen again by using data from the different agencies concerned in the review.

Ethical Considerations

Social workers are in a privileged position when working with service users because of their power to obtain confidential information. The principle of confidentiality in their work promotes trust between the service user and social worker. The principle is supported by the regulations placed on public services which help service users discuss sensitive issues that they may not be able to disclose to others. Protecting an individual's right to a personal life as provided in Article 8 of the *Human Rights Act 1998* (Chapter 2) encourages autonomy and empowers the individual to make decisions regarding their own life. However, a conflict may arise for the social worker when the need to share information and the need to breach confidentiality in the public interest is a legitimate aim when safeguarding individuals. Social workers must follow the law and balance the decisions made, as well as taking account of the ethical considerations. The BASW *Code of Ethics* helps the social worker navigate their way through these ethical considerations (see: BASW *Code of Ethics*, 3 Ethical Practical Principles, paras 5 and 10, at: www.basw.co.uk/about-basw/code-ethics).

Development of Data Protection Law and Social Policy

The EU has had a significant impact on UK policy regarding data protection, confidentiality and information sharing. Data protection law has seen significant reforms since 1995 to protect individuals' data during a time of evolving technology. For example, to ensure that personal information stored about individuals was not misused, the

UK enacted the *Data Protection Act 1998* and, following the reforms made in the EU General Data Protection Regulations (GDPR) 2017, the *Data Protection Act 2018* was passed (see *EU: The History of the GDPR* at: https://edps.europa.eu/data-protection/data-protection/legislation/history-general-data-protection-regulation_en).

After the UK left the EU on 31 January 2020, the pre-existing EU rules on data protection remained in place until the end of the Brexit transition period (31 December 2020). From 1 January 2021, the Data Protection, Privacy and Electronic Communications (Amendments etc.) (EU Exit) Regulations 2019 came into force to ensure the continuation of data protection law in the UK.

Confidentiality

UK law has long recognised, at common law, that breach of confidentiality is a civil wrong unless disclosure is justified in the public interest. Case law, which has developed since the nineteenth century, has often involved the activities of celebrities, but it has important implications for social work practice. The following case provides an overview of the development: the legal principle of confidentiality is determined by the case of *Attorney-General* v *Guardian Newspapers Ltd* (No. 2) (1990).

> A duty of confidence arises where someone receives information in circumstances where he or she agrees or has notice that the information is confidential, and it would be just in all the circumstances that they should be prevented from disclosing that information to others.

The principal of confidentiality under the common law is that consent is required before disclosing information to another party. However, as discussed below, there are times when breaching confidentiality is necessary specifically in relation to safeguarding people at risk of harm.

The Right to Privacy

Since the early 1990s, case law has made a distinction between the law of confidentiality and the right to privacy, see *Kaye* v *Robertson* (1991) and *Wainwright* v *Home Office* (2002). These cases highlighted the gap in UK law between the recognised breach of confidentiality and the lack of protection against invasion of privacy which existed at that time. The HRA 1998 incorporated the ECHR rights into UK law (Chapter 2) and an individual's right to a private life was recognised under Article 8. However, since its inception there has been a conflict between an individual's Article 8 rights and another party's Article 10 rights, which provides for freedom of expression. The relevance of this distinction to social work practice can be found in the Caldicott principles.

In 1997, a review was conducted by Dame Fiona Caldicott because of concerns in the NHS about confidentiality and the development of information technology (IT).

The six principles outlined in the review have significance for social work practice when working with other agencies (see box below).

1. Justify the purpose(s). Every proposed use or transfer of patient identifiable information within or from an organisation should be clearly defined and scrutinised, with continuing uses regularly reviewed, by an appropriate guardian.
2. Do not use patient identifiable information unless it is absolutely necessary. Patient identifiable information items should not be included unless it is essential for the specified purpose(s) of that flow. The need for patients to be identified should be considered at each stage of satisfying the purpose(s).
3. Use the minimum necessary patient-identifiable information. Where use of patient identifiable information is considered to be essential, the inclusion of each individual item of information should be considered and justified so that the minimum amount of identifiable information is transferred or accessible as is necessary for a given function to be carried out.
4. Access to patient identifiable information should be on a strict need-to-know basis. Only those individuals who need access to patient identifiable information should have access to it, and they should only have access to the information items that they need to see. This may mean introducing access controls or splitting information flows where one information flow is used for several purposes.
5. Everyone with access to patient identifiable information should be aware of their responsibilities. Action should be taken to ensure that those handling patient identifiable information – both clinical and non-clinical staff – are made fully aware of their responsibilities and obligations to respect patient confidentiality.
6. Understand and comply with the law; every use of patient identifiable information must be lawful. Someone in each organisation handling patient information should be responsible for ensuring that the organisation complies with legal requirements (see: https://assets.publishing. service.gov.uk/government/uploads/system/uploads/attachment_data/ file/192572/2900774_InfoGovernance_accv2.pdf)

   A seventh principle was endorsed by the Department of Health following a further review because of concerns about information sharing of patient data.
7. The duty to share information can be as important as the duty to protect patient confidentiality. Health and social care professionals should have the confidence to share information in the best interests of their patients within the framework of the existing principle.

Public Interest Defence

Lord Laming's inquiry into the death of Victoria Climbié highlighted the need to share information over the restrictions of data protection.

Exchange of information between professionals

17.115 Throughout this Inquiry it was said repeatedly that when there is professional concern about the welfare of a child, the free exchange of information is inhibited by the Data Protection Act 1998, the Human Rights Act 1998, and common law rules on confidentiality. The evidence put to the Inquiry was that unless a child is deemed to be in need of protection, information cannot be shared between agencies without staff running the risk that their actions are unlawful. This either deters information sharing, or artificially elevates concern about the need for protection – each of which is not compatible with serving well the needs of children and families. Clearly these matters are complicated. There must be a balance struck between the protection of a child and the right to privacy.

(GOV.UK, 2003: *The Victoria Climbié Inquiry*, CM5730)

Following the recommendations made by the inquiry, the Government has supplied guidance which was updated in 2018.

In addition to the ... General Data Protection Regulation ... GDPR and Data Protection Act 2018, practitioners need to balance the common law duty of confidence, and the rights within the Human Rights Act 1998, against the effect on children or individuals at risk, if they do not share the information. If information collection and sharing is to take place with the consent of the individuals involved, providing they are clearly informed about the purpose of the sharing, there should be no breach of confidentiality or breach of the Human Rights Act 1998. If the information is confidential, and the consent of the information subject is not gained, then practitioners need to decide whether there are grounds to share the information without consent. This can be because it is overwhelmingly in the information subject's interests for this information to be disclosed. It is also possible that a public interest would justify disclosure of the information (or that sharing is required by a court order, other legal obligation or statutory exemption). In the context of safeguarding a child or young person, where the child's welfare is para-mount, it is possible that the common law duty of confidence can be over overcome. Practitioners must consider this on a case-by-case basis. As is the case for all information processing, initial thought needs to be given as to whether the objective can be achieved by limiting the amount of information shared – does all of the personal information need to be shared to achieve the objective?

(HM Government, 2018)

The above guidance is a good example of how the recommendations from reviews and research can impact on social policy. The recommendations following the Laming review were integrated into guidance in the form of a policy document and subsequently amended to aid practitioners in their decisions regarding information sharing.

The public interest defence has developed in tort law specifically to deal with the conflict between freedom of speech and the right to private life. Tort law is the branch of law that deals with wrongdoings committed by one party against another. For social work practice, the public interest defence is one that practitioners rely on for protection when making the decision to share confidential information without the consent of the service user. The defence means that confidential information can be shared where it can be shown that it is in the public interest to do so. For example, the defence is used if the practitioner thinks that disclosing the information will protect the individual and others or society from harm. The reasons for disclosure must be evidenced and the practitioner must show that they adhered to the principles above. See the case of *W* v *Egdell* [1990] Ch 359 regarding a psychiatrist's duty of confidence to his patient where Lord Bingham, in his judgment in the case, stated the following.

> There is one consideration which in my judgment, as in that of the judge, weighs the balance of public interest decisively in favour of disclosure. It may be shortly put. Where a man has committed multiple killings under the disability of serious mental illness, decisions which may lead directly or indirectly to his release from hospital should not be made unless a responsible authority is properly able to make an informed judgment that the risk of repetition is so small as to be acceptable. A consultant psychiatrist who becomes aware, even in the course of a confidential relationship, of information which leads him, in the exercise of what the court considers a sound professional judgment, to fear that such decisions may be made on the basis of inadequate information and with a real risk of consequent danger to the public is entitled to take such steps as are reasonable in all the circumstances to communicate the grounds of his concern to the responsible authorities. I have no doubt that the judge's decision in favour of Dr. Egdell was right on the facts of this case.

Information Sharing

Making the correct decision about when and how to share information about a service user is important for social workers and social work students. It is one that should be made, where possible, with a manager.

> The seven golden rules for sharing information are:
>
> 1. Remember that the General Data Protection Regulation (GDPR), Data Protection Act 2018 and human rights law are not barriers to justified information sharing but provide a framework to ensure that personal information about living individuals is shared appropriately.
>
> *(Continued)*

2. Be open and honest with the individual (and/or their family where appropriate) from the outset about why, what, how and with whom information will, or could be shared, and seek their agreement, unless it is unsafe or inappropriate to do so.
3. Seek advice from other practitioners, or your information governance lead, if you are in any doubt about sharing the information concerned, without disclosing the identity of the individual where possible.
4. Where possible, share information with consent, and where possible, respect the wishes of those who do not consent to having their information shared. Under the GDPR and Data Protection Act 2018 you may share information without consent if, in your judgement, there is a lawful basis to do so, such as where safety may be at risk. You will need to base your judgement on the facts of the case. When you are sharing or requesting personal information from someone, be clear of the basis upon which you are doing so. Where you do not have consent, be mindful that an individual might not expect information to be shared.
5. Consider safety and well-being: base your information sharing decisions on considerations of the safety and well-being of the individual and others who may be affected by their actions.
6. Necessary, proportionate, relevant, adequate, accurate, timely and secure: ensure that the information you share is necessary for the purpose for which you are sharing it, is shared only with those individuals who need to have it, is accurate and up to-date, is shared in a timely fashion, and is shared securely (see principles).
7. Keep a record of your decision and the reasons for it – whether it is to share information or not. If you decide to share, then record what you have shared, with whom and for what purpose.

(HM Government, 2018; see: https://assets. publishing.service.gov.uk/government/uploads/system/ uploads/attachment_data/file/721581/Information_sharing_ advice_practitioners_safeguarding_services.pdf)

When working with adults at risk of harm, the *Care Act 2014* principles (Chapter 12) provide for the need to empower the service user by supporting them to make their own decisions and giving informed consent of their care. Prevention requires being proactive and reporting issues that may put the service user or anyone else at harm. The principle of partnership and accountability covers the need to share information with other agencies in supporting the service user, but also in being accountable for the decision of information sharing and following the regulations set out in the DPA 2018 and GDPR.

Relevant Legislation

The *Data Protection Act 1998* was enacted following an EU data directive that required member states to implement the provisions into national law as they saw fit. However, the development of the internet and the need to protect individual citizens' rights to a private life and ensure that the data collected was protected also needed to be addressed. The EU General Data Protection Regulations (GDPR) meant that member states had to ensure that national law was implemented to recognise them. The *Data Protection Act 2018* was implemented to recognise the principles in the GDPR and to update the UK's law on data protection.

The main elements of the *Data Protection Act 2018* are:

General data processing

- Implements GDPR standards across all general data processing.
- Provides clarity on the definitions used in the GDPR in the UK context.
- Ensures that sensitive health, social care and education data can continue to be processed while making sure that confidentiality in health and safeguarding situations is maintained.
- Provides appropriate restrictions to rights to access and delete data to allow certain processing currently undertaken to continue where there is a strong public policy justification, including for national security purposes.
- Sets the age from which parental consent is not needed to process data online at age 13, supported by a new age-appropriate design code enforced by the Information Commissioner.

Law enforcement processing

- Provides a bespoke regime for the processing of personal data by the police, prosecutors and other criminal justice agencies for law enforcement purposes.
- Allows the unhindered flow of data internationally while providing safeguards to protect personal data.

Intelligence services processing

- Ensures that the laws governing the processing of personal data by the intelligence services remain up-to-date and in line with modernised international standards, including appropriate safeguards with which the intelligence community can continue to tackle existing, new and emerging national security threats.

Regulation and enforcement

- Enacts additional powers for the Information Commissioner who will continue to regulate and enforce data protection laws.
- Allows the Commissioner to levy higher administrative fines on data controllers and processors for the most serious data breaches, up to £17m (€20m) or 4% of global turnover for the most serious breaches.
- Empowers the Commissioner to bring criminal proceedings against offences where a data controller or processor alters records with intent to prevent disclosure following a subject access request.

(DCMS, 2018)

To summarise the above, all public and private organisations must ensure that they protect the information they have and store it securely. The information must be held with the consent of the individual where possible and only shared if the data controller (the person holding the data) can establish why the information needs to be shared. Finally, the information stored must be accessible to the individual it relates to.

The Information Commissioner's Office (ICO) was set up to uphold information rights in the public interest. It investigates breaches of data protection and imposes penalties if a breach has been found. A maximum fine of up to £17.5 million or 4 per cent of the total annual worldwide turnover in the preceding financial year, whichever is higher. The ICO can also take the following actions:

- issue warnings and reprimands;
- impose a temporary or permanent ban on data processing;
- order the rectification, restriction, or erasure of data; and
- suspend data transfers to third countries.

Part 3 of the DPA 2018 places a duty on organisations to report certain types of data breaches to the ICO within 72 hours of becoming aware of the breach if 'left unaddressed such a breach is likely to have a significant detrimental effect on individuals. For example:

- result in discrimination;
- damage to reputation;
- financial loss; or
- loss of confidentiality or any other significant economic or social disadvantage.'

(ICO, n.d.(a))

Freedom of Information

The public have a right to ask for official information that public bodies hold unless an exemption applies. The purpose is to ensure transparency and accountability of public bodies and their actions.

Public bodies also have an obligation to make official information available to the public, as follows.

The *Freedom of Information Act 2000* provides public access to information held by public authorities. It does this in two ways:

public authorities are obliged to publish certain information about their activities; and
members of the public are entitled to request information from public authorities …

Public authorities include government departments, local authorities, the NHS, state schools and police forces. However, the Act does not necessarily cover every organisation that receives public money. For example, it does not cover some charities that receive grants and certain private sector organisations that perform public functions.

Recorded information includes printed documents, computer files, letters, emails, photographs, and sound or video recordings.

The Act does not give people access to their own personal data (information about themselves) such as their health records or credit reference file. If a member of the public wants to see information that a public authority holds about them, they should make a data protection subject access request.

(ICO at: https://ico.org.uk/for-organisations/guide-to-freedom-of-information/?template=pdf#:~:text=The%20Freedom%20of%20Information%20Act,request%20information%20from%20public%20authorities)

Exemptions to a freedom of information request include where the process of collating the information would cost too much or take too much staff time to deal with, or if the request is vexatious, or it repeats a previous request from the same person. Exemptions also include information requested that is in relation to government policy, in cases of a criminal investigations or include the security services.

Remedies for Breach of Confidentiality

A legal remedy is a decision made by the court to correct a wrong committed against another party. Examples of remedies in relation to a breach of confidentiality are provided in Figure 4.1.

Injunctions	This orders the wrongdoer to do or not to do something.
Damages	Financial compensation awarded to the party that has been wronged.
A court order	An order for delivery and destruction of materials breached.
An account for profits	A remedy that requires any profits made from the breach to be surrendered.

Figure 4.1 Remedies

Consent

The following section considers the importance of gaining consent when needing to share information regarding children and adults. In practice, gaining the consent of the individual is the first principle that needs to be followed but, as we can see above, there are many circumstances when a social worker must decide to share confidential information without the consent of the individual concerned. When working with adults, gaining consent before sharing information is paramount. If they lack the capacity to give consent to the sharing of their information, the social worker must use the principles provided by the *Mental Capacity Act 2005* (Chapter 14). The MCA also applies to those from the age of 16. Furthermore, the law states that a 16- and 17-year-old can make their own decisions if they have the capacity. However, when working with children under the age of 16, the requirements for gaining consent rest with the child, their parents and, if necessary, medical opinion.

The Gillick competency test (see Chapter 6) is used to determine whether a child between the ages of 12 and 16 understands the consequences of the decision they are being asked to make and therefore whether they have the competency to make that decision. It is a test used by many frontline practitioners in health and social care, and therefore one that needs to be understood by the social workers. The test was introduced following a case that set the precedent for gaining consent from children.

Gillick v West Norfolk & Wisbeck Area Health Authority [1986] AC 112 House of Lords

The case concerned a mother who sought a declaration by the court that it would be unlawful for a doctor to prescribe contraceptives to girls under 16 without the knowledge or consent of their parent.

The Department of Health and Social Security (DHSS) had issued guidance on family planning services, which contained a section dealing with contraceptive advice and treatment for young people. It stated that clinic sessions should be available for people of all ages, that in order not to undermine parental responsibility and family stability the department hoped that attempts would always be made to persuade children under the age of 16 who attended clinics to involve their parent or guardian at the earliest stage of consultation, and that it would be most unusual to provide contraceptive advice to such children without parental consent.

It was also stated that to abandon the principle of confidentiality between doctor and patient in respect of children under 16 years might cause some not to seek professional advice at all, thus exposing them to risks such as pregnancy and sexually transmitted diseases, and that in exceptional cases it was for a doctor exercising his clinical judgement to decide whether to prescribe contraception. Mrs Gillick, the mother of five girls under the age of 16 years, wrote to her local area health authority seeking an assurance from them that no contraceptive advice or treatment would be given to any of her daughters while under 16 years of age without her knowledge and consent. The area health authority refused to give such an assurance and stated that, in accordance with the guidance, the final decision must be for the doctor's clinical judgement. Mrs Gillick began an action by a declaration that the guidance gave advice which was unlawful and wrong, and which adversely affected parental rights and duties. The Court of Appeal allowed Mrs Gillick's appeal on the grounds that a girl under 16 was incapable either of consenting to medical treatment or of validly prohibiting a doctor from seeking the consent of her parents, and that the advice contained in the DHSS guidance was contrary to law. This meant, therefore, that any doctor who treated a girl under 16 without the consent of her parent or guardian would be infringing the inalienable and legally enforceable rights of parents relating to the custody and upbringing of their children which, save in an emergency, could not be overridden otherwise than by resort to a court exercising its jurisdiction to act in the best interests of the child.

The DHSS appealed the decision and the House of Lords found in their favour, stating the following:

1. that a girl under the age of 16 years had the legal capacity to consent to medical examination and treatment, including contraceptive treatment, if she had sufficient maturity and intelligence to understand the nature and implications of the proposed treatment;
2. that the parental right to control a minor child deriving from parental duty was a dwindling right which existed only in so far as it was required for the child's benefit and protection; that the extent and duration of that right could not be ascertained by reference to a fixed age, but depended on the degree of intelligence and understanding of that particular child and a judgment of what was best for the welfare of the child.

The case also provided for the Fraser Guidelines which are used by medical professionals when giving advice to children on contraception and sexual health while upholding their wishes for confidentiality. The principle of consent in relation to working with children and their families is expanded in Chapters 6 and 7.

Thought Box

*   How do you think an assessment for Gillick competency should be carried out?
*   What questions would you ask a child under 16 to establish if they have 'sufficient maturity and intelligence to understand the nature and implications of the proposed treatment'?

Gaining Consent from Adults

When providing care to an adult, professionals need to gain consent from the 'relevant person', which means the service user or a nominated representative. If a young person from the age of 16 or an adult lacks capacity to consent as determined under the Mental Capacity Act 2005, then the best interests of the individual must be established. The regulations provide for this to be undertaken by an appointed lasting power of attorney, deputy or nearest relative if they are being treated under the *Mental Health Act 1983*, which determines the law regarding consent during detention for treatment of a mental disorder. The principle of consent is discussed further in Chapters 13 and 14.

Accessing Medical and Care Records

Social workers need to know about service users' access to their records and what, if anything, can be withheld. The DPA 2018 provides for people to access data held about them.

Section 45

Right of access by the data subject

1. A data subject is entitled to obtain from the controller—

    (a) ... confirmation as to whether or not personal data concerning him or her is being processed, and

    (b) where that is the case, access to the personal data and the information set out in subsection (2) ...

Schedule 3 of the GDPR provides for exemptions to access specifically for health, social work, education and child abuse data. The exemptions include:

- ... the extent that complying with the right of access would be likely to prejudice carrying out social work because it would be likely to cause serious harm to the physical or mental health of any individual. This is known as the 'serious harm test' for social work data.
- This exemption can apply if you receive a request (in exercise of a power conferred by an enactment or rule of law) for child abuse data. If you are unsure whether the data you process is 'child abuse data', see paragraph 21(3) of Schedule 3, Part 5 of the DPA 2018 for a definition ...

(ICO: see exemptions at: https://ico.org.uk/for-organisations/
guide-to-data-protection/guide-to-the-general-data-
protection-regulation-gdpr/exemptions/#ex21)

Further guidance for social workers can be found on the CQC website (see: www.cqc.org.uk/sites/default/files/Accessing%20medical%20and%20care%20records%20900092.pdf).

E-professionalism

A developing area of social work practice is that of social media. There are many useful attributes that social media can bring to social work practice, specifically in relation to best practice. However, the use of social media has many disadvantages for both the social work practitioner and student, especially when on placement.

Social Work England, the regulating body for social work practice states:

'As a social worker, I will not ... use technology, social media or other forms of electronic communication unlawfully, unethically, or in a way that brings the profession into disrepute.' *R (on application of) Ngole* v *University of Sheffield* 2019 highlights the significance of this quotation.

R (on application of) Ngole v *University of Sheffield* 2019

A student appealed against the refusal of his judicial review challenge to the respondent university's decision to remove him from a course of study. The appellant, a devout Christian, had been enrolled on an MA degree course, successful completion of which led to registration and practice as a qualified social worker. On enrolment, the appellant had signed an agreement confirming that he had read the Health and Care Professions Council (HCPC) guidance on standards of conduct and ethics. He posted comments on social media expressing views on same-sex marriage and homosexuality. The university instituted disciplinary proceedings. The appellant denied having discriminated against anybody. The university's fitness to practise committee found him to be in breach of his professional requirements to keep high standards of professional conduct and to ensure that his behaviour did not damage public confidence in the profession. The Court of Appeal found that even though professional regulations had to be followed and maintained to uphold social work practice values, the decision of the university to expel the student was a disproportionate outcome, taking into account his Article 10 rights to freedom of expression.

The British Association of Social Workers (BASW) provides guidelines for social workers when using social media in practice (see box below).

Social workers should ensure that their online presence is professionally appropriate. Social workers should apply the same principles, expectations and standards for interacting and communicating with people online as in other areas of practice (3.1) ...

... For students, the same issues about boundaries and confidentiality are relevant and the same precautions should be taken with regard to placements. Discretion should be used in relation to using university networks to ensure there is a distinction between personal and professional communication.

Chapter Summary

This chapter has:

- identified the difference between the law on confidentiality and an individual's rights to privacy;
- examined when confidential information should be shared in social work practice and outcomes of serious case reviews;
- discussed the current law on data protection and the responsibilities that are attached to holding information and the rights of those whose data is stored;
- highlighted the policy and ethical considerations in relation to information sharing and confidentiality relevant to social work practice.

Exercises

1. Does English law include a law of confidentiality and/or privacy?
2. What changes has the *Data Protection Act 2018* brought and how does it impact on social work practice?
3. Consider the key points on whether to share information against someone's wishes from this scenario:

> Delia is 15 and has had mental health problems in the past. She visits her GP for a routine check on her medication and asks for advice on contraception as she is in a new relationship with Donny. She tells her GP that she loves Donny but is concerned because he sometimes gets violent towards her. The GP asks Delia if she has discussed her concerns about Donny with her parents and wanting to use contraception. Delia says she hasn't as her parents would be very cross that she was seeing Donny and states that she knows the GP can't tell them because of doctor patient confidentiality and she has rights.

Answers can be found in the Appendix.

Further Reading

BASW, SocialMedia: www.basw.co.uk/system/files/resources/Social%20Media%20Policy.pdf (accessed 28 February 2020). This provides further clarification of the expectations of social workers and students in relation to the increasing use of social media.

Walker, R. (n.d.) The English Law of Privacy – An Evolving Human Right (supremecourt.uk/docs/speech_100825.pdf).

5

Social policy and ethical considerations relevant to the legal context of social work

- consider practice dilemmas associated with the Social Work England *Professional Standards*;
- understand 'responsibility' for and within practice and as a determiner of those viewed as 'deserving' of care and support.

Introduction

The study of social policy and ethics in relation to social work practice are distinct topics that require an in-depth understanding. The following chapter introduces the two subjects to enable the reader to understand the interdisciplinary nature of them in relation to the legal topics examined in this book.

Social policy concerns the need to provide for citizens in society to ensure that their well-being is maintained. Citizens' needs include, *inter alia*, the provision of health and social care services, education, housing and welfare. The organisations responsible for implementing policy that affects social work practice are government, international bodies and voluntary organisations. The policy section of this chapter discusses the relevance of policies made in their legal context. Not only should a social worker know the law and their statutory duties, but they also need to be critically reflective in their practice when making decisions for the benefit of service users. This means that when addressing service users' concerns, it is not only necessary to adhere to the law, but also to consider other issues that are impacting on the service user. For example, a family that requires housing, which the housing department are dealing with, may also have mental health issues that negatively impact on their lives. The social worker must follow the law in relation to their housing needs, but also ensure that other issues affecting their lives are addressed.

The second part of the chapter considers how ethics, values and policy issues must be taken into account in accordance with the professional ethics requirements of the professional registration body, Social Work England, set out in the *Professional Standards for Social Workers*.

Development of Social Policy Studies in Social Work

Social work education and social policy became interlinked at the beginning of the twentieth century, but it was not until after the Second World War that social policy studies were embedded academically in social work education. This was as a result of the development of the welfare state established in 1948 following the adoption of the recommendations in the Beveridge Report (1942), which had identified the problems of ill-health and poverty that many people faced. Beveridge wanted government to establish a system that would provide a minimum standard of living 'from cradle to grave'. The minimum standards of living included improvements to education and housing, and the creation of the National Health Service, funded by taxation.

The Beveridge Report

William Beveridge (1879–1963) was a social economist who, in November 1942, published a report entitled 'Social Insurance and Allied Services' that would provide the blueprint for social policy in post-war Britain. Beveridge had been drawn to the idea of remedying social inequality while working for the Toynbee Hall charitable organisation in East London. He saw that philanthropy was simply not sufficient in such circumstances and a coherent government plan was necessary. By the outbreak of war, Beveridge found himself working in Whitehall where he was commissioned to lead an inquiry into social services. His vision was to battle against what he called the five giants: idleness, ignorance, disease, squalor and want. His 'from cradle to grave' social programme that, among other proposals, called for a free national health service alienated some politicians, but it struck a chord with the public, which would influence Clement Atlee's Labour Government to implement Beveridge's proposals.

(The Beveridge Report: www.nationalarchives.gov.uk)

Since the 1970s, governments have supported the policy of decentralisation. This means that local authorities and the voluntary sector should be responsible for the welfare of residents within their communities using public funds provided by central Government. One reason for this policy is that, because local organisations understand the needs of their residents better, more power should be placed in the hands of local communities. An example of this can be found in the *Localism Act 2011*:

> The Localism Act contains a wide range of measures to devolve more powers to councils and neighbourhoods and give local communities greater control over local decisions like housing and planning.

As seen in Chapter 1, the journey of an Act of Parliament involves scrutiny by the House of Commons and House of Lords. An example of the debates concerning the Localism Bill prior to its enactment in 2011 is given in the box below.

There is an obsessive view, which I suspect comes mainly from civil servants at the centre in Whitehall, that local authorities cannot be trusted to get on and do things sensibly unless they are provided with thousands of pages of detailed rules telling them exactly how they should do them. It is inefficient, because it means that people cannot adjust things to what is sensible for their area. A huge amount of time and resources is wasted at the centre in putting all these documents together and getting agreement on them – it even wastes parliamentary time; and time is wasted in monitoring all the rules and regulations, with people having to account for the way in which they do things, and then in changing them all when things are not going right. It is a ridiculous way to carry on.

Surely now is the time, in a Bill called Localism, to call a halt to it.

(Lord Greaves, Hansard, Col. 1404, 23 June 2011, Vol. 728)

Hansard is a record of the debates held in Parliament for that day and provides an understanding of the development of policy that ministers bring to Parliament. Many are held following petitions from voluntary organisations. It is a valuable resource in the study of social policy and one that will help with future academic essays and dissertations.

Social Policy and Legal Context

Social policy begins by identifying and understanding specific social problems and collating evidence to enable positive change. From there, the government can outline what needs to be done to address the problem, how they will achieve this and what methods and approaches are required. However, there are times when legislation is needed to make policy changes. An example was the *Local Government Act 1988*, which caused a furore when Parliament amended the Act by inserting a new s.28 to prohibit the promotion of homosexuality in teaching or by publishing material. The amendment resulted following concerns that some Labour councils were promoting homosexuality. A clause, described in the box below, was introduced to address this.

A clause prohibiting the promotion of homosexuality by local authorities was then introduced by David Wilshire in the Committee Stage of the Local Government Bill 1987–88 on 2 December 1987. He supported his introduction of the clause with a dossier of examples of the sort of activity it aimed to curtail, ranging from local authority advertisements for lesbian and gay officers, to extracts from the books *Positive Images* and *Jenny lives with Eric and Martin*. This now notorious picture book (depicting a day in the life of a young girl in Denmark who lived with her gay father and his partner) was intended as a resources guide for teaching about homosexuality. According to a guide to Section 28 published by Liberty, only one copy of the book was in circulation. It was held in an Inner London Education Authority teacher's centre and the Chief Education Officer of ILEA had ruled that it should not be made available in school libraries.

(Research Paper 00/47, The Local Government Bill [HL]: the 'Section 28' debate, Bill 87 of 1999–2000)

However, the enactment of s.28 meant that a local authority could be liable for the breach and that LGBT+ children would be disadvantaged. Organisations such as Stonewall were established, which lobbied Parliament and eventually managed to see the repeal of the section in 2003.

One of the many defects of the section is that it is not clear and has never been tested by the courts. If it were so tested, it would not achieve any of the objectives which its original proponents sought from it.

What it has done is create an appalling atmosphere among teachers and social workers who believe that they cannot touch on some of the most difficult problems which people bring to them and that they cannot give them information, education and counselling. That is the effect, not its legal effect, and it is therefore inappropriate for the face of primary legislation ...

My Lords, I am aware of the report from the Institute of Education and believe it to be well founded on the experience of schoolteachers and headteachers. That is one of the main motivations behind our desire to see the repeal of the section and to provide a sensible, calm and caring context in which sexual relationships are advised on by schoolteachers, social workers and youth workers. The continuation of the section has a pernicious effect, and we ought to remove it.

(Lord Whitty, Hansard, Local Government Act 1988:
Section 28 HL Deb, 03 February 2000, Vol. 609, cc347–50)

The importance of voluntary sector groups lobbying Parliament to ensure fair practice for all is highlighted above. Lobbying is the process by which an individual or preferably a group of individuals urge Parliament to support a campaign that will change or develop policy.

There are times when Parliament has to act in emergency situations that will impact on the well-being of the citizen. An example of this is the legislative development to provide for social welfare due to the Coronavirus pandemic in 2020, which had a global impact on lives and welfare. Provisions in the *Coronavirus Act 2020* covered many issues that affect social work practice. These include changes to local authorities' statutory duties under the *Care Act 2014* which allowed LAs to suspend their duty to ensure that provision of care is given to those most in need. However, LAs still had to ensure that they would provide care where there was potential for a breach of an individual's human rights. Social workers working as youth offending officers were also affected by the Act because of concerns that the increased powers given to the police were 'heavy handed'.

Relevance to Social Work Practice

The examples provided above have all illustrated the importance of social policy to social work practice. As a practitioner, it is necessary to understand the impact that policy decisions and potential legislation will have on practice. Furthermore, it is necessary to ensure that a holistic approach is practised when making decisions with service users. The study of social policy helps social workers to think critically about their practice.

Thought Box

Consider the impact that Covid-19 has had on social policy and social work practice.

See: www.basw.co.uk/system/files/resources/basw_social_working_during_the_covid_19_pandemic_initial_findings_26.01.21.pdf

Key Ethical Values and Principles Relevant to Social Work

This chapter examines the ways in which consideration of social work values and ethical issues is important for social work practice. It also examines Social Work England's (SWE) *Professional Standards*, and how these duties and requirements relate to legal issues in practice and looks at some of the current issues facing professionals.

Ethical approaches (also described as moral philosophy) in Western countries derive from ancient Greece and affect how people make decisions and lead their lives. It concerns how individuals, organisations and society can make judgements/guide actions about what is bad and what is good.

Taken from the Greek word *ethos*, which can mean custom, habit or character, the term 'ethics' can be seen to cover such matters as:

- How can I lead a good life?
- What are my rights and responsibilities in terms of others and society in general?
- How can I make moral decisions? How might I, or others, make determinations about what is good and what is bad?

Ideas about ethics arise and develop over time, and can come from religious groups, philosophical traditions and from cultures. They underpin debates on topics such as abortion, human rights and professional conduct.

Often, ethics is considered as an ethereal, distant, impenetrable concept, and of no value to daily life. However, ethical ideas are used every day, usually unconsciously, in terms of, relationships with colleagues, service users and carers, and in developing and maintaining relationships with friends, family and acquaintances. Ethics will, for example, be concerned with whether these relationships should always be underpinned by honesty and loyalty, or whether exceptions can ever be made legitimately.

This chapter contends that ethics, and ethical decision-making, can be seen to be based around some relatively accessible ideas that involve consideration of what is a good action, how this can be determined and how people try to apply this to their thinking, their actions and in making decisions about what do. In fact, people do this every day when balancing up their professional and personal lives, and in how they act with colleagues and service users and carers.

Three key ethical ideas underpin what is examined. The work of Banks (2012) and Beckett et al. (2017) clearly and helpfully set out the differences and similarities between these three approaches: Kantian, utilitarian and virtue ethics.

Immanuel Kant (1724–1804) was a German philosopher who argued that individuals are free to act as moral agents, are responsible for their own actions and have individual rights and liberty. The Kantian approach also sees individuals as having a duty to respect others. This then leads to the concept of self-determination, but then raises problems of how this fits with the self-determination of others if there is a conflict between them. Kant emphasises the individual person's rights and duties, particularly the principles of liberty and justice.

Utilitarianism is about the greatest good for the greatest number of people by way of increasing, for example, pleasure (or absence of pain), happiness or well-being. Utilitarianism stresses the notion of the public good, looking to the consequences of actions with respect to the principles of utility and justice. However, this could be used, for example, to argue that certain groups of people who are not 'productive' economically should not be given any welfare benefits, as we are not ensuring the 'survival of the fittest' or the greatest common good (unless we believe that providing services to people who are not economically productive is a good thing in itself and makes us better people and a better society). Jeremy Bentham (1748–1832), an English philosopher and social reformer, introduced the idea that everyone's interest should count for one unit in such calculations – no more, no less – no matter what their standing or status in society.

This fits well with social work ethical codes and the idea that everyone should be equal and treated equally. However, as already stated, how does this help when social workers have to balance the rights of one person against the rights of others – for example, in safeguarding adults and children at risk of harm? What rights do parents have and what are the rights of people detained under the *Mental Health Act 1983*? On a wider basis, during the Covid-19 pandemic in 2020, debates took place about how to balance the rights of individuals to do what they wish to do against the rights of others not to get infected, and to what extent individuals' freedom of movement could be limited to achieve a possible balance.

A third key approach is that of virtue ethics. While there are many versions of virtue-based approaches, many of them are based on Aristotle's work (a Greek philosopher, 384–322 BC), and on religious traditions. They have in common an emphasis on the moral character of the person carrying out the actions, as opposed to ideas of obligations, duties or principles, and outcomes of actions, which are often emphasised in Kant's and Bentham's work. Elements of virtue might be argued to include integrity, honesty, truthfulness and kindness – all important values for social work; a person of true 'virtue' should *always* tell the truth.

Fundamental and core issues for social work are its basis in individual rights and social justice. However, in the case study below it will be considered whether keeping information confidential and/or honesty must always be judged to be absolutely the right things to do. Respect for all persons, no matter their status, ethnicity, sexuality, LGBTQ+ status or any other attribute, is key to social work approaches and non-judgemental approaches, which means accepting and valuing the individual for who they are. This relates to a key element of Social Work England's *Professional Standards* to 'Assess the influence of cultural and social factors over people and the effect of loss, change and uncertainty in the development of resilience' (s.3.14). The area of individual rights also relates to a key feature of social work values in relation to anti-oppressive practice. Social Work England states:

Social workers understand the multiple and intersecting oppressions and disadvantages that impact people, families and communities. They use their professional power in a positive way with their employer and other professionals to uphold standards and decisions and to challenge structures. (SWE, 2019b: 7)

Biestek (1962), a key and early writer on professional social work, emphasised non-judgemental acceptance and confidentiality, as does the SWE (2019a) – e.g. 'Value each person as an individual, recognising their strengths and abilities' (s1.1, SWE, 2019a). However, this does not mean that social workers are always accepting of someone's behaviours – for example, in work with people who commit crimes or who abuse others. It is also necessary to consider the role of utilitarianism set out above, where a good action is judged not on the basis of an individual's rights, but in relation to the outcomes with reference to the greatest good of the greatest number.

See further discussion of these points in Chapters 10, 15 and 20.

Textbooks provide different emphases and insights on these (and wider) issues. For example, Banks (2012) sets out how, in using utilitarian principles, there are assumptions about human beings being free individuals, while society requires compromises to freedom. Banks discusses one form of utilitarianism, rule utilitarianism, which sets out how people use 'rules' they construct to speed up the process of moral reasoning and decision-making, as they are not able to examine philosophically every action and decision in full. If they did, it would mean that workers would never manage to take any actions! In addition, Banks points out that utilitarianism does not necessarily explain how social workers should weigh up the outcomes of actions to be able to determine whether they are for the greatest good of the greatest number.

Beckett et al. (2017) places emphasis on defining values and ethics, and looking at the moral philosophy that informs social work values and ethics, including those from religion. It discusses throughout the application of its key focus on 'realism' as a necessary precondition for effective social work, examining the real-world applications and tensions between ethical rhetoric and reality. Barsky (2019) is set in the context of social work practice in the USA. It gives pointers on how to integrate knowledge, self-awareness, methods and critical thinking abilities to try to deal with ethical issues in social work. It particularly addresses ideas on the use of social work values such as respect, personal and professional integrity, social justice, human relationships and competence.

The following section identifies important ideas and tools that can help social workers consider how to apply the values of social work, first to service users and carers, but also to their employing agencies and to Social Work England. Social Work England *Professional Standards Guidance* (SWE, 2019b) states that

Ethics in the context of social work is about the professional responsibilities and values social workers have and how they conduct themselves inside and outside the workplace. ... The British Association of Social Workers (BASW) and the International Federation of Social Work (IFSW) both have codes of ethics that social workers in England follow.

(SWE, 2019b: 7)

(Note: The Social Work England *Professional Standards* (2019) used in this chapter are accurate at the time of publication. However, they are subject to periodic review and may be amended from time to time. Please refer to the Social Work England website for the latest version: www.socialworkengland.org.uk/standards/professional-standards/)

In examining SWE's requirements it can be seen that the different Standards may be in competition with each other. The IFSW ethical code (2018) referred to above by SWE states that 'Principles of social justice, human rights, collective responsibility and respect for diversities are central to social work.' It also addresses the dual role of social work and its control as well as care functions:

> Social workers often work with people to find an appropriate balance between competing human rights. … Social workers respect and promote people's rights to make their own choices and decisions, provided this does not threaten the rights and legitimate interests of others.

The following part of the chapter uses case studies, reflective exercises and thought boxes to aid in the application of these issues as applied to service user groups. It also helps to make judgements about, and be able to justify actions to SWE, about why the social worker's actions were 'good' actions (e.g. Banks, 2012; Barsky, 2019; Beckett et al., 2017; Gray and Webb, 2010).

Case study – Moral dilemmas

One ethical issue that affects social workers is whether they should always be honest. Look at the following case example, then consider the issues arising in the Thought Box that follows.

During a visit to a service user (A) the social worker finds them to be in great mental distress, which is part of their mental health problems. The social worker knows that A has a history of being violent to others because of the delusions A has when in this type of vulnerable and frightened state. A becomes agitated and asks the social worker to promise not to let anyone else know of any concerns the social worker may have about them, as they are afraid of being admitted to hospital again against their will. Does the social worker do this to protect themselves and then subsequently break that promise? Or does the social worker make clear that they will have to tell other agencies of the situation and risk compromising the rights of A under the law and policies to protect the social worker's interests and rights, health and safety, if they were to become violent towards them?

In the example above, it can seem that there are conflicting elements in SWE *Professional Standards* on how social workers might determine and justify a good action in terms of being 'honest' (s.2.1), 'respecting people's privacy' (s.2.2) and 'treating confidential information about people in line with the law' (s.2.6). At the same time, social workers are told to 'Make sure that relevant colleagues and agencies are informed about identified risks and the outcomes and implications of assessments and decisions I make' (s.3.9); 'Use my assessment skills to respond quickly to dangerous situations and take any necessary protective action' (s.3.12).

Thought Box

Justifying my actions and decisions

If social workers are asked to articulate and justify their approaches, decisions and actions in circumstances relating to their social work practice, consider how, and on what basis, they may be able to clearly set out the reasons for that course of action, based on their understanding and interpretation of social work values and the *Professional Standards*.

Chapter Summary

The chapter has:

- identified the significance of social policy to social work practice and academic study;
- examined the importance of social work values and ethics in practice;
- considered practice dilemmas associated with the Social Work England *Professional Standards*;
- set out the ways in which to consider ethical principles in terms of helping to identify and decide actions based upon such ethical dilemmas in social work practice and how to interpret the sometimes conflicting requirements in SWE's *Professional Standards*;
- discussed ways in which such considerations can aid social workers in delivering their professional requirements required by SWE.

Case study – Ethical principles

M is in his early forties, lives alone at home and is an avid supporter of his local football team. He subscribes, through the Club, to their own TV network, watching matches home and away. He has many contacts with fans across the country and throughout the world, linking through Twitter, Facebook and Instagram. He is known for his funny and frequent posts, attracting many thousands of followers. While active on social media, M has not been out of his second-floor flat, above a shop on the main road, for years. No one knows why M stopped going out and whether this was sudden or gradual. Now M is reliant on neighbours and shopkeepers for his shopping. Always describing himself as 'big boned', M has gained considerable weight in recent years, weighing now approximately 40 stones. He struggles to move around the flat unaided and is no longer able to get down the stairs to the front door. M is worried about how he would escape if there was a fire in the flat or shop below. His weight is causing acute health complications, but he is unable to attend outpatient appointments. He has tried to diet, but loses motivation and will power, being at home alone with little encouragement. His weight is increasing. M's GP has reported that his patient is suffering from severe depression, but is concerned about the consequences of prescribing medication, given possible side effects and further increases in weight. M complains that 'they all' blame him for how things are and that no one attempts to understand how he has reached such a point in his life. He has referred several times to feeling like 'ending it all'. No one, he feels, appreciates the consequences for him and what he describes as a never-ending cycle of isolation, inactivity, eating, isolation and inactivity. M's biggest fear is that he will die suddenly at home, alone. He worries that emergency services would not be able to get him out of the flat without removing the front window and lifting him down. For M this would be the ultimate humiliation.

As the social worker in the above situation, what ethical considerations might you use to reflect on whether you should be completely honest with the service user who is in mental distress that may help you put in operation the apparently conflicting SWE requirements set out here?

Answers can be found in the Appendix.

Further Reading

British Association of Social Workers (2014) *The Code of Ethics for Social Work,* available at: www.basw.co.uk/about-basw/code-ethics

International Federation of Social Workers (IFSW) (2018) Global social work statement of ethical principles, available at: www.ifsw.org/global-social-work-statement-of-ethical-principles/

Littlechild, B. and Hawley, C. (2010) Risk assessments for mental health service users: ethical, valid and reliable? *Journal of Social Work,* first published online on 4 August 2009 as doi:10.1177/1468017309342191, then in print in April 2010, 10 (2).

Social Work England (2019a) *Professional Standards,* available at: www.socialworkengland.org.uk/standards/professional-standards/

Social Work England (2019b) *Professional Standards Guidance,* available at: www.socialworkengland.org.uk/standards/guidance-documents/professional-standards-guidance/

Part 2

Social Work with Children and Families

6

The Law, Social Policy and Ethics Relating to Children and Families

Chapter Objectives

By the end of the chapter, readers will be able to:

- understand the law, social policy and ethics relating to children and families relevant to social work practice;

(Continued)

- identify who are defined as 'children in need' and their families and under-stand the services that local authorities must or can provide;
- understand the context in which the law operates and its relevance to social work;
- apply the rules to the practice of social work with children and families.

Introduction

This chapter provides an overview of the law specifically relevant to children and fami-lies in England. Although England, Wales, Scotland and Northern Ireland have different systems in place to protect children, all the relevant legal rules are predicated on the same principles – that is, that children (people under the age of 18 in England, Wales and Northern Ireland (16 in Scotland)), because of their age and vulnerability, need to be protected from harm. Important provisions of the *Children Act 1989* (CA) are examined, as well as the role of organisations/bodies that have a remit to protect children's rights. This includes the important responsibilities that the law places on parents and guardians of children, how the courts determine disputes between parents about the upbringing of their children and a local authority's responsibilities to 'children in need'.

Ethical Principles

An important ethical principle relevant to working with children and families is the need to respect the right to self-determination. The law recognises that children under the age of 16 can have the capacity to make decisions for themselves, and therefore have a right to confidentiality (see *Gillick* v *West Norfolk & Wisbech Area Health Authority*, UKHL 7 (1985) (Chapter 4). However, in *Bell* v *Tavistock and Portman NHS Foundation Trust* [2020] EWHC, the High Court held that children under 16 with gender dys-phoria 'are unlikely to be able to give informed consent' to take puberty-blocking drugs and any proposed treatment must first be sanctioned by a court. Where children do have the capacity to make a relevant decision, this means that the information cannot be shared with the child's parents without the child's consent unless disclosure is justi-fied in the 'public interest' because it is necessary to safeguard and protect children from harm (see Chapters 4 and 10 for further discussion).

Social Policy and Children

'Social policies play a key role in the lives of children and their families, and children rely very heavily on welfare services for their present and future well-being' (Ridge, 2015). Important areas of social policy that directly impact on children's lives include access to education and healthcare, as well as the social service and welfare provision. The cost of housing, low pay and recent reforms of the benefits system have been identified as key factors in the increase of numbers of children living in poverty (see Chapters 19 and 20, and the Children's Commissioner blog: Fact checking claims about child poverty (2020)). This is relevant as the social worker's role is not just to protect children from abuse and neglect, but to help improve the well-being of children and their families by helping them to access appropriate services. Social workers should also act as advocates for reform. Since the *Children Act*, which makes the welfare of the child paramount, there has been growing recognition that children's voices should be heard when decisions are taken about them. See: *Munro Review of Child Protection: Final Report – A child-centred system* (DfE, 2011).

Important Legislation Relating to Children and the Law

Children Act 1989

Education Act 1996

Crime and Disorder Act 1998

Children Act 2004

Childcare Act 2006

Children, Schools and Families Act 2010

Children and Families Act 2014

Childcare Act 2016

Children and Social Work Act 2017

The *Children Act 1989* provides the legal framework for the care and protection of children; it has been amended several times over the last 20 years to reflect changing social norms, developing social policies and as a result of high-profile child abuse cases (Chapter 10). It is supported by important guidance, *Working Together to Safeguard Children: Statutory guidance on inter-agency working to safeguard and promote the welfare of children* (the Statutory Guidance (2018) updated in 2020), which is issued under s.7 of the *Local Authority Social Services Act 1970* (see Chapter 1). It sets out, in practical terms, what social workers must do at all stages of a local authority's involvement in supporting, protecting and safeguarding children (Chapter 7).

Protection of Children's Rights

Both domestic law (law made in the UK) and international law (law made as a result of agreement between the UK and other countries) seeks to protect children's basic rights and give children a voice. An underpinning principle is that children should enjoy these rights regardless of age, race, language, sex, disability, sexual orientation, or any other status. The following are important organisations/bodies that are relevant to protecting children and have important implications for social work practice.

The Children's Commissioner for England (CCE)

The CCE was established in 2005 following a recommendation in the Victoria Climbié Inquiry: *Report of an Inquiry by Lord Laming* (2003) (see Chapter 7). The role is to promote and protect the rights of children, especially the most vulnerable, by speaking up for them so that policy-makers can consider their views and interests. There is also a Children's Commissioner for Wales and a Children and Young People's Commissioner for Scotland. Examples of the work undertaken by the CCE includes supporting children in care and care leavers, highlighting the problems of vulnerable children such as those with mental health problems, those excluded from school, at risk of neglect or who are living with parents with health problems. The CCE has an advice service, Help at Hand. They regularly publish reports to highlight important problems – for example, *Bleak Houses: Tackling the crisis of family homelessness in England* (August 2019) which makes important recommendations about how homelessness can be prevented, and the use of temporary accommodation.

Thought Box

How effective has the CCE been in influencing government policy?

The Children and Family Court Advisory and Support Service (CAFCASS)

CAFCASS is an independent organisation established by Part II of the *Criminal Justice and Courts Services Act 2000* to safeguard and promote the welfare of the children involved in family court proceedings. It gives advice to the court and provides information, advice and other support for children and their families. Family proceedings include private law cases – i.e. disputes between parents about the care of their child – and public law cases (applications by LAs for care and supervision orders) (Chapter 7), and adoption applications (Chapter 8). CAFCASS makes recommendations on what it considers the 'child's best interests' (s.1, CA 1989). In care proceedings, the CAFCASS worker is known as the Children's Guardian (CG) – i.e. the voice of the child in court. Section 41, CA 1989 places a duty on the CG to safeguard the interests of the child (Practice Direction 16A – Representation of Children (2017)). The CG will appoint a solicitor to represent the child, talk to the parents, the child (if old enough) and, where relevant, teachers, social workers and health visitors before compiling their report. The LA's care plan will be analysed and advice given to the court on what should happen.

Two international treaties that are also important are:

1. The **United Nations Convention on the Rights of the Child (UNCRC)** is a legally binding international agreement setting out the civil, political, economic, social and cultural rights of every child, regardless of their race, religion or abilities (see Chapter 9).
2. **The European Convention on Human Rights** (see Chapter 2).

The *Children Act 1989* (CA 1989)

The law makes special provision for children in relation to a range of issues designed to give children certain rights and aimed at protecting them from harm.

Welfare of the Child (s.1, CA 1989)

All decisions that the family courts make that involve children – that is, whether it is a private or a public law action – are determined by 'the 'welfare principle' (s.1, *Children Act 1989*) which provides:

- the welfare of the child is the court's paramount consideration;
- delay is likely to prejudice the welfare of the child;
- the court should not make an order unless to do so would be better for the child than making no order (the 'no order principle').

The 'paramountcy principle' means that the best interests of the child takes priority over the rights and interests of parents and others.

In reaching such decisions the courts are required to have regard to the following s.1 (3):

a) the ascertainable wishes of the child;
b) the child's physical, emotional and educational needs;
c) the likely effect on the child of a change of circumstances;
d) the child's age, sex, background and any relevant characteristics;
e) any harm the child is suffering or likely to suffer;
f) the capability of the parents of meeting the child's needs (if relevant); and
g) the range of powers available to the court.

What is a 'Family'?

Radical changes have also taken place in the last 20 years to the construct of what constitutes a 'family':

and children in the 21st century live increasingly complex lives in a range of diverse family settings. Policies seek to respond to social and demographic change but changing ideologies and constructions of childhood will also affect how governments formulate policies and provide services. (Ridge, 2015)

These changes are reflected in the determination of parental responsibility (see below).

Parental Responsibility (ss.2–4, CA 1989)

Parental responsibility (PR) means:

> all the rights, duties, powers, responsibilities and authority which by law a parent of a child has in relation to the child and his property (s.3).

In practical terms, this means that parents are responsible for providing their child with a home, and maintaining and protecting them from harm. Parents must also ensure that their child receives appropriate education, necessary medical treatment and their property is looked after. They can also determine their child's religion and appoint a guardian to look after them – for example, in the event of death or while working abroad.

The duty to support a child financially is not dependent on the parent(s) having PR, nor is PR dependent on whether the parent lives with the child. The Child Maintenance Service has enforcement powers to ensure that appropriate financial support is provided by the person with PR (see: https,//assests.publishing.gov.uk/government/uploads/system/uploads/attachment_data/file/325266/receiving-child-maintanence.pdf).

The natural parents' PR ends if their child is adopted (s.46, *Adoption and Children Act 2002*); the adoption order gives the adoptive parent(s) PR for their adopted child (Chapter 8). However, where a child lives with other than his birth parents but is not the subject of an adoption order – for example, where a family member takes responsibility for looking after that child – PR remains with the parent(s) but may be shared with the person looking after the child or the LA if the child is subject to a care order. In these circumstances the parents' ability to exercise PR is restricted as day-to-day decision-making rests with the person(s) looking after the child. Both same-sex parents have PR for the child if they were civil partners at the time of the appropriate 'treatment' – e.g. donor insemination.

A person with PR does not have an automatic right of contact with the child (s.34, CA 1989) (Chapter 7). Where contact is disputed, contact with an absent parent is determined by the child's best interests (s.1, CA 1989).

Who has PR?

A birth mother (including a surrogate mother) has PR for her child from birth. PR is transferred from the surrogate mother to the commissioning parent(s) on the grant of a Parental Order by the family court. A father will also have PR for the child if he is married to the child's mother when the child was born (or, in Scotland, when the child was conceived); there is a rebuttable presumption that a husband is the father of the child. An unmarried father can obtain PR by:

1. jointly registering the child's birth with the mother (from 1 December 2003); or
2. obtaining a parental agreement with the mother; or
3. obtaining a parental responsibility order from the court.

Step-parents do not automatically acquire PR on marriage to the child's father or mother, but can obtain it by entering into a parental responsibility agreement (with written consent of every person who has PR for the child) or by order from a court. A parent does not lose PR on divorce.

Parents are also responsible for disciplining their child. Section 58, CA 2004 makes it unlawful for a parent to smack their child unless this amounts to 'reasonable punishment' (which is not defined). It is illegal for schools, nurseries and childcare workers to smack another person's child. Unreasonable forms of punishment are criminal offences (see Chapter 16).

Thought Box

What is 'reasonable punishment' and should any smacking of a child be unlawful? The *Children (Equal Protection from Assault) (Scotland) Act 2019* changed the law in Scotland from November 2020 by removing the 'reasonable chastisement' defence in assault cases.

Disputes about the Care of a Child (s.8, CA 1989)

Parents who have PR but cannot agree about the child's welfare – e.g. who the child should live with, spend time with or have contact with, their schooling, medical treatment or whether the child should live abroad – can apply to the family court for one of the following orders (private law proceedings) under s.8, CA 1989:

1. **A Child Arrangements Order** is an order that decides who a child lives with, who they spend time with or have contact with and for how long. They can be used to settle disputes between parents when the relationship has broken down or in cases where children live with other than their birth parents. Some orders contain very detailed arrangements while others are more open. See *B & C (Children: Child Arrangement Order)* [2018] EWFC B100. An enforcement order can be obtained (under s.11J, CA 1989) if the court is satisfied 'beyond reasonable doubt' (the criminal burden of proof) that a person has failed to comply with the order.

2. A **Specific Issue Order** is an order that determines a specific question about how PR should be exercised – e.g. which school the child should go to, whether the child's name should be changed, or whether the child should have a particular medical treatment – e.g. circumcision or the MMR vaccine (see *EG* v *JG* [2013] *EW* v *JG* [2013] EW Misc 23 CC, which involved a dispute between the parents about the schooling of their children).

3. A **Prohibited Steps Order** is an order to prevent one parent from making a decision about the child's upbringing when the other parent disagrees. See *Re A and B (Prohibited Steps Order at Dispute Resolution Appointment)* [2015] EWFC B16 which involved an appeal by the father against an order requiring him to refrain from involving his children in political activities.

Applications for s.8 orders are made to the family court; CAFCASS will be involved if the court requires it to be. See the final report of the Ministry of Justice (MoJ), Assessing risk of harm to children and parents in private law children's cases (October 2020). LAs cannot apply for a child arrangements order, but can apply for a specific issue or prohibited steps order (see: www.gov.uk/government/consultations/assessing-risk-of-harm-to-children-and-parents-in-private-law-children-cases).

Local Authorities' Duty to Provide Court Reports (s.7, CA 1989)

Under s.7, a court can require the LA or CAFCASS to provide a welfare report in any s.8 private law proceedings. The court will specify the issues they want addressed and, if there is evidence of domestic abuse, will require a 'safety and risk assessment'. The court will usually set a timetable for submission of the report, often between 12 and 16 weeks. The report should provide a history of LA involvement with the family, the profile of the child and each adult who is a party to the proceedings, a summary of the assessment, comments on the welfare checklist (s.1), and conclusions and recommendations (see *MS* v *MN* [2017] EWHC 324 (Fam)).

Section 37, CA 1989 allows the court, when considering a s.8 CA application, where appropriate, to make an interim care or supervision order instead, and can direct the LA to investigate the child's circumstances (see *Re F (Children) [2014]* EWCA Civ 1474). If it is concluded that the LA should provide services to the family, a detailed description of the services must be appended. The social worker responsible for producing the report will generally need to attend the court hearing.

Wardship

In cases where issues concerning the welfare of a child cannot be resolved under the CA 1989, the family court can exercise its 'inherent jurisdiction' – that is, the right to make decisions on any matter that comes before it unless it is specifically prohibited from doing so by case law or Act of Parliament. The child must be under 18 and either 'physically present' or 'habitually resident' in England and Wales – that is, show that this is their main home and where they intend to stay. If a child is made a 'ward of court', the court becomes the legal guardian and, although day-to-day care and control still rests with the individual looking after them (e.g. a parent or LA), the court's consent is required when making important decisions about the child's life. See, for example, the decision in *Re S (Wardship)* [2016] EWFC B1.

The most common examples of wardship cases are orders to stop the press publishing names to prevent 'undesirable association', orders for emergency medical treatment, orders to return children to and from another country, and to protect a child from a forced marriage.

Education

Education is compulsory from the age of 5 until 16 (children can be home-schooled). Once a person is 16, they must either 1) stay in full-time education; 2) start an apprenticeship or traineeship; or 3) spend 20 hours in paid or voluntary work while attending part-time education.

If a child is absent from school without good reason, local councils and schools can take legal action to enforce attendance by using one or more of the following orders.

1. A Parenting Order (s.8 *Crime and Disorder Act 1998*) requires attendance at parenting classes to improve a child's or children's school attendance.
2. An Education Supervision Order (s.36 *Children Act 1989*) requires the appointment of a supervisor to help get the child(ren) into education.
3. A School Attendance Order (s.437, *Education Act 1996*) gives a parent 15 days to ensure that the child is registered with a school or is being home-schooled. Failure to do this can result in prosecution or a fine (a local council can impose a fine of £60 (£120 if not paid within 21 days); non-payment after 28 days can result in prosecution).

Section 444(1) of the *Education Act 1996* provides that where a child is absent from school without authorisation (whether the parent knows or not), the parent is guilty of an offence punishable with a fine up to £1,000.

Section 444(1A) provides that if a child is absent without authorisation with parental knowledge, the offence is punishable by a fine of up £2,500 and a prison sentence of up to three months.

The following defences apply:

- Absence because of sickness or an 'unavoidable' emergency.
- Absence because the day was set aside exclusively for religious observance.
- The LA had failed to make the necessary travel arrangements for the child when it had a duty to do so (see: Sentencing Council, 2017).

The LA has a duty to investigate (s.47, CA 1989) where children are absent from school because of abuse or neglect (s.31, CA; see Chapter 7).

Leaving home

Once a child reaches the age of 16, they can choose to leave home; before a child is 16 a parent cannot legally tell them to leave. However, for a child to find accommodation without parental support may be difficult as private landlords often require a 'guarantor' (usually a parent) to pay the rent if it is not paid. Furthermore, access to state benefits may be restricted (see Chapter 19).

Children's services have a duty to accommodate 16- and 17-year-olds excluded from the family home if assessed as a 'child in need' within s.17, CA 1989 (see below). If the child falls within the criteria set out in s.20, CA 1989, the child will become a looked after child (see Chapter 7).

Consent

There is a presumption that anyone aged 16 and over (s.2, *Mental Capacity Act 2005*) (Chapter 14) has the capacity to make their own decisions and therefore 16- and 17-year-olds can, for example, give consent to medical treatment without parental involvement (see above).

> Sexual activity with a child under 13 is a criminal offence as, by law (s.5, *Sexual Offences Act 2003*), they cannot give valid consent to any form of sexual activity. The maximum sentence is life imprisonment. It will also be a safeguarding issue within s.31, CA 1989 (Chapter 7). Sexual activity with a child between the ages of 13 and 16 is also an offence, but Home Office Guidance (Home Office, 2004, Children and Families: Safer from Sexual Crime – the *Sexual Offences Act 2003*) provides that teenagers under 16 will not be prosecuted where both parties mutually agree and are of a similar age. Once 16, a person can give valid consent to sexual activity.

Where a person over 18 years holds a position of trust (for example, a social worker or teacher) in respect of a person under 18 years old (e.g. pupil, service user, etc.), any sexual activity with that person will constitute a breach of trust and a criminal offence regardless of the child's capacity to consent (s.16, *Sexual Offences Act 2003*).

If a child lacks capacity (that is, they are under 16 and do not have the requisite understanding to give valid consent) to give consent – for example, to medical treatment – someone with PR (see above) can consent for them if that is in the child's best interests. If the person with PR refuses to consent, this can be overruled by the courts, as can a competent child's refusal to give consent to life-saving treatment (see University of Leeds, n.d.). All children with the relevant level of understanding can expect to be involved in decisions about their welfare (s.1, CA 1989).

LA Support for Children and Families (ss.17–30, CA 1989)

Part III of the *Children Act 1989* sets out the legal rules governing support for children and families provided by LAs in England. Wales, Scotland and Northern Ireland have separate legislation.

The following are the important provisions applicable to England.

The provision of services for children in need (CiN), their families and others (ss.17– 30, *Children Act 1989*)

---

s.17(1), *Children Act 1989* provides two important underpinning principles and places 'a general duty' on local authorities in England:

a) To safeguard and promote the welfare of children within their area who are in need, and
b) So far as is consistent with that duty, to promote the upbringing of such children by their families, by providing a range and level of services appropriate to those children's needs.

s.17(3) states:

> Any service provided by an authority in the exercise of functions conferred on them by this section may be provided for the family of a particular child in need or for any member of his family, if it is provided with a view to safeguarding or promoting the child's welfare.

In March 2020, there were 389,260 children in need in England (GOV.UK statistics). 'Children in need' are children who require additional help to enable them to reach their potential. The *Statutory Guidance* (2018) states (Chapter 1) that relevant children should receive the help they need from local organisations that should ensure:

- that help is given as soon as the need arises;
- effective measures are taken to identify children and families who would benefit from early help;
- effective assessments for early help;
- the availability of the relevant help;
- getting the right help at the right time;
- responding appropriately to referrals; and
- sharing information with relevant practitioners and organisations.

s.17(10), CA states that 'a child is a child in need' if:

a) he is unlikely to achieve or maintain, or to have the opportunity of achieving or maintaining, a reasonable standard of health or development without the provision for him of services by a LA under this part;
b) his health or development is likely to be significantly impaired, or further impaired, without the provision for him of such services; or
c) he is disabled.

Section 17(11) CA provides:

> For the purposes of this Part, a child is disabled if he is blind, deaf or dumb or suffers from mental disorder of any kind or is substantially and permanently handicapped by illness, injury or congenital deformity or such other disability as may be prescribed, and in this Part –
>
> 'development' means physical, intellectual, emotional, social or behavioural development and 'health' means physical or mental health.

There is evidence that children with disabilities are more vulnerable to abuse because they are more likely to be socially isolated, unable to resist abuse, have impaired communication skills and are vulnerable to bullying and at greater risk of exclusion from school (discussed further in Chapter 7). See: Islington Safeguarding Children Board: Disabled Children: www.islingtonscb.org.uk.

Part 3 of the *Children and Families Act 2014* sets out the duties owed by LAs, health bodies, schools and colleges to provide for children and young people with special educational needs. LAs must maintain a register of disabled children which includes undertaking a needs assessment, and providing:

*   information about the services available;
*   an educational, health and care plan; and
*   a range of services.

Section 2 of the CSDPA 1970 provides a list of services that LAs must provide for disabled children (see: www.legislation.gov.uk/ukpga/1970/44/section/2).

Direct payments can be made to a person with PR for a disabled child; a disabled person with PR for a child; and to a disabled child aged 16 or over. Each LA has eligibility criteria to prioritise need in relation to the resources available.

The Common Assessment Framework (CAF) 'is a standardised approach for the assessment of children and their families, to help with the early identification of additional needs and promote a coordinated service response'. Families can refuse to be assessed; if they do agree, they can choose what information to share. The social worker's assessment is an 'evaluative judgement', which can only be successfully challenged if either it was not carried out properly or the decision is 'irrational' – i.e. one that a reasonable LA would not make. In *R (on the application of AC & SH) v London Borough of Lambeth* [2017] EWHC 1796, the LA's assessments were found to be 'procedurally unfair'; a fresh assessment was ordered. Similarly, in *R (AM) v Havering LBC* [2015] EWHC 1004 Admin, the LA had acted irrationally in deciding that the children were not CiN as the family were homeless and unable to find accommodation.

Section 17(4A) requires LAs to ascertain the child's wishes and feelings, and give 'due consideration' (having regard to their age and understanding) to the wishes expressed before deciding what services to provide. If a child is assessed as a 'child in need' (CiN), the LA must provide services set out in a CiN plan which delineates the nature of the support required and why; which agency will provide that support; the expected outcomes; the time frame and provision for regular reviews (three months after the start of the CiN plan and then at least every six months).

Support provided can include the following.

Accommodation (s.17(6) and S20)

An LA can provide accommodation for a homeless family for whom the LA housing department does not have a statutory duty – e.g. because the family is 'intentionally homeless' (Chapter 19). However, the duty under s.17 is a 'general duty' – i.e. LAs *may* provide for the family to be accommodated together, but do not have a specific duty to do so. In *R v Barnet LBC ex parte G*; *R v Lambeth LBC (ex parte W)* and *R v Lambeth LBC (ex parte A)* [2003] UKHL 57, the House of Lords decided that, although most homeless children will be 'CiN', s.17 did not impose an obligation on the LA to provide accommodation to enable a dependent child to live with their family.

Thought Box

Is this decision incompatible with s.17(1)(b)?

Note: Children accommodated under s.17, CA are not 'looked after children' (Chapter 7) because they are neither subject to a care order nor voluntarily accommodated by the LA under s.20, CA.

s.20 CA: LA duty to provide accommodation

In contrast to s.17(6), s.20, CA1989 imposes on LAs a duty to provide accommodation to children in need in their area in the following circumstances:

- where no one has parental responsibility for the child;
- where a child is lost or has been abandoned; or

- the person who has been caring for the child is prevented (whether or not permanently) from providing the child with suitable accommodation or care.

The duty arises when the child's welfare is likely to be 'seriously prejudiced' if they are not provided with accommodation. Accommodation can be with foster parents, in a residential home or a residential specialist school if they have special educational needs. In deciding where to accommodate the child, the LA must ascertain and consider the child's wishes and feelings, and must safeguard and promote the welfare of the child. Bed and breakfast accommodation is not considered suitable, even in an emergency. An LA also has a power to accommodate a child to safeguard and promote their welfare, even if a person with PR can accommodate the child. Such children will be 'looked after' by the LA. In *R (on the application of G)* v *Southwark London Borough Council* [2009] UKHL 26, the local authority argued unsuccessfully that G, aged 17, had been accommodated by the housing department under s.17 CA rather than by social services under s.20. As a result, the children leaving care provisions applied (see also Chapter 19).

Help in kind or in cash (s.17(6))

LAs can also provide help in kind or cash – e.g. for a child and family to have a holiday, respite care, make cash payments or give vouchers for food and clothing. LAs can provide homeless young people with a deposit and rent in advance instead of providing accommodation directly where appropriate. Services provided under s.17 are not 'public funds' for the purposes of the immigration rules (Chapter 18).

Services (s.18)

Section 18 of the CA 1989 requires LAs to provide day care for pre-school CiN and out-of-school activities (including in school holidays) for school-aged children in need. They must also provide advice, guidance and counselling, recreational activities, home helps, family holidays, family centres and help with maintaining the family home in appropriate circumstances. The specific duties and powers of the LA are set out in Part 1 of Schedule 2 of the CA, which includes a duty to prevent children suffering ill-treatment or neglect, and to reduce the need to bring care proceedings – e.g. by finding alternative accommodation for domestic violence perpetrators to ensure children's safety (Chapters 7, 16 and 19).

Section 17 support is dependent on establishing that the relevant 'child' is under 18. In *R (on the application of FZ)* v *Croydon LBC* [2011] EWCA Civ 59, the court held that the LA's assessment of an unaccompanied asylum seeker, FZ's age, was flawed because he did not have an appropriate adult with him when he was assessed. A new assessment was ordered. See Assessing Age, Home Office (2019) (www.gov.uk/government/publications/assessing-age-instruction).

Young carers (s.17ZA)

Young carers are defined under the *Carers (Recognition and Services) Act 1995* as 'Children and young people under 18 who provide or intend to provide a substantial amount of care on a regular basis.' Section 17ZA places on LAs a duty to take 'reasonable steps' to identify young carers in their area, if there is 'an appearance of need' and assess whether they require support.

> The assessment must take into account the young carer's willingness to continue as a carer, the impact on their education, physical and mental health, recreational activities and whether they work or wish to work. (Local Government Association report (January 2018) *Meeting the Health and Wellbeing Needs of Young Carers*)

If a young carer is assessed as requiring support, LAs must either:

- provide support directly to the young carer; or
- demonstrate that the young carer is receiving adequate care and support from another source.

See: *The Young Carers (Needs Assessments) Regulations 2015* at: www.legislation.gov.uk/uksi/2015/527/made. There are an estimated 800,000 young carers in the UK (The Children's Society).

Chapter Summary

This chapter has:

- provided an overview of the law relevant to children and families and highlights the relevant social policy and ethical implications;
- examined the organisations/bodies that play an important role in protecting children;
- examined LA's duties to children in need and explained the social worker's role in the assessment process;
- considered the implications for social work practice.

Exercises

1. What changes have there been to the construct of a family in recent years?
2. In what ways do children live 'increasingly complex lives' and what policies are needed to give recognition to this?
3. Identify the circumstances where the determination of whether a person has PR for a child is relevant to social work practice.
4. Read the *R (on the application of G)* v *Southwark London Borough Council* [2009] UKHL 26 case report and explain why the court came to that decision.

(Continued)

5. What is the 'no delay' principle?

   a) The 'no delay' principle is for social workers to use.
   b) The 'no delay' principle means any delay in making an order is likely to be detrimental to the child.
   c) The 'no delay' principle prevents a local authority applying for an order.
   d) The 'no delay' principle means that parents can contest orders being made in relation to their children.

6. When working with safeguarding children, who is the primary client for the social worker?

   a) The child(ren).
   b) The parents.

7. Who is the 'no order' principle aimed at?

   a) Social workers.
   b) The courts.
   c) To prevent local authorities applying for court orders.
   d) The 'no order' principle means that parents can contest orders being made in relation to their child/ren.

8. How many principles are there in s.1 of the *Children Act 1989*?

   a) 1
   b) 2
   c) 3
   d) 4

9. Are all children with severe learning difficulties children in need under s.17, CA 1989?

   a) Yes
   b) No

10. Can parents who have a child aged 6 who falls within the definition of a child in need in s.17, CA 1989 refuse to allow their child to be assessed under the CAF?

    a) Yes
    b) No

11. Consider whether the following children are 'children in need' and, if so, which category in s.17(10) applies:

    1. A, aged 10, lives with his mother who suffers from depression, and his older sister, aged 17, who is in full-time education at a sixth form college some distance away. He is frequently absent from school because his mother is unwell and his sister cannot take him. The school have found it very difficult to engage with A's mother about the impact of his absences on his education.

2. B is aged 8 and has special educational needs. She goes to her local school but is subject to bullying, fails to interact with the other children and the school are concerned about her deteriorating behaviour.
3. C is aged 3 and often attends nursery unkempt and very hungry. He is underweight and often listless.

Answers can be found in the Appendix.

Further Reading

DfE (2018) *Working Together to Safeguard Children.* London: DfE. Crown copyright.

DSCF (2003) *Every Child Matters*: House of Commons, September. London: HMSO. Crown copyright.

DSCF (2009) *Safeguarding Disabled Children, Practice Guidance.* London: DSCF. Crown copyright.

GOV.UK (2009) *Every Child Matters: Change for Children, Statutory Guidance to the UK Border Agency on promoting and safeguarding the welfare of children,* available at: https://assets.publishing.service.gov.uk/government/uploads/system/uploads/attachment_data/file/25

Home Office (2004) *Children and Families: Safer from Sexual Crime – the Sexual Offences Act 2003.* London: Home Office Communications Directorate.

London Safeguarding Children Partnership (2017) *London Child Protection Procedures: Children with Disabilities,* available at: www.londoncp.co.uk/disabled_ch.html

Lord Laming (2003) *The Victoria Climbié Inquiry: Report of an Inquiry by Lord Laming,* available at: www.gov.uk/government/publications/the-victoria-climbie-inquiry-report-of-an-inquiry-by-lord-laming

Parton, N. (2004) From Maria Colwell to Victoria Climbié: reflections on a generation of public inquiries into child abuse. *Child Abuse Review,* 13(2): 80–94.

7

Child Protection and Safeguarding under the *Children Act 1989*

Chapter Objectives

By the end of this chapter, readers will be able to:

- understand the social policy, ethical principles and legal duties relevant to local authorities' duty to safeguard children;
- understand the legal rules and ethical implications that apply to the compulsory removal of children from their families and the role of social workers in the safeguarding process;
- apply the law, ethical principles and social policy to case scenarios.

Introduction

It is essential for social workers working in child protection to know and understand how the law, social policy and ethical principles apply to social work practice. This chapter examines the legal rules that give the courts power to make an order for the removal of a child from their family by a local authority. It also examines the role that social workers play in this process and the obligations that LAs owe to children who are 'looked after' by them. The relevant legal rules are set out in the *Children Act 1989* and case law provides practical examples of the application of these rules. *Working Together to Safeguard Children: Statutory Guidance on Inter-agency Working to Safeguard and Promote the Welfare of Children* (DfE, 2018, updated in 2020) sets out what 'individuals, organisations and agencies must and should do to keep children safe' (para. 9) and states that 'a child centred approach is fundamental to safeguarding and promoting the welfare of every child' (para. 10).

Compulsory intervention into family life should only be justifiable, both legally and ethically, if it results in better outcomes for the children involved. Media attention often focuses on the poor outcomes experienced by looked after children, evidenced by poor educational achievement (Jay and McGrath-Lone, 2019) and over-representation in the criminal justice statistics (see the response by the Youth Justice Board for England and Wales (2015) to *Keeping Children in Care out of Trouble: an Independent Review chaired by Lord Laming*). The independent inquiry into the Rotherham sexual abuse scandal revealed that over a third of the children affected by sexual exploitation were known to children's services because of child protection concerns and neglect, but the system had failed to protect them (see Jay (n.d.) *Independent Inquiry into Child Sexual Exploitation in Rotherham, 1997–2013*). Boys in care (56 per cent) outnumber girls (44 per cent) and Black, Asian and Minority Ethnic children (BAME) are over-represented with 24 per cent of looked after children of BAME origin compared with around 16 per cent of the general population under 18. The most significant disproportionality relates to Black and mixed-heritage children; Asian children are slightly underrepresented among those with looked after status (DfE, 2017 and Bateman et al., 2018). Research also suggests that looked after BAME children may lack 'genuinely warm relationships' with foster carers and social workers, which 'negatively impacts on their emotional well-being' (Coward, 2015). Despite the evidence cited above, research has also shown that most children in care have good experiences and believe that it was the right choice for them (Biehal et al., 2014).

Thought Box

Why do you think that BAME children are over-represented in the looked after children statistics and what implications does this have for social work practice?

Definition of Safeguarding

The *Statutory Guidance* (DfE, 2018, updated 2020, pp. 5–6) defines safeguarding and promoting the welfare of children as:

- protecting children from maltreatment;
- preventing impairment of children's health or development;
- ensuring that children grow up in circumstances consistent with the provision of safe and effective care;
- taking action to enable all children to have the best outcomes.

In pursuit of these objectives the law places legal obligations on LAs to prevent and protect children from harm. Social workers are key to the implementation of these objectives and therefore need to know the law, have the necessary legal skills to apply the law and recognise that such decisions involve making ethical judgements. Social workers are also well placed to advocate for law reform where improvements are needed in the services available to meet the needs of their service users.

Ethical Principles Relevant to Safeguarding Children

An important ethical principle relevant to safeguarding requires a social worker to work in the child's best interest (which is also a legal prerequisite (s.1, CA 1989)). This means that where the exercise of a 'right' (e.g. of self-determination) threatens the rights, safety and legitimate interests of others, it can be overridden because disclosure can be justified in the 'public interest' (Chapter 4), even when consent to such disclosure is refused by the person who made the allegations (BASW, *Code of Ethics*) and even though the disclosure could result in conflict between parents and other family members. This principle is reflected in s.11, *Children Act 2004* and the *Statutory Guidance* (DfE, 2018, updated 2020, para. 28). The relevant ethical issues are further examined in Chapter 10.

Social Policy and Safeguarding Children

Safeguarding law has developed in a piecemeal fashion in response to concerns prevalent at a given time. These concerns have shaped the social policies that underpin the resulting legislation (see Chapter 10 for the history of child protection law and the issues that influenced the inclusion of important provisions in the *Children Act 1989*).

The death of Victoria Climbié in 2000 and the subsequent inquiry chaired by Lord Laming, which found that the NHS, the police and social services had missed 12 opportunities to save her, led to the *Children Act 2004*. This legislation established the new role of Children's Commissioner (Chapter 6) and placed a duty on local authorities to work together and share information with other agencies to 'improve the well-being of children'. It also required local authorities to appoint directors of children's services.

The murders of two 10-year-old girls by their school's caretaker in 2002 led to the *Safeguarding Vulnerable Groups Act 2006* which established an Independent Safeguarding Authority (now the Disclosure and Barring Service (DBS)). Employers use the DBS service to ensure that they do not recruit unsuitable people to work with children and adults at risk. Employers also have an obligation to refer a person to the DBS if they have 'dismissed, planned to dismiss, or changed the employee's role in their organisation because the employee harmed or might have harmed a child or adult at risk of harm' (*Barring Referrals: Your Guide to How and When to Make One* (DBS, n.d.)).

The DBS maintains two lists: one of people barred from working with children and the other of people barred from working with adults at risk. The person reported will be given the opportunity to make representations to the DBS before a decision is made to include them on the list (see: www.gov.uk/government/organisations/disclosure-and-barring-service).

Despite these developments, child abuses have continued to make the headlines. The death of Baby P in 2007 resulted in Lord Laming's second report (*The Protection of Children in England: A Progress Report* (2009)) which found that 'too many local authorities had failed to adopt the reforms which followed the Climbié inquiry'. An independent review of the child protection system was commissioned by the government in 2010 and Professor Munro's report, *A Child-centred System*, was published in 2011. An independent inquiry into child sexual abuse was set up in 2014, chaired by Professor Alexis Jay, following the Jimmy Saville sex abuse scandal and the 'serious concerns that some organisations had failed and are continuing to fail to protect children from sexual abuse'. See the interim report of the *Independent Inquiry into Child Sexual Abuse* (Jay, 2018). The *Children and Families Act 2014* was passed to 'give greater protection to vulnerable children' and reformed adoption law to ensure that 'more children who need loving homes are placed faster' (Government press release: 'New changes to the law to give greater protection to vulnerable children' (March 2014, GOV.UK)). The *Children and Social Work Act 2017* was passed to improve support for looked after children and care leavers and established a central Child Safeguarding Review Panel for cases of 'national importance'.

The Department for Education launched a 'wide-ranging, independent review to address poor outcomes for children in care, as well as strengthening families to improve vulnerable children's lives' (DfE, 2021).

Thought Box

Do vulnerable children need better protection and, if so, what reforms are necessary?

Safeguarding Policies and Shared Working

While the law imposes specific duties on all LAs to safeguard children and adults at risk, the duty to safeguard is not the exclusive responsibility of LAs. The NHS (i.e. doctors, nurses and other healthcare professionals; NHS England) also has statutory responsibilities in this area (*Safeguarding Policy*, 2015), as do schools (*Keeping Children Safe in Education*, GOV.UK, 2015), the police and all organisations who have contact with or work with children (e.g. sports clubs and charities) (see Brigden, 2014).

Shared working between the different agencies and professionals is an important requirement set out in the *Statutory Guidance* (2018, updated 2020, para. 11).

All organisations/agencies with responsibility for the care of children have a duty to safeguard children must also have a safeguarding policy that sets out what will be done to keep children safe. This includes LAs, schools, the NHS, the Church (*Promoting a Safer Church: Parish Safeguarding Handbook*, Church of England, 2018), police, youth groups and any other organisations that work with children.

Statistics at 31 March 2020:

- There were 389,260 children in need at 31 March 2020.
- There were 51,510 children in need on child protection plans.
- Domestic violence by the parent was identified as a factor in 169,860 episodes of need and remains the most common factor.
- The number of section 47 CA enquiries started were 201,000.
- The number of initial stage child protection conferences (ICPCs) was 77,470 and 39 per cent of the enquiries led to an initial child protection conference.
- The number of children looked after in England was 78,150.

(https://explore-education-statistics.service.gov.uk/)

Types of child abuse

Abuse can take various forms, including the following.

Physical abuse is deliberately physically hurting a child. It might take a variety of different forms, including hitting, pinching, shaking, throwing, poisoning, burning or scalding, drowning or suffocating a child.

Emotional abuse is the persistent emotional maltreatment of a child. It is also sometimes called psychological abuse and it can have severe and persistent adverse effects on a child's emotional development.

Sexual abuse is any sexual activity with a child. You should be aware that many children and young people who are victims of sexual abuse do not recognise themselves as such. A child may not understand what is happening and may not even understand that it is wrong. Sexual abuse can have a long-term impact on mental health.

Neglect is a pattern of failing to provide for a child's basic needs, whether it is adequate food, clothing, hygiene, supervision or shelter. It is likely to result in the serious impairment of a child's health or development.

If you're worried that a child is being abused, advice for practitioners can be obtained from HM Government (2015): https://assets.publishing.service.gov.uk/government/uploads/system/uploads/attachment_data/file/419604/What_to_do_if_you_re_worried_a_child_is_being_abused.pdf

Important Provisions in the *Children Act 1989*

Child protection investigations, conferences and child protection plans

Section 47 of the *Children Act 1989* requires LAs to investigate when they are informed that a child who lives in their area is:

- the subject of an Emergency Protection Order (see below);
- in police protection (see below);
- suffering or likely to suffer significant harm.

The investigation must be carried out in accordance with the local protocol and must be completed within 45 days. If immediate protection is required, the LA, National Society for the Prevention of Cruelty to Children (NSPCC) or the police must use their statutory powers to safeguard the child. Multi-agency working is crucial to the process and the LA should initiate a strategy discussion to identify the levels of risk and agree any necessary action (*Statutory Guidance*, 2018, updated 2020, para. 78). LA social workers are key to this process.

A Child Protection Conference (CPC) will be convened if, following the investigation, the LA reasonably believes that the child is suffering or likely to suffer significant harm. This is a meeting between family members, the child (where appropriate) and the professionals who are involved with the family about the child's future safety, health and development. It will consider all the relevant information to determine how best to safeguard the child. Parents can request minutes of the conference which can only be shared with their solicitor. A child protection plan will be drawn up by the LA which sets out how the child can be kept safe, how further harm is to be prevented and what support the LA will provide for the child and the family (see: *Best Practice for the Implementation of Child Protection Plans: London Safeguarding Children's Board* (2015) at: www.londoncp.co.uk/best_prac_cpp.html).

Emergency protection

The following are important ways in which children who are believed to be at risk of harm can be safeguarded; they are time limited.

Child assessment orders (s.43)

An LA or the NSPCC can apply to the court for a child assessment order if they have reasonable grounds to believe that a child 'is suffering or likely to suffer significant harm' and they need to assess the child's health and development to determine whether the 'threshold criteria' is met but cannot make the assessment without the order. It lasts for a maximum of seven days. The court can order the child to be removed from the home if that is the only way an assessment can be made or it can make an emergency protection order instead (in practice, applications for child assessment orders are rare).

Emergency Protection Orders (EPOs) (s.44)

Any person, including an LA and the NSPCC, can apply to the court for an order to remove a child if there is 'reasonable cause to believe that a child is likely to suffer significant harm if either they are not removed, or if they are removed from where they are living'. The order is for eight days, renewable by a further seven days. The parents should be informed of the application unless it is believed that significant harm to the child might result. The LA should consider whether the parents will agree to the child being accommodated under s.20 (i.e. voluntarily – Chapter 6) or whether they should make an application for an interim care or supervision order instead (s.38). If an emergency protection order (EPO) is granted, the LA has PR, but s.44(5) places limits on its exercise. The court must give directions about contact (s.44(6)). Under s.44A, the court can make an order (with the other party's consent) excluding an alleged abuser from the home (this allows the child to stay in the home with the other parent/carer). At the end of the 15 days, the LA will have to return the child to their home or obtain an interim care order (ICO) (s.38).

Police protection (s.46)

A police officer who has reasonable cause to believe that a child is likely to suffer significant harm can (without application to a court) take the child into police protection. The police must inform the LA and the child (if they appear capable of understanding) and the parents. Section 17(1)(e) *Police and Criminal Evidence Act 1984* gives the police power to enter private premises without a warrant in an emergency ('to save life or limb'). Police protection lasts for 72 hours and on expiry the child will be returned home unless the LA has made application for an EPO or ICO.

Note: The police can remove a child without first obtaining a court order; a local authority cannot.

Care and supervision (ss.31–42)

Part IV of the *Children Act 1989* sets out the criteria that must be established before a court can make a care or supervision order and the court's powers in the legal process. A court can only make a care or supervision order on the application of a local authority or the NSPCC if it is satisfied on the balance of probabilities – that is, more likely than not – that the criteria has been met (see *Re H and R (Child Sexual Abuse: Standard of Proof)* [1996] 1 FLR 80).

Section 31(2) states that a court can only make a care or supervision order if it is satisfied:

a) that that the child is suffering or likely to suffer significant harm; and
b) that the harm, or likelihood of harm, is attributable to—

   i) the care given to the child, or likely to be given to him if the order were not made, not being what it would be reasonable to expect a parent to give to him; or
   ii) being beyond parental control.

The threshold criteria

The criteria set out in s.31(2) is called the 'threshold criteria' and it is the LA's (or NSPCC's) duty to provide the necessary evidence to satisfy the court 'on the balance of probabilities'. However, even if the threshold criteria is established, the court also needs to be satisfied that a care order is in the child's best interests in s.1 CA (see Chapter 6). The same criteria apply both to the grant of a care and a supervision order.

Lady Hale, in the case of *Re J* [2013] UKSC 9, said:

> Reasonable suspicion is a sufficient basis for the authorities to investigate and even to take interim protective measures, but it cannot be a sufficient basis for the long-term intervention, frequently involving permanent placement outside the family, which is entailed in a care order.

'Harm' is defined broadly to include s.31(9) and (10):

- physical, emotional and sexual abuse;
- neglect;
- impairment suffered by seeing or hearing the ill-treatment of another (where children witness domestic violence);
- prolonged school absences.

Whether harm is 'significant' is a question of fact for the court to decide. In *Humberside CC v B* [1993] 1 FLR 257 it was held that 'significant means considerable, noteworthy or important' and in *Y (Children)* [2014] EWCA that it must be 'something unusual, more than commonplace human failure or inadequacy'. The courts will consider the seriousness, frequency and duration of the harm suffered and whether it is premeditated. A single event may have a sufficiently harmful effect to be 'significant', but continuing acts (e.g. of neglect) can have a cumulative impact on the child and be 'significant' (*Care Proceedings: Re F (Interim Care Order)*, CA, 14 May 2007).

The risk that a child 'is *likely* to suffer significant harm' – that is, is likely to suffer future harm – must be 'real and substantial'. If the risk is based on past disputed facts (e.g. who was responsible for causing harm to a child in the past) the court must decide where the truth lies. This can be inferred from previous behaviour. In *Re J* [2012] EWCA Civ 380, the LA wanted care orders for three children whose mother had been 'in a pool of possible perpetrators' (along with the father of the child) of causing her older child's death. Because there was insufficient proof that the mother was the perpetrator, neither a care nor supervision order could be made because the 'likelihood' of the children suffering harm could not be established on the balance of probabilities. *In the matter of B (A Child)* [2013] UKSC 33, a child was removed from her parents at birth and made subject to a care order because the court was satisfied that the child would be at risk of future psychological or emotional harm (this could be inferred from previous behaviour).

Section 31(10) provides that the question of whether the harm suffered 'is significant turns on the child's health or development', which must be compared with 'what could reasonably be expected of a similar child'. The courts will take into account whether the child has reached the relevant developmental milestones (see *Early Years Foundation*

Stage Profile Handbook): https://assets.publishing.service.gov.uk/government/uploads/system/uploads/attachment_data/file/942421/EYFSP_Handbook_2021.pdf), and whether there have been prolonged school absences that have adversely impacted on the child and the characteristics of the child, including their age, state of health and other relevant factors.

In *Re T (A Child: Care Order: Beyond Parental Control: Deprivation of Liberty: Authority to Administer Medication)* [2017] EWFC B1, the court held that a child found to be 'beyond parental control' did not, in this case, impute fault on the parents' part. In *Z (A Child)* [2018] EWFC 25, the court found that the parents had done all they could to access appropriate care for Z, but 'had been let down' by the NHS and Child and Adolescent Mental Health Service (CAMHS). The court made a care order and Z was accommodated in a low-security unit.

The standard of the 'reasonable parent' is an objective standard; their age and/or vulnerability is not relevant in determining whether the threshold criteria has been met. Reasonable parents are expected to keep their children safe, access healthcare when appropriate and have their children educated. However, a parent's vulnerability (e.g. because of their mental health or learning disability) is relevant to the question of whether appropriate support could be provided by the LA to prevent the need for a care or supervision order, as well as the willingness of the parent to accept that support (*B (A Child) (Fact Finding)* [2019] EWFC B46 – Establishing the Legal Threshold under s.31 *Children Act* (12 December 2019)).

A care order gives the LA parental responsibility (Chapter 6), which is shared with the child's parents (or any other person who has PR for the child). The LA cannot change the child's religion or their name, and should normally involve parents in decisions about medical treatment. The child can be placed with the parents, relatives, foster carers or in a children's home. If a decision is made for the child to remain with the family, the LA can remove the child at any time and, in an emergency, without giving the parents notice. A care order automatically discharges an existing s.8 *Children Act* order (see Chapter 6) and any supervision order or interim care order in place for that child. A child who is subject to a care order is 'a looked after child'. A care order ends when the child is 18, but a care order cannot be made once a child has reached the age of 17 (s.31(3)).

Supervision orders

A supervision order places a duty on the LA to 'advise, assist and befriend' and parents must allow the LA reasonable contact with the child. The LA does not acquire PR for the child and the child is not 'looked after' by the LA. It lasts initially for a year and can be extended to a maximum of three years. The order will usually require the child to live at a specified address and the parent is required to inform the supervisor of any change of address. The child can be required to attend 'at a specified place, take part in specified activities, meet with the supervisor at a specified time and place and submit to medical examination'. The court can, on an application for a care order, decide that a supervision order should be granted instead, and vice versa.

Re FC (A Child: Care or Supervision Order) [2016] EWFC B90 (16 November 2016)

This case involved a child of 16 months whose mother had learning difficulties; all her previous children had been taken into care. The LA applied to the court for a supervision order. The child's guardian argued that a supervision order would not be appropriate in this case because it would not ensure that the LA would be involved throughout the whole of FC's childhood. The court held that the 'threshold criteria' was met and a care order was in the child's best interests. The decision was upheld on appeal.

Note that the LA can decide that a child subject to a care order can remain at home with their parent(s) but, if they do, the LA can remove the child at any time without involving the court, as the court, when they granted the care order, gave the LA authority to do this. However, it should be part of the LA's care plan that they provided to the court (see *In the Matter of D (A Child)* [2014] EWFC 6).

Section 31A states that when an application is made to the court which could result in a care order being made, the relevant LA must prepare a plan for the future care of the child within the time limit set by the court. Section 31A (3) states that the care plan 'must give any prescribed information and do so in the prescribed manner'. Section 31(3) requires the court to consider the permanence provisions of the section 31A plan for the child concerned (see Chapter 21).

Non-means-tested legal aid is available to parents and those with parental responsibility in care or supervision proceedings. The child(ren) will also be eligible for non-means-tested legal aid; the child's guardian is responsible for appointing a solicitor to represent the child in those proceedings.

Interim care and supervision orders

Section 38(1) gives the court power to make an interim care or supervision order which can last for up to eight weeks on the first application and is renewable for further periods of 28 days. The court must be satisfied that there are reasonable grounds for believing that the child is suffering or likely to suffer significant harm within s.31(2)) (*Re T (Interim Care Order: Removal of Children Where No Immediate Emergency)* [2015] EWCA 453).

Section 38A gives the court the power to exclude an alleged abuser from the home where there is reason to believe that, if the abuser was excluded, the child would not be at further risk of harm. A power of arrest can be attached to such orders – that is, if the excluded abuser breaks the order s/he can be arrested without the need to obtain a warrant from the court. The other parent/carer must give consent to the exclusion.

An appeal against an order can be made by the child, parents or LA within 28 days of the order being made. The LA complaints procedure can also be used (see *Statutory Guidance for Local Authority Children's Services on Representations and Complaints Procedures* (DfE, 2006)).

The public law outline

Practice Direction 12A – Care, Supervision and other Part 4 Proceedings: Guide to Case Management: www.justice.gov.uk/courts/procedure-rules/family/practice_directions/pd_part_12a (sets out detailed rules on how care applications must be managed). The rules include the following:

1. A pre-proceedings meeting.
2. A list of the documents the LA must file with the court which include:

   - a social work chronology;
   - a current assessment;
   - a care plan;
   - any other relevant documents.

3. The Case Management Hearing.
4. The Resolution Hearing.
5. The timetable for the proceedings, which states (5.1) that the application must be disposed of:

   (a) without delay; and
   (b) in any event within 26 weeks beginning with the day in which the proceedings were issued.

Contact

Section 34 provides a statutory presumption in favour of contact – that is, the LA must allow the child 'reasonable contact' with his parent(s), guardian and any other person with PR for the child. The LA also has a general duty to promote contact with the wider family, including siblings and grandparents. The court can attach conditions to contact (e.g. that it is supervised or indirect (contact by telephone, letters or emails, etc.). The court can make an order allowing the LA to refuse contact with a named person (but cannot prevent contact if the LA wants to allow it). The LA can prevent contact for up to seven days to 'safeguard the child's welfare' but will need the court's permission if it wants a longer period (see *Re K* [2008] EWHC 540 and *Re W (Child) (Parental Contact: Prohibition) [2000] Fam 1*).

LA Duties to Children Looked After by Them (ss.22 and 23)

The Care Planning, Placement and Case Review Regulations, 2010 provide detailed rules about an LA's duties in respect of looked after children. It includes the duty to assess the child's needs (including health needs), prepare a plan setting out how those needs are to be met, a plan for contact with the child's family, a placement plan and the support available. The regulations also detail the frequency of visits required, the advice, support and assistance available for the child, and the requirement for periodic reviews. The LA must ascertain and consider the child's wishes and feelings (if appropriate) and those of the parent (or anyone with PR or any other relevant person (s.22(4)). The child's religion, racial origin, cultural background, whether they should be placed with their siblings and whether the placement should be near the family home should also be considered.

Care Orders and Human Rights Law

Removing a child from their family is potentially an interference with protection given under the European Convention on Human Rights (ECHR) incorporated into law by the *Human Rights Act 1998* (see Chapter 2). The Convention rights which are particularly relevant to child protection are: 1) the right to be free from inhuman and degrading treatment (Art. 3); 2) the right to respect for privacy and family life (Art. 8) and 3) the right to a fair hearing (Art. 6). For a discussion of these provisions, see 'How important is the Human Rights Act for vulnerable children and families?', briefing by Family Rights Group, October 2014.

In *Re G (Care; Challenge to the Local Authority's Decision)* [2003] EWHC 551, [2003] 2 FLR 42, the judge (Mumby, J.) stated:

> This as it seems to me is a classic example of the kind of case where, whatever may have been the case previously, the Human Rights Act 1998 gives parents treated as badly as the parents in this case appear to have been ... effective remedies for breach by a local authority of either the substantive or procedural requirements of Article 8.

He listed the importance of the following when an LA is considering making an application for a care order.

- Inform the parents promptly of its plans.
- Give factual reasons.
- Give an opportunity for parents to answer an allegation.
- Provide an opportunity to make representations.
- Allow parents the opportunity to attend and address any crucial meetings.

The implications of this list for social work practice are clear.

Children Leaving Care

Section 23 of the CA 1989 places certain duties on LAs to certain children who leave the care system, and this support must be provided until they are 25.

The support includes the following:

- a personal adviser;
- a 'pathway plan' setting out the advice and support needed;
- ensuring that (until the age of 18) they have accommodation and sufficient money;
- help to continue living with a foster parent until aged 21 if wanted;
- bursaries if staying in full-time education;
- a home allowance to help with the costs of setting up home;
- help with finding work and accessing benefits;
- a six-monthly review.

See: Leaving Care, The Children's Commissioner, at: www.childrenscommissioner. gov.uk/help-at-hand/leaving-care-your-rights/

Child Protection and the Criminal Law

Child abuse and neglect are also crimes for which perpetrators can be prosecuted. The standard of proof in criminal cases is 'beyond reasonable doubt' (i.e. there is no other logical explanation) and not 'on the balance of probabilities', which applies to the grant of care orders. The following legislation is relevant:

Section 1, *Children and Young Persons Act 1933* (any person of 16 years and older who has responsibility for a child and who 'wilfully assaults, ill-treats, neglects, abandons … that person shall be guilty of a criminal offence'.

Sections 20, 27 and 47 *Offences Against the Person Act 1861* (inflicting bodily injury, with or without a weapon, s.20, exposing children whereby life is endangered, s.27 and assault occasioning actual bodily harm, s.47.

Sexual Offences Act 2003, which includes rape, sexual activity without consent and specific child sex offences contained in ss.9–29.

Section 5, *Domestic Violence, Crime and Victims Act 2004* (and the *Amendment Act 2012*) which includes the offences of causing or allowing a child to suffer serious physical harm, as well as causing or allowing a child to die; and the offence of failing to protect a girl from the risk of female genital mutilation.

Chapter Summary

This chapter has:

- provided an outline of the relevant legal rules (illustrated by reference to case law) applicable to safeguarding children and references to the social policy and ethical implications;
- explained the duties that LAs owe to looked after children who have been removed from their families to be made safe;
- explained the assessments that LAs are required carry out and the court orders available, the criteria for obtaining them and the implications for social work practice.

Exercises

1. Consider whether the harm is significant in the following scenarios and justify your decision by reference to the legal rules/decided cases:

   a) A child aged 4 months is found with a broken wrist.
   b) A child aged 6 months has bruising around the mouth.
   c) A child aged 2 has 20 random bruises of different ages around the knees and lower leg.
   d) A child aged 3 has serious burns on her face.
   e) A child aged 4 is found wandering alone along a busy road.

2. Read the decision in *A Local Authority* v *R-B* [2019] EWCA Civ 1560 and answer the following questions:

   1. In what court was the case heard?
   2. What orders did the local authority ask the court to make?
   3. If the court granted those orders, what would be the outcome for baby J?
   4. What decision did the court make?
   5. Why did the court reach the decision it did?

Answers can be found in the Appendix.

Case study – Child protection

M and F have 3 children, C a girl of 4, D a boy of 7 and E a girl of 11. M suffers from depression and F, who is currently unemployed, spends much of his time in the local betting shop.

(Continued)

C attends a nursery where there are concerns that she is failing to thrive and is always hungry. D went to school last week with bruising on his face which he said had been caused by F. E suffers from attention deficit hyperactivity disorder (ADHD) and attends a special school. Both M and F are failing to meet E's needs.

1. Identify the key legislation (including the specific sections) relevant to this scenario.
2. What do you think the LA should do and why?

Answers can be found in the Appendix.

Further Reading

Munroe, E. (2020) *Effective Child Protection* (3rd edn). London: SAGE.

8

Adoption and Fostering: Law, Ethics and Social Policy

Chapter Objectives

By the end of this chapter, readers will be able to:

- explain the legal rules, ethical and social policy considerations relevant to adoption and fostering;
- understand the significance of these rules for social workers;
- apply the important legislation, and policy and ethical considerations to social work practice;
- consider the impact of the rules on children and their families.

Introduction

This chapter examines the social policy, law and ethics relevant to adoption. Adoption is the legal process that removes parental responsibility for a child from the natural parents and transfers it to the adoptive parents. It severs permanently the legal relationship between the natural parents and the child. It has been described as 'the most draconian interference in family life possible', *Down Lisburn Health and Social Services Trust and another (AP) (Respondents)* v *H (AP) and another (Appellants)* [2006] UKHL 36 para. 34. It is justified on public policy grounds by the need to ensure, where this is possible, that children who cannot be looked after by their natural parents are provided with permanent homes by adoptive parents who can meet their needs instead of entering or remaining in the care system. The UK has the highest number of adoptions in Europe and is one of only a small number of European countries that allows, in certain circumstances, children to be adopted without parental consent (see Penton-Glynne, 2016, for a comparison).

Ethical Considerations

Adoption is, however, often seen as 'a controversial area of social policy' (Featherstone et al., 2018). The BASW Enquiry in 2016 into to the role of the social worker in adoption noted that the use of 'non-consensual adoption across the UK has sparked disagreements between the judiciary and government (see *Re T* [2018] EWCA Civ 650), criticism from many birth parents whose children have been adopted against their wishes, and questions within the social work profession itself about the ethics of this increasingly politicised area of practice'. It also points out that adoption has been promoted as 'the gold standard' in England in recent years which is not replicated in the other parts of the UK.

The BASW Enquiry also found that professional ethics are not used sufficiently 'to inform adoption practice' and 'a human rights discourse in social work in relation to adoption is under-developed'. The BASW *Code of Ethics* requires social workers to challenge 'unjust policies and practices' and places 'a duty to bring to the attention of their employers, policy makers, politicians and the general public situations where resources are inadequate or where distribution of resources, policies and practice are oppressive, unfair, harmful or illegal'. It also noted that

> social workers usually have responsibilities to more than one service user at a time, such as in a family situation so that what is right for one member of a family may not be for another. This underlines the need for ethical talk to be embedded in cultures of critical reflection and dialogue. However, little evidence was given to the Enquiry that such cultures were routinely available to social workers.
> (www.basw.co.uk/system/files/resources/basw_55505-10_1.pdf)

The Enquiry made the following recommendations.

1. The use of adoption needs to be located and discussed in the context of wider social policies relating to poverty and inequality.
2. UK governments should collect and publish data on the economic and social circumstances of families affected by adoption.

3. The current model of adoption should be reviewed and the potential for a more open approach considered.
4. There needs to be further debate about the status of adoption and its relationship to other permanence options.
5. BASW should develop further work on the role of the social worker in adoption and the human rights and ethics involved.

Thought Box

How difficult is it for social workers employed by LAs to challenge policies that their employers are required by law to implement?

Social Policy and the History of Adoption Law

At common law there was no mechanism for transferring 'parental rights and duties' (now 'parental responsibility') to another person. Adoption of a child was informal and often secretive; adoptive parents had no rights, and the biological parent could subsequently reclaim custody of their child, often when they had reached working age (then as low as 8) so they could help contribute to the household income. This happened even if they had had no contact with their natural parents for years and whether or not they had contributed to their care. The *Adoption and Children Act 1926* provided for the first time a mechanism for the irrevocable transfer of parental rights and duties from natural to adoptive parents if the following two conditions were satisfied:

a) the competent and independent consideration of the child's welfare; and
b) the informed consent of the natural parents.

The law at that time allowed a birth mother to veto the suitability of the prospective adoptive parents, but this was repealed by the *Adoption Act 1949*. Adoption services were historically provided by voluntary organisations (e.g. Dr Barnardo's) and they played an important role in protecting children whose families were unable or unwilling to care for them. LAs were first given power to act as adoption agencies by the *Adoption Act 1958* (they now have a statutory obligation to provide such services). However, voluntary organisations still play an important role in both adoption and fostering.

Following the introduction of the *Children Act 1989*, it became clear that further reforms to adoption law were necessary and the recommendations in the White Paper Adoption: A New Approach [2000] DoH Cm. 5017 led to the *Adoption and Children Act 2002* (ACA). This, subject to subsequent amendments, forms the basis of the current law in England and Wales. For a guide to the key provisions, see the *Adoption and*

Children Act 2002, Cullen (2021) and *Statutory Guidance on Adoption: For local authorities, voluntary adoption agencies and adoption support agencies* (DfE, 2013).

In *Adoption: A Vision for Change* (March 2016), the DfE set out the Government's adoption vision for 2020. It included:

- improving social work training;
- reducing the time children wait to be adopted;
- providing better adoption support.

The DfE gave regional Adoption Agencies (AAs) £650,000 in October 2019 to find more adoptive parents and in January 2020 wrote to directors of children's services urging them to prioritise adoption for children in the care system. This reflects ongoing government support for adoption as a way of obtaining permanence for looked after children.

Government policy is also reflected in the Children's Minister's letter to Directors of Children's Services in 2020: 'Adoption as a permanence option' which expressed concern about falling numbers of adoptions and confirmed that adoption was a government priority as 'it is a route to permanence for children in care'. It also stated: 'We are determined to see adoption pursued whenever it is in a child's best interests and to develop a fully regionalised system where all children are matched with adoptive parents without undue delay' (https://assets.publishing.service.gov.uk/government/uploads/system/uploads/attachment_data/file/859403/Adoption_letter_final.pdf).

In March 2020, there were 80,080 children in the care of local authorities in England, and 3,440 looked after children were adopted in that year. There were 3,880 children who had had an adoption best interest decision made but were not yet placed and 2,440 children had a placement order but were not yet placed. The average number of days between a child entering care and moving in with their adoptive family was 459 (Statistics England/CoramBAAF, see: corambaaf.org.uk/practice-areas/looked-after-children-statistics).

Adoption and Children Act 2002 (ACA)

Who can adopt? (ss.49–51)

The following rules apply:

- Couples who are married, have entered into a civil partnership, or two people living as partners in an enduring family relationship, or a single person.
- The prospective adopter(s) must be at least 21 years of age.
- At least one of the couple must be domiciled in the UK or both must have been habitually resident in the UK for at least a year – that is, deemed to have a permanent home in the UK.

The recruitment and assessment process for prospective adopters

Prospective adopters are required formally to register an interest with an adoption agency; the registration cannot be refused on grounds of ethnicity, age, sexual orientation, religious beliefs or because they do not share the same religious beliefs, culture or ethnicity as children waiting for adoption. While these characteristics can be considered when matching prospective adopters with a particular child, the decision on suitability to adopt must be based on the ability of the prospective adopter(s) to parent the child and meet their needs (with appropriate support where necessary).

Black children are more likely to be in care (8 per cent) and less likely to be adopted (2 per cent) compared with their share of the under-18-year-old population (5 per cent) (Adopted and Looked After Children (November 2020): www.ethnicity-facts-figures.service.gov.uk/health/social-care/adopted-and-looked-after-children/latest).

The formal assessment process has two stages.

1. *The pre-assessment process*, which includes police and health checks, taking up references, counselling and preparation to help prospective adopters decide whether to proceed with their application. Prospective adopters who are not found to be suitable must be given a clear written explanation.
2. *The assessment process*, which starts when the prospective adopter(s) notify the AA that they wish to proceed with their application. Any necessary training must be provided and a formal assessment made of the suitability of the prospective adopter(s). The assessing social worker must draft a report for the Adoption Panel (see below). If there are any concerns about their suitability, a second opinion should be obtained. The report must be shared with the prospective adopter(s) (but not the medical report and references).

If a prospective adopter is found to be unsuitable, they can request a review of the decision or ask to have the decision referred to the Independent Review Mechanism for Fostering and Adoption (see Disagreeing with a qualifying determination about fostering, adopting, or protected adoption information (2020 guidance) at: www.GOV.UK).

First4Adoption was set up in 2013 to provide a national adoption information service for people interested in adopting. They provide impartial information and put people in touch with adoption agencies in their area. Coram currently provide the service under licence from the DfE.

Fostering for adoption

Since the introduction of the *Children and Families Act 2014*, prospective adopters who are registered foster parents and who have been approved as adopters can foster a child with the prospect of adopting that child. The aim is to reduce the number of foster placements a child has had before being adopted. There must, however, be clear evidence that the child is unlikely to be able to be cared for by the birth parents.

Adoption Panels

Adoption Panels are multidisciplinary bodies that are required to consider the cases referred to them by the AA and make recommendations about:

- whether a child should be placed for adoption;
- the suitability of prospective adopters;
- whether a child should be placed for adoption with a specific prospective adopter.

Adoption Panels can also advise on contact arrangements, whether a Placement Order should be applied for, the number, age, background, sex and likely needs of the children a prospective adopter should be able to adopt, and whether adoption support is needed. Prospective adopters must be invited to attend the panel meeting before a recommendation is made (*R* v *London Borough of Newham (on the application of A, T and S)* [2008] EWHC 2640), although there is no obligation for them to attend. The panel can request additional information before finalising their recommendations. The Adoption Panel's recommendation should be shared with the prospective adopters.

Once it has been decided that a child should be placed for adoption, a suitable prospective adopter should be identified within six months (three months if the child is less than 6 months old).

Placement for adoption by Adoption Agencies (ACA, s.18)

An Adoption Agency can only place a child (of 6 weeks or older) for adoption with prospective adoptive parents where:

- the parent(s) of the child has consented to the placement. Unmarried fathers with PR can give or withhold consent (*Re J (Adoption: Contacting Father)* [2003] EWHC 199); or
- the LA has obtained a placement order from the court.

Children placed for adoption by a LA are 'looked after' children for the purposes of the CA 1989 (Chapter 7). A baby less than 6 weeks old can only be placed for adoption with parental consent which had been given voluntarily.

Placing children for adoption with parental consent (ACA, ss.19–20)

AAs can place a child for adoption if parental consent has been given unconditionally on the prescribed form (A107) and it has not been withdrawn. Consent can be given in advance, but it can be withdrawn in writing at any time until the application for an adoption order is made. If parents do not consent, the LA must obtain a placement order (PO) (s.21) from the family court which authorises the LA to place a child for adoption (only LAs can obtain a PO). The court cannot make a PO unless:

- the child is subject to a care order; or
- the court is satisfied that the threshold criteria in s.31 CA (Chapter 7) is met and it is in the child's best interests; or
- the child has no parent or guardian.

While the PO is in force, the LA has PR and, if the child is placed for adoption with prospective adopters, they will share PR with the LA. A PO suspends an existing s.8 order and a care or supervision order. Only an AA can remove a child placed for adoption under a PO.

Dispensing with parental consent (ACA, s.52)

A court cannot dispense with parental consent unless it is satisfied that either:

- the parents or guardian cannot be found; or
- the child's welfare requires the consent to be dispensed with.

In *Re M-H (Placement Order: Correct Test to Dispense with Consent)* [2014] EWCA Civ 1396, the mother accepted that she could not parent the child but wanted regular contact, which was considered more likely if her child was placed in long-term foster care. The judge granted a placement order; the mother appealed. The appeal was dismissed. The needs and characteristics of the child and the harm suffered is the court's overriding consideration.

In *Re R (a child)* [2014] EWCA Civ 1146, the judge said: 'Where adoption is in the child's best interests, local authorities must not shy away from seeking, nor courts from making, care orders with a plan for adoption, placement orders and adoption orders.' The PO remains in place until it is revoked by an adoption order (or the child marries or reaches the age of 18).

In *Re B (A Child)* [2013] UKSC 33 and *Re B-S (Children)* [2013] EWCA Civ 1146, the courts emphasised that social workers, in their final plans in care and adoption cases, should ensure that:

- the recommendation for permanence is proportionate to both the level of risk and the level of harm; and
- where adoption is the final plan, it makes clear that 'nothing else will do' – the fact that adoption would be the best likely outcome is not enough.

Section 23 of the ACA allows for the variation of a PO (to substitute one LA for another) and s.24 gives the LA or the child the right to apply to the court to revoke the PO before the child has been placed for adoption. Under s.30 it is an offence for any authority other than the AA to remove a child from the placement.

> ## Thought Box
>
> In adoption cases, is the need for the LA to prove that 'nothing else will do' contrary to government policy?

Residence requirements

Section 42 of the ACA provides that the following residence requirements must be satisfied before an application for an adoption order can be made.

- For a child placed for adoption by an AA or where the applicant is a parent of the child, the child must have lived with the prospective adopter(s) for a minimum of ten weeks.
- For a child whose parent's partner wants to adopt, the child must have lived with the applicant for at least six months.
- For a child whose LA foster parents want to adopt, the child must have lived with the foster parents for one year.
- In all other cases, the child must have lived with the applicant(s) for not less than three years during the preceding five years.

Applications for adoption

Once an application for adoption has been made, the child can only be removed by order of the court or by the LA. If a LA foster parent gives notice of their intention to adopt, the child can only be removed with leave of the court or the LA, or, if the child is accommodated under s.20 of the CA, by a person who has PR for the child (Chapter 6). If a child who is accommodated under s.20 has lived with a foster carer for five years or more, or if an application for leave to make an application to adopt has been made, the parent/person with PR cannot remove the child.

There are four preliminary requirements that must be satisfied before an adoption order (AO) can be made:

- The residence requirements are met (see above).
- The AA must submit a report to the court on the suitability of the applicants and the relevant welfare issues (s.43).
- CAFCASS must prepare a welfare report to safeguard the child's interests.
- In all non-agency placements, the LA must be informed of and submit a court report on the suitability of the prospective adopter(s) (s.44).

Post-placement visits

Once a child is placed with their adoptive parent(s), the AA must visit in the first week, and then weekly until the first review (four weeks after placement). The adopted child should be seen and spoken to alone unless the child refuses, or it is inappropriate because of their age and understanding. A written report must be made after each visit and placed on the child's case file. If, before an AO is made, the placement breaks down, the placing authority must find another placement for the child.

Adoption orders (s.46, ACA)

The effect of an AO is to end the legal relationship between the child and the natural parents. The adoptive parent(s) have PR and the natural parents' PR ends, as do their liabilities under the *Child Support Act 1991* (their duty to maintain the child). The child is no longer 'a looked after child'. Parents need leave of the court to oppose the making of an AO; to be successful, they must provide evidence of a change in their circumstances (e.g. successful rehabilitation from addiction). In *Re B-S (Children)* [2013] EWCA Civ 1146 (above), the court held that, although there had been a change in the birth mother's circumstances, the welfare checklist (s.1, CA) had to be applied and because this indicated that the children 'were in particular need of stability and care' it was 'entirely improbable' that the mother would succeed in her claim. The judges made clear that the LA's and children's guardian's reports must address all the options realistically possible for the child, with arguments for and against each option, and provide a fully reasoned recommendation necessary to meet the requirements in Articles 6 and 8 of the ECHR (Chapter 2); judges must provide a proper evaluation of those options before reaching their decision.

The child's name cannot be changed until the adoption order is made unless the court gives leave, or the birth parent or guardian has given written consent. If a person wants to adopt a stepchild, they must inform the LA and go through the same assessment process as other adoptive parents. The LA social worker must provide a report on the suitability of the adopter and the child's best interests.

AAs are expected to support adopters to provide adopted children with the information they need to make sense of what has happened to them. Life story-books can help children who have been separated from their birth parents to remember their early lives.

Since 2015, adoptive parents are entitled to adoption leave and pay, subject to the relevant eligibility rules (comparable to the maternity and paternity pay and conditions; see: www.gov.uk/adoption-leave-and-pay). An Adoption Support Fund was also established in 2015 which can provide financial assistance to help children recover from past harmful experiences and help them bond with their adoptive parent(s). These therapies include intensive family support, cognitive therapy and music therapy. Extra funding (Pupil Premium Plus) is available to enable state schools to provide additional support to all children subject to care orders or adopted from care (the current rate is £2,300 per year).

Disclosure of information about a person's adoption

Sections 56–63 of the ACA requires the AA to keep the specified information for a minimum of 100 years and treat the contents of the case records as confidential (e.g. birth certificate, birth details, birth family tree, photographs, any significant mementoes, etc.). There are detailed rules about when an AA must disclose this information – for example, to an enquiry held by the Children's Commissioner, the courts or to CAFCASS. Section 57 restricts the circumstances in which disclosure of s.56 information can be made.

B and B v A County Council [2006] EWCA Civ 1388

In *B and B v A County Council* [2006] EWCA Civ 1388, the adoptive parents requested the LA to keep their identity and the area in which they lived secret from the birth family. The LA failed to do this and, as a result, the family had to move. The adoptive family claimed damages in negligence from the LA for psychiatric injury and loss. It was held that the LA owed a duty to ensure that the adopted parents' personal information was not disclosed and were negligent because they had failed to guard against a detrimental event occurring.

The Adoption Contact Register (ACR) allows an adopted person to find their birth relatives and a birth relative find an adopted person. Once an adopted person is 18, they can apply to have their name added to the register, as can a birth relative over 18. The specified form must be completed and a fee is payable (see: www.gov.uk/adoption-records).

An intermediary agency can be used to trace a birth relative or adopted person; the ACR allows people to state that contact is not wanted. The register is not open to public inspection or search. There is no statutory obligation for adoptive parents to inform their adopted child that they were adopted, but many AAs advise parents to introduce the word 'adoption' as early as possible.

Post-adoption contact

Section 46(6) of the ACA requires the court to consider any existing or proposed arrangements for contact and consider the views of the parties to the adoption proceedings, which includes, where relevant, the child. Sections 1(4)c and 1(4)(f) ACA, which make the child's welfare of paramount consideration in adoption proceedings, must be applied in such cases. The *Children and Families Act 2014* inserted new provisions into the ACA 2002 (contained in ss.51A and 51B), which gives the court a specific power to make post-adoption contact orders. The following people can apply:

- any relative (by blood, marriage or adoption);
- any person who had PR for the child immediately before the adoption order was made;
- any person entitled under s.26 of the ACA 2002;
- any person who the child has lived with for at least one year.

Re B (A child) (Post-Adoption Contact) [2019] EWCA Civ 29 was the first case to consider the implications of s.51A of the ACA 2002. The court confirmed that post-adoption contact, where the adoptive parents do not agree, would only be ordered in exceptional circumstances. The judgment provides suggested good practice, which includes the need for AAs to ensure that social workers and prospective adopters understand the developing research in this area, and social workers and the children's guardian consider the significance of the research. Where post-adoption contact is considered a realistic option, prospective adopters should be told. Sibling contact should be considered separately from parental contact.

Intercountry Adoptions

If a foreign child has been 'adopted' abroad and brought into the UK by their adopters, the adoption will only be recognised if the child is from one of the states listed in Adoption (Designation of Overseas Adoptions) Order 1973 or recognised as valid within the Hague Convention (an international agreement to safeguard intercountry adoptions and child abductions). If neither applies, the child must be adopted in this country.

If a foreign child is brought into the country for adoption, the Adoptions with a Foreign Element Regulations 2005 must be complied with. This requires prospective adopters to apply in writing to an AA/LA for an assessment of their suitability to adopt a child and provide the AA/LA with any information required to inform the assessment. A fee is payable (currently £1,975). Children should be visited by the adoptive parents in their own country before being brought into the UK.

Under s.9 of the *Children and Adoption Act 2006*, the Secretary of State can place restrictions on the adoption of children into the UK from any country where there is concern about their practices. Detailed rules are set out in Annex C of the ACA 2002: 'Further information on adoptions with a foreign element'. A child who is resident in the UK cannot be removed from the UK for the purpose of adoption unless an order is obtained under s.84 of the ACA. Adopters can apply to register an overseas adoption with the General Register Office.

The Adoption and Special Guardianship Leadership Board was established in 2018 to provide leadership to help improve permanency outcomes for looked after children subject to adoption or special guardianship orders.

Alternatives to Adoption

The following are alternatives to adoption.

> *Residence under a child arrangements order* (s.8, CA) can potentially be obtained by both relatives and non-relatives of a child as an alternative to adoption. The order gives the person(s) with whom it is decided that the child should live parental responsibility for the child (see Chapter 6).

> *Step-parents can acquire PR* (s.4A, CA) as an alternative to adopting the child (see Chapter 6).

Special guardianship (s.14A, CA) was introduced by the ACA 2002 and the rules were inserted into s.14, A–F, CA 1989.

Applications for special guardianship (SG) can be made by the following:

- individuals;
- jointly by two or more people, but not the child's parents;
- LA foster parents with whom the child has lived for at least a year;
- a relative with whom the child has lived for at least a year;
- any person with whom the child has lived for three of the last five years;
- the child's guardian;
- an individual named in a child arrangement order with whom the child lives;
- anyone with the consent of those with PR; and
- if the child is subject to a care order, any person who has the consent of the LA.

A court can make a special guardian order (SGO) in any proceedings concerning the welfare of the child, even if it has not been applied for; this includes adoption proceedings. Prospective applicants need to give the LA three months' written notice of their intention to apply unless they have made a competing application for an adoption order. The LA must prepare a report about the suitability of the applicant(s) and whether parental contact should be allowed. If an SGO is made, the special guardian obtains PR, which can be exercised to the exclusion of others with PR except another SG, or in cases where the consent of more than one person with PR is required. Special guardianship retains the link with the natural parents (unlike most adoptions). SGOs can be varied or discharged (unlike an Adoption Order). LAs are required to arrange for Special Guardianship support services to be provided. If a child is looked after by the LA prior to the SGO being made, the child will qualify for advice and assistance in accordance with the children leaving care provisions (if they apply; see s.24(1A) of the CA (Chapter 7)). A child is entitled to therapeutic support from the Adoption Support Fund if they were in LA care before the SGO was made. See: Special Guardianship: a review of the evidence (Nuffield Family Justice Observatory [2019]) which focuses on the judgment in *P-S (Children)* [2018] EWCA Civ 1407 where the court refused to make an SGO in favour of the paternal grandparents before the children had lived with them and made a care order instead. In 2020, 3,700 SGOs were made, compared with 3,400 adoption orders (see: DfE, 2020). The statistics show that 5 per cent of SGOs break down, compared with 15 per cent of child arrangement orders (s.8, CA) and 0.7 per cent of adoptions. See: Special guardianship: Statutory guidance for local authorities on the Special Guardianship Regulations 2005 (as amended by the Special Guardianship (Amendment) Regulations 2016) (January 2017).

Long-term Fostering

Around 75 per cent of looked after children are placed with foster parents. The regulatory framework (which LAs and independent fostering agencies must comply with) is set out in the *Fostering Services: National Minimum Standards* (DfE, 2011) and The Fostering Services (England) Regulations [2011]. Statutory guidance on fostering services for looked after children is available on the GOV.UK website *Children Act 1989: Fostering services* (DfE, 2011). The regulations provide the framework for the delivery of fostering services, the assessment of foster carers and the support that fostering service providers (including LAs) are expected to provide. The guidance sets out the functions and responsibilities of LAs and independent fostering agencies for looked after children.

The Care Planning and Fostering (Miscellaneous Amendments) (England) Regulations 2015 created a statutory concept of 'long-term fostering' and applies when the following conditions are met.

- Foster care is the child's plan for permanence as recorded in their care plan.
- The foster carer has agreed to be the child's foster carer until they cease to be looked after.
- The child's responsible authority has confirmed the arrangement to the foster carer, the child and their birth parents.

The responsible authority must assess the foster carer's ability to meet the child's needs and determine the support which is necessary to achieve this. The child's views must be considered, and their family and the Independent Reviewing Officer must be consulted (see: Long-term fostering in England, The Fostering Network: www.thefosteringnetwork.org.uk).

Foster parents have a right to full information about the child they are to foster and are entitled to an allowance based on the type of care provided and the age of the child. LAs have recommended pay rates. Foster carers are not employees of the LA (and therefore have no employment protection rights), although in *Johnstone* v *Glasgow City Council* (2017) an employment appeal tribunal held that the foster carers in this case were employees because of the control exercised by the council (see: www.gov.uk/employment-tribunal-decisions/mr-j-johnstone-mrs-c-johnstone-v-team-foster-care-glasgow-city-council-4103972-2016-4103973-2016).

In *Armes* v *Nottinghamshire County Council* [2017] UKSC 60 the LA was held vicariously liable (without the need to prove negligence on the LA's part) for the physical and emotional abuse perpetrated by a foster mother and the sexual abuse perpetrated by a foster father against the foster child in their care, and in *W* v *Essex County Council* [2000] 2 WLR 601 the LA was held to owe the foster family a duty of care when allocating a child to their care.

Private Fostering Arrangements

Sections 66–72 of the *Children Act 1989* regulate the 'private arrangements for the fostering of children'. Private fostering involves the placement of a child under 16 (or under 18 if the child has a disability) for 28 days or more in the care of a person who is not the child's parent or a relative, friend or other person connected with the child. See: The Children (Private Arrangements for Fostering) Regulations [2005].

Section 105 of the CA defines a relative as a 'grandparent, brother, sister, uncle or aunt (whether of the whole or half-blood, or by marriage or civil partnership), or step-parent. Private foster carers can, however, come from the extended family – e.g. cousins or great aunts or uncles.

A private carer who proposes to foster a child must inform the LA at least six weeks before the placement is due to start (or as soon as possible if the placement starts earlier). The regulations set out the information required, which includes the child's name, sex, date and place of birth; their health and eating preferences and hobbies; their religious and cultural or ethnic background; and educational provision.

An LA social worker must carry out an inspection within seven days of receiving the information to establish whether the placement is suitable and make recommendations. If the placement is found to be unsuitable and the child cannot be returned to the parents, the LA must decide what steps to take to safeguard the child's welfare. If the LA considers that the child is 'a child in need' (Chapter 6), the LA must provide appropriate services and support. If the fostering arrangement comes to an end, the LA must be given notice, in writing, within 48 hours of the event. Section 70 makes it a criminal offence not to comply with the regulations without 'reasonable excuse'.

Private foster carers do not get PR for the child, although they can make day-to-day decisions about the child's welfare. The latest available statistics state that 1,560 children were cared for in private fostering arrangements on 31 March 2015.

Re L (A Child) (Jurisdiction: Private Fostering) 2015 EWHC 1617

In *Re L (A Child) (Jurisdiction: Private Fostering)* 2015 EWHC 1617, L was privately fostered in the UK. Her father (F) and sisters lived in Romania. L had made repeated allegations that her father had sexually abused her and her sisters. Following the breakdown of the private fostering arrangement, L was taken into police protection to prevent her removal from the UK and then made subject to an ICO (Chapter 7). The LA was criticised for failing to ensure that L had retained contact with her siblings while in foster care and considered that it had contributed to the breakdown of the private fostering arrangement.

Chapter Summary

This chapter has:

- provided an outline of the development of adoption law, the relevant legal rules and the emphasis on finding permanent homes for children who cannot live with their birth families and explains the role that social workers play in the adoption process;

- referenced the important social policy and ethical issues relevant to adoption and the application to social work practice;
- considered the alternatives to adoption, including special guardianship and long-term fostering and how fostering (including private fostering) is regulated.

Case study – Achieving permanence for children in care

A, aged 10, B, aged 6, C, aged 2 and D, aged 11 months were recently made subject to care orders because of neglect and abuse. E, their mother, is a substance abuser; she has refused all attempts to engage in rehabilitation. A and B's father, F, was not married to E and has had no contact with them for the past five years. C and D's father, G, is in prison for armed robbery. B has spina bifida and requires considerable care. A and B are living with their paternal grandmother (H) and C and D are with foster parents who live some way away. E has very little contact with any of her children. C and D are of mixed race; their foster parents are white. They are said to be well settled and the foster parents have expressed an interest in adopting them. You are keen to achieve permanence for the children.

Identify the relevant law, ethics and social policy of this case study, and explain how it applies to the facts. What human rights considerations are relevant here?

Answers can be found in the Appendix.

Further Reading

Mahmood, S. and Doughty, J. (2019) *Child Care and Protection: Law and Practice* (6th edn). London: Wildy, Simmonds & Hill.

O'Halloran, K. (2018) *Adoption Law and Human Rights*. London: Routledge.

Pearce, N. and Budworth, R. (2020) *Adoption Law: A Practical Guide*. Oxford: Wiley.

9

The Youth Justice System

Introduction

The youth justice system (YJS) and social work practice requires close consideration. Many social workers decide to practise in the youth justice system – for example, in youth offending teams. The role of the social worker in these teams is a crucial one in supporting and helping to prevent children and young people not to reoffend. The following chapter provides an overview of the policy approaches that have developed the law and their impact on governmental decisions about children and young people who offend.

Social Work Ethics in the Youth Justice System

Children and young people who commit crime can be an emotive issue that is exacerbated by the media, the public's response to children committing crime and government policy. Yet the children involved may have complex needs that require consideration of the causes of their offending behaviour. This is significant for social workers in practice, as can be seen in the strategic social worker and the professional capabilities framework (BASW). (See: Strategic social worker 3 – Diversity and equality: Recognise diversity and apply anti-discriminatory and anti-oppressive principles in practice, at: www.basw.co.uk/professional-development/professional-capabilities-framework-pcf/the-pcf/strategic-social-worker/diversity-and-equality)

Thought Box

Following the ethical principles established in Chapter 5, consider the ethical dilemmas involved in punishment and the responsibility of children and young people who have offended along with the accountability of their parents.

Social Policy Approaches in the Youth Justice System

The legal developments of the youth justice system in the UK began in earnest from the Industrial Revolution. It recognised that children, who often worked long hours in poor conditions in factories, were vulnerable and children should be treated differently from adults (see Bateman and Hazel, 2014). However, for the purposes of social work practice, the most significant developments and policies that have impacted on children and young people came from the New Labour government in the 1990s following the James Bulger murder by two 10-year-old boys in 1993. The public outcry for justice against the two boys was so intense that Tony Blair's government adopted policies that would appease the need for justice. This stance reinforced the punishment approach that had already developed in dealing with children and young people who offended (Sabbagh, 2016).

Punishment

The criminal justice or punishment approach is a punitive method of dealing with young offenders and politically is seen as a tough stance on youth offending. The young offender is viewed as exercising choice in their actions and should therefore be held responsible for them. Sanctions reflect this stance through retribution rather than rehabilitation (Sabbagh, 2016).

Welfare

The welfare approach has its origins in the reforms of the late nineteenth century through advocates such as the social reformer Mary Carpenter (1807–1877), who founded a 'ragged school' and 'reformatories'. Institutions such as reformatory schools became established as a response to the need to segregate young people and adult offenders. This approach was a means of meeting the needs of the young offender and to provide treatment in recognition of their offending behaviour (Arthur, 2010).

Developmental approach

The early developmental model of youth justice reform championed the belief that the fewer interventions by the state in dealing with youth offending, the better the outcome would be for all. The focus was on youth crime of a non-serious nature and placed the onus on parents and schools who could assist the child as they 'grew out of crime' and matured, rather than stigmatising them through the YJS. This approach has grown scientifically with input from neuroscience which shows how parts of the brain react in the decision-making process (Blakemore, 2008) and is very much at the fore of youth justice currently, with leading reports identifying the need to consider the brain development of the child in the youth justice system. Examples are the sentencing guidelines that courts use:

> Children and young people are inherently more vulnerable than adults due to their age and the court will need to consider any mental health problems and/or learning disabilities they may have, as well as their emotional and developmental age.
>
> (Sentencing Council, 2017)

Actuarialism

Actuarialism focuses on preventing offending through early identification of the risk factors that cause individuals to offend. This approach aims to manage the propensity to offend through targeted interventions designed from the data of crime audits. Examples are the pre-school intellectual stimulation programmes that have been shown to contribute to a reduction in later youth offending (Farrington and Welsh, 2007). Other examples include the dispersal by police of young people gathered in public areas in order to prevent the occurrence of anti-social behaviour. The negative consequence of this preventative strategy is the labelling of young people as criminals based on their propensity to offend, as distinct from their actual offending (Sabbagh, 2016).

Responsibilisation

Responsibilisation as a policy approach has been used at different times in the history of criminal justice, in all societies, and has recently re-emerged as restorative justice. The purpose of this approach is to repair the harm caused by the young person. Initially, the purpose was to be offender-focused, meaning that the aim was to rehabilitate the young offender by making them responsible for their crime. This approach has had some success in the YJS and one of the reasons for its success is the multi-agency approach that has been used to deliver it. Also, it is argued that young people are more likely to admit guilt than their adult counterparts, which then makes a restorative justice approach appropriate for their sentence. However, there has been a shift in this approach, and it is now very much victim-centred or sometimes victim-led. This shift is to ensure that the victim feels that justice has been done, as distinct from the focus being on the offender.

An example can be seen in the sentence of a referral order, which includes a form of restorative justice attached to it (Sabbagh, 2016).

Children first, offenders second

The current policy approach that has been adopted by the YJS is to identify the child or young person who has offended as a child rather than as an offender (Haines and Case, 2015). In line with the UK's international obligations, this approach highlights the need to recognise the child through their biological age, brain development and therefore vulnerability. This means addressing their needs that led to them offending rather than punishing them. This approach promotes the use of diversion from the traditional youth justice procedures, prevention from reoffending and making adults responsible for the child's behaviour. This also means including the agencies involved in the youth justice system and utilising a multi-agency approach.

United Nations Convention on the Rights of the Child (UNCRC)

The UNCRC provides for children's rights and specifically for vulnerable children, among whom children and young people who offend are included. In all actions concerning children, whether undertaken by public or private social welfare institutions, courts of law, administrative authorities or legislative bodies, the best interests of the child shall be a primary consideration.

The UK must submit a report every five years to the UNCRC showing how it is implementing the provisions through domestic law. The 2010 policy paper, drafted under the Labour government, emphasised how the UK met its legal obligations within, for example, the *Children Act 1989*. However, the definition of parental responsibility in the CA is a generic one and focuses on who has parental responsibility, as distinct from what is expected of parents in their duties for their child (see Chapter 6). The latest report from the Children's' Commissioner to the UNCRC highlights the discrimination that children are subject to in different parts of the UK (para. 6, see: www.childrenscommissioner.gov.uk/wp-content/uploads/2020/12/cco-uncrc-report.pdf).

Current Data from the Youth Justice Board

In the year ending March 2020:

- There were just over 58,939 arrests of children (aged 10–17) by the police in England and Wales. This decreased by 74 per cent over the last ten years, but increased by 1 per cent in the last year.

(Continued)

- Black children accounted for 17 per cent of arrests, which is 7 percentage points higher than ten years ago.
- Around 7,200 youth cautions were given to children in England and Wales. This is a decrease of 90 per cent compared with the year ending March 2010, with a decrease of 16 per cent in the last year. (Youth Justice Board, 2020)

The data from the Youth Justice Board provides a picture of children and young people caught up in the youth justice system from initial arrest. In 2020, there was an increase for the first time in arrests and a 0.2 per cent drop in the reoffending rate. However, the reoffending rate is still higher than it was in 2008. Reoffending is defined as committing any offence within the 12-month period following sentencing for the initial crime.

Overrepresentation of BAME Children and Young People in the YJS

There is a disproportionate number of ethnic minority children in the criminal justice system. Arrests of Black children have increased over the last ten years, with the latest figures showing a decrease in first-time entrants to the YJS, but an increase in reoffending rates for Black children and young people. Arrests of Black children accounted for 17 per cent (around 8,600) in the latest year, 7 percentage points higher than the proportion ten years ago.

> Arrests of Mixed (around 4,000) and Asian and Other (just over 4,000) children both made up 8 per cent of the total in the latest year and have also seen changes in proportions over the last ten years, albeit on a smaller scale. (Youth Justice Board, 2020)

The *Lammy Review* (GOV.UK, 2017), which examined the disproportionate numbers of BAME children and young in the youth justice system, highlighted the following.

- BAME children were more likely to plead not guilty to an offence, which could result in a custodial sentence whereas pleading guilty was more likely result in a community sentence.
- BAME defendants were more likely to receive a custodial sentence than their white counterparts.
- BAME children serving custodial sentences were more likely to feel discriminated against by staff and have mental health needs.
- BAME children's offences were recorded on the police national database for minor crimes which could be seen for criminal checks when applying for jobs. (p. 5)

Recommendations from the report included renaming Youth Offending Panels (YOP) to Local Justice Panels which 'should take place in community settings, have a stronger emphasis on parenting, involve selected community members and have the power to hold other local services to account for their role in a child's rehabilitation' (p. 10). A youth offending panel includes a member of the youth offending team (YOT) and at least two other members from the community as recruited by the YOT.

The report also identified the responsibility of parents:

> Behind many young offenders are adults who either neglect or exploit them. The youth justice systems appear to have given up on parenting. Last year, 55,000 young offenders were found guilty in the courts, but just 189 parenting orders were issued by the youth justice system. Only 60 involved BAME young people. Parents need support alongside accountability. (p. 6)

Parental responsibility is a factor that may impact on social work practice when making decisions in supporting families in need – for example, as found in the *Children Act 1989*, s.31(2)(ii), threshold criteria, being beyond parental control (see Chapter 7).

Age of Criminal Responsibility

The age of criminal responsibility in England, Wales and Northern Ireland is 10 years old; it is one of the youngest ages globally and has been criticised by international bodies as being too young (CRC, 2016). The criticism of criminalising children at the age of 10 years is that it may damage them and encourage further criminal behaviour, as well as prevent them from moving on with their lives because they have a criminal record. The following link shows the different ages of criminal responsibility in Europe: https://archive.crin.org/en/home/ages/europe.html. The table in the link highlights how the age of criminal responsibility in England and Wales is out of step with other European countries and its obligations under international and European law. However, until 2019 Scotland's age of criminal responsibility was 8 years old; this has now been raised to 12 years old.

A child who commits a crime in England and Wales who is under the age of 10 can still be dealt with by the police and local authorities. For example, the child may be put under a child safety order, which is an order of the court that provides for a child to be supervised by a responsible officer, such as a youth offending officer, to help prevent any further crime being committed and address the initial offending behaviour.

Youth Offending Teams (YOTs)

Many social workers choose to work as youth offending officers in youth offending teams. Youth offending officers have the task of maintaining the law and preventing recidivism by young offenders. Research indicates that children in the youth justice system trust their youth offending officer more than any other person they experience in the youth justice system (Sabbagh, 2017).

Youth offending teams work with young people who get into trouble with the law. YOTs look into the background of a young person and try to help them stay away from crime.
They also:

- run local crime prevention programmes;
- help young people at the police station if they're arrested;
- help young people and their families at court;
- supervise young people serving a community sentence;
- stay in touch with a young person if they're sentenced to custody.

(GOV.UK, Youth offending teams)

YOTs work with children between the ages of 10 and 18 years and with those under the age of 10 to prevent them from offending. They work to agreed minimum standards as set out by the Ministry of Justice.

The aim of these standards is to:

- provide a framework for youth justice practice and ensure that quality is maintained;
- encourage and support innovation and good practice to improve outcomes for children who commit crime;
- ensure that every child lives a safe and crime-free life, and makes a positive contribution to society;
- align with the YJB's child-first, offender-second principle;
- assist the YJB and inspectorates when they assess whether youth justice services are meeting their statutory requirements.

(MOJ, 2019)

Legal Aid, Sentencing and Punishment of Offenders Act 2012

The *Legal Aid, Sentencing and Punishment of Offenders Act 2012* (LASPO) provided for changes to sanctions for young offenders in terms of traditional diversionary measures. For example, instead of reprimand and final warnings for minor offences, they are now termed 'youth cautions' or 'youth conditional cautions'. A caution is an out-of-court disposal whereby the perpetrator must admit to the offence and the caution. It is not a conviction but can be considered by the courts for future offences.

The Green Paper Breaking the Cycle (2010) led to the LASPO Act making use of out-of-court disposals and the need to ensure that young people are kept away from the YJS when possible. However, the deep end of incarceration for young people would be more controversial as the Act placed financial responsibility on local authorities for young offenders in custody. This has been achieved by making a designated local authority responsible for a child on remand through the local authority's statutory duty for looked after children. It can be argued that this was a cost-saving exercise by the coalition government to reduce central government's financial obligation towards young offenders in custody.

Youth Courts

The youth court is found in the magistrates' court. Magistrates are volunteers from the community without necessarily having any previous legal experience; however, they do receive legal training (see Chapter 1). They are meant to represent the community the defendant belongs to so that justice is fair to both the victim and the perpetrator. Magistrates deal with both criminal and family law cases, which means that the decisions they make will be of significance in social work practice. The panel is made up of three magistrates and one legal adviser who provides the magistrates with advice on the law and procedure during the hearing. For criminal cases, they deal with minor crimes ranging from minor assault to theft. Their sentencing powers are limited to reflect the minor crimes they deal with, which range from referral orders to the maximum sentence of a detention training order.

It could be argued that the court's role in society is to administer justice rather than becoming concerned with the reasons why the offender has committed the crime. However, in the youth courts the offender and their parents can make the court aware of how their circumstances may have contributed to the young person offending. Furthermore, the courts take into consideration a pre-sentence report by the YOT, which identifies areas of the young offender's background that will assist the court in passing their sentence (see Chapter 21).

For more serious offences such as murder, rape and robbery, the child will be tried in the Crown Court. The trial is before a jury and the sentences range from community sentences to prison.

Sentencing Guidelines

In 2017, the sentencing guidelines that courts use when sentencing children and young people were updated to reflect the current policy positions identified above. For example, in the principles set out below, both the developmental approach and the child-first, offender-second approach has been adopted.

Section one: general approach

Sentencing principles

1.1 When sentencing children or young people (those aged under 18 at the date of the finding of guilt) a court must have regard to:

(Continued)

- the principal aim of the youth justice system (to prevent offending by children and young people);
- and the welfare of the child or young person.

1.2 While the seriousness of the offence will be the starting point, the approach to sentencing should be individualistic and focused on the child or young person, as opposed to offence focused. For a child or young person, the sentence should focus on rehabilitation where possible. A court should also consider the effect the sentence is likely to have on the child or young person (both positive and negative) as well as any underlying factors contributing to the offending behaviour.

1.3 Domestic and international laws dictate that a custodial sentence should always be a measure of last resort for children and young people and statute provides that a custodial sentence may only be imposed when the offence is so serious that no other sanction is appropriate (see section six for more information on custodial sentences).

1.4 It is important to avoid 'criminalising' children and young people unnecessarily; the primary purpose of the youth justice system is to encourage children and young people to take responsibility for their own actions and promote re-integration into society rather than to punish. Restorative justice disposals may be of particular value for children and young people as they can encourage them to take responsibility for their actions and understand the impact their offence may have had on others.

1.5 It is important to bear in mind any factors that may diminish the culpability of a child or young person. Children and young people are not fully developed, and they have not attained full maturity. As such, this can impact on their decision making and risk-taking behaviour. It is important to consider the extent to which the child or young person has been acting impulsively and whether their conduct has been affected by inexperience, emotional volatility or negative influences. They may not fully appreciate the effect their actions can have on other people and may not be capable of fully understanding the distress and pain they cause to the victims of their crimes. Children and young people are also likely to be susceptible to peer pressure and other external influences and changes taking place during adolescence can lead to experimentation, resulting in criminal behaviour. When considering a child or young person's age their emotional and developmental age is of at least equal importance to their chronological age (if not greater).

1.6 For these reasons, children and young people are likely to benefit from being given an opportunity to address their behaviour and may be receptive to changing their conduct. They should, if possible, be given the opportunity to learn from their mistakes without undue penalisation or stigma, especially as a court sanction might have a significant effect on the prospects and opportunities of the child or young person and hinder their re-integration into society.

(www.sentencingcouncil.org.uk/wp-content/uploads/Sentencing-Children-and-Young-People-definitive-guideline-Web.pdf)

> ## Thought Box
>
> Can you identify where in the sentencing guidelines the developmental approach and the child-first, offender-second approach has been adopted. Furthermore, what principles from the *Children Act 1989* are apparent in the principles above?

The guidelines also provide a table that shows different types of offence and the recommended sentences for them. Some of the offences will include support from social services – for example, county lines, which involves the exploitation of vulnerable young people and adults by gang members to move drugs from the city to more rural, suburban areas.

The Crown Prosecution Service (Legal Guidance: Drug Offences (2021)) states:

> The 'runners' are invariably children, often boys aged 14 to 17 years, who are groomed with money and gifts and forced to carry out day to day dealing. Runaway and missing children are also used by gangs to expand inner city drugs empires into county towns. Children as young as 11 years of age have been reported as being recruited into the highly sophisticated gangs.
>
> Gang members enter relationships with young women in order to secure a location for drugs to be stored in the new area. In addition, violence is used against drug users to coerce them to become runners, enforce debts, and use their accommodation as an operating base.

This is significant for social work practice when working with families, as they may need to apply relevant provisions in the *Children Act 1989* – for example, s.20 which places a duty on the local authority to provide accommodation for a child in their region if they are a child in need (see Chapter 6). This may be because the child has no one who has parental responsibility (PR) for them or if parents with PR agree to allow the local authority to accommodate their child while retaining PR (see Chapter 6). This applies to children who have been involved in gangs to support them away from contact with the gang members.

Out-of-court Disposal

The purpose of out-of-court disposals is to ensure that justice is seen to be done, but that the disposal is proportionate to the offence and helps reduce the reoffending rate. Depending on the severity of a crime a young person commits, the police have the discretion to deal with it based on certain factors, as shown in Figure 9.1 (MOJ, 2013).

Community resolution	Youth caution	Youth conditional caution
• Non-statutory. • Local discretion on implementation, following Association of Chief Police Officers (ACPO) guidance and Home Office counting rules. • Victim's wishes to be taken into account. • Young person's agreement required in order to participate and accept community resolution. • Best practice is for police to notify YOTs of all community resolution.	• Statutory disposal. • YOT notified. YOT will use their expertise to determine the need for assessment and intervention. • Assessment required for second and subsequent formal disposals. • Non-compliance with voluntary interventions will inform future disposal decisions. • Guidance recommends joint decision-making process involving YOT and police to determine appropriate disposal.	• Statutory disposal. • Police are empowered to offer a youth conditional caution with proportionate rehabilitative, punitive and reparative conditions as an alternative to prosecution. • YOT will screen and advise police on appropriate conditions to prevent reoffending. • YOT responsible for monitoring compliance. • Non-compliance may result in prosecution for original offence.

Figure 9.1   Out-of-court disposals

Source: Authors, based on Youth Justice Board for England and Wales (2019)

Referral Orders

A referral order is a statutory community-based order in which the court 'refers' the child to a youth offender panel, which is convened by volunteer members of the community and held at an informal venue. The panel, along with the child, will agree a contract of work with which the child is expected to comply. There is a distinct focus on restorative justice. Compliance is regularly reviewed by the panel. Referral orders were introduced in the *Youth Justice and Criminal Evidence Act 1999* (and are now provided for in the *Powers of Criminal Courts (Sentencing) Act 2000*), and are the community-based orders most often used by the courts when dealing with 10- to 17-year-olds, particularly for first-time offenders who plead guilty (MOJ, 2018).

Referral orders are made for children convicted for the first time who have pleaded guilty to the offence or, in some cases, for a second time if a certain period of time has elapsed. Their purpose is to give the child a chance to address the consequences of their actions and help support them. This is another initiative to reduce reoffending by working with first-time offenders. However, this is a court order, which means that it remains on the Police National Computer, a system that stores and shares information on criminal records. Once it is 'spent' (this means at the end of the agreed referral period and once all the conditions have been completed), it does not need to be disclosed on a basic disclosure and barring service (DBS) check, but has to be disclosed for enhanced checks.

Youth Rehabilitation Order (YRO)

6.23 A YRO is a community sentence within which a court may include one or more requirements designed to provide for punishment, protection of the public, reducing re-offending and reparation.

6.24 When imposing a YRO, the court must fix a period within which the requirements of the order are to be completed; this must not be more than three years from the date on which the order comes into effect.

6.25 The offence must be 'serious enough' in order to impose a YRO, but it does not need to be an imprisonable offence. Even if an offence is deemed 'serious enough' the court is not obliged to make a YRO.

6.26 The requirements included within the order (and the subsequent restriction on liberty) and the length of the order must be proportionate to the seriousness of the offence and suitable for the child or young person. The court should take care to ensure that the requirements imposed are not too onerous so as to make breach of the order almost inevitable.

6.27 The available requirements within a YRO are:

- activity requirement (maximum 90 days);
- supervision requirement;
- unpaid work requirement (between 40 and 240 hours);*
- programme requirement;
- attendance centre requirement (maximum 12 hours for children aged 10–13, between 12 and 24 hours for young people aged 14 or 15 and between 12 and 36 hours for young people aged 16 or over – all ages refer to age at date of the finding of guilt);
- prohibited activity requirement;
- curfew requirement (maximum 12 months and between 2 and 16 hours a day);
- exclusion requirement (maximum 3 months);
- electronic monitoring requirement;
- residence requirement;*
- local authority residence requirement (maximum 6 months but not for any period after the young person attains the age of 18);
- fostering requirement (maximum 12 months but not for any period after young person attains age of 18);**
- mental health treatment requirement;
- drug treatment requirement (with or without drug testing);
- intoxicating substance requirement;
- education requirement; and
- intensive supervision and surveillance requirement.**

* These requirements are only available for young people aged 16 or 17 years old on the date of the finding of guilt.

** These requirements can only be imposed if the offence is an imprisonable one *and* the custody threshold has been passed. For children and young people aged under 15, they must be deemed to be a persistent offender.

(Sentencing Council, 2017)

Detention and Training Order

As the title suggests, the detention and training order is a sentence that combines incarceration and a period of training to help support the young person away from offending. This is the highest sentence a magistrate can give to young people who offend. The sentence lasts between four and twelve months; the first half is spent in detention and the second half in an education or training setting that is monitored by the youth offending team.

Detention Institutions

There are three types of institutions that accommodate children and young people who have been sentenced to a period of detention (see Figure 9.2).

Youth offending institution	Secure training centre/school	Secure children's home
• For children between the ages of 15 and 18 years and young adults between the ages of 18 and 21 years. • There are five YOIs in England and Wales. • A focus on behaviour management, education and supporting emotional, mental and physical needs.	• For children between the ages of 10 and 17 years. • There are three STCs, one of which is to become the first secure school since the Charlie Taylor review of the youth justice system in 2016. • Children who are given custodial sentences and are considered vulnerable are sent to these centres and schools.	• For children between the ages of 10 and 17 years. • There are 15 privately managed secure children's homes in England and Wales. • For vulnerable children and some who are given custodial sentences. • Low child-to-staff ratio with a focus on education and healthcare.

Figure 9.2   Types of detention institution

Currently being piloted are secure schools, which were a recommendation that came from the Charlie Taylor review of the YJS in 2016 (MOJ), the aim being to provide a child-focused institution that enables the child's rehabilitation through education, healthcare and physical exercise within a secure environment (MOJ, 2018).

Restorative Justice (RJ)

As discussed above, restorative justice has its origins in the youth justice system under the responsibilisation approach. It is an approach that is being widely used in the YJS in diverting children and young people away from the youth justice system. It enables the victim and the offender a chance to communicate and address the harm that has been caused by the offence.

The process can be delivered by a face-to-face meeting between the perpetrator and the victim or between a number of people in a community who have been victim to the offence. Another approach is that of indirect communication, which can take the form of messages, written or through recordings, being passed between the perpetrator and the victim(s). All of these approaches are facilitated by a trained RJ practitioner (RJC, 2015)

Before RJ can take place, there must be an identifiable victim, both parties must consent to the process and the offender must plead guilty to the offence. The process is not always straightforward as the parties may not be willing to undertake the process at the same time. However, there are trained RJ facilitators who will work with both parties in order to achieve a positive RJ outcome. RJ provides an opportunity for the victim to be heard, but some criminal actions by children and young people highlight how they are also victims.

National Referral Mechanism (NRM)

As highlighted above with the example of county lines, children and young people are more likely to be victims of crime by being drawn into the youth justice system. Modern slavery is an example of this. Many children are trafficked into the UK from overseas, but children can also be trafficked from one part of the UK to another. The International Labour Organization website provides further detail about child trafficking (see: www.ilo.org/ipec/areas/Traffickingofchildren/lang--en/index.htm).

Social workers working with children and young people who are experiencing the abuse highlighted above may need to refer the case to the NRM. The NRM framework was introduced to fulfil the UK's obligation to the Council of Europe Convention on Action Against Trafficking in Human Beings. If the police, local authority or other organisations working with vulnerable children identify a child as being a victim of trafficking, they must refer the case to the NRM. The NRM supports those agencies in providing advice, accommodation and protection for victims of trafficking (see Chapter 18).

Chapter Summary

This chapter has:

- provided an overview of the policy developments and subsequent legislation that has impacted on the youth justice system specifically since the late 1990s;
- highlighted the relevance of social work practice in the youth justice system;
- introduced the current sentencing guidelines and the possible sentences for certain offences;
- identified how many children and young people are victims who then become caught up in the youth justice system.

Exercises

Look at the sentencing guidelines and decide what sentences you would give for the following scenario.

1. G and C have two children – P, who is 12 years old and T, who is 16; both live at home. The family are of Eastern European origin. G and C have found it stressful raising the boys. P has been staying out late and coming home with expensive new items. C says that P's behaviour is getting harder to manage, which is creating a lot of tension between her and G. T was accommodated by the local authority two years ago and placed with foster carers but is now back home. C said that T had become involved with some 'druggies', was constantly fighting with C and keeps taking money from her purse and they cannot cope with his behaviour.

How can social services and the youth offending team help the children and their families?

Answers can be found in the Appendix.

Further Reading

MOJ (2019) *Standards for Children in the Youth Justice System*. Ministry of Justice/Youth Justice Board.

10

Social policy and ethical considerations relevant to working with children and families

Chapter Objectives

By the end of this chapter, readers will be able to:

- understand the importance of social policy considerations on the development of child protection law;
- understand the application to social work practice;
- apply ethics and values to social work with children and families.

Introduction

Social policy is concerned with the promotion of welfare and well-being, and embraces the notion that the state (which includes central and local government, as well as voluntary organisations) should have a role in helping people lead safe, fulfilling and healthy lives. The influence of social policy on the development of the law and practice of child protection is important for social workers to understand as the policies have implications for service users and social work practice. Important changes in policy in this area have been made in the last hundred years; the reasons for these policy changes and their effectiveness in safeguarding vulnerable children requires examination.

The chapter also examines key issues from the perspective of social work ethics and values, and discusses how these can be used to meet the sometimes conflicting demands of Social Work England's (SWE) *Professional Standards*. Respect for individuals and decisions about when to breach confidentiality can pose ethical dilemmas for social work with children and families. Important examples examined in this chapter include resistance and disguised compliance, cultural sensitivity versus cultural relativity, and issues of domestic violence.

Social Policy and Safeguarding Children

The life of children born into poverty in nineteenth-century Britain was typified by poor diet, poor housing, high mortality rates (averaging 149 child deaths per 1,000 of the population compared with 3.8 deaths per 1,000 of the population in 2018), labouring in unsafe factories, workhouses and child prostitution. The poor were originally 'looked after' by their local parish, funded by a tax on parish householders. By the end of the eighteenth century, opposition to the costs led to outbreaks of violence. The *Poor Law Amendment Act 1834* which resulted provided for able-bodied people needing poor relief to live in workhouses where they were required to work in exchange for food and accommodation (many people at the time regarded poverty was a result of indolence). Orphaned and abandoned children, as well as the physically and mentally ill, were also accommodated in workhouses; there was no access to education. (The grim conditions are portrayed in *Oliver Twist* by Charles Dickens.)

Charities subsequently played an important part in law reform. Dr Barnado was so shocked at the conditions of children in the East End of London that he set up a 'ragged school' in 1867 and subsequently children's homes to provide a more humane alternative to the workhouse. It was against this backdrop that other charitable organisations were founded. The NSPCC (as it is now called) was established in 1884 and launched a sustained campaign to end child cruelty. This led to the *Prevention of Cruelty to, and Protection of, Children Act 1889*, which gave the state, for the first time, the power to intervene in the relationship between parents and children. Police were given powers to enter people's homes where children were thought to be in danger and ill-treatment of children was made a crime, as was begging. Guidelines on child labour were also included. Gradually, more voluntary organisations were established to help combat deprivation and child abuse – e.g. the Church of England Children's Society and National Children's Homes (now Action for Children)

The social policy objectives were clear: the state and voluntary organisations should be the vehicles to ensure that children were protected from serious harm. However, there have always been, throughout the development of policy and law in this area, policy-makers who were and are reticent about giving the state too much power.

---

s.1 *The Prevention of Cruelty to, and Protection of, Children Act 1889* provided:

Any person over sixteen years of age who, having the custody, control, or charge of a child, being a boy under the age of fourteen years, or being a girl under the age of sixteen years, wilfully ill-treats, neglects, abandons, or exposes such child, or causes or procures such child to be ill-treated, neglected, abandoned, or exposed, in a manner likely to cause such child unnecessary suffering, or injury to its health, shall be guilty of a misdemeanour, and, on conviction thereof on indictment, shall be liable, at the discretion of the court, to a fine not exceeding one hundred pounds, or alternatively, or in default of payment of such fine, or in addition to payment thereof, to imprisonment, with or without hard labour, for any term not exceeding two years ...

Subsequent legislation, which increased state intervention into people's lives, included the *Children Act 1908* which made the registration and inspection of foster carers of children under the age of 7 compulsory; extended the offence of child cruelty to include neglect (e.g. a child under the age of 7 being left unattended near an open fire); established Borstals as an alternative to children being sent to adult prisons; established juvenile courts; banned capital punishment for children under the age of 18 and the sale of cigarettes to the under-16s. The *Punishment of Incest Act 1908* made it illegal for the first time for a man to have sexual intercourse with his grand-daughter, daughter, sister, half-sister or mother. The *Employment of Women, Young Persons and Children Act 1920* placed further restrictions on the employment of children and the *Children and Young Person's Act 1932* extended the powers of juvenile courts and made local authorities, rather than the police, responsible for bringing to court children in need of care and attention. Supervision orders were introduced for children at risk. The *Children and Young Persons Act 1933* consolidated much of the existing law; some important sections of this Act remain in force (see: www.legislation.gov.uk/ukpga/Geo5/23-24/12).

Subsequent Reforms

The four-day public inquiry in January 1945 into the death of 13-year-old Dennis O'Neill caused by ill-treatment by his foster parents found that they had been selected 'without adequate inquiry' into their suitability and there had been a 'serious lack of supervision by the local authority'. The public outcry led to the *Children Act 1948*, which was seen both as a landmark in public childcare law and an important part of the developing welfare state. It 'marked a change in emphasis, from mere provision to meeting the developmental needs of the individual child' (see: Cabinet Papers: Protection of Children, National Archives, for further information at: www.nationalarchives.gov.uk/cabinetpapers/themes/protection-children.htm).

In a paper comparing the *Children Act 1948* with the *Children Act 1989*, it was noted that 'for the state to take on responsibility for children who were vulnerable, neglected or in other ways receiving inadequate parenting was a remarkable development in its time' (*Children Act 1948* and *1989*: similarities, differences, continuities (Hughes, 1988)).

The *Children and Young Persons Act 1963* reformed the treatment of young offenders in juvenile courts, raised the age of criminal responsibility from 8 to 10 years and emphasised the importance of care and protection in the treatment of young offenders. The *Children and Young Persons Act 1969* reduced the powers of juvenile courts to make orders, preferring care and supervision by probation officers and social workers as an alternative to criminal sanctions. It also made provision to raise the age of criminal responsibility from 10 to 14 years, but this was never implemented.

The *Child Care Act 1980* provides that:

> It shall be the duty of every local authority to make available such advice, guidance and assistance as may promote the welfare of children by diminishing the need to receive children into or keep them in care under the Children Act 1948 ... or to bring children before a juvenile court; and any provisions made by a local authority under this subsection may, if the local authority think fit, include provision for giving assistance in kind or, in exceptional circumstances, in cash.

Material assistance to prevent the need for children to be taken into care continues to be an important aspect of a LA's powers and duties (it is available to families with 'children in need' (s.17, CA 1989; see Chapter 6)).

Thought Box

If the families of children in need require 'material assistance', why is this not provided by the Department of Work and Pensions through the benefit system (see Chapter 19)?

Children Act 1989

The Act saw a major shift in public policy relating to the protection of vulnerable children in part as a response to a number of high-profile deaths of children from abuse which had shocked the public. Two examples involved children who were known to social workers. The public inquiry into the death of Maria Colwell (who died in 1973), who was the subject of supervision order (Scott, 1975), led to the setting up of 1) child protection committees to coordinate the safeguarding of children in local areas, 2) inter-agency child protection conferences to consider specific cases of child abuse and neglect and 3) child protection registers to identify children at risk.

The death of Jasmine Beckford in 1984, who was in the care of Brent LBC, also led to a public inquiry in 1985. The report criticised magistrates, health visitors, teachers and especially social workers for their part in permitting what the Report described as 'a predictable and preventable homicide'. The recommendations played an important part in the changes brought about by the *Children Act 1989*, including the introduction of the 'paramountcy principle' (Chapter 6).

The Cleveland Inquiry, chaired by Butler-Schloss, was set up to investigate concerns about children living in Cleveland, who had been taken into LA care after some had been wrongly diagnosed as having been sexually abused.

> The *Report of the Inquiry into Child Abuse in Cleveland* (1987) concluded that:
>
> Family support and child protection were not two necessarily conflicting and incompatible priorities: both required similar attitudes, approaches, and skills. Even parents who were suspected of abuse retained a sense of responsibility for their children which should be nurtured, not crushed; and even the implementation of legal powers required respect, communication, the willingness to listen, and the desire to reach agreements—not least with the victims themselves.

Two other important influences on the underpinning principles contained in the *Children Act 1989* were:

1. the decision of the House of Lords in *Gillick* v *West Norfolk and Wisbech Area Health Authority* [1986] AC 112 which determined that children younger than 16 could give consent to medical treatment if they had the required requisite capacity (see Chapter 4). This decision had and still has important implications for the involvement of children in decisions that affect them.
2. The recommendations of the Law Commission Review of Child Law, Guardianship and Custody (1988) HC594 were to make the law 'clearer, simpler and fairer'. It also made other important recommendations for law reform, including

replacing 'parental rights' with 'parental responsibility', obtaining the views of the child, as well as how decisions about residence and contact of children whose parents no longer live together (now called child arrangement orders) should be made, and the grounds for making care and supervision orders (Chapter 6).

The important principles embodied in s.1 of the *Children Act 1989* are a reflection of the developments in the 1970s and 1980s. The Act has been amended on several occasions since it first became law (Chapters 6 and 7).

> ## Thought Box
>
> Is there too much state intervention in family life? On what basis is it justifiable for the state to intervene?

Recent Developments

In July 2016, the DfE published *Putting Children First*, with the aim of reforming and improving children's social care by 2020. In 2017, it added a further commitment 'to ensure that all vulnerable children, no matter where they live, receive the same high quality of care and support by 2022', and published a 'roadmap' for how it intends to transform children's social care services. It identified the following as crucial:

- a highly capable and skilled social work workforce;
- high-performing services everywhere;
- a practice and learning system that enables, identifies and spreads excellence and innovation.

The House of Commons Public Accounts Committee (2019) criticised the Government's 'slow progress' in reforming children's services and called on it to 'improve both the quality and the cost-effectiveness of children's social care in measurable ways by its goal of 2022' (Children's Social Care Services in England: House of Commons Briefing Paper, 28 June 2019).

A former Children's Commissioner commented:

> The act (CA 1989) was seen at the time to be a major step forward in promoting the best interests of children. It exposed the need for vulnerable children to be protected and heralded the development of the principles for the safeguarding of children that we now take for granted. But although legislation is critically important in setting benchmarks, fine words can be so easily hijacked by cuts in resources. Today, there is a lack of political and public will to put the needs of children, and especially their rights, at the heart of policy and practice. (Aynsley-Green, 2019)

> ## Thought Box
> What reforms do you consider are necessary to protect 'vulnerable' children?

Ofsted inspections have shown an overall improvement in the effectiveness of local authorities' children's services in England.

> As at 31 March 2019, the proportion of LAs judged good or outstanding for overall effectiveness increased to 46%. After each LA's first Single Inspection Framework (SIF) inspection it was 36%. The proportion judged inadequate has dropped from 22% after each LA's first SIF, to 13%. (Ofsted, 2019)

The Adoption and Children (Coronavirus) (Amendment) Regulations 2020 (SI No 445), which came into force on 24 April 2020, made changes to ten sets of children's social care regulations with no Parliamentary scrutiny. On 10 June 2020, Parliament debated the renewal of the provisions. For a discussion on the implications for safeguarding children, see: https://article39.org.uk/2020/06/11/safeguards-for-children-in-care-house-of-commons/

Ethical Issues

The ethics and value base for social workers in relation to child safeguarding and working with families is based, at its core, on the need for social workers to respect everyone they work with, regardless of, for example, being differently abled, their sexual orientation, ethnicity, and where oppression and discrimination may affect their rights and the services they receive. There is also a duty to advocate for the needs of all service users and carers regardless of their attributes. In doing so, social workers should be as honest as possible with service users and carers, share their concerns, agree what needs to be addressed, how, and any advocacy the social worker will endeavour to carry out either jointly or on their behalf (Littlechild et al., 2020).

SWE's *Professional Standards* require social workers to observe the following:

- Value each person as an individual (1.1)
- Respect and promote the human rights, views, wishes and feelings of the people I work with, balancing (the) rights and risks (1.2)
- Work in partnership with people to promote their wellbeing and achieve best outcomes, recognising them as experts in their own lives (1.3)
- Recognise differences across diverse communities and challenge the impact of disadvantage and discrimination on people and their families and communities (1.5)
- Recognise and use responsibly, the power and authority I have when working with people, ensuring that my interventions are always necessary, the least intrusive, proportionate, and in people's best interests (1.7). (Social Work England, 2019)

In the last 30 years, social work with children and families has become increasingly dominated by state intervention and child safeguarding, as discussed above. This has resulted in families having more involuntary engagements with services; they often complain that these interventions are 'intrusive and oppressive' (Parton, 2014; Lonne et al., 2015). This is a key feature for social workers to consider in terms of their skills, methods and application of values in practice. One of the debates in policy and practice in recent years has been in relation to balancing the two conflicting demands of parental rights and the concomitant rights of children. Section 1 of the *Children Act 1989* states that the needs of children are paramount. The *Statutory Guidance* (2018) (updated 2020) states that:

> A key principle of the Children Act 1989 is that children are generally best looked after within the family, save where that is not consistent with their welfare, with their parents playing a full part in their lives and with least recourse to legal proceedings.
>
> (DfE, 2018: 4)

This, however, might conflict with how best to support women suffering domestic violence where child safeguarding issues are also involved, but where disempowerment and control over both the child and adult victims is also a feature (see, for example, Humphreys and Bradbury-Jones, 2015).

This means that social workers should respect and value parents while not necessarily condoning their behaviour and their actions towards their children. Therefore, where a parent has some form of mental health challenge, learning disability or misuses drugs, this in itself should not affect how the family is supported in relation to the requirements under the *Children Act 1989*, and the ethical and professional codes.

However, as described in Chapter 5, in everyday practice social workers have to balance up these important values with their knowledge of the needs of people who are abused in some way, and the legal duty to protect them over and above others in that situation: 'Recognise the risk indicators of different forms of abuse and neglect and their impact on people, their families and their support networks' (3.4) and to 'respond quickly to dangerous situations and take any necessary protective action' (3.12). This also includes how the two SWE *Professional Standards* directives – 1) to be open, honest, reliable and fair (2.1) and 2) to respect and maintain people's dignity and privacy (2.2) – are to be balanced. If one parent informs the social worker of domestic violence but does not want this shared with the abuser, it may well be necessary to inform other agencies as part of safeguarding children procedures at a time when telling the parents may put the children at further risk. The same is true if a child discloses abuse; a promise cannot be made that this will be kept a 'secret'. The *Statutory Guidance* (2018) makes mandatory the 'effective sharing of information between practitioners and local organisations and agencies is essential ... keep children safe ... Practitioners should be proactive in sharing information as early as possible ...', points emphasised by the

DfE's (2018, updated 2020) information-sharing advice for safeguarding practitioners (see also Chapter 4).

Thought Box

Domestic violence, abuse and social work interventions and virtue ethics.

- Should we always be honest with service users?
- Should we always maintain confidentiality?

What do these ideas mean when working with someone subject to domestic violence where this was discussed in private and the perpetrator subsequently wants to know what was discussed with the victim? This means weighing up the rights of an abused adult not to have this information disclosed against the need to protect the children, which could require disclosure. Similarly, if a child discloses that they are a victim of sexual abuse, but only after first obtaining an assurance that the conversation was confidential, can that promise be broken? How can such situations be prevented?

If there is a conflict of interest, whose needs should take priority – those of parents or children? (The *Children Act 1989* makes this clear.) How should parents be trusted? What empowering and strength-based approaches should be considered? (See, for example, Forrester et al., 2008; Wilson et al., 2011.) How can service users be included in assessments and shared decision-making as required in Social Work England *Professional Standards* to 'Work in partnership with people to promote their wellbeing and achieve best outcomes, recognising them as experts in their own lives'? (1.3).

It can be seen that there are potential conflicts between valuing and trusting people, and including them in assessments and interventions in a strengths-based manner, while also looking at possible conflicts of interests. The case study and questions below highlight these concerns. A consideration of the ethical approaches that can help in making these decisions is also included.

Working with Resistant Parents in Child Protection

This section examines work with the small proportion of parents in child safeguarding work who are resistant – for example, by demonstrating disguised compliance or being violent or aggressive to safeguarding children's staff (Littlechild et al., 2016; Brandon et al., 2020; Fauth et al., 2010). If one or both parents is an abuser, they may use strategies and tactics they have learned over a long period of time in order to keep members of the family silent about the abuse (Littlechild and Bourke, 2006). This clearly breaches the child's right to safety and well-being, but it is necessary to work with parents in a respectful way as much as possible while ensuring the protection of the child, and the requirements of the *Children Act 1989* and the Gillick competence judgment (Chapter 4).

> Lord Laming stated in his report on the death of Victoria Climbié that:
>
> > Adults who deliberately exploit the vulnerability of children can behave in devious and menacing ways. They will often go to great lengths to hide their activities from those concerned for the well-being of a child. [Social work] staff have to balance the rights of a parent with that of the protection of the child. (Lord Laming, 2003: 13)
>
> He judged that social workers need to practise 'respectful uncertainty', applying critical evaluation to any information they receive and maintaining an open mind.

The two key elements from SWE *Professional Standards* that relate to these areas are:

- Recognise and respond to behaviour that may indicate resistance to change, ambivalent or selective cooperation with services, and recognise when there is a need for immediate action. (3.15)
- Practise in ways that demonstrate empathy, perseverance, authority, professional confidence and capability, working with people to enable full participation in discussions and decision making. (2.4)

Both of these are key considerations to take into account when considering the rights of each of those involved in the case study at the end of this chapter. The report into the death of Jasmine Beckford (discussed above) stated 'thou shalt not *not* intervene'. Social workers' legal and professional duties require engagement with the child as much as possible based on the Gillick competence criteria set out above.

Parents may not always deliberately set out to cover up child abuse; if a parent has mental health problems, a learning disability or misuses drugs they may be fearful of what will happen from social work interventions.

Cultural Relativism versus Cultural Sensitivity

One of the proud traditions of social work is that it is the first profession to champion the rights of BAME groups who are often oppressed and unfairly discriminated against. This has gained new impetus after the killing of George Floyd in the USA in 2020 and the reactions to this globally, and highlighted in statements by BASW (see: BASW (2020) statement: George Floyd: 'BASW wholly condemns the murder of George Floyd and the frightening circumstances that led to it').

The Child Welfare Inequalities Project studied 6,000 children in England on child protection plans and 8,000 children in care and established that there are extreme inequalities between ethnic groups in the proportions of children being looked after in care in England (Bywaters et al., 2019). This knowledge places a duty on social workers to try to counterbalance the processes and decision-making that have led to disadvantage for the families and children they work with (Bywaters et al., 2020).

It is also well established that most Minority Ethnic groups in England experience socioeconomic (SEC) disadvantage. There are, however, wide disparities in child protection rates between ethnic categories – for example, Indian rates are lower than Pakistani and Bangladeshi, and White British; Black African rates are lower than Black Caribbean. 'Black Caribbean' children at all levels of neighbourhood deprivation are more likely than 'White British' children to be in care. However, the authors determined that little attention has been given to these issues in children's services, and there is a need to provide better guidance for practice (Bywaters et al., 2019).

Morris et al. (2018) in their research findings on work with child protection social workers in deprived communities found that social workers rarely attributed or reflected on the wider inequalities affecting such groups and did not take account of issues around ethnicity. The implications for practice mean that practitioners should be alert to possible biases which affect the rights and needs of service users when making assessments and decisions (see SWE *Professional Standards*, and particularly sections 1.5, 1.6, 1.7 4.4, 3.5, 3.7, 3.14, 4.2, 4.8, 6.1).

SWE *Professional Standards* provide: 'Value the importance of family and community systems and work in partnership with people to identify and harness the assets of those systems' (1.4), including in the areas of cultural sensitivity, 'recognis(ing) differences across diverse communities and challenge the impact of disadvantage and discrimination on people and their families and communities' (1.5). It is a social worker's responsibility to understand as much as possible about the cultural identities of the people, families and communities they are working with. In addition, the welfare checklist (s.1, CA) requires the courts to consider 'his [*sic*] age, sex, background and any characteristics of his which the court considers relevant', which includes cultural and religious background'. Social workers must provide the courts with this information in their reports.

Social workers must be able to carry out work confidentially which is culturally sensitive, recognising and working with the strengths of different cultural practices, while at the same time avoiding cultural relativity, which can put children at risk (Littlechild, 2012; NSPCC, 2014). If social workers have little and/or prejudiced knowledge (Dingwall et al., 1983, 2014) they will not have the confidence to challenge parents who raise matters of race or religion to distract attention from a focus on the child (NSPCC, 2014: 4). Social workers should also set out to parents clearly and honestly what their role is.

Chapter Summary

This chapter has:

- examined the development of social policy around child protection and considered the implications for social work practice from the perspectives of children, young people, parents and carers;
- critically examined ideas, knowledge and approaches within an examination of social work ethical principles, values and professional standards, which can be applied to social work practice to aid reflection, consideration and actions in relation to what can be real dilemmas that can arise in practice.

Case study – Ethical issues for safeguarding child interventions

M (23) and her partner A (27) have three children – J (6), K (18 months) and L (6 months). The family is Black British. A was recently released from prison for drug-related offences and also assaults against M.

They live in a housing association flat in an area of high social need and deprivation. Neither work and they live on benefits.

M has very few social activities or friends that she engages with. She seems to depend on A a great deal, but also becomes frustrated and angry at what she sees as his neglectful attitude towards herself and children. Both the two older children have a child protection plan in place with concerns about neglect and the effect of witnessing domestic abuse perpetrated by A to M.

J has attended school irregularly, and the school has some concern about the state of hygiene and behaviour when he does attend. As part of the child protection plan, A should be attending a treatment agency for alcohol and drug addictions. You discover that he has not been attending as much as he should.

A place in a Children's Centre was found for K due to concerns from the health visitor and the social worker involved with the family that her development was being delayed, and there were queries about possible neglect and emotional abuse. K's attendance has been erratic and A has hardly engaged, claiming that he is too busy looking for work. L was not taken for his six-monthly health check.

There has been a report to the police from M of physical assault on her over the weekend, and the police who attended had concerns about the children witnessing the incident. As the family's social worker, you must now decide what to do.

How should a social worker set about working with each of the family members, using ethically justifiable methods and approaches, as referenced to the SWE *Standards*? In doing this, consider how the three main areas of social work ethical decision-making – individual rights, utilitarianism and virtue ethics – may affect these? In particular, how should the rights of each person be balanced against the rights and needs of the others in this situation?

M	A	J	K	L
Individual rights issues for M	Individual rights issues for A	Individual rights issues for J	Individual rights issues for K	Individual rights issues for L
Rights of others in the family	Rights of others in the family	Rights of others in the family	Rights of others in the family	Rights of others in the family

Figure 10.1   Key issues

Answers can be found in the Appendix.

Further Reading

Dale, D. (1986) A child in trust: the report of the inquiry into the case of Jasmine Beckford, *The British Journal of Criminology*, 26(2): 173–8, April.

Kirton, D. (2015) *Child Social Work Policy & Practice*. London: SAGE.

Rains, R.E. (1991) The Cleveland enquiry protecting children and their families from abuse: the Cleveland crisis and England's Children Act 1989. *Case Western Reserve Journal of International Law*, 23(2).

Part 3

Social Work with Adults

11

Adult Social Care and the Care Act 2014

Chapter Objectives

By the end of this chapter, the reader will be able to:

- identify the scope of an LA's duties under the *Care Act 2014*;
- understand the legal rules, social policy and ethical principles relevant to the LA's discharge of its duties under the *Care Act 2014*;
- apply the rules to social work practice.

Introduction

The *Care Act 2014* (the Care Act) repealed most of the existing adult social care law – for example, the *National Assistance Act 1948*, the *Chronically Sick and Disabled Persons Act 1970* relating to adults and the *Carers (Recognition and Services) Act 1995*, and recodified much of that law. It also made some significant reforms to adult social care law, including placing on LAs new duties and responsibilities about care and support for adults. It is largely based on the Law Commission's Report on Reform of Adult Social Care (Law Com. No. 326, 2011) which had criticised the existing law as 'complex and outdated'. However, one of their key recommendations for a single Act of Parliament with a detailed Code of Practice has not been implemented; instead, many of the details are set out in accompanying regulations and guidance.

Ethical Issues and Adult Social Care

Marketisation of social care from 1990 and the austerity budgets from 2010 onwards have had, it is argued, a detrimental impact on social work practice as the crisis in social care 'has generated a particularly hostile environment for professional social workers, because of the swingeing cuts to welfare services in general'. It is also argued that 'ethics stresses the need for social workers to seek to maximise opportunities for a fulfilling life for older people. However, lack of resources may stand in the way and care systems run the risk that they will further disadvantage older service users and reinforce ageist attitudes' and 'older people can end up feeling devalued' (Lloyd and Sullivan, 2018). See also: *Professional Capabilities Framework* (BASW, 2018) and Chapter 15.

Social Policy Considerations

Because of the growing numbers of over 65s in the population (see the Office for National Statistics, 2016), there have been increasing concerns about the cost of old age, including the cost to the NHS, the cost of social care and who should pay. There have also been problems around older people in hospital causing 'bed blocking' because of delays in organising social care on discharge (see 'Delayed transfers of care', Nuffield Trust, May 2020). As a result, there has been debate about how social policy should respond to these challenges (see Age UK and the Alzheimer's Society). However, there is also criticism that ageing is often considered a negative development as it assumes a 'natural period of decline'. In 'A social policy on ageing: to reduce the costs of old age, we must improve the entire life course' (LSE blogs, 24 June 2018), Alan Watkins argues that the focus of social policy should be on the prevention of chronic conditions which are known triggers and are often preventable – e.g. diabetes, stroke and heart disease. He further argues that 'it is not ageing that is the focus of official social policy ortho-doxy but old age'.

The reforms made in the *National Health Service and Community Care Act 1990* out-sourced much of social care provision to private companies. There are now over 5,500 different care home providers and 10,000 regulated home care providers. As a result, LAs are no longer the major commissioner of adult social care services as 'the pri-vatisation of care alongside tighter access to local-authority-funded care has resulted in a large growth of self-funding "customers"' (see GOV.UK, 2017, Competition and Markets Authority Care Homes Market Study Report). Cuts in funding have resulted in 400,000 fewer older people receiving publicly funded care in the period between 2009/10 and 2015/16, and around one in ten people aged 65 face future lifetime care costs of over £100,000 (The Health Foundation, 2019).

The coronavirus pandemic disproportionately impacted on older people and on people with underlying health problems (The Health Foundation, 2020) and saw high rates of coronavirus infection in care homes and high death rates (Scobie, 2021) as well as increasing the amount of unmet need. For an analysis see: 'How Covid-19 has magnified some of social care's key problems' (The King's Fund, 2020) and 'The social care system is failing the people who rely on it and urgently needs reform (The King's Fund, 2021).

Thought Box

Consider what reforms you think are needed in adult social care.

The Local Authority's Obligations under the *Care Act 2014*

The Act established a new set of criteria which all LAs must comply with and which should ensure that it reaches those most in need. It places on LAs the following obligations:

- To promote 'well-being' (see s.1 below).
- To prevent the need for care and support by helping and encouraging people to lead healthier lives.
- To provide information about care and support services available in their area which allows people to make informed choices and stay in control of their lives (see s.4 below).

It also places an obligation on LAs to 'integrate with the NHS', although this is not a new initiative. The *National Health Service Act 2006* placed a duty on clinical commissioning groups (CCGs) to work with LAs. The *Health and Social Care Act 2012* established health and well-being boards to encourage integrated working between health and social care, and a forum for health and social care to work together to improve the health and well-being of their local population. This has seen the NHS and a local authority 'jointly commissioning' services and pooling budgets (NHS, 2017: 29–37). See also: Nuffield Trust, 2019.

LAs also have an obligation to support 'high quality' social care providers. This obligation was introduced because of the collapse in 2012 of Southern Cross Healthcare, which was the largest private provider of care homes both for both older and younger adults. A Serious Case Review in 2011 found that one of their homes was 'rife with institutionalised abuse' and was 'mismanaged and understaffed' (Southern Cross, Orchid View, September 2009–October 2012). A 'Southern Cross-style collapse in care home market cannot be ruled out', a study for the Care Quality Commission (CQC), warned that high provider debts, local authority fees and pay rises could lead to a 'financial crisis' (Stothart, 2014).

The *Care Act 2014* also provides for the following:

- a commitment to personalised services;
- new national minimum standards for workforce training;
- a new code of conduct emphasising dignity and respect;
- increased legal rights for carers;
- improved access to housing aids and adaptations.

Section 78(1) of the *Care Act 2014* provides the following: 'A LA must act under the general guidance of the Secretary of State in the exercise of its functions.' The *Care and Support (Eligibility Criteria) Regulations* [2015] SI No 313 (the Eligibility Regulations) also include an 'Explanatory Memorandum', together with the Care and support statutory guidance (*Statutory Guidance*, June 2020), which sets out how local authorities should meet the legal obligations placed on them by the *Care Act 2014* and its accompanying regulations (see: www.gov.uk/government/publications/care-act-statutory-guidance/care-and-support-statutory-guidance).

Well-being

Section 1(1) places on LAs a 'general duty' to promote an individual's well-being which is 'at the heart of care and support' and sets out what the LA must do to comply. The obligation is defined in para. 1.5 of the *Statutory Guidance* as 'a broad concept … relating to the following areas in particular:

- personal dignity (including treatment of the individual with respect);
- physical and mental health and emotional well-being;
- protection from abuse and neglect;
- control by the individual over day-to-day life (including over care and support provided and the way it is provided);
- participation in work, education, training or recreation;
- social and economic well-being;
- domestic, family and personal;
- suitability of living accommodation;
- the individual's contribution to society.'

R (on the application of JF) v Merton LBC [2017] EWHC 1619

In *R (on the application of JF)* v *Merton*, the LA were ordered to undertake a fresh assessment of JF's care as the LA had failed in its obligation to put the person being assessed at the centre of the process.

> ## *R (Davey)* v *Oxfordshire CC* [2017] EWCA Civ 1308
>
> In *R (Davey)* v *Oxfordshire CC*, a 41-year-old disabled man with quadriplegia brought judicial review proceedings against the LA's decision to reduce his weekly personal budget by 42 per cent because it would result in his spending more time alone and possibly affect his ability to retain his existing care team. The LA successfully argued that they had considered the possible impact on D's well-being of the changes and there was insufficient evidence that his care team would need to change. The court concluded that there was no breach of s.1.

Preventing need for care and support (s.2)

Section 2.1 of the *Statutory Guidance* states: 'It is critical to the vision in the Care Act that the care and support system works to actively promote wellbeing and independence and does not just wait to respond when people reach a crisis point.' There is, however, little explanation about how this can be translated into practice (see Marczak et al., 2019). LAs should identify the services available in their area and provide (or arrange for another agency to provide) the appropriate resources to help people remain healthy and independent. A good example is the provision of support for people discharged from hospital – for example, following a stroke or a fall, who may need help to regain skills and confidence. Another is to involve volunteers in 'prevention-focused' initiatives (Local Government Association, 2017).

Information and advice (s.4)

An LA must provide information and advice about the care and support services in its area which is 'accessible and proportionate' and includes information on the following:

- how these services can be accessed;
- the cost implications;
- how independent financial advice about care and support can be accessed;
- how to raise concerns about the safety and/or well-being of an adult with care and support needs.

See, for example: Transforming adult social care: access to information advice and advocacy (Local Government Association, 2009), and Adult Social Care: Quality Matters (GOV.UK, 2019).

Assessment of a person's need for care and support (s.9)

The *Care Act 2014* made important changes to how an adult's eligibility for care and support is determined. It is no longer based on an assessment of the level of risk, but on whether a person is unable to achieve desired 'outcomes' without support. The statutory guidance sets a 'national minimum eligibility threshold for meeting an adult's care and support needs and a carer's support needs' (para. 2 of the Explanatory Memorandum to the Eligibility Criteria Regulations). It provides the framework for determining 1) whether any assessed care and support needs meet the threshold for LA support and 2) whether the person being assessed is unable to achieve one of the specified outcomes set out in Regulation 2.

When carrying out assessments to determine whether an adult has needs for care and support, the LA must ensure that the assessments:

- focus on the adult's needs and the outcomes they want to achieve;
- are provided to anyone who appears to have *some* need for care and support – i.e. they are not limited to those people who the LA thinks will be eligible;
- do not take account of unrelated factors such as a person's finances;
- must be carried out with involvement from the adult and, where appropriate, their carer or nominee.

See the diagram on the assessment process (6.1.2 Care and Support Statutory Guidance (DH), 2018) at: www.gov.uk/government/publications/care-act-statutory-guidance/care-and-support-statutory-guidance

Refusing an assessment (s.11)

If an adult refuses an assessment for care and support, the LA is not required to assess unless:

1. the adult lacks capacity to refuse and LA is satisfied that assessment would be in that person's best interests; or
2. the adult is experiencing, or is at risk of, abuse or neglect; or
3. the adult changes his or her mind.

If the LA subsequently thinks that the person's needs or circumstances have changed, the LA has a duty to assess, but assessment being subject to the person's further right to refuse unless provisos 1 or 2 in the list above applies. Similarly, if a carer refuses a carer's assessment, the LA is not required to assess unless the carer changes their mind or the LA thinks that the carer's needs or circumstances have changed. If so, the LA must assess but assessment being subject to the carer refusing again.

Independent advocates (s.67)

An LA must arrange for an 'independent advocate' to represent and support a person being assessed if they have 'substantial difficulty understanding and participating fully in the assessment process. In *R (on the application of SG)* v *Haringey LBC* EWHC 2579 (Admin) the LA's failure to provide SG with an independent advocate made the assessment unlawful as, without an advocate, SG was unable to influence the outcome of the assessment.

Specified outcomes (para. 2(2) Eligibility Criteria)

The following outcomes determine whether the person has eligible needs:

- managing and maintaining nutrition;
- maintaining personal hygiene;
- managing toilet needs;
- being appropriately dressed;
- maintaining a safe and habitable environment;
- developing and maintaining personal and family relationships;
- accessing work, training or education;
- accessing community services;
- carrying out caring responsibilities for a child.

A person is unable to achieve an outcome if either they:

- cannot do it without assistance; or
- is able to do it without assistance but doing so causes significant pain, distress or anxiety.

CP v North East Lincolnshire Council [2019] EWCA Civ 1614

In *CP v North East Lincolnshire Council*, a 22-year-old woman with complex and multiple disabilities sought a judicial review of the Council's assessment of her care needs and the calculation of her personal budget. The dispute centred on the LA's refusal to fund the cost of her weekly attendance at an activity centre run by a charity which her father had set up and was actively involved in. The LA did, however, fund the cost of taking CP to and from the centre. The court held that the LA was in breach of its duty under s.26, CA 2014 to meet a person's care and support needs, which were recognised by the LA's decision to fund the cost of taking her there. Although the LA subsequently agreed to pay the cost, CP was awarded compensation for the period it did not fund.

The eligibility criteria (s.13)

Section 13.7 states that needs meet the eligibility criteria if 'they are of a description specified in the regulations', or 'they form part of a combination of needs of a description so specified'.

The adult's need for care and support will meet the criteria if:

1. their care and support needs are as a result of a physical or mental condition;
2. because of their needs they cannot achieve at least two of the specified outcomes;
3. as a result, there is a significant impact on their well-being.

Care and support plans (s.13(2))

Where an LA has assessed an adult as eligible for care and support, it must prepare a care and support plan (in consultation with the person, their nominee or carer) and provide the person with a copy. It must specify:

- the needs identified;
- whether, and to what extent, those needs meet the eligibility criteria;
- which needs the authority will meet and how;
- how this will affect the outcomes the person wishes to achieve;
- the cost to the LA of meeting those needs;
- how the adult might delay or prevent future needs arising.

It must also specify where the needs are to be met by direct payments, information on the amount and frequency of those payments.

Challenges to the care and support plan can be made through the LA's complaints procedure (see: www.lgo.org.uk/adult-social-care/). If a complainant disagrees with the LA's response, they can complain to the Local Government and Social Care Ombudsman (www.lgo.org.uk). A challenge can also be made by an action for judicial review (see *CP* v *NE Lincolnshire*, above). It is usually necessary to be legally represented in judicial review cases; legal aid may be available.

Meeting a person's care and support needs (s.8)

Section 8(1) provides the following examples of what may be provided to meet a person's assessed care needs under ss.18–20:

a) accommodation in a care home (within s.3 *Care Standards Act 2000*) or in premises of some other type;
b) care and support at home or in the community;
c) counselling and other types of social work;
d) goods and facilities;
e) information, advice and advocacy.

Section 8(2) allows an LA to meet the needs provided under ss.18–20 by arranging for the services to be provided by 'someone other than itself', by providing the service itself', or by making direct payments'. Section 14 gives LAs the power to charge for the services required to meet the person's needs, but is restricted to the cost incurred by the LA. The Regulations provide that an LA cannot charge for services where the person's income falls below a specified amount (The Care and Support (Charging and Assessment of Resources) Regulations, 2014).

Under Reg. 3, a LA is prohibited from charging for the following:

- the cost of aids and minor adaptations to help with care at home (subject to a limit of £1,000);

- the first six weeks of 'intermediate care and reablement support services' provided by the LA – i.e. a programme of care and support which is limited in time and is aimed at helping the person to be able to live independently at home.

Section 17 requires LAs to assess the financial resources – i.e. carry out a 'means test' of a person to determine whether their income (there is a 'minimum income guarantee' after deduction of housing costs) and capital (the capital maximum is, at date of publication, £23,250) is sufficient to require the person to pay for the care they need (see Part 3 of the Regulations). Where the assessed person is married or has a civil partner, the assessment must be based on the individual's income and capital, not on their joint resources.

Residents (or temporary residents) in care homes must have a personal expenses allowance (£24.40 per week at date of publication). The proposed cap on the total amount of care costs a person would have to meet (the 'accrued costs') recommended by the Dilnot Commission on Funding of Care and Support (DoH, 2011) is incorporated into s.15; it has not yet been implemented.

The duty to meet a person's needs for care and support (s.18)

If the needs assessment determines that a person has eligible care and support needs, s.18 places on the LA a duty to meet those needs if:

a) the person is ordinarily resident in the LA area; or
b) is present in the LA area and has no settled home; and
c) the person consents to the LA meeting their needs; or
d) if they lack capacity, a 'best interests' decision (under the MCA 2005) has been made to meet those needs.

The Care and Support (Charging and Assessment of Resources) Regulations 2014 set out the maximum that an LA can charge. LAs have discretion whether to charge for meeting a person's care and support need unless the care and support required is free of charge (para. 8.2). An LA may still charge for services provided to a person who is assessed as having financial resources above the upper limit but lacks capacity. Section 19 provides LAs with a power to meet a person's care and support needs when s.18 does not create a duty to meet those needs.

Social Security benefits

The following non-means-tested benefits may be claimable to help meet care costs on top of LA funding. Attendance Allowance, Disability Living Allowance (DLA) and Personal Independent Payment (PIP) are benefits to help disabled people meet the extra costs incurred by their disability (see Chapter 19). They can only be considered in the LA's financial assessment if the LA are meeting those needs. If not, enough of the benefit must be kept so the person can meet the disability-related needs the LA is not meeting – e.g. extra washing, special diets, extra heating and bedding, special clothing, gardening and transport costs. Other benefits may also be claimable, such as carer's allowance, pension credit, council tax reduction and discount, and the warm home discount scheme (see Chapter 19 and GOV.UK).

Hurley & Ors v Secretary of State for Work and Pensions [2015] EWHC 3382 (Admin)

In *Hurley & Ors v Secretary of State for Work and Pensions*, it was held that the inclusion of the Carer's Allowance when determining the benefits cap (see Chapters 4 and 19) was unlawful, as it indirectly discriminated against disabled people and carers providing the care.

Personal budgets (s.26)

A 'personal budget' is a statement that sets out the total cost of the care required to meet the person's assessed needs; the amount the person must pay towards the cost of that care (determined by the LA's financial assessment); and any costs that the LA must make towards the agreed care package. Where the provisions in s.18 apply, the personal budget must set out the cost to the LA of meeting those needs and, if the cost includes 'daily living costs' – e.g. day care, live-in care, rehabilitation adaptations, supported living, meals delivered to a person's home, etc. – the amount attributable to those costs.

Direct payments (Care and Support (Direct Payments) Regulations 2014)

Direct payments are a means of supporting disabled people to live more independently as they give greater flexibility and choice for people to decide how their care needs are best met. LAs must give people the option of having direct payments to buy the care they need. It allows people to employ carers directly or contract with a chosen domiciliary care agency instead of having the care arranged by the LA. Direct payments can also be used to fund social activities – for example, visiting friends, going to the gym, swimming, accessing education, training and employment, as well as providing for day-to-day care needs. Direct payments cannot usually be used to pay close relatives to provide the care unless the LA considers it necessary to meet people's care and support needs. An 'authorised person' – e.g. a family member or friend – can be appointed to manage the payments on behalf of a person who lacks mental capacity.

The LA can refuse to provide a person with a direct payment if the LA considers that there is not a 'suitable person' to manage the payments. The legislation also prevents the following groups from receiving direct payments:

- offenders subject to court orders;
- people detained under the *Mental Health Act* on leave from the hospital (s.17) or conditionally discharged detained patients subject to Home Office restrictions (s.41);
- people subject to guardianship (s.8) or supervised discharge (s.25A).

Deferred Payment Agreements and loans (s.34)

Deferred Payment Agreements (DPAs) were introduced as part of the government's commitment to ensuring that people should not be forced, during their lifetime, to sell their home to pay for care home fees. The rules are set out in the Care and Support (Deferred Payment) Regulations 2014. The LA will pay the person's care charges on condition they are repaid at a later date (in effect, the LA lends the person money to pay their care home fees). A legal charge is placed on the person's home to ensure that the LA recovers the money when the property is sold. LAs can charge interest on the 'loan'. The LA should offer everyone who owns their own home and receives care and support the option of a deferred payment arrangement (see: *Which?*, 2019).

The *Care Act 2014* and Accommodation

Section 8 expressly provides that LAs can provide accommodation in a care home or 'other premises' to meet a person's care and support needs. However, an assessment under the *Care Act 2014* can also help with the following.

1. Establishing 'priority need' under s.188(1) *Housing Act 1996*. This requires the LA housing department to provide accommodation to an applicant where there is reason to believe that the applicant may be homeless, eligible for assistance and in priority need – s.189(1)(c) *Housing Act 1996* (see Chapter 19).
2. Showing that the accommodation is not reasonable for the (disabled) person to continue to occupy (s.175(3), *Housing Act 1996*). The accommodation can be unreasonable because of its physical condition, location, affordability, overcrowding or where there is risk of violence. If the accommodation is 'unreasonable', the person is considered 'statutorily homeless'. In *Lomax v Gosport BC* [2018] EWCA Civ 1846, the Court of Appeal held that the LA had failed to consider the impact of isolation on L's mental state (L was seriously disabled and wheelchair bound, and wanted accommodation nearer her family). An LA must also satisfy the 'public sector equality duty' (PSED) under the *Equality Act 2010* which requires them to take into account a disabled person's needs (Chapter 4).
3. Preventing homelessness. Section 4(2) *Homelessness Reduction Act 2017* places on LAs a duty to take reasonable steps to help a person stay in their current accommodation or help them secure alternative accommodation (Chapter 19).
4. Improving priority on the LA's allocations scheme (waiting list). If a person thinks that the LA has not properly considered their health, welfare or disability needs, they should be helped to provide the LA with relevant supporting evidence from health and social care professionals to give them higher priority. A request to review the LA's decision can also be made (help can be obtained from, for example, Shelter, Citizens Advice, local councillors or the person's MP).
5. Defending a possession claim.
6. Obtaining supported housing or a place in a care home (s.8 above)

Age UK estimates that there are 1.4 million people who have difficulty with the activities of daily living who do not receive all the help they need and 160,000 who receive no help at all. A survey in 2017 found that most people do not feel that care has improved since the introduction of the *Care Act 2014* (McNicoll, 2017).

Assessment of carers' needs for support (s.10)

The eligibility of carers for support is determined by reference to the following three conditions.

1. They need support because they are providing an adult with necessary care.
2. As a result of providing that care, their physical or mental health is being compromised, or is at risk of being compromised, or they are unable to achieve any of the outcomes set out in the regulations.
3. The consequence of being unable to achieve the outcomes has, or is likely to have, a significant impact on their well-being.

Section 10(1) requires the LA to assess a carer's need for support 'where it appears they may have needs for support' to determine:

a) whether the carer does have needs for support (or is likely to do so in the future);
b) if the carer does, what those needs are (or are likely to be in the future).

Anyone over 18 can ask for a carer's assessment. An advocate can be requested to help a carer in the assessment process. A carer (who may be a family member) is someone who regularly looks after a person who is ill, elderly or who has a disability and provides help with the following (deemed 'necessary care'):

*   washing, dressing, or taking medicines,
*   taking them out,
*   taking them to hospital and doctor's appointments,
*   shopping, cleaning and laundry,
*   paying bills and organising finance,
*   giving emotional support,
*   keeping someone company,
*   watching over someone who cannot be left alone.

(See: www.nhs.uk/conditions/social-care-and-support-guide/
support-and-benefits-for-carers/carer-assessments/)

Care provided by a carer under a contract, or as voluntary work, does not fall within s.10.

Section 10(4) provides that the LA's duty to carry out a carer's assessment applies regardless of their view about the level of the carer's need for support, their financial resources or those of the adult needing care.

The assessment must include (s.10(5)) an assessment of:

- whether the carer is able, and likely to continue to be able, to provide the necessary care;
- whether the carer is willing, and will continue to be willing, to provide the care;
- the outcomes the carer wants to achieve;
- whether, and if so to what extent, support could help achieve the desired outcomes.

The assessment must also take into account:

- whether the carer works or wants to work;
- whether the carer takes part in, or wants to take part in education, training or recreation;
- whether, and if so to what extent, there are alternatives to the provision of support which could help achieve the outcomes that the carer wants to achieve;
- whether the carer would benefit from the provision of anything under s.2 (prevention) or s.4 (information and advice), or of anything that might be available in the community.

The outcome of the assessment can include the following:

- giving the carer breaks;
- gym membership and exercise classes to relieve stress;
- help with taxi fares if the carer does not drive;
- help with gardening and housework;
- training how to lift safely;
- introducing carers to local support groups;
- advice about benefits.

Children under the age of 18 who care for adults are provided with care and support from children's services until they reach 18 (Chapter 6).

People Subject to Immigration Control and the Care Act 2014

A person who is subject to immigration control (defined by s.115, *Immigration and Asylum Act 1999*) who has care and support needs (including the need for accommodation), which arises solely because of destitution (extreme poverty) preventing them from being able to look after themselves (or the physical effects/anticipated effects of destitution) cannot have their needs met under the *Care Act 2014* (see Chapter 18).

However, if their need for care and support arises from a disability or infirmity, the provisions of the *Care Act* can apply. See *R (SG) v Haringey LBC and SSHD* [2015] EWHC 2579 SG involving a destitute, homeless asylum seeker suffering from severe mental health problems and *R (Westminster) v National Asylum Support Service* [2002] UKHL 38 which held that asylum seekers who were 'infirm' but whose infirmity 'was not a consequence of their destitution' should have their need for accommodation assessed as part of their adult social care package.

Non-means-tested Care

As well as the social care provided by LAs under the *Care Act 2014*, which is means-tested, there are two ways of receiving care which are not means-tested.

1. Section 117 *Mental Health Act 1983* (see Chapter 13) places on LAs and CCGs a duty to provide free after-care (regardless of means) for people who have been detained under s.3 or s.37. The free after-care provided must be related to mental health needs only (its rationale is to stop readmission to hospital) and not any other needs that a person may have. It includes both care in the community and care in a care home.
2. NHS Continuing Healthcare (CHC) involves the provision of a package of care and support services to meet the needs of someone who has a 'primary healthcare need', which includes medical care as well as accommodation and social care. In *R v North and East Devon Health Authority ex p Coughlan* [1999] EWCA Civ 1871, the Court of Appeal held that 'where a person's need is primarily for health care then the health service must fund the whole of the nursing home placement' and 'social services departments can only provide nursing to a person in a nursing home where it is a service "ancillary or incidental" to the accommodation provided'.

Eligibility for NHS continuing healthcare is determined by the NHS. The National Framework for NHS CHC and NHS-funded nursing care (DoH, 2018; s.2, *NHS Act 2006*) requires a multidisciplinary needs assessment involving the LA. CHC funding must be met by the NHS (it is not means-tested, as NHS care is free at the point of delivery). The CCG must arrange a care and support package to meet the person's assessed needs. Care can be provided in a care home, nursing home or in the community. Assessment often takes place before discharge from hospital (see: www.nhs.uk/conditions/social-care-and-support-guide/money-work-and-benefits/nhs-continuing-healthcare/). See also *R (on the application of Wolverhampton Council) v South Worcestershire CCG and* Shropshire CCG [2018] EWHC 1136 (Admin).

People cared for in nursing homes are entitled to the 'nursing care element' of the care home fees paid for by the NHS (NHS-funded nursing care) if they are not eligible for CHC funding. The nursing element is payable whether the person or the local authority are paying the remainder of the fees. The rate at date of publication was £165.56 per week (see: www.nhs.uk/conditions/social-care-and-support-guide/money-work-and-benefits/nhs-funded-nursing-care/).

A 'fast-track' process applies to people who have 'a rapidly deteriorating condition that may be entering the terminal phase' and may require the urgent provision of CHC funding (NHS continuing healthcare funding fast-track tool, GOV.UK, 2018).

Exercise

In *R (on the application of Cornwall Council (Respondent)) v Secretary of State for Health* [2015] UKSC 46 PH, a young man with physical and learning dis-abilities who was born in Wiltshire in 1986, was accommodated under s.20 of the *Children Act 1989* (Chapter 6) in 1991. He was placed with foster parents in Gloucestershire who then moved to Cornwall. When PH became 18, he was unable to stay with his foster carers and was placed in a home in Somerset. His care package cost £80,000 per annum. Which Council had to pay and why?

The answer can be found in the Appendix.

Chapter Summary

This chapter has:

- set out the powers and duties of LAs in relation to the provision of adult social care and outlines the important underpinning principles;
- discussed relevant social policy and ethical considerations;
- explained the assessment criteria relevant to people who have care and support needs, and their carers;
- provided practical examples of how the law is applied in practice.

Case study – Adult social care: working with families: the legal, ethical and social policy considerations

Consider the legal, ethical and social policy considerations of the people involved in the following case study.

Bhindi and Chandra are both in their 80s. Bhindi has severe arthritis and is in constant pain with poor mobility and finds it increasingly difficult to manage the stairs; there is no downstairs toilet. Chandra had a stroke three months ago which has affected his short-term memory. He spent several weeks in hospital, but both Bhindi and Chandra refused an offered care package as they did not want strangers coming into their home and said it was their daughter's responsibility to look after them. They live in their own home which has been poorly maintained over recent years.

Their daughter, Dhara, lives 5 miles away and although she has been trying to provide full-time care for her parents, she is now exhausted and wants to return to her own home. Bhindi and Chandra both receive attendance allow-ance. Their son, Ekram, who lives nearby, refuses to help.

Dhara thinks her parents should go into a care home but knows that they will refuse to consider this.

Answers can be found in the Appendix.

Further Reading

Braye, S. and Preston-Shoot, M. (2019) *The Care Act 2014: Wellbeing in Practice* (Transforming Social Work Practice Series). London: Learning Matters.

Feldon, P. (2017) *Get in on the Care Act: The Care Act 2014*. London: Local Government Association (2014).

Feldon, P. (2017) *The Social Worker's Guide to the Care Act 2014* (Critical Skills for Social Work). St Alban's: Critical Publishing.

The King's Fund (2018) *Key Challenges Facing the Adult Social Care Sector in England*. London: The King's Fund.

The King's Fund (2021) *The Social Care System is Failing the People who Rely on it and Urgently Needs Reform*. London: The King's Fund.

Mandelstam, M. (2017) *Care Act 2014: An A–Z of Law and Practice*. London: Jessica Kingsley.

Marczak, J., Wistow, G. and Fernandez, J.-L. (2019) Evaluating social care prevention in England: challenges and opportunities: *Journal of Long Term Care*, pp. 206–17, 4 December.

McNicoll, N. (2017) Service users give mixed verdict on Care Act's impact. *Community Care*, 28 June.

Watkins, A. (2018) A social policy on ageing: to reduce the costs of old age, we must improve the entire life course. LSE blogs, 24 June.

12

Safeguarding Adults

Chapter Objectives

By the end of this chapter, readers will be able to:

- understand the legal rules, social policy and ethical principles relating to adult safeguarding and their implications for social work practice;
- understand the duties of LAs and other agencies to safeguard adults;
- apply the law, ethics and social policy to case scenarios relevant to social work practice.

Introduction

Safeguarding is concerned with protecting the health, well-being and human rights of people at risk of harm. However, there is concern that incidents of abuse often go unreported because some victims fear that the consequences of disclosure might result in more abuse. They can also fear the possible impact on family relationships and may lack knowledge about the services that are available to provide help. Safeguarding law and practice aims to prevent abuse and neglect happening, promote the safety and well-being of those at risk, penalise perpetrators and learn lessons when things go wrong. Social workers play a pivotal role in safeguarding adults at risk of harm, and it is vital to understand the relevant legal rules, ethical principles and the social policy objectives and the implications for social work practice. The following are examples of social work decision-making which requires this knowledge and understanding.

- Whether to deprive a person of their liberty because they are the victim of abuse and neglect.
- Whether a person has the capacity to make decisions about, for example, where they live or to refuse medical treatment.
- Whether sensitive information should be disclosed because of concerns that a person is a victim of financial abuse.
- Whether appropriate intervention is necessary to protect a person (with or without capacity) from harm perpetrated against them by a family member.

Section 14.7 Care and Support Statutory Guidance (DHSC, 2020) states:

> Safeguarding means protecting an adult's right to live in safety, free from abuse and neglect. It is about people and organisations working together to prevent and stop both the risks and experience of abuse or neglect, while at the same time making sure that the adult's wellbeing is promoted including, where appropriate, having regard to their views, wishes, feelings and beliefs in deciding on any action. This must recognise that adults sometimes have complex interpersonal relationships and may be ambivalent, unclear or unrealistic about their personal circumstances.

Ethical Considerations

The right to autonomy is protected by human rights law (Chapter 2), by provisions in the *Mental Capacity Act 2005*, and it is an important ethical principle incorporated into BASW's *Code of Ethics* to be applied in social work practice. However, dilemmas may arise when making decisions about whether a person needs safeguarding or whether they have the right to make 'unwise' decisions.

Social Policy and Adult Safeguarding

Historically, the incidence of adult abuse, particularly of older people, did not receive the same media attention as child abuse. In recent years public awareness has increased considerably.

> Elder abuse can be defined as 'a single, or repeated act, or lack of appropriate action, occurring within any relationship where there is an expectation of trust which causes harm or distress to an older person'.

It is a global social issue which affects the Health and Human Rights of millions of older persons around the world, and an issue which deserves the attention of the international community. (UN, n.d.: Department of Economic and Social Affairs: Ageing)

Since 2011, a World Health Elder Abuse Awareness Day has been held each year on 15 June.

A total of 475,560 concerns of abuse were raised during 2019–20, an increase of 14.6 per cent on the previous year. The impact of the coronavirus (Covid-19) outbreak on these statistics is not yet known (see NHS Digital, 2019).

Manthorpe and Stevens (2014) chart the 'emergence of "elder abuse" as a social problem' and the policy developments that have resulted. This includes adult safeguarding (s.42, *Care Act 2014*) and the regulation of the social care workforce. Regulation 19 of the *Health and Social Care Act 2008 (Regulated Activities) Regulations 2014* aims to ensure that social care providers only employ 'fit and proper' staff and the regulation of social care providers (now provided by the CQC). Most policies are formulated by the DHSC, often after considering the views of pressure groups (such as Age UK). See also the *Safeguarding Vulnerable Groups Act 2006* discussed below and in Chapter 7.

People with learning disabilities are also at particular risk of abuse; see: 'Staff abused women at learning disability unit, finds CQC' which resulted in the hospital being closed and staff members dismissed 'after CCTV footage showed workers emotionally and physically abusing service users' (*Community Care*, 23 September 2020). See also Disability and domestic abuse risk, impacts and response (GOV.UK, 2015).

The Statement of Government Policy on Adult Safeguarding (DH, 2013) provided:

2.1 The Government's policy objective continues to be to prevent and reduce the risk of significant harm to adults from abuse or other types of exploitation, whilst supporting individuals in maintaining control over their lives and in making informed choices without coercion.

2.2 The Government believes that safeguarding is everybody's business, with communities playing a part in preventing, identifying and reporting neglect and abuse. Measures need to be in place locally to protect those least able to protect themselves.

Different Types of Abuse

Abuse includes the following.

- Sexual abuse – e.g. indecent exposure, harassment and rape.
- Physical abuse – e.g. misuse of medication, withholding food and drink, restraint.
- Psychological abuse – e.g. threats, verbal and emotional abuse, controlling behaviour, isolation.
- Domestic abuse – e.g. assault, rape, emotional abuse, controlling behaviour.
- Discriminatory abuse – e.g. unfair treatment because of age, race, disability (Chapter 3).
- Financial abuse: e.g. theft, being coerced into spending money or altering a will.
- Modern slavery (see Chapter 18).

(NHS, 2021: Abuse and neglect of vulnerable adults)

The factors that exacerbate the risk of abuse include social isolation, dependency, poor staffing levels, lack of training, alcohol, drug and mental health problems – e.g. dementia – and a victim's inability to communicate their concerns (see WHO, 2020: Elder abuse).

Sources of Safeguarding Law

The law relating to safeguarding adults comes from the following sources (see Chapters 1 and 2):

- legislation;
- decisions of the High Court exercising its inherent jurisdiction;
- human rights law.

Key Safeguarding Legislation

In addition to the *Care Act 2014*, the following legislation has important implications for safeguarding law and practice.

Mental Health Act 1983

The origins of mental health law date back to the thirteenth century when the king claimed wardship over 'all natural fools and idiots' (Killapsy, 2006). The current law is contained in the *Mental Health Act 1983* (amended by the *Mental Health Act 2007*). It provides for the assessment, admission and treatment of people suffering from mental disorder and gives rights to, and provides safeguards for, people who are compulsorily detained in hospital, which includes help to challenge their detention (see Chapter 13).

Sexual Offences Act 2003

Sexual relations with a person who lacks capacity is an offence under ss.30–33 *Sexual Offences Act 2003*. Sections 38–44 of the *Sexual Offences Act 2003* prohibits sexual activity between a care worker and a person with a mental disorder while the relationship continues. It applies to doctors, nurses, care workers in homes, workers providing services in clinics or hospitals and volunteers. The offences apply, whether or not the victim appears to consent, and whether or not they have the legal capacity to consent. Section 74 made the offence of rape easier to prove; it states: 'a person consents if he agrees by choice and has the freedom and capacity to make that choice'.

Mental Capacity Act 2005

The general principles underpinning the Act are that everybody (aged 16 and over) is presumed to have capacity, that people should be supported to make their own decisions, wherever this is possible, and that anything done for or on behalf of people without capacity must be in their best interests and must be the least restrictive intervention possible (see Chapter 14).

Section 44 of the *Mental Capacity Act 2005* created a new offence of ill-treatment or neglect:

1. if a person (D):

   a) has the care of a person (P) who lacks, or whom D reasonably believes to lack, capacity, and
   b) is the donee of a lasting power of attorney, or an enduring power of attorney created by P, or
   c) is a deputy appointed by the court for P.

2. D is guilty of an offence if he ill-treats or wilfully neglects P.

R v Patel [2013] EWCA Crim 965

In *R v Patel*, a nurse was on duty in a care home when a patient suffering from pneumonia had a cardiac arrest and died. No CPR was attempted, despite it being a requirement in the relevant practice standards. P argued in her defence that, because the survival rate in such cases was low, CPR would probably not have saved the patient's life. Her conviction for wilful neglect was upheld by the Court of Appeal because she had not provided the treatment she should have done.

Safeguarding Vulnerable Groups Act 2006

This Act established an Independent Safeguarding Authority (ISA); it also introduced a new vetting and barring scheme, and placed a statutory duty on everyone working with vulnerable groups (with both children and adults) to register and undergo a vetting process. The ISA, which is part of the Disclosure and Barring Service (DBS), maintains an adult barred list – i.e. a list of people considered unsuitable to work with vulnerable adults (see also Chapter 7).

Public Health Act 1984

The *Public Health Act 1984* gives local authority environmental health officers the power to enter, clean and disinfect premises for the prevention of infectious diseases.

Housing Act 1988

Section 8 of the *Housing Act 1988* provides grounds for a landlord to evict a tenant in breach of the tenancy agreement or for causing a nuisance.

Care Act 2014

The *Care Act 2014* embodies the following six important principles relevant to safeguarding, which are set out in 14.3 of the *Statutory Guidance* (2020):

1. Empowerment (supporting and encouraging people to make their own decisions).
2. Prevention (taking action before harm occurs).
3. Proportionality (making the least intrusive response to the threatened harm).
4. Protection (representing and supporting those in greatest need).
5. Partnership (working in partnership with other relevant services to prevent, detect and report abuse and neglect).
6. Accountability (ensuring transparency and accountability in safeguarding practice).

Section 42 places on local authorities, for the first time, a statutory duty 'to make enquiries' where they have 'reasonable cause to suspect an adult in its area (whether or not they ordinarily live there):

a) has needs for care and support (whether or not known to the local authority);
b) is experiencing, or is at risk of, abuse or neglect, or
c) as a result of those needs is unable to protect himself or herself against the abuse or neglect or the risk of it.'

The enquiry should establish whether any action is needed to prevent or stop abuse and neglect, and if so what action is necessary. All the relevant people involved will usually be interviewed, including any witnesses to the abuse. The person's views and the outcome they want to achieve must be considered, and an assessment made of their need for protection and support (see: Safeguarding Adults (NHS England): www. england.nhs.uk/wp-content/uploads/2017/02/adult-pocket-guide.pdf).

The *Statutory Guidance* (2020) states:

14.81 Professionals and other staff need to handle enquiries in a sensitive and skilled way to ensure distress to the adult is minimised. It is likely that many enquiries will require the input and supervision of a social worker, particularly the more complex situations and to support the adult to realise the outcomes they want and to reach a resolution or recovery. For example, where abuse or neglect is suspected within a family or informal relationship it is likely that a social worker will be the most appropriate lead. Personal and family relationships within community settings can prove both difficult and complex to assess and intervene in.

14.82 While work with the adult may frequently require the input of a social worker, other aspects of enquiries may be best undertaken by others with more appropriate skills and knowledge. For example, health professionals should undertake enquiries and treatment plans relating to medicines management or pressure sores.

Safeguarding Adults Board

Section 43 of the *Care Act 2014* requires every LA to establish a Safeguarding Adults Board (SAB) to lead adult safeguarding in their local area. The SAB is made up of three statutory partners – the local authority, NHS clinical commissioning groups (CCGs) and the Chief Officer of Police – whose role is to provide strategic leadership and promote public awareness of adult abuse. The SAB's three core duties are:

1. To publish a strategic plan that sets out how their objectives will be met, and the contribution made by member and partner agencies.
2. To publish an annual report setting out the effectiveness of their work.
3. Commission adult safeguarding reviews where an adult in its area dies from actual or suspected abuse or neglect and there is concern that more could have been done by partner agencies to prevent the death.

A Serious Case Review (SCR) must be commissioned by an SAB when:

- an adult in its area dies because of abuse or neglect, whether known or suspected, and where there is concern that the relevant agencies (see below) could have done more to protect the adult;
- it is known or suspected that the adult has experienced significant abuse or neglect;
- an SCR can also be arranged where the lessons learned could be used to prevent future harm or death.

Self-neglect

Self-neglect is recognised in legislation as a category of abuse for the first time. The *Care Act 2014, Statutory Guidance* (2010) states that self-neglect:

14.17 covers a wide range of behaviour [that involves] neglecting to care for one's personal hygiene, health or surroundings and includes behaviour such as hoarding. It may not necessarily prompt a section 42 enquiry. An assessment should be made on a case-by-case basis. A decision on whether a response is required under safeguarding will depend on the adult's ability to protect themselves by controlling their own behaviour. There may come a point when they are no longer able to do this without external support.

The death of Robert Crane (RC) in September 2014 in a fire in his flat provides an important example of the difficulties that can arise for social workers and other professionals in cases of self-neglect. RC lived alone in a council flat; he suffered from bipolar disorder and was well known to the mental health and adult social care services as well as the police, the fire services and the housing department. It was known that he regularly lit fires and stockpiled flammable items. Care teams and housing department staff who visited him had found evidence of hoarding. RC refused to engage with a community care assessment and was judged to have had the capacity to make that decision. The subsequent SCR identified 'missed opportunities to intervene'. They found that the relevant services involved 'had failed to take RC's mental health history into account when assessing his capacity' and 'failed to recognise that his inability or unwillingness to engage with services was a risk in itself'. There was also concern that the potential impact of his behaviour on others living in the tower block had not been considered sufficiently.

Other Agencies with Safeguarding Responsibilities

Safeguarding is a multi-agency responsibility, not the exclusive responsibility of LAs. The following organisations also have safeguarding responsibilities, and all must have clear procedures and policies that set out the framework for managing safeguarding interventions and must ensure that their staff comply with the provisions. All the organisations set out below are either health and care providers, regulators, or involved with law enforcement and thus have an important role to play in protecting people from abuse and/or reporting it when it happens.

- The NHS (including GPs, hospitals and the ambulance service).
- Safeguarding Adults Board.
- The Probation Service.
- The police service.
- Care homes and domiciliary care agencies.
- Service and professional regulators – e.g. Care Quality Commission, General Medical Council, Social Work England.
- Voluntary organisations working in adult health and social care.

Care Quality Commission (CQC)

The CQC was established by the *Health and Social Care Act 2012* to regulate health and care services in England. This includes the following:

- GP practices and dentists;
- hospitals, hospices and the ambulance service;
- care homes and home care agencies;
- children's services;
- mental health services.

It inspects, monitors and regulates the relevant services to ensure they meet the necessary standards of quality and safety. Its safeguarding role is to ensure that care providers have effective procedures in place to keep children and adults safe from abuse and neglect. Enforcement action can be taken (both civil and criminal) where appropriate. See: Safeguarding service users from abusive and improper treatment: www.cqc.org. uk. See also: Report a concern about an attorney, deputy or guardian: www.gov.uk/report-concern-about-attorney-deputy-guardian

The Court of Protection (COP)

The COP is a 'superior court of record' – i.e. has the status of the High Court – and can set precedents and enforce its own decisions. Its jurisdiction was created by Part 2 of the *Mental Capacity Act 2005*. The COP makes decisions on financial or welfare matters for people who lack capacity (see Chapter 14). See the following case as an example of a safeguarding decision made by the COP.

> ## A (Capacity: Social Media and Internet Use: Best Interests) [2019] EWCOP 2
>
> In *A (Capacity: Social Media and Internet Use: Best Interests)*, A was aged 21 and had a learning disability 'with an impairment in adaptive social and executive functioning'. There was particular concern about the risks of his being able to access the internet unsupervised as he was known to search compulsively for sites showing pornography and extreme sexual activity. The court accepted that the LA's 'internet access and safety care plan', which restricted his access, allowed his phone contract to be capped and allowed staff to check his mobile phone messages daily, was in A's best interests.

The COP can make a 'statutory will' (or change a will) on behalf of a person who lacks capacity. Application can be made when the person is not able to understand:

- what making or changing a will means;
- what property they own or what money they have;
- how making or changing a will could affect the people they know.

In 'Taking capacity seriously?' (Keene et al., 2019), the authors found that in 70 per cent of cases the subject of the proceedings had either a learning disability or dementia, and the most common issue was to determine residence, care and contact.

The Official Solicitor and Public Trustee (OSPT) and the Attorney General

The OSPT helps 'vulnerable' people who lack capacity (children and adults) 'take advantage of the services offered by the justice system' to prevent social exclusion. The Official Solicitor acts either as a litigation friend (acting on an incapacitated person's behalf in any litigation) or as a solicitor for adults who lack capacity and cannot manage their affairs and where there is no one else willing to act. Her jurisdiction is limited to civil, family or COP cases. The Official Solicitor also acts in international child abduction cases and international maintenance claims.

The Public Trustee's primary function is to act as trustee for an estate where there is no executor (if there is a will) or administrator (if no valid will) and no other person is willing to act. The Public Trustee can also be appointed where the beneficiary of the will is either a child or adult who lacks capacity. The Attorney General is the government's chief legal adviser who, in adult safeguarding cases, has authority to represent those who cannot represent themselves.

The Inherent Jurisdiction of the High Court

The inherent jurisdiction of the High Court is based on the common law doctrine that a 'superior court' has jurisdiction (acting on the Crown's behalf) to hear any matter that comes before it unless an Act of Parliament or rule limits that authority. It enables the High Court to protect people who cannot protect themselves (both children and adults), whether or not they lack capacity. Examples of relevant case law where the inherent jurisdiction was invoked because the *Mental Capacity Act 2005* did not apply include the following in the box below.

XCC v AA and others [2012] EWHC 2183 COP

In *XCC v AA and others*, DD had severe learning difficulties and was taken to Bangladesh by her parents and married to AA (her cousin). On return to the UK, XCC (a LA) applied for a declaration that the marriage was invalid. The COP, exercising its inherent jurisdiction, declared 1) that DD did not have capacity to marry or consent to sexual relations; 2) that the marriage was not valid in the UK (although it was in Bangladesh) because DD lacked capacity; 3) it was in DD's best interests for the marriage to be annulled; and 4) if a person is unable to give consent the marriage is a forced marriage within the *Forced Marriage (Civil Protection) Act* (2007) (Chapter 16). Note: marriage is not a 'welfare' issue within the provisions of the MCA 2005.

In the following two cases the inherent jurisdiction of the High Court was invoked because the vulnerable adults did not lack capacity and thus the MCA could not be used.

Re SA (Vulnerable Adult with Capacity: Marriage) [2006] *1 FLR 867*

In *Re SA (Vulnerable Adult with Capacity: Marriage)*, a 'vulnerable adult' was defined as 'someone who, whether or not mentally incapacitated, and whether or not suffering from any mental illness, or mental disorder, is or may be unable to take care of him or herself, or unable to protect him or herself against significant harm or exploitation' or 'is incapacitated from making the

---

relevant decision by reason of such things as constraint, coercion, undue influence or other vitiating factors'. In this case, SA was deaf and could not speak, and was unable to communicate with her parents who wanted to take her to Pakistan for an arranged marriage. SA wanted the right to exercise a veto on any chosen potential spouse.

DL v *A Local Authority* [2012] EWCA Civ 253

In *DL* v *A Local Authority*, DL, who lived with his elderly parents, was said to have been verbally and physically aggressive towards them, controlled their contact with other people, including health and social care professionals, tried to coerce his father to transfer the house into his name and tried to pressurise his mother to go into a care home. Both parents were assumed to have capacity. The court held that where the will of a vulnerable adult of any age was overborne and where the facts justified it, the courts should provide protection.

Human Rights Law and Adult Safeguarding

The *Human Rights Act 1998* incorporates into English law the provisions of the European Convention on Human Rights (ECHR) (Chapter 2). There is a very large body of case law on the ECHR. Set out below are some cases that illustrate the impact that the ECHR has on aspects of safeguarding. See *HL* v *UK* [2004] ECHR 471 (the 'Bournewood' case), the European Court of Human Rights (ECtHR) and *MH* v *UK* [2013] ECHR 1008 where the ECtHR held that UK law was incompatible with Article 5 because MH did not have effective access to a mechanism by which she could challenge the lawfulness of her detention (see the Independent Review of the Mental Health Act: Interim Report, GOV.UK, 2018 and White Paper, Reforming the Mental Health Act (DHSC, 2021)).

J Council v *GU and others* [2012] EWHC 3531

In *J Council* v *GU and others*, GU was detained in a private care home under the DoL provisions in the *Mental Capacity Act 2005*. GU suffered from 'autism, obsessive-compulsive disorder, dissocial personality disorder and paedophilia and lacked capacity to make important decisions'. The court had to decide whether the restrictions on his freedom to maintain private correspondence (which involved monitoring his phone calls and letters, and regular searches) complied with Article 8 of the ECHR. Had GU been detained in a high-security hospital, restrictions and monitoring of his personal correspondence would have been subject to the *Mental Health Act, Code of Practice* (2015), para,

(Continued)

4.27, but there are no equivalent safeguards in the MCA, *Code of Practice* (2016). The judge made clear the need for Parliament to plug the gap. A policy was drawn up to require the protection of Article 8 rights to be overseen by the local NHS trust and CQC (see: CQC, 2018: Guidance for care home providers: Protect people's privacy when you use surveillance).

UN Convention on the Rights of Persons with Disabilities (UNCRPD)

The UNCRPD was adopted on 13 December 2006. The UK became a signatory in 2009, but the provisions have never been incorporated into UK law and therefore cannot be relied on directly in the courts. In *M v A Hospital* [2017] EWCOP 19, it was noted that the UNCRPD aims to ensure that 'disabled people have full equality under the law'. Disabilities include long-term physical, mental, intellectual and sensory impairments which can restrict sufferers from participating in society on an equal basis to others. Article 1 states:

> The purpose of the present Convention is to promote, protect and ensure the full and equal enjoyment of all human rights and fundamental freedoms by all persons with disabilities, and to promote respect for their inherent dignity.

There has been persistent criticism of the UK's approach to protecting disabled people's rights. A UN Enquiry into the Rights of Persons with Disabilities in the UK in 2017 concluded that Government reforms to the welfare system from 2010 onwards have led to 'grave and systematic' violations of disabled people's rights. 'The UK's 2019 response to the observations of the UN Committee on the Rights of Persons with Disabilities' can be accessed on the GOV.UK website. The UN Rapporteur's report on extreme poverty also accused the UK of violating the human rights of disabled people as a result of 'sustained and widespread cuts to social support' as disabled people 'had been hardest hit by tax and welfare reforms' (www.ohchr.org).

Gaining Access to People Suspected to be at Risk of Abuse or Neglect

There are a number of legal provisions that can be used to gain entry to a property where it is suspected that a vulnerable person is at risk of abuse or neglect. These include the following.

s.17   The *Police and Criminal Evidence Act 1984* gives the police the power to enter a person's property (without a warrant) 'to save life or limb or prevent serious damage to property'. In *Baker* v *CPS* [2009] EWHC 299, the court held that the term 'saving life or limb' was outdated, but it required evidence of a fear that serious injury to a person has or might occur. Concerns about a person's welfare are insufficient (*Syed* v *DPP* [2010] 174 JP 97). Under s.17, the police can also enter property to arrest a person suspected of committing an indictable (serious) offence.

The police also have the power, at common law, to enter premises to arrest a person to prevent a breach of the peace – i.e. where there is reasonable grounds to believe that harm has been or will be caused to a person.

s.16(2)   The *Mental Capacity Act 2005* gives the COP the power to make an order to allow access to an adult who is assessed as lacking capacity and there are concerns about their welfare.

s.115   The *Mental Health Act 1983* gives Approved Mental Health Professionals (AMHPs) the power to enter and inspect premises where a person suffering from a mental disorder is living (other than a hospital), where it is suspected that a person is not receiving proper care.

s.135   The *Mental Health Act 1983* gives the magistrates court the power (on application from an AMHP) to issue a warrant to allow police to enter property (using force if necessary) where there is reasonable cause to suspect that a person may be suffering from a mental disorder and a) is being ill-treated or neglected, or b) is living alone and unable to care for themselves (see Chapter 13).

Thought Box

Social workers have no power of entry under the *Care Act 2014* to people's property, even when they suspect an adult is at risk of abuse or neglect. Should they have such power?

Chapter Summary

This chapter has:

- provided an outline of adult safeguarding law, the social policy and relevant ethical principles and explains where the law comes from;
- provided case law examples of how the law is applied in practice;
- explained the duty of a LA to make enquiries where there is reasonable cause to suspect an adult is at risk of abuse or neglect, and the implications for social work practice;
- explained the role of other agencies with responsibilities in this area of law and discussed how those responsibilities are discharged.

Case studies – Safeguarding adults at risk of harm

Identify the legal rules relevant to the scenarios and discuss how they might be used (if at all) to safeguard the people involved.

1. Mr A is 55; he suffers from Korsakoff syndrome (a chronic memory disorder caused by vitamin B deficiency) brought about by alcohol misuse. He lives alone and has consistently refused help from both NHS mental health services and adult social care. His neighbours are very concerned about him, but he refuses to let anyone into his flat to provide help.

2. Ms B is aged 43 and has a learning disability. She lives with her parents and goes to a day-care centre three days a week. Her parents are becoming increasingly frail and are finding it difficult to look after her, but refuse to let carers come into their home. The staff of the day-centre have become very concerned, as Ms B often comes to the centre hungry and unkempt. Today, she has a number of unexplained bruises on her body.

3. Mr C, aged 25, suffers from autism. He lives with his mother and a sister, aged 16, who is still at school. His mother is finding it very difficult to look after Mr C and has told her daughter that she will take him to Pakistan to get married 'so he will have someone to look after him when I'm gone'. The sister tells her friend's mother who is a social worker.

4. Mrs D has dementia and is in a care home. She is very unsettled and frequently tries to 'escape'. When her daughter visited yesterday, she found her very drowsy with a large bruise above her right eye. The staff told the daughter that Mrs D had fallen out of bed. The daughter is concerned that she is being forced to take medication which she does not need and should not be given.

5. Mr E is aged 93 and very frail, but has the capacity to deal with his financial affairs. He has a carer four times a day. His only son lives in Australia. When you arrive to assess him today, Mr E says that he has just had a call from his bank to tell him that £2,500 has been taken from his bank account. Mr E is very distressed.

6. Ms F, aged 56, suffers from multiple sclerosis and lives with her partner, Ms G. They jointly own their two-bedroomed flat. Ms F now needs care at night, particularly with toileting. Ms G considers that Ms F would be better off in a residential home as Ms G says she cannot (and will not) provide Ms F with the care she needs. Ms F is very distressed as she does not want to go into a care home or use incontinence pads at night. She has no other friends or family she can get help from. She rings the Adult Social Care Team (ASC) for help.

Answers can be found in the Appendix.

Further Reading

Institute of Public Health (2021) Report on Adult Safeguarding Focus Groups with Health and Social Care Service Users, available at: publichealth.ie/report-on-adult-safeguarding-focus-groups-with-health-and-social-care-service-users

Starns, B. (2019) *Safeguarding Adults Together: A Multi-agency Practice Guide.* St Alban's: Critical Publishing.

13

Mental Health Law

Introduction

It is imperative for professionals working with service users suffering from a mental health disorder to understand the relevant law, the social policies that have informed the law, and the ethical issues involved in their care and treatment. For some practitioners, such as approved mental health professionals (AMHPs), this will influence the decisions they make when assessing a person to determine what treatment is in their best interests. This chapter provides an overview of mental health law in England and Wales relevant to social work study and practice.

Ethical Implications

Ethical considerations for social workers working with patients requiring mental health treatment include how to balance their rights against what is in their best interests while being detained, being treated for their condition and when receiving care in the community. The latter treatment promotes empowerment of the individual, but it is also necessary to ensure that they are not open to abuse or infringe other people's rights during treatment. The ethical principles that correlate with this approach can be seen in the Kantian theory discussed in Chapter 5 – for example, making decisions based on duty and morality, but also considering the conflict with this and the social worker's own values. To help understand this from a practical perspective, the *Strengths Based Approach Framework* provides guidance for social workers when assessing the needs of a service user with mental health requirements. It states that the assessment must be person-centred and a collaborative process (DHSC, 2019a: 38).

Development of Mental Health Law and Social Policy

Prior to the late nineteenth century, the law regarding people with mental illness was punitive and labelled individuals using terminology that is now regarded as offensive. This terminology was reflected in legislation that provided for the compulsory admission and treatment of people suffering from mental illness. The *Lunatic Act 1845* introduced asylums to treat the 'insane', recognising a need for treatment along with institutionalisation. In relation to confinement, the *Lunacy Act 1890* introduced a process of certification for confinement which had time limits attached. The 1890 Act was the main piece of legislation regulating mental health services up to the inception of the NHS (Turner et al., 2015). However, one of the issues that developed politically from this was the growth in people being detained in asylums. The *Mental Health Act 1959* followed the Percy Report (Hansard, 1957) that recommended principles that included the following.

> - mental and mental deficiency services should be brought into line wherever possible with general health services and compulsion used only when positively necessary for the protection of society or in the interests of the patient.
> - to expand the community services, including residential services, for all groups of mental patients.
> - the recognition in the future of three main groups of patients – mentally ill, psychopathic, severely sub-normal – instead of two as now ...
>
> (Hansard, 1957)

Reforms have been ongoing as knowledge grows in relation to our understanding of mental health. For example, reforms in the definition of mental disorder were made in the MHA 1959, the MHA 1983 and were further amended by the MHA 2007.

The Development of the Definition of Mental Disorder

The *Mental Health Act 1959* defined mental disorder as 'mean(ing) mental illness, arrested or incomplete development of mind, psychopathic disorder, and any other disorder or disability of mind'. Hospital admission was decided medically rather than by the courts and provided for the integration of mental health services into the NHS. The closure of the Victorian asylums began in the 1960s, but few community services were developed as an alternative. The *Mental Health Act 1983* was passed with the aim of providing informal treatment for most people suffering from mental disorder while also setting out the criteria for compulsory admission and treatment.

The 1983 definition of mental disorder was amended by the *Mental Health Act 2007*.

Section 1 now provides that 'mental disorder means any disorder or disability of the mind; and "mentally disordered" shall be construed accordingly …'. This broadened the definition of mental disorder and amended the exclusions to the definition. The MHA 2007 explanatory notes clarify the amendments made to the original MHA 1983 definition. The exclusions from mental disorder included the removal of promiscuity or other immoral conduct, sexual deviancy and clarification of the use of alcohol and drugs.

---

24. Clinically, neither promiscuity nor 'other immoral conduct' by itself is regarded as a mental disorder, so the deletion of that exclusion makes no practical difference. Similarly, sexual orientation (homo-, hetero- and bi-sexuality) alone is not regarded as a mental disorder. However, there are disorders of sexual preference which are recognised clinically as mental disorders. Some of these disorders might be considered 'sexual deviance' in the terms of the current exclusion (for example paraphilias like fetishism or paedophilia). On that basis, the amendment would bring such disorders within the scope of the 1983 Act.
25. The use of alcohol or drugs is not, by itself, regarded clinically as a disorder or disability of the mind (although the effects of such use may be). However, dependence on alcohol and drugs is regarded as a mental disorder.
26. The effect of the exclusion inserted by this section is that no action can be taken under the 1983 Act in relation to people simply because they are dependent on alcohol or drugs (including opiates, psycho-stimulants or some solvents), even though in other contexts their dependence would be considered clinically to be a mental disorder.
27. It does not mean that such people are excluded entirely from the scope of the 1983 Act. A person who is dependent on alcohol or drugs may also suffer from another disorder which warrants action under the 1983 Act

(Continued)

(including a disorder which arises out of their dependence or use of alcohol and drugs or which is related to it). Nor does it mean that people may never be treated without consent under the 1983 Act for alcohol or drug dependence. Like treatment for any other condition which is not itself a mental disorder, treatment for dependence may be given under the 1983 Act if it forms part of treatment for a condition which is a mental disorder for the purposes of the 1983 Act (see section 7 below for the definition of medical treatment).
(MHA, Explanatory notes, Part 1, Chapter 1, paras 24 and 25, at: www.legislation.gov.uk/ukpga/2007/12/notes/division/6/1/1/4)

The above determines that dependency on alcohol and drugs is not in itself enough for a person to be detained under the MHA, unless it is associated with a mental disorder – e.g. drug-induced delirium or a psychotic disorder; see 2.12 MHA *Code of Practice*.

In relation to people with learning disability, s.1 (2A) MHA now provides:

But a person with learning disability shall not be considered by reason of that disability to be—

(a) suffering from mental disorder for the purposes of the provisions mentioned in subsection (2B) below; or

(b) requiring treatment in hospital for mental disorder for the purposes of sections 17E and 50 to 53 below, unless that disability is associated with abnormally aggressive or seriously irresponsible conduct on his part.

This means, therefore, that people with an intellectual disability can only be detained under the MHA without suffering from a mental disorder if they behave 'abnormally aggressively or seriously irresponsibly' (see Hollins et al., 2019).

The MHA *Code of Practice* also provides guidance for practitioners in identifying which groups fall within the definition of mental disorder (see Chapter 2, MHA *Code of Practice*: https://assets.publishing.service.gov.uk/government/uploads/system/uploads/attachment_data/file/435512/MHA_Code_of_Practice.PDF).

The over-representation of people of colour in the mental health system is considered further in Chapter 15.

Thought Box

Consider the ethical issues that arise when working with service users from different groups who may or may not fall within the broad definition of a mental disorder. Use the information from the *Code of Practice* and Mental Health Foundation above to relate to the definition of a mental disorder as found in s.1, MH 1983 (as amended, MHA 2007).

Mental Health Act 1983 (as amended by the Mental Health Act 2007)

The Act provides for informal and compulsory admission to hospital for people suffering from a mental disorder. It also provides for the compulsory treatment of people detained under the Act. Compulsory treatment can be given irrespective of whether or not the patient has capacity to consent to the treatment (although there are safeguards set out in Part IV). The *Code of Practice* (which 'shows professionals how to carry out their responsibilities under the Mental Health Act 1983, and provide high quality and safe care') sets out the five guiding principles that should be considered when making all decisions in relation to care, support or treatment provided under the Act (p. 9).

- Least restrictive option and maximising independence.
- Empowerment and involvement.
- Respect and dignity.
- Purpose and effectiveness.
- Efficiency and equity.

The MHA 1983 provides detailed rules about the detention, care and treatment of people suffering from mental disorder and includes the mentally ill involved in the criminal justice system. The key sections that social workers need to know and understand are discussed below.

Section 131: informal admission

Voluntary admission into hospital first became possible in the 1930s, which meant that an individual could admit and discharge themselves from treatment. This is the favoured approach to mental health treatment as it is a voluntary decision that recognises the individual's rights. However, as discussed in the following chapter, this route of entry for treatment can be contentious – see: *HL* v *UK* 45508/99 [2004] ECHR 471. A voluntary patient (s.131) has the freedom to refuse treatment and medication, and can leave the hospital when they want to, although medical professionals are able to use compulsory powers to detain and treat such patients if considered necessary. The following provides an overview of compulsory detention for assessment and treatment under the MHA.

Section 2: compulsory admission for assessment and treatment

s.2(2) An application for admission for assessment may be made in respect of a patient on the grounds that—

(a) he is suffering from mental disorder of a nature or degree which warrants the detention of the patient in a hospital for assessment (or for assessment followed by medical treatment) for at least a limited period; and

(b) he ought to be so detained in the interests of his own health or safety or with a view to the protection of other persons.

14.27, s.2 should only be used if:

- the full extent of the nature and degree of a patient's condition is unclear;
- there is a need to carry out an initial in-patient assessment in order to formulate a treatment plan, or to reach a judgement about whether the patient will accept treatment on a voluntary basis following admission;
- there is a need to carry out a new in-patient assessment in order to reformulate a treatment plan, or to reach a judgement about whether the patient will accept treatment on a voluntary basis.

(MHA *Code of Practice*, p. 118)

In s.2(2), the 'nature' of the illness has been defined as the mental disorder that the patient experiences and 'degree' is defined as the symptoms of the mental disorder (*R Smith* v *MHRT South Thames Region* [1998] EWHC 832. An application for admission under s.2 must be made either by an Approved Mental Health Professional (AMHP) or the nearest relative (see below). The person must be assessed by two doctors, one of whom must be approved under s.12 of the MHA and have 'special experience in the diagnosis or treatment of mental disorder'; the other should be known to the patient – for example, their general practitioner. Detention under s.2 is for up to 28 days and cannot be renewed. However, the 28-day time scale may be extended if an application has been made to a court to displace the nearest relative (including cases where the nearest relative objects to the patient being detained for treatment under s.3 of the Act). A patient detained under s.2 has the right to appeal to the Mental Health Tribunal within 17 days of their detention or they can ask the hospital managers to discharge them (see below).

Section 3: admission for treatment

s.3(2) An application for admission for treatment may be made in respect of a patient on the grounds that—

(a) he is suffering from [F1 mental disorder] of a nature or degree which makes it appropriate for him to receive medical treatment in a hospital; and
(b) ...
(c) it is necessary for the health or safety of the patient or for the protection of other persons that he should receive such treatment and it cannot be provided unless he is detained under this section [F3]; and
(d) appropriate medical treatment is available for him.

A patient can be detained under s.3 if they are an informal patient or detained under ss2, 4 or 5 of the Act. Section 3 can also be used to detain a patient in the community where they are already known to the mental health services. The detention can last for up to six months and be renewed by the responsible clinician for a further six months. Like s.2, two doctors and an applicant must be involved in the assessment of the patient. The AMHP is required to consult with the nearest relative who can object to the application for admission (see *Re GM (Section 3 of the Mental Health Act 1983)* [2000] EWHC 642 (Admin). The MHA *Code of Practice* provides further guidance when s.3 can be used (see MHA *Code of Practice*, 14.28).

Section 4: admission for assessment in cases of emergency

Section 4 of the MHA is used for an emergency application for detention to assess the patient, which may be made by the AMHP or the nearest relative (see *Re GM*, above) and only requires one medical recommendation. The applicant must have seen the patient personally within the previous 24 hours. A s.4 detention lasts for up to 72 hours and should then become a s.2 unless the patient agrees to stay, is discharged or another medical recommendation is provided as s.2 requires (15.2–15.8 of the MHA *Code of Practice* provides guidance on the use of s.4).

Section 5: application in respect of patient already in hospital

Inpatients can be detained under this section by a nurse, ward doctor or approved clinician to enable an assessment of their mental state. Section 5(2) allows a ward doctor or approved clinician to detain and assess an informal inpatient for a period up to 72 hours. Section 5(4) allows a nurse qualified in mental disorders to detain an inpatient for up to six hours if they feel that the patient is suffering from a mental disorder that would put them and others at risk.

Medical Treatment and the MHA

The provision of treatment under the MHA must be appropriate and take account of the patient's wishes and feelings. The MHA of the *Code of Practice* provides the following.

24.3	In the Act medical treatment includes nursing, psychological intervention and specialist mental health habilitation, rehabilitation and care.
24.4	The Act defines medical treatment for mental disorder as medical treatment which is for the purpose of alleviating or preventing a worsening of a mental disorder or one or more of its symptoms or manifestations.
24.5	This includes treatment of physical health problems only to the extent that such treatment is part of, or ancillary to, treatment for mental disorder (e.g. treating wounds self-inflicted as a result of mental disorder). Otherwise, the Act does not regulate medical treatment for physical health problems.

The definition is important as it determines the types of treatment that can be given to detained patients without their consent and means that detained patients who have capacity to consent to treatment can lawfully refuse treatment for a physical illness but not for treatment of their mental disorder. There are, however, safeguards set out in Part IV of the Act that require second opinion doctors (SOADs) to decide whether treatment given to a detained patient who refuses to consent or is incapable of consenting is clinically justifiable (see below and *Re C (adult refusal of medical treatment)* [1994] 1 All ER 819). For a discussion of the covert administration of medication to detained patients, see Chapter 14.

Sections 135 and 136: police powers to remove to a place of safety

Police powers under the MHA 1983 *Code of Practice* are provided for under the following guidelines.

> 16.3 The purpose of a section 135(1) warrant is to provide police officers with a power of entry to private premises, for the purposes of removing the person to a place of safety for a mental health assessment or for other arrangements to be made for their treatment or care. The warrant must be applied for by an AMHP and can be granted by a magistrate when the person is believed to be suffering from mental disorder and is being ill-treated, neglected, or kept otherwise than under proper control, or is living alone and unable to care for themselves. (MHA *Code of Practice*, p. 139)

An AMHP must apply for the warrant and have considered where the place of safety should be. The purpose is to assess the mental state of the person, who can be detained under s.135 for 24 hours; this can be extended for up to another 12 hours if necessary.

> 16.17 Section 136 is an emergency power that allows for the removal of a person who is in a place to which the public have access, to a place of safety, if the person appears to a police officer to be suffering from mental disorder and to be in immediate need of care or control, if the police officer believes it necessary in the interests of that person, or for the protection of others. The person should then receive a mental health assessment, and any necessary arrangements should be made for their on-going care. (MHA *Code of Practice*, p. 141)

The *Policing and Crime Act 2017*, ss.80–3 amended ss.135–6 of the MHA 1983. They include:

- it is now unlawful to use a police station as a place of safety for anyone under the age of 18 in any circumstances;

- a police station can now only be used as a place of safety for adults in specific circumstances, which are set out in regulations;
- the previous maximum detention period of up to 72 hours has been reduced to 24 hours (unless a doctor certifies that an extension of up to 12 hours is necessary).

Compulsory Treatment in the Community

Compulsory care and treatment can also be provided in the community in three ways.

Section 7: application for guardianship

Guardianship falls under the responsibility of the local authority or someone appointed by them. The role involves the patient being able to receive care and treatment in the community rather than in hospital. Guardianship can only be provided for following a completed medical recommendation and an application from an AMHP, or in rare instances a nearest relative. The application must show that the following grounds are met.

---

s.7 Application for guardianship

(1) A patient who has attained the age of 16 years may be received into guardianship, for the period allowed by the following provisions of this Act, in pursuance of an application (in this Act referred to as 'a guardianship application') made in accordance with this section.

(2) A guardianship application may be made in respect of a patient on the grounds that—

    (a) he is suffering from mental disorder, F1 ... of a nature or degree which warrants his reception into guardianship under this section; and

    (b) it is necessary in the interests of the welfare of the patient or for the protection of other persons that the patient should be so received.

Guardians have the following powers.

- they have the exclusive right to decide where a patient should live, taking precedence even over an attorney or deputy appointed under the Mental Capacity Act 2005 (MCA). The Court of Protection also lacks jurisdiction to determine a place of residence of a patient whilst that patient is subject to guardianship and there is a residence requirement in effect
- they can require the patient to attend for treatment, work, training or education at specific times and places (but they cannot use force to take the patient there), and
- they can demand that a doctor, approved mental health professional (AMHP) or another relevant person has access to the patient at the place where the patient lives.

(MHA, *Code of Practice*, 30.3)

<u>Section 17: leave of absence during detention</u>

An inpatient being detained and treated under sections 2 and 3 of the MHA can be given leave of absence during the detention, where appropriate. This must be authorised by the responsible clinician and for a specified period. If it is for more than seven consecutive days, a community treatment order (see below) should be considered.

Community treatment orders (CTOs)

A patient detained under section 3 or part 3 of the MHA 1983 may be subject to a CTO. They can be made in respect of patients of any age and must be authorised by the responsible clinician with the agreement of the AMHP. Conditions will be placed on the CTO and, following the treatment under a CTO, the patient will be eligible for s.117 aftercare. The CTO can last up to six months and can be renewed by the responsible clinician. Challenge of the CTO can be made to the mental health tribunal.

Sections 17 and 17A have been the cause for political debate, specifically the review into the murders committed by John Barratt and Michael Stone, both of whom had been treated under the MHA.

Thought Box

Consider the concerns that the media portray regarding community treatment and the subsequent fears the pubic have.

The *Code of Practice* provides a summary of the differences between ss.7 and 17, and a CTO (Figure 18, p. 350, see: https://assets.publishing.service.gov.uk/government/uploads/system/uploads/attachment_data/file/435512/MHA_Code_of_Practice.PDF).

Aftercare

Following detention and treatment for a mental disorder a patient is entitled to free aftercare under s.117 of the MHA 1989. This is provided by the local authority and clinical commissioning group (CCG) with the aim of providing services to prevent readmission into hospital (MHA *Code of Practice*, 33.2 and 33.3).

Mental Health Act 1983, Code of Practice

This guidance, unlike legislation, is not mandatory. It should be used by social workers to demonstrate that an informed decision-making process has been followed. A CQC report in 2019 found that the *Code of Practice* was not being used as it should be. See the case of *R (on the application of Munjaz)* v *Mersey Care NHS Trust* [2005] UKHL 58 which held that 'Although the code of practice issued pursuant to the Mental Health

Act 1983 s.118(1) provided guidance and not instructions, a hospital had to consider the code with great care and depart from it only if it had cogent reasons for doing so.'

Key Roles

Social work with service users who suffer from a mental health disorder requires knowledge of the key roles found in the MHA.

The nearest relative

The nearest relative has rights and responsibilities for people being detained and treated for a mental disorder, as discussed above (see: *TW* v *Enfield Borough Council* [2014] EWCA Civ 362 [2014] MHLO 2). Their role is a contentious one and is being considered for reform. A person's nearest relative is determined by the Act rather than by the patient (unlike the choice of next of kin).

Section 26 provides that the patient's NR is determined by the relative highest on the following list:

a)   husband or wife (or civil partner);
b)   son or daughter;
c)   father or mother;
d)   brother or sister;
e)   grandparent;
f)   grandchild;
g)   uncle or aunt;
h)   nephew or niece.

There are caveats to the list – for example, a nearest relative must be 18 years and over. See s.26(5) for further disqualifications. The nearest relative can also be displaced under s.29 (see Chapter 2: www.legislation.gov.uk/ukpga/1983/20/contents).

The MHA 2007 added 'unsuitability' to the categories provided for when a NR can be displaced: see *JT* v *UK* 26494/95 [2000] ECHR 133.

Although nearest relatives can make applications for detention under the MHA, in practice this is usually done by an AMHP.

Approved Mental Health Professional (AMHP)

AMHPs are approved by local social services authorities to carry out certain duties under the MHA, including making applications for detention. They are responsible for identifying and contacting the nearest relative, arranging for doctors to carry out assessments and coordinating key agencies, such as police and the ambulance service in the admission process. AMHPs are independently responsible for the decision to detain a person and must arrange conveyance to hospital. They have a key responsibility to ensure that people's human rights are upheld and that the guiding principles set out in the MHA *Code of Practice* (2015) are followed. They must ensure that the least restrictive option is at the forefront of the process. AMHPs have other duties and powers under the MHA in relation to community treatment orders, guardianship, applying to a court to displace a NR or taking over the NR role and applying to court for warrants under s.135, MHA (National Workforce Plan for Approved Mental Health Professionals (AMHPs) (2019)). AMHPs can be registered social workers, chartered psychologists, first-level nurses or registered occupational therapists. They must undertake specialist training.

Approved Clinician (AC)

Section 145 of the MHA 1983 provides for the meaning of an Approved Clinician and their roles under the Act. These include using the powers under s.5, report writing for patients with a criminal conviction and advising the nearest relative regarding the possible discharge of the patient. The following professionals can undertake specialised training to become an AC:

- doctors;
- chartered psychologists;
- first-level nurses;
- registered occupational therapists;
- registered social workers.

Responsible Clinician

A Responsible Clinician does not need to be a doctor, but must be an approved clinician and, in certain circumstances such as assessment under ss.2 and 3, a registered medical practitioner will be required to make decisions concerning the patient's detention and treatment. An AMHP will also make decisions alongside the responsible clinician, as discussed above, about whether a person should be subject to a CTO. The responsible clinician has overall responsibility for the care and treatment of people assessed and treated under the *Mental Health Act 1983*.

Hospital Manager

Hospital Managers are independent of the hospital, CCGs and local authority; they are not employees or officers of the hospital. Their role includes the power under s.23 to discharge a detained patient; they inform patients of their rights relating to discharge from detention and from a CTO (see MHA *Code of Practice*, Chapter 37).

Hospital Managers' hearings are less formal than a mental health tribunal, and are made up of three panel members who are independent of the hospital and the team treating the patient. The patient can ask for discharge via this hearing and the hospital managers can decide if a patient's detention should be renewed once the official time limit is due to end.

Second Opinion Appointed Doctor (SOAD)

A SOAD is a consultant psychiatrist with at least five years' experience and is appointed by the Care Quality Commission. A SOAD safeguards the patient if they are refusing treatment or lack capacity to consent to the treatment. They ensure that the treatment being given is necessary, and the rights and wishes of the patient have been considered when administering it (see MHA, *Code of Practice*, Chapter 25).

Independent Mental Health Advocate (IMHA)

Section 30 of the MHA 2007 states that the local authority should enable a qualifying patient to be supported by an IMHA where possible. IMHAs can support nearly all patients being detained for treatment, guardianship and CTOs. They are independent of the mental health service and assist patients to understand their rights and the law surrounding their detention. The MHA *Code of Practice* (Chapter 6) states that their role includes providing information relating to their rights, the rights of the NR, explaining sections of the MHA that apply to them and the conditions these might impose on the patient.

Mental Health Tribunal (MHT)

A deprivation of liberty without consent can be a breach of a patient's rights under Article 5 of the ECHR (Chapter 2). Challenges to detention are safeguards for patients who feel their detention is unlawful and therefore a breach of their human rights. The patient or their nearest relative can apply to the tribunal to challenge their detention, which would be held in the hospital or, if subject to a CTO, another appropriate place. MHTs are made up of a legal representative (the judge), a registered medical professional and a third member who must have health and social care experience. The panel decide, on the balance of probabilities, whether the patient should remain under compulsory detention for treatment of a mental disorder. The social worker plays an important part in this process as they, along with the responsible clinician and other parties supporting the patient, will be required to complete a report for the panel. The decision of the tribunal can be to:

- order the patient's release;
- recommend that they are transferred to a different hospital;
- ask for treatment in the community;
- recommend leave of absence to prepare for return to the community.

If the patient feels there has been a mistake in the decision-making process or the decision itself, they may be able to appeal to the upper tribunal.

Children and Young People under the MHA

The MHA applies to all ages, which means that children and young people can also be compulsorily detained for assessment or treatment under the Act, but not for guardianship.

Young people can also be admitted as informal patients if they have given consent and are Gillick competent (see Chapters 4 and 6). The *Code of Practice* identifies children as being under the age of 16 and young people between 16 and 17 years old. This is significant for practitioners in establishing when parental responsibility (PR) (determined by ss.2 and 3 of the *Children Act 1989*) can be used to override the wishes of the child/young person (see Chapters 6 and 7). If a competent child or a young person with capacity refuses treatment, it may be necessary for the court to make the decision to detain and treat them compulsorily under the Act. Furthermore, confidentiality (see Chapter 4) and the wishes of the child remain, but the scope of parental responsibility is still considered (see Thomas et al., 2015). See also the MHA *Code of Practice*, 19.39, regarding parental consent on admission and/or treatment of a child under the MHA 1983.

The development of case law in the area of deprivation of liberty for children and young people is ongoing, as can be seen in the following case law.

RK v BCC [2011] EWCA Civ 1305	The court considered the following cases in their decision. 'The decisions of the European Court of Human Rights in *Neilson* v *Denmark* [1988] 11 EHRR 175 and of this court in *Re K* [2002] 2WLR 1141 demonstrate that an adult in the exercise of PR may impose, or may authorise others to impose, restrictions on the liberty of the child.' *Parents could not consent to DoL.*
Re D (A Child: deprivation of liberty) [2015] EWHC 922 (Fam)	'The observations of *Thorpe LJ in RK v BCC and others* [2011] EWCA Civ 1305 to the effect that a parent may not lawfully detain or authorise the deprivation of liberty of a child (a) were obiter; (b) did not correctly state the legal position; (c) were arguably inconsistent with the views of Lords Neuberger and Kerr in Cheshire West ...' *Parents could authorise the DoL.*
D (A Child) (2019) UKSC 42	'There is no scope for the operation of parental responsibility to authorise what would otherwise be a violation of a fundamental human right of a child.' *Parents could not authorise a DoL.*

Figure 13.1   Development of case law (DoL) for children and young people

Reforms

The *Mental Health Act 2007* amended both the MHA 1983 and the MCA 2005. This followed a long period of deliberation around reforms to mental health law in the UK, which included extended powers of compulsion in the community.

Following a review of the MHA by Sir Simon Wesseley, *Modernising the Mental Health Act: Increasing choice, reducing compulsion*, was published in 2019. It provides recommendations on modernising the current mental health system, addressing the problem of rising detentions under the MHA 1983, and the disproportionate number of BAME people being detained under the MHA. The recommendations include the following.

- Those detained under the Act will be allowed to nominate a person of their choice to be involved in decisions about their care. Currently, they have no say on which relative is contacted. This can lead to distant or unknown relatives being called upon to make important decisions about their care when they are at their most vulnerable.
- People will also be able to express their preferences for care and treatment, and have these listed in statutory 'advance choice' documents.
- The right to an early challenge to compulsory treatment.

This led to the publication of a White Paper, Reforming the Mental Health Act (2020), with the proposed reforms that aim to tackle:

- racial disparities in mental health services;
- better meet the needs of people with learning disabilities and autism;
- ensure appropriate care for people with serious mental illness within the criminal justice system (www.gov.uk/government/consultations/reforming-the-mental-health-act/reforming-the-mental-health-act).

See also *Reforming the Mental Health Act* (DHSC, 2021a) which sets out the Government's response to the White Paper.

Chapter Summary

This chapter has:

- provided an overview of the *Mental Health Act 1983* (as amended by the 2007 Act);
- identified the key roles relevant to social work practice;
- considered the implications of the MHA for children, young people and their parents;
- discussed the proposed current reforms of mental health law in England and Wales.

Case study – *Mental Health Act 1983* provisions case study

Fatima is 19 years old and has just been granted refugee status in the UK after fleeing from the war in Syria. Fatima's English is poor and she has been socially isolated since living here; she has no family or friends who live in the UK. Fatima's GP has become increasingly concerned about her mental

(Continued)

health as she appears very depressed and has expressed suicidal thoughts. Fatima was recently cautioned by the police for anti-social behaviour in the local supermarket. The GP has asked the local mental health team to make an urgent visit to see Fatima as the GP wants her to be detained under the *Mental Health Act 1983*.

1. What specific legislative provisions in the *Mental Health Act 1983* are relevant to this scenario relating to assessment, detention and treatment?
2. Briefly explain what the terms below mean and their possible relevance to the facts in the scenario:

   a) approved mental health professional;
   b) community treatment order;
   c) responsible clinician.

Further Reading

Thomas, V., Chipchase, B. and Rippon, L. (2015) The application of mental health legislation in younger children. *British Journal of Psychiatry Bulletin*, 39(6): 302–4, December.

Turner, J., Hayward, R., Angel, K., Fulford, B., Hall, J., Millard, C. and Thomson, M. (2015) *The History of Mental Health Services in Modern England: Practitioner Memories and the Direction of Future Research*. Cambridge: Cambridge University Press.

14

Mental Capacity and the *Mental Capacity Act* 2005

Chapter Objectives

By the end of the chapter, readers will be able to:

- understand the law relating to mental capacity;
- identify key case law relating to mental capacity;
- consider the provisions in the *Mental Capacity Act 2005*;
- consider areas of conflict between mental capacity, mental health and ethics that impact on social work practice.

Introduction

Mental capacity law has traditionally been intertwined with the development of mental health law and has only developed recently as a distinct body of law to provide protection for people who lack capacity to make their own decisions. This chapter provides an overview of the development of the law relating to mental capacity and its significance to social work practice. It includes references to important cases that demonstrate how the law developed historically and examines the important provisions in the *Mental Capacity Act 2005*. This includes the criteria used for determining whether a person has capacity and the implications for health and social care professionals who are required to assess capacity in the course of their work, which includes social workers, paramedics, doctors, nurses and the police. The chapter also examines how the law protects people who are assessed as lacking capacity.

Ethical Principles

Virtue ethics relates well to this area of the law and social work practice (see Chapter 5) as it focuses on the qualities of character needed by professionals when they make decisions or take actions on another person's behalf. In relation to mental capacity, this could be a social worker deciding what is in a service user's best interests (see s.4, MCA, below). The MCA *Code of Practice* provides a framework for how decisions about what is in a person's best interest should be made.

> 5.7 When working out what is in the best interests of the person who lacks capacity to make decisions or act for themselves, decision-makers must take into account all relevant factors that it would be reasonable to consider, not just those that they think are important. They must not act or make a decision based on what they would want to do if they were the person who lacked capacity. (MCA: *Code of Practice*, p. 68)

Development of the Law and Social Policy in Relation to Mental Capacity

The law surrounding those who cannot give valid consent was historically based on the common law of necessity. The law was developed to protect those making decisions where this was necessary because it was in a person's best interests – for example, when a person could not consent to medical treatment. *Re F (Mental Patient: Sterilisation)* [1990] 2 AC 1 is a leading case where the court was required to determine the lawfulness of carrying out a medical procedure (sterilisation) where the patient did not have capacity to consent. The court held that 'Under the common law doctors were able to operate on adults unable to consent to or to refuse treatment by reason of emergency or mental disability if the treatment was in the patient's best interest'. Although court involvement was not strictly necessary, the court should be consulted where sterilisation of a person lacking capacity was being considered 'due to its special characteristics and effects'.

Prior to the MCA 2005, the law about decision-making for people who lacked capacity developed in a piecemeal way. Policy and the subsequent legislation were the result of extensive consultations and review. The ethos of the Bill presented to Parliament was based on the principle that 'everyone has the right to make their own decisions and must be assumed to have capacity to do so unless it is proved otherwise' (HC, 2004).

Mental Capacity Act 2005

The *Mental Capacity Act 2005* brought together the principles from the common law of necessity into one piece of legislation. It provides protection to those who lack capacity, due to a mental impairment or the temporary effects of drugs and alcohol, unlike the *Mental Health Act 1983* which provides protection for people with mental illness, irrespective of their capacity to consent. The Act also provides for individuals with capacity to be able to make decisions regarding their future health and social care needs, as well

Section 1	Provides the five principles to be followed by all individuals working with people who may lack capacity: 1. The following principles apply for the purposes of this Act. 2. A person must be assumed to have capacity unless it is established that he lacks capacity. 3. A person is not to be treated as unable to make a decision unless all practicable steps to help him to do so have been taken without success. 4. A person is not to be treated as unable to make a decision merely because he makes an unwise decision. 5. An act done, or decision made, under this Act for or on behalf of a person who lacks capacity must be done, or made, in his best interests. 6. Before the act is done, or the decision is made, regard must be had as to whether the purpose for which it is needed can be as effectively achieved in a way that is less restrictive of the person's rights and freedom of action.
Section 2	Provides the definition and the diagnostic stage of the two-stage test for assessment of a lack of capacity: 1. For the purposes of this Act, a person lacks capacity in relation to a matter if at the material time he is unable to make a decision for himself in relation to the matter because of an impairment of, or a disturbance in the functioning of, the mind or brain. 2. It does not matter whether the impairment or disturbance is permanent or temporary …

Section 3	Provides the second part of the two-stage test, the functional stage:
	
	1. For the purposes of section 2, a person is unable to make a decision for himself if he is unable –
	
	   a) to understand the information relevant to the decision;
	   b) to retain that information;
	   c) to use or weigh that information as part of the process of making the decision, or
	   d) to communicate his decision (whether by talking, using sign language or any other means) …

Section 4	Provides for the best interest checklist that must be adhered to when making decisions for an individual who lacks capacity. An exception to this provision is if the patient has made an advance decision.

Figure 14.1   Part 1, MCA 2005

as their finances, by appointing a lasting power of attorney or making an advanced decision (see below). The Act applies to everyone working with or making decisions on behalf of people who lack capacity. The provisions of the Act highlight the importance of the human rights principles when assessing a person's capacity to make a decision or when it may be necessary to deprive them of their liberty.

There are three parts to the MCA 2005. Part 1 contains provisions for assessing capacity and ensuring that the best interests of the individual are met if they are assessed as lacking capacity (see Figure 14.1).

Applying assessment principles in practice

Section 1 provides the principles that apply to the MCA, the fundamental one being the presumption of capacity. This means that the burden of proof is on the professional or the court (the decision-maker) to determine whether the person lacks capacity or not. The standard of proof is the balance of probabilities, which means that the assessment must determine that it is more likely than not that the patient lacks capacity. The judgment in the case of *Heart of England NHS Foundation Trust* v *JB* [2014] highlights the care that decision-makers must take when assessing a patient. The decision-maker must show evidence at each stage of the two-stage test of how the patient meets both the functional test and the impairment of the mind they are suffering from.

For helpful guidance on the MCA, which includes guidance on helping people make their own decisions and how to make best interest decisions, see: www.nhs.uk/conditions/social-care-and-support-guide/making-decisions-for-someone-else/mental-capacity-act/

It is also important to remember that there should be an accurate record explaining how the decisions were made and what information was taken into account in the decision-making process, as there could subsequently be a legal challenge or complaint (see Chapter 21).

Section 4: best interest considerations

This section provides for the process of identifying what is in the best interests of the patient assessed as lacking capacity when a decision is needed to be made on their behalf. The best interest checklist focuses on what the patient would have wanted if they had been able to make that decision rather than what the professional considers to be the best outcome.

> 5.7 When working out what is in the best interests of the person who lacks capacity to make a decision or act for themselves, decision-makers must take into account all relevant factors that it would be reasonable to consider, not just those that they think are important. They must not act or make a decision based on what they would want to do if they were the person who lacked capacity. (MCA, *Code of Practice*, p. 68)

Ethical Considerations when Assessing Capacity

When assessing capacity and making decisions about what is in a person's best interests, under the MCA ethical considerations may arise – for example, when assessing service users with learning disabilities.

A learning disability affects the way a person learns new things throughout their lifetime. It affects the way a person understands information and how they communicate. This means they can have difficulty:

- understanding new or complex information;
- learning new skills;
- coping independently.

Around 1.5 million people in the UK have a learning disability. It is thought that up to 350,000 people have a severe learning disability (NHS: www.nhs.uk/conditions/learning-disabilities/).

When applying the MCA, the ethical considerations that a social worker must take into account might conflict with family members' views about the incapacitated person's best interests, or they may conflict with decisions taken by medical practitioners about the patient's best interests. BASW provides guidance for practitioners when working with adults with learning disabilities (see BASW, 2019a).

Thought Box

Consider the ethical dilemmas that may arise when advocating for a service user with a learning disability who lacks capacity under the MCA.

Deprivation of Liberty (DoL)

Sections 4A and B of the MCA 2005 provide the safeguards in relation to individuals who lack capacity to give consent to treatment while being deprived of their liberty. Without these safeguards, an individual's Article 5 rights under the ECHR would be breached. The following case set the precedent for the safeguards that are necessary when an individual has been deprived of their liberty because of the need to provide them with care or medical treatment.

HL v United Kingdom (45508/99)

The applicant, who suffered with autism and lacked capacity to consent to medical treatment, alleged that he had been detained in a psychiatric institution as an 'informal patient' in violation of Article 5(1) and that the procedures available to him for a review of the legality of his detention did not satisfy the requirements of Article 5(4) of the Convention.

H applied for a judicial review against his unlawful detention and sought damages. The House of Lords held that the hospital could rely on the common law doctrine of necessity to justify his detention and treatment.

However, the European Court of Human Rights (ECtHR) held that there had been a violation of Arts 5(1) and 5(4). The ECtHR found that it was irrelevant that H did not resist his admission and subsequent detention as the right to liberty outweighed this consideration. They also found against the defence of necessity, as the law of necessity did not provide any procedural rules, nor did it allow the detention to be reviewed in accordance with Art. 5. Without these safeguards, the detention was deemed arbitrary as it was based solely on the hospital's assessment.

The case highlighted the UK's lack of protection for those without capacity to give consent to a deprivation of liberty for medical treatment. As a result of this judgment, the government implemented the safeguards in ss.4A and B of the MCA 2005. The safeguards require that any DoL by a hospital or care home must be authorised by a supervisory body (the local authority) that must ensure that the correct assessments have been carried out before determining whether the DoL is lawful.

Assessment	What it means for the individual
Age assessment	They must be over 18.
Mental health assessment	They must be suffering from a mental disorder as identified under the *Mental Health Act 1983*.
Mental capacity assessment	They must lack the capacity to make a decision regarding their stay in hospital or a care home.
Eligibility assessment	They must not be detained under the MHA at the same time as a DoL, as found in Schedule A1, MCA.
Best interests assessment	Must meet the criteria set out in Schedule 1, MCA.
No refusals requirement	DoL must not conflict with a lasting power of attorney, court appointed deputy or advance decision by the patient.

Figure 14.2   Assessment criteria

Furthermore, DoLs only applied to people aged 18 years and over (see *Birmingham City Council* v *D* [2016] EWCOP 8.

Definition of DoLs

Being able to identify what is a deprivation of liberty is important for social workers to determine whether there has been a potential breach of Article 5 rights. The case of Cheshire West is the precedent for this. There is a summary in Chapter 2; an analysis is set out in the box below.

> ### *P (by his litigation friend the Official Solicitor) (Appellant) v Cheshire West and Chester Council and another (Respondents) and P and Q (by their litigation friend, the Official Solicitor (Appellants) v Surrey County Council (Respondent)* [2014] WLR(D) 140
>
> These appeals concern the criteria for judging whether the living arrangements made for a mentally incapacitated person amount to a deprivation of liberty. If they do, the deprivation must be authorised by a court or by the procedures known as the deprivation of liberty safeguards (DoLs) in the *Mental Capacity Act 2005* ... and subject to regular independent checks.
>
> P and Q (otherwise known as MIG and MEG) are sisters who became the subject of care proceedings in 2007 when they were respectively 16 and 15. Both have learning disabilities. MIG was placed with a foster mother to whom she was devoted and went to a further education unit daily. She never attempted to leave the foster home by herself but would have been restrained from doing so had she tried. MEG was moved from foster care to a residential home for learning disabled adolescents with complex needs. She sometimes required physical restraint and received tranquillising medication. When the care proceedings were transferred to the Court of Protection in 2009, the judge held that these living arrangements were in the sisters' best interests and did not amount to a deprivation of liberty. This finding was upheld by the Court of Appeal.
>
> P is an adult born with cerebral palsy and Down's syndrome who required 24-hour care. Until he was 37 he lived with his mother, but when his health deteriorated the local social services authority obtained orders from the Court of Protection that it was in P's best interests to live in accommodation arranged by the authority. Since November 2009, he has lived in a staffed bungalow with other residents near his home with one-to-one support to enable him to leave the house frequently for activities and visits. Intervention is sometimes required when he exhibits challenging behaviour. The judge held that these arrangements did deprive him of his liberty but that it was in P's best interests for them to continue. The Court of Appeal substituted a declaration that the arrangements did not involve a deprivation of liberty, after comparing his circumstances with another person of the same age and disabilities as P.
>
> The Supreme Court allowed the appeals. MIG, MEG and P had all been deprived of their liberty.
>
> *(Continued)*

Reasons for the judgment

The DoLs were introduced into the Act (MCA 2005) following the case of *HL v United Kingdom* [45508/99] (see above), which found that the treatment of a severely mentally disabled adult after his informal admission to hospital amounted to a deprivation of his liberty by the hospital. The purpose of DoLs is to secure an independent professional assessment of a) whether the person concerned lacks the capacity to make his own decision about whether to be accommodated in the hospital or care home for care or treatment, and b) whether it is in his best interests to be detained via a process that complies with Article 5 of the HRA and provides a right to challenge the detention.

The European Court of Human Rights (ECtHR) has established general principles relating to the deprivation of liberty of people with mental disorders or disabilities. The general principles make it clear that it is important not to confuse the question of the benevolent justification for the care arrangements with the concept of deprivation of liberty. Human rights have a universal character and physical liberty is the same for everyone, regardless of their disabilities. What would be a deprivation of liberty for a non-disabled person is also a deprivation for a disabled person. *The key feature is whether the person concerned is under continuous supervision and control and is not free to leave.* The person's compliance or lack of objection, the relative normality of the placement and the purpose behind it are all irrelevant to this objective question.

It follows that in P's case the judge applied the right test and his decision should be restored. MIG and MEG were also both under *continuous supervision and not free to leave* the place where they lived. The deprivation of their liberty was the responsibility of the state and therefore different from similar constraints imposed by parents in the exercise of their ordinary parental responsibilities. Accordingly, the decisions of the courts below must be set aside and a declaration made that their living arrangements constitute a deprivation of liberty. Periodic independent checks are needed for such vulnerable people to ensure that the arrangements remain in their best interests. See www.supremecourt.uk/cases/docs/uksc-2012-0068-press-summary.pdf

The judgment of the Supreme Court meant that the acid test for a definition of a deprivation of liberty is:

- Are they under continuous control and supervision?
- Are they free to leave?
- Is their care and treatment imputable to the state, which means is there state involvement in their treatment?

For an interesting discussion about whether to deprive a person of their liberty and weighing the inherent risks for the person involved if they were not detained, see: *Westminster City Council* v *Sykes* [2014] EWCOP B9 (24 February 2014).

Covert Administration of Medication

Covert administration of medication is treatment given to a patient without their knowledge and most often put into their food or drink. This action must only be carried out if the patient lacks capacity or is being treated for a mental health disorder and it is in their best interests. NICE provides guidance for professionals when treating a patient covertly (NICE, 2014, 1.15). If safeguards are not followed, this action could be unlawful and a breach of a person's human rights (see Chapter 2).

The court in the case of *AG* v *BMBC & Anor* [2016] EWCOP 37 provided further guidance to professionals in the circumstances of covert medication being administered. The case highlights the safeguards and monitoring requirements that professionals need to take when administering medication covertly. It also highlighted the potential for breaches of Articles 8 and 5 rights as the treatment could fall within the definition of DoLs.

Mental Capacity (Amendment) Act 2019

The Act provides for the liberty protection safeguards to replace the provision in the MCA for DoLs.

The key points are:

- Requires a Code of Practice to include guidance on the Liberty Protection Safeguards (LPS) and what would be considered a deprivation of liberty.
- LPS can be used in more settings than just hospitals and care homes, such as private and domestic settings.
- Authorisations can include transport arrangements.
- LPS apply to 16 years upwards.
- DoL needs to be authorised by a 'responsible body' prior to the DoL taking place.

At the time of writing, the Code of Practice is still being developed, and the DoLs and the LPS are running alongside each other until the LPS Code of Practice is completed (planned for April 2022; fact sheets were published in DHSC, 2021b).

The Mental Capacity Act 2005: Code of Practice

The *Mental Capacity Act 2005*: *Code of Practice* provides guidance that helps professionals and others understand the legal obligations placed on them. This is a great help to professionals as the legal language used in Acts of Parliament can be hard to decipher. As with the *Mental Health Act*: *Code of Practice*, the guidance is not mandatory, but it is recommended that practitioners follow it in case they are required to justify their actions under the Act – e.g. by a court.

The categories of people who are required to have regard to the *Code of Practice* include anyone who is:

- an attorney under a Lasting Power of Attorney (LPA) (see Chapter 7);
- a deputy appointed by the new Court of Protection (see Chapter 8);
- acting as an Independent Mental Capacity Advocate (see Chapter 10);
- carrying out research approved in accordance with the Act (see Chapter 11);
- acting in a professional capacity for, or in relation to, a person who lacks capacity working;
- being paid for acts for or in relation to a person who lacks capacity.

The last two categories cover a wide range of people. People acting in a professional capacity may include:

- healthcare staff – e.g. doctors, dentists, nurses, therapists, radiologists, paramedics, etc.;
- social care staff (social workers, care managers, etc.);
- others who may occasionally be involved in the care of people who lack capacity to make the decision in question, such as paramedics, housing workers or police officers.

People who are being paid for acts for or in relation to a person who lacks capacity may include:

- care assistants in a care home;
- care workers providing domiciliary care services;
- others who have been contracted to provide a service to people who lack capacity to consent to that service.

However, the Act applies more generally to everyone who looks after, or cares for, someone who lacks capacity to make decisions for themselves. This includes family carers or other carers. Although these carers are not formally required to have regard to the *Code of Practice*, the guidance given in the *Code* will help them to understand and apply the Act. They should follow the guidance in the *Code* as far as they are aware of it. (MCA: *Code of Practice*, p. 2)

Section 5: MCA

Section 5 provides protection from liability for decision-makers if they can show that they have followed the criteria set out in the MCA. It does not, however, provide protection from criminal liability or in negligence. For example, reasonable restraint can be used if its purpose is to prevent the patient seriously harming themselves and is proportionate. If the patient is likely harm to others, then the common law defence of necessity would apply. If a person needs to be deprived of their liberty in an emergency, the provisions set out in ss.4A and B need to be followed.

Court of Protection

The Court of Protection (CoP) as provided for under Part 2 of the MCA 2005 was created to protect individuals who lack capacity and is given certain powers. The table below explains some of these powers that are relevant to social workers when working with service users who lack capacity.

Lasting Power of Attorney (LPA): s.9, MCA	This allows an individual to appoint somebody to make decisions for them should they lack the capacity to do so in the future. There two types of LPA, one for health and welfare and one for finance. CoP can remove an LPA or settle disagreements.
Make a declaration: s.15, MCA	The court can make a declaration as to whether an individual lacks capacity and the lawfulness of acts carried out on behalf of the individual, including the lawfulness of a deprivation of liberty.
Appoint deputies: s.16, MCA	If there is not an LPA, the court can appoint a deputy to make decisions for the individual relating to health, welfare and finance. The CoP can also remove them.
Advance decisions: s.24, MCA	CoP can decide if these are valid.

Figure 14.3   CoP powers

Lasting Power of Attorney

Before the MCA, the law provided for an 'enduring power of attorney' (EPA), which allowed a person (the donor) to appoint an attorney (the donee, a person(s) chosen by the donor) make financial decisions on their behalf in the event they lost capacity. The MCA replaced EPAs with LPAs, which now means that a 'donor' can appoint a 'donee' (called an attorney) to make decisions regarding health and welfare on behalf of the donor once they lack the capacity to do so themselves, as well as financial decisions (a donor can give the donee the power to make both types of decision or only one type). The decision to appoint an LPA by the donor must be made while they have the capacity; they can revoke the decision at any time while they have the capacity. This LPA must be registered with the Office of the Public Guardian (OPG) for it to be valid. The OPG's roles include:

- taking action where there are concerns about an attorney, deputy or guardian;
- registering lasting and enduring powers of attorney, so that people can choose who they want to make decisions for them;
- maintaining the registers of attorneys, deputies and guardians;
- supervising deputies and guardians appointed by the courts, and making sure they carry out their legal duties;
- looking into reports of abuse against registered attorneys, deputies or guardians.

(GOV.UK (n.d.) Office of the Public Guardian)

There are instances when a donee of a LPA may not act in the best interests of the donor. This can be referred to the OPG who, if necessary, can ask the Court of Protection to decide whether the LPA should be revoked. An example of this, where an attorney misused the donor's money, is illustrated in *The Public Guardian* v *CS & PL* [2015] EWCOP30.

Independent Mental Capacity Advocates

This role was created by the MCA 2005 to provide rights for those deemed to lack capacity under the MCA. They are there to help the patient understand their rights and advocate for them. They ensure that the MCA provisions are being followed and advise the patient when they are not. It is the responsibility of the local authority to provide an IMCA once instructed by the relevant body or decision-maker. IMCAs must come from a background that involved working with people who require advocacy skills such as the health, social care and the legal sector. They must also undertake the required training (OPG606, *Making Decisions: The Independent Mental Capacity Advocate (IMCA) Service*).

Advanced Decisions

An advanced decision, or a 'living will', is a decision a person over the age of 18 can make to refuse a specific type of treatment at some time in the future in the event they have lost capacity. The treatment being refused must be specified in the statement and it must, if valid, be enforced by the medical team and family members. This area of the law is a contentious one and has produced much case law, as can be seen in *Re QQ [2016] EWCOP 22* where the court found that QQ's advance decision was not valid as she did not have capacity at the time of making it.

Overlap Between the MCA and MHA

Chapter 13 provided an overview of the *Mental Health Act 1983*, which has very different aims from the *Mental Capacity Act 2005*. For example, the MCA provides protection for individuals who lack capacity, but the MHA provides for the detention and compulsory treatment of people suffering from a mental disorder irrespective of capacity. This means that the MHA overrides the MCA if an individual requires admission and treatment. However, there can be an overlap between the two regarding the safeguards required when depriving a patient of their liberty and informal admission under the MHA.

GJ v *The Foundation Trust et al* [2010] Fam 70

The claimant, who was suffering from alcohol-related dementia and diabetes, was at risk of self-neglect and a consequent worsening of his mental and physical health. He was admitted to hospital for assessment under s.2 of the *Mental Health Act 1983* following two hypoglycaemic attacks caused by neglecting to have his insulin injections; he was detained for treatment under s.3 of the 1983 Act. He was subsequently discharged to a residential care home and, when that placement broke down, was returned to hospital and made the subject of a standard authorisation under the deprivation of liberty safeguards set out in Schedule A1 to the *Mental Capacity Act 2005*. This provided for the lawful deprivation of liberty of a person with a mental disorder who lacked the capacity to consent. The claimant objected to being detained, claiming that he was 'ineligible to be deprived of liberty' for treatment of his mental disorder and applied for an order terminating the standard authorisation on the ground that his detention was unlawful.

[It was held] that the *Mental Health Act 1983*, when it applied, had primacy over the *Mental Capacity Act 2005* in the sense that the relevant decision-makers under both Acts should approach the questions which they had to answer relating to the application of the 1983 Act on the basis of an assumption that an alternative solution was not available under the 2005 Act.

The case above discussed the role of decision-makers, including social workers, in making such decisions. The judgment concluded that if a patient fell within the scope of both the MHA and the MCA, the detention should fall under the MHA as it had primacy over the MCA. This provided some clarity for practitioners. Patients detained under the MHA have better rights to challenge their detention through a mental health tribunal.

AM v SLAM & Sec of State for Health [2013] UKUT 0365 (AAC)

Here, the circumstances do not raise issues relating to a) treatment for mental and/or physical disorder or problems (as in *GJ v Foundation Trust*) or b) discharge from hospital. Rather, they relate to whether the Appellant should be discharged from detention under s.2 because her assessment in hospital should be carried out and authorised under the MCA and its DoLs.

Decision-makers who have to address the application of the provisions of the DoLs are faced with complicated legislative provisions and their difficulties are compounded when they have to consider the relationship between the MHA and the MCA. Regular visitors to the provisions need to remember the daunting task they set for lawyers and non-lawyers who have to apply them.

There is and was effective common ground that a) AM had a mental disorder, b) she needed a cognitive assessment and c) she needed treatment in the form of taking tablets. The way in which the case for discharge was put is not that AM should be discharged home, but that she should be discharged from s.2 detention in hospital. The argument was that, as she would stay there on a voluntary basis, her s.2 detention was not 'necessary' and so it was not 'warranted' if those provisions were read compatibly with Article 5(1)(e) of the ECHR.

The outcome of the case rested on the basic philosophy of the MCA, which embodies the principle that a person who lacks capacity must be treated in the least restrictive way; that principle, however, also underpins the MHA. The overlap between the MCA and MHA remains problematic.

Chapter Summary

This chapter has:

- identified the law on mental capacity that social workers need to use in practice;
- discussed key areas that impact on social workers and their service users in relation to deprivation of liberty and the new liberty protection safeguards;
- analysed case law to gain an understanding of how the law protects those who lack capacity;
- highlighted the practice problems arising from the overlap between the MCA and the MHA.

Exercise

1. Identify whether the following scenarios are a deprivation of liberty:

    a) P lives in a residential care home and is physically unable to leave his room without the help of staff, family or friends who come to visit him. He can make a call to staff when he wants to leave his room as they only check in on him when making their routine rounds throughout the day.
    b) P is in a private room and is checked continuously throughout the day, due to his physical and mental condition.

2. Shirley is known to the local mental health team as she suffers from depression; she is also a diabetic and is refusing to take her medication, which leaves her delirious. Should Shirley be treated under the *Mental Health Act 1983* or the *Mental Capacity Act 2005*?
3. How is Article 5 of the *Human Rights Act 1998* relevant to the *Mental Capacity Act 2005*?
4. What is the impact of the Cheshire West case described above in relation to the *Mental Capacity Act 2005*?

Answers can be found in the Appendix.

Further Reading

AG v *BMBC & Anor* [2016] EWCOP 37

Mental Capacity Act 2005: Code of Practice (2007) Norwich: TSO, available at: https://assets.publishing.service.gov.uk/government/uploads/system/uploads/attachment_data/file/497253/Mental-capacity-act-code-of-practice.pdf (accessed 18 April 2020).

15

Social policy and ethical considerations relevant to working with adults

- have a greater understanding of the policy reforms of the *Mental Capacity Act* and the *Mental Health Act 1983*;
- highlight the over-representation of BAME people with mental health needs and consider the reasons for this;
- consider the application of ethics and values in adult safeguarding;
- recognise the need to whistleblow when there is negligent or abusive conduct.

Introduction

Three main areas that encapsulate social policy and subsequent reforms can be found in the care for adults at risk of harm, mental capacity, mental health policy and legislation. Reforms in all these areas are ongoing and therefore input from social policy sources are plentiful and are considered below. The second part of the chapter examines key areas of social work ethics and values in relation to mental capacity, mental health and safeguarding issues, including the need to whistleblow where agencies or institutions abuse or neglect vulnerable people.

Terminology

The word 'vulnerable' was defined in the *No Secrets: guidance on protecting vulnerable adults in care* as a person

> who is or may be in need of community care services by reason of mental or other disability, age or illness; and who is or may be unable to take care of him or herself, or unable to protect him or herself against significant harm or exploitation.
>
> (DoH, 2000)

However, the Law Commission, in their report on reform of Adult Social Care (Law Com No 326) (2011) regarded the term 'vulnerable' as stigmatising and used the terms 'adult at risk of harm' and 'adult with care and support needs' (Johnson and Boland, 2019). This terminology has been incorporated into the *Care Act 2014*. It is important for social workers to be aware of the broad range of terminology used in practice and keep up to date with any changes in terminology which could be perceived as discriminatory.

Social Policy Relating to Adults

Chapter 12 identified the complex and outdated law relating to the protection of adults at risk contained in the *National Assistance Act 1948*, the *Chronically Sick and Disabled Persons Act 1970* and the *Carers (Recognition and Services) Act 1995*. The *Care Act 2014* recodified much of the law and part of the focus became the well-being of adults at risk of harm. Some of the provisions of the Act were based on recommendations in the Law Commission's Report on reform of Adult Social Care (2011) and the Mid Staffordshire public inquiry (UK Parliament: The Francis Report (UK Parliament, 2013)). They included, *inter alia*, ensuring that the needs of the individual were being met using eligibility criteria to assess their needs, carers' assessments and the safeguarding of adults at risk of harm. See: Reforming the Law on Adult Social Care and Support: The Government's Response to the Law Commission Report 326 on Adult Social Care (DH) July 2012 which summarises the Law Commission's proposals and sets out the Government's response, at: https://assets.publishing.service.gov.uk/government/uploads/system/uploads/attachment_data/file/136454/2900021-Reforming-the-Law-for-Adult-Care_ACCESSIBLE.pdf; and the Report of the Mid Staffordshire NHS Trust Public Inquiry (2013), at: www.gov.uk/government/news/francis-report-on-mid-staffs-government-accepts-recommendations

The reports highlight how data and information collated from stakeholders in health and social care impact on social policy in practice. They also provide examples of how social policy informs the reform of existing legislation.

As a result of the recommendations, professional standards, including those of the SWE, had to include duties of candour and protection for whistleblowing.

Whistleblower

A whistleblower is an employee who reports certain types of wrongdoing, generally while at work. A whistleblower is protected by law and should not be treated unfairly because of the reporting of wrongdoing while at work.

The wrongdoing reported should be in the public interest and affect the general public. The concern can be raised at any time regarding an incident that happened in the past, is happening now or may happen in the near future. Whistleblowing for Employees can be found at: www.gov.uk/whistleblowing

---

Thought Box

Read the recommendations made by the Law Commission in the Government's response and the inquiry (see links above). How effective do you think these recommendations and subsequent legislative provisions in the *Care Act 2014* have been to date?

Social Policy and Reform of the *Mental Capacity Act 2005*

As identified in Chapter 14, policy and the reform of mental capacity law is ongoing, with consultations and reports highlighting the relevant issues that need reform and making recommendations for how the law should be reformed. For example, the Law

Commission report on Mental Capacity and Deprivation of Liberty, HC 1079 (2017) Law Com no 372 included consultation with stakeholders and made recommendations. The *Mental Capacity (Amendment) Act Bill 2018* impact assessment set out the policy considerations that the government wanted to achieve based on the recommendations of the Law Commission. These included the creation of a simplified legal framework that would provide improved outcomes for people whose liberty was being deprived and their family or unpaid carers. Furthermore, it was to include other settings where a deprivation of liberty could occur and ensure that the individual's Art. 8 rights were being met. Read the full report at: https://publications.parliament.uk/pa/bills/cbill/2017-2019/0323/ MCAB%20Impact%20Assessment%20FINAL.rtf%20SIGNED.pdf

The legislative process as discussed in Chapter 1 allows for interested groups to express their concerns regarding proposed changes to legislation. For example, the Law Society of England and Wales provided a Parliamentary Brief on the *Mental Capacity (Amendment) Bill 2017–19* during the House of Commons Second Reading, which raised concerns about the need for the best interests of the individual to be at the heart of the decision-making process to deprive a person of their liberty. They were concerned that the new safeguards took away the right to challenge the detention.

A case that relates to this concern and highlights the significance of an individual being able to challenge their deprivation of liberty is *RD & Ors (Duties and Powers of Relevant Person's Representatives (RPRs) and Section 39D IMCAs)* [2016] EWCOP 49. The court had to consider the rights of five older patients with various conditions affecting their mental capacity to make decisions regarding their detention, bringing an application to the court and the role of the relevant persons representative (RPRs) and independent mental capacity advocates (IMCAs). The significance of the judgment was that it provided guidance for the RPRs, which included the need to consider whether the patient would wish to and have the capacity to apply to the Court of Protection to challenge their detention. Furthermore, the guidance elaborates on the need for patients' preferences to be considered in relation to their wishes and feelings about the proceedings, their actions and emotional behaviour in their placement that would be relevant to the proceedings. Read para. 86 found at: www.bailii.org/ew/cases/EWCOP/2016/49.html

See Chapter 14 for a discussion on the *Mental Capacity (Amendment) Act 2019*, which created the new Liberty Protections Safeguards (LPS).

Thought Box

Read the RD & Ors case above and identify the guidance provided by the judge under s.21A at para. 86 regarding the decision to make an application challenging detention under the MCA.

Further concerns about the amendments to the MCA and DoLs relate to 16- and 17- year-olds being drawn into the scope of liberty protection safeguards and the interplay with the *Children Act 1989*. Human rights factors were pushed to the fore in the debate on the final draft of the Bill. The controversy over protecting rights also related to the overlap between detention under the MCA 2005 and the MHA 1983.

In 2017, the Government announced a review of the *Mental Health Act 1983* (as amended). Some of the recommendations are highlighted in Chapter 13. One of the key themes of the review is to improve choice and decision-making for patients. This includes the choices made in relation to decisions about detention and treatment where the patient lacks the requisite mental capacity. An ongoing conflict between which Act should be used to lawfully detain an individual has been highlighted in Chapter 14, but the reforms propose to help ameliorate this conflict.

The Interface with the *Mental Capacity Act*

For historical reasons, the MHA and *Mental Capacity Act* have grown up separately and operate under different court structures. This makes for neither clarity nor simplicity. We recognise that in the short to medium term it would not be possible to merge the two systems (by what is known as a 'fusion act') and there is at present no firm agreement as to whether this would be a sound long-term aim. In the meantime, choices will have to be made as to which system to use in relation to decisions about detention and treatment where the patient lacks the requisite mental capacity.

We are firmly of the opinion that the decision should be made on the basis of whether the patient is 'objecting' to what is proposed (using objecting in the usual sense of the word, as opposed to being unable to consent or dissent, as in the sense of the Cheshire West judgment – see Chapter 2). That is a decision with which professionals are familiar and is in keeping with the history and existing functions of the two Acts. It also has the virtue of simplicity – namely, if objecting, the MHA should be used; if not and the person lacks capacity, the MCA should be used. Of course, it is necessary to note the differences between the two regimes in terms of safeguards and after-care, differences that we believe are proportionate to the differences in intrusion into a person's life between the two Acts.

Some harmonisation could be achieved by 'cross-ticketing' judges of the Court of Protection and the Mental Health Tribunal to hear cases where a person is subject to both the MHA and the MCA, and by ensuring recognition in both regimes of advance decision-making, and the position of those who hold powers of attorney and of deputies. All this must be considered in the context of the Liberty Protection Safeguards currently under consideration in Parliament. We have to recognise that in this area we are on shifting sand. See: DHSC, 2019b: 14.

Over-representation of Black and Minority Ethnic Patients in the MHA Detention Statistics

Another major concern that the review highlighted was the over-representation of ethnic groups in compulsory detentions under the Act, which highlighted the question why ethnic minority groups do not have or access 'pre-crisis' treatment. Many factors were found to try to explain this detriment: 'Involving longstanding experiences of discrimination and deprivation, with a lack of understanding of the human dynamics of what is happening and some crucial gaps in trust between service users and providers' (GOV.UK, 2021, Detentions under the *Mental Health Act 2020*, p. 20).

A useful table from the above report shows the disparities of ethnic minority groups and the use of compulsory detention under the MHA 1983. See Number of detentions under the Mental Health Act per 100,000 people, by aggregated ethnic group, at: www.ethnicity-facts-figures.service.gov.uk/health/mental-health/detentions-under-the-mental-health-act/latest. This includes the disproportionate use of CTOs in ethnic minority groups. One of the recommendations is that an organisational competency framework should be developed with the remit of improving mental health outcomes for ethnic minority groups. Another is to provide culturally appropriate advocacy services for BAME groups, which would help to provide for their needs specific to their diverse communities (see DHSC, 2019).

BAME groups are also over-represented in the coercive elements of mental health work, and some of the possible causes are examined by the Lankelly Chase Foundation (2014). It found that while people of African Caribbean background have lower reported rates of common types of mental illness such as depression compared with other ethnic groups, they are more likely to be diagnosed with severe mental illness and 3–5 times more likely than any other group to be diagnosed and admitted to hospital for schizophrenia. Importantly for social workers, it found that in 50 per cent of studies exploring the reasons for such disparities 'race-based' explanations (including negative stereotyping) are cited. It could be argued that social work agencies and systems can amplify and compound these inequalities, and that social workers have a duty to examine how they combat this with their own and other agencies, and with other professionals. Furthermore, they should examine their own potential biases and prejudices, even if they are unconscious and unintended (Garraway, 2015). To highlight this point, the recommendations below were taken from *Modernising the Mental Health Act: Increasing choice, reducing compulsion; Final report of the Independent Review of the Mental Health Act 1983* (2018); the relevant SWE *Professional Standards Guidance* (SWE, 2019b) has been added.

Ensuring the provision of culturally appropriate advocacy services (including Independent Mental Health Advocates) for people of ethnic minority backgrounds, in doing so responding appropriately to the diverse needs of individuals from diverse communities. (See: SWE, 2019a – 1.5: Recognise differences across diverse communities and challenge the impact of disadvantage and discrimination on people and their families and communities.)

- Raising the bar for individuals to be detained under the Mental Health Act, as well as any subsequent use of Community Treatment Orders. (See: SWE, 2019a – 1.6: Promote social justice, helping to confront and resolve issues of inequality and inclusion; 3.13 – Provide, or support people to access advice and services tailored to meet their needs, based on evidence, negotiating and challenging other professionals and organisations, as required.)

- Providing the opportunity for people to have more say in the care they receive, ensuring that people from ethnic minority backgrounds are involved in the care and treatment plans developed for them and thus increasing the likelihood that they are more acceptable. (See: SWE, 2019a, 3.13; 2.4; Practise in ways that demonstrate empathy, perseverance, authority, professional confidence and capability, working with people to enable full participation in discussions and decision-making.)
- Increasing the opportunities available to challenge decisions about the care offered and received in a more meaningful way. (See: SWE, 2019a: 6.3 – Inform people of the right to complain and provide them with the support to do it, and record and act on concerns raised to me. See also whistleblowing section below.)
- Addressing endemic structural factors through the piloting and evaluation of behavioural interventions to combat implicit bias in decision-making.
- Reducing the use of coercion and restrictive practices within inpatient settings, including in relation to religious or spiritual practices. (See: SWE, 2019a, 1.5 above.)
- Seeking greater representation of people from ethnic minority backgrounds, especially those of Black African and Caribbean heritage in key health and care professions.
- Endorsing ongoing work to explore how the use of restraint by police is reduced, encouraging police services to support people experiencing mental distress or ill health as a core part of day-to-day business.
- Extending the powers of the *Mental Health Units (Use of Force) Act*, 'Seni's Law', to seclusion.
- Improving the quality and consistency of data and research on ethnicity and use of the *Mental Health Act* across public services, including criminal justice system organisations and Mental Health Tribunals.
- Giving individuals the ability to choose which individuals from their community are involved with, and receive information about, their care. (See: SWE, 2019a, 2.4, 3.13, 1.4 – Value the importance of family and community systems and work in partnership with people to identify and harness the assets of those systems.)

The above recommendations were taken from *Modernising the Mental Health Act: Increasing choice, reducing compulsion; Final report of the Independent Review of the Mental Health Act 1983 (2018)* and *SWE Professional Standards*, found at: www.socialworkengland.org.uk/media/1640/1227_socialworkengland_standards_prof_standards_final-aw.pdf

One of the recommendations highlighted above led to the introduction of the *Mental Health Units (Use of Force) Act 2018*. This is also known as Seni's Law, and resulted from the death of Olaseni Lewis, who was a voluntary inpatient in a mental health unit in 2010. He died after being restrained by 11 police officers who used force that was unreasonable and disproportionate. Following a petition from his family, the local MP introduced a Private Members Bill (see Chapter 1) that subsequently became an Act of Parliament. The Act makes provision for the oversight and management of the appropriate use of force in relation to people in mental health units. Institutions now have a duty to train their staff on the use of restraint, record instances when restraint has been used and for the police to use body cameras when called to help restrain patients in mental health units.

Ethics and Values

The following section examines key issues from SWE's *Professional Standards* (2019a), and how social workers might consider applying these standards in relation to mental capacity, mental health and safeguarding vulnerable adults. This includes the need to whistleblow where there is evidence of abuse or neglect in agencies or institutions. It was noted in Chapters 5 and 10 that, as far as possible, based on social work values and SWE *Standards*, social workers need to encourage and use their skills and methods (including task-centred (Littlechild et al., 2020) and strengths-based approaches (Wilson et al., 2011)) to enhance and prioritise empowerment, self-determination and shared decision-making (see sections of SWE's *Standards* below). However, social workers have a dual role: to take account of the rights of service users and balance the rights of other people involved, paying particular regard to SWE's *Professional Standards* (2019a).

> Duties with regard to the dual role regarding empowerment, self-determination and shared decision-making:
> '2.2 Respect and maintain people's dignity and privacy', against the need to break confidentiality, as set out in Chapters 5 and 10. Such a dual role means that, in accordance with '2.3 Maintain professional relationships with people and ensure that they understand the role of the social worker', social workers need as far as possible and as honestly as best they can to set out their role without producing risk for the service user, carers or themselves.

Mental Capacity Act and Mental Health Act Issues

While working to SWE's *Professional Standards* (2019a), social workers must keep in mind how best to 'Value each person as an individual, recognising their strengths and abilities (1.1), and Work in partnership with people (1.4)', where a service user's wishes or ability to make the decision is in question, and where the safeguards under the MCA and MHA should be considered. There may be pressure from relatives, carers or other professionals to take coercive measures, but part of the social work role is to advocate for non-coercion where appropriate for the service user (s.1.2). Attention should be given to the individual's rights, which include their right to be protected for their safety and well-being if they cannot do this themselves. This can also include ensuring proper consultation with family and carers, and fits with duties in s.3.3 to 'Apply my knowledge and skills to address the social care needs of individuals and their families commonly arising from physical and mental ill health, disability, substance misuse, abuse or neglect, to enhance quality of life and wellbeing.'

Beckett et al. (2017) set out how professional social workers have challenges when balancing the rights of different people involved in mental health situations. They may be acting as Approved Mental Health Professionals (AMHP) and be required to consider whether a person should be deprived of their liberty under the *Mental Health Act* and the associated *Code of Practice*. Social work's ethical standards and values require social workers to consider the rights of the person with a diagnosed mental health problem and whether they need to be detained for their own or others' safety, taking into account the rights of all those involved. This may also require consideration of the utilitarianism theory – that is, the greatest good of the greatest number. This is a key area for social workers to consider, not least because they may:

1. be called before a mental health tribunal to justify their actions/decisions, and
2. in the event of a complaint made against them, potentially be investigated by the SWE.

As Beckett et al. (2017) discuss, ethical codes and professional standards are there to guide social workers' practice about how to make decisions in ethically challenging scenarios in the 'real world'.

With regard to mental health interventions, as seen in Chapter 13, these should be informal wherever possible, which is reflected in SWE *Standards* 1.7. Where it is in accordance with the legislation, and the person is being assessed under the MHA, the elements set out above to ensure the person's rights to least restrictive alternatives should be foregrounded. Social workers are working/coordinating with other agencies and must, as set out in the *Professional Standards* 2.6, 'Treat information about people with sensitivity and handle confidential information in line with the law.' Furthermore, in implementing SWE's 3.6, 'Draw on the knowledge and skills of workers from my own and other professions and work in collaboration, particularly in integrated teams, holding onto and promoting my social work identity.' Therefore, professional ethics issues need to frame social work interventions with the person themselves, the carers and other agencies – e.g. the local MH NHS Trust, voluntary organisations/support services – to provide services that can be part of supporting people and making themselves and others safe. If the person is sectioned under the MHA, the social worker should ensure that the person is informed of their rights (SWE, 2019a, 1.2), which includes providing appropriate means of communication (SWE, 2019a, 2.5) and their right to appeal and have an advocate to act on their behalf.

If it is suspected that a person from a BAME community is subject to unfair discrimination, the social worker needs to consider how, and with whom, they can challenge such discrimination (SWE, 2019a, 1.5, 'Recognise differences across diverse communities and challenge the impact of disadvantage and discrimination on people and their families and communities'). This may be particularly important when a social worker is acting as an AMHP where there is potential to breach a person's rights (as set out above).

Adult Safeguarding

Similar ethical issues arise for social workers to consider in safeguarding vulnerable adults as in safeguarding children (discussed in Chapters 5 and 10). This includes whether to maintain confidentiality, resistance and disguised compliance, cultural sensitivity and issues of domestic violence. However, it is necessary also to recognise the differences between the two service user groups, as made clear in government guidance, such as the Department of Health and Social Care: *Care and Support Statutory Guidance* (2020), which states: 's1.14g – The need to protect people from abuse and neglect'. In any activity which a local authority undertakes, it should consider how to ensure that the person is and remains protected from abuse or neglect. These issues and how social workers apply them are informed by SWE *Standards*, ss.1.5, 1.7, 2.3, 2.5, 2.6 and 3.6 (all quoted above – for example, s.3.4: 'Recognise the risk indicators of different forms of abuse and neglect and their impact on people, their families and their support networks', should also frame actions and decisions.

Whistleblowing

If a social worker cannot be sure that a service user's best interests and safety are being met, they may need to raise concerns within the context of their whistleblowing duties and may need to escalate concerns if these are ignored by managers.

BASW (2014a) has published a valuable guide on the issues surrounding whistleblowing for social workers and advice on when whistleblowing may be necessary. It states that 'being prepared to whistle blow is one of the practice principles in the BASW Code of Ethics'.

Social Work England's *Professional Standards* relating to whistleblowing are:

- 6.1 Report allegations of harm and challenge and report exploitation and any dangerous, abusive or discriminatory behaviour or practice.
- 6.2 Reflect on my working environment and where necessary challenge practices, systems and processes to uphold Social Work England's professional standards.
- 6.3 Inform people of the right to complain and provide them with the support to do it, and record and act on concerns raised to me.
- 6.5 Raise concerns about organisational wrongdoing and cultures of inappropriate and unsafe practice.

The impetus for the changes in the codes was to protect social workers and staff in agencies where this might be needed. This goes back to the bravery and commitment of social worker Alison Taylor, whose actions resulted in her making public the abuse that was taking place in a number of North Wales young people's residential units (*The Guardian*, 2012). It is illegal for an employer to subject any of its workers to negative consequences because of making a 'protected disclosure' under the *Public Interest Disclosure Act 1998* (BASW, 2014a).

The BASW *Code of Ethics* (2014b) s.3:9 concerns 'Being prepared to whistleblow' in that Social workers should be prepared to report bad practice using all available channels including complaints procedures and if necessary, use public interest disclosure legislation and whistleblowing guidelines.

Chapter Summary

This chapter has:

- examined three main areas in relation to the many reforms and debates about how to protect some of the most vulnerable people in our society;
- considered the policy and ethical values relevant to working with vulnerable adults, and those with mental capacity and mental health challenges;
- discussed the need to whistleblow on abusive or neglectful agencies or institutions;
- highlighted the over-representation of Black and ethnic minority mental health patients in the compulsory detention statistics.

(Note: The Social Work England *Professional Standards* (2019) used in this chapter are accurate at the time of publication. However, they are subject to periodic review and may be amended from time to time. Please refer to the Social Work England website for the latest version: www.socialworkengland.org.uk/standards/professional-standards

Exercises

1. A social worker working with a person suffering from dementia wishes to remain at home. They are living with other members of their family, but the family members' health and well-being are being severely undermined by caring for the person. Is it right to plan for the person to go to a residential unit, even though they cannot really fully consent to this, because the social worker thinks it may be in their overall best interests, and in the best interests of the rest of the family?

2. You are the social worker for a person in a care home. Assume this is a resident at Sweet Pea Care Home under a Care Plan. You receive concerns from their relatives that they have found them dishevelled and seemingly

(Continued)

neglected and fearful on some visits. The managers say that the person's mental/physical state is a function of the disabilities the person has and, despite raising concerns, no safeguarding process has been enacted. If you make known your concerns within your agency, but there is no response from managers apart from you being told off and a decision that they will not pursue the matter further, what can you do?

Answers can be found in the Appendix.

Further Reading

The Lankelly Chase Foundation Report (2014) *Ethnic Inequalities in Mental Health: Promoting Lasting Positive Change*, available at: lankellychase.org.uk/

The NHS has produced useful guidance for practitioners on different forms of abuse and neglect in relation to vulnerable adults and responding to their needs. See: www.nhs.uk/conditions/social-care-and-support-guide/help-from-social-services-and-charities/abuse-and-neglect-vulnerable-adults/

Part 4

Social Work in Practice Contexts

16

Domestic Abuse

Chapter Objectives

By the end of this chapter, readers will be able to:

- understand the various forms of domestic abuse;
- understand and apply to case studies the current legislation that protects individuals affected by domestic abuse;
- understand the current reforms to domestic abuse legislation and the practical implications;
- apply the social policy and ethical implications to social work practice.

Introduction

The significance of understanding the law surrounding domestic abuse is necessary for social work practice as it underpins the ethos of well-being. Using the skills learned in higher education and in practice, a social worker can identify domestic abuse and the services required to support a person experiencing it. Police-recorded incidence of domestic abuse is increasing and, as the data below suggests, this may be due to a greater awareness of the issues and subsequent reporting by victims. Social workers require an understanding of the preventative orders and remedies available for individuals experiencing domestic abuse and all the diverse groups it can affect.

Ethical Principles

Consideration of faith, religion and cultural differences is a requirement for social workers when working with individuals experiencing domestic abuse. An example can be found in forced marriage for those with intellectual disabilities. The law in the UK protects individuals who do not or are not able to consent to marriage (see below). However, some families who care for relatives with intellectual disabilities encourage 'forced' marriage as a way of securing long-term care for them. Current research involving the South Asian communities in the UK highlighted the perception that long-term care through forced marriage was an ideal solution for their relative. The research states that forced marriages seemed to be more prevalent in the South Asian community. In establishing the reasons why families felt this was their only way of providing long-term support for their relative was a feeling that their local community and members of the same ethnic and religious group were not supportive of them because of lack of acceptance of individuals with intellectual disability (McCarthy et al., 2020).

For social workers working with families in these situations, ethical considerations include the social worker's understanding of the cultural beliefs of different communities and the abuse of the rights of the parties concerned in the marriage. One of the recommendations from the research is to provide further training to various agencies such as social workers, police and registrars in identifying the practice (McCarthy et al., 2020).

Current Policy and Reform of Domestic Abuse Legislation

The *Domestic Abuse Bill* gained Royal Assent in April 2021 (see Landmark Domestic Abuse Bill receives Royal Assent (GOV.UK)). The provisions within the Act are based on the *Domestic Abuse Bill 2020* policy paper which set out the summary in the box below.

The Bill will:

- create a statutory definition of domestic abuse, emphasising that domestic abuse is not just physical violence, but can also be emotional, coercive or controlling, and economic abuse;
- establish a Domestic Abuse Commissioner, to stand up for victims and survivors, raise public awareness, monitor the response of local authorities, the justice system and other statutory agencies and hold them to account in tackling domestic abuse;
- provide for a new Domestic Abuse Protection Notice and Domestic Abuse Protection Order;
- place a duty on local authorities in England to provide support to victims of domestic abuse and their children in refuges and other safe accommodation;

- prohibit perpetrators of abuse from cross-examining their victims in person in the family courts in England and Wales;
- create a statutory presumption that victims of domestic abuse are eligible for special measures in the criminal courts (for example, to enable them to give evidence via a video link);
- enable domestic abuse offenders to be subject to polygraph testing as a condition of their licence following their release from custody;
- place the guidance supporting the Domestic Violence Disclosure Scheme ('Clare's law') on a statutory footing;
- ensure that where a local authority, for reasons connected with domestic abuse, grants a new secure tenancy to a social tenant who had or has a secure lifetime or assured tenancy (other than an assured shorthold tenancy) this must be a secure lifetime tenancy;
- extend the extraterritorial jurisdiction of the criminal courts in England and Wales, Scotland and Northern Ireland to further violent and sexual offences.

See: Domestic Abuse Bill Factsheet: www.gov.uk/government/publications/domestic-abuse-bill-2020-factsheets/domestic-abuse-bill-2020-overarching-factsheet

A response from Refuge, a provider of services for people experiencing gender-based violence highlights why the law needed reforming in this area. See: https://publications.parliament.uk/pa/cm5801/cmpublic/DomesticAbuse/memo/DAB33.htm

During the lockdown as a result of Covid-19, domestic abuse cases increased because perpetrators were at home more and the impact of lockdown exacerbated what was an already potentially tense situation in some households. See: Domestic abuse during the coronavirus (Covid-19) pandemic, England and Wales: November 2020 (GOV.UK).

A government campaign encouraged friends and neighbours to be aware of potential signs of domestic abuse, which include:

- being withdrawn, or being isolated from family and friends;
- having bruises, burns or bite marks;
- having finances controlled, or not being given enough to buy food or pay bills;
- not being allowed to leave the house, or stopped from going to college or work;
- having your internet or social media use monitored, or someone else reading your texts, emails, or letters;
- being repeatedly belittled, put down or told you are worthless;
- being pressured into sex;
- being told that abuse is your fault, or that you're overreacting.

(Home Office, 2018; see: www.gov.uk/guidance/domestic-abuse-how-to-get-help?gclsrc=aw.ds)

Campaigners have raised concerns about migrant women who have no recourse to public funds (see Chapters 18 and 19) and who are not provided protection in the Act (Step Up Migrant Women UK; see: https://stepupmigrantwomen.org/).

Furthermore, the needs of the LGBTQ community should be considered in relation to domestic abuse. Stonewall offers guidance for those in LGBTQ relationships relating to domestic abuse and highlights through ONS data and research that the LGBTQ community are less likely to report experiences of domestic abuse than other groups. Social workers should be able to signpost all the groups identified above to relevant resources for prevention of abuse and the necessary support.

Current Data on Domestic Abuse

The following data from the Office for National Statistics (ONS) shows the current statistics for domestic abuse in England and Wales.

- According to the Crime Survey for England and Wales year ending March 2020, an estimated 5.5 per cent of adults aged 16 to 74 years (2.3 million) experienced domestic abuse in the last year.
- There was no significant change in the prevalence of domestic abuse experienced in the last year compared with the year ending March 2019.
- The police recorded a total of 1,288,018 domestic abuse-related incidents and crimes in England and Wales (excluding Greater Manchester Police) in the year ending March 2020.
- Of these, 758,941 were recorded as domestic abuse-related crimes, an increase of 9 per cent from the previous year.
- As the survey showed no change, the increase in police-recorded crime may reflect improved recording by the police and increased reporting by victims.

See: ONS, Domestic abuse prevalence and trends, England and Wales: year ending March 2020, for detail on the abuse-related crimes found at: www.ons.gov.uk/ peoplepopulationandcommunity/crimeandjustice/articles/domesticabuseprevalence-andtrendsenglandandwales/yearendingmarch2020

Definition of Domestic Abuse

The definition of domestic abuse is provided for under s.1 of the *Domestic Abuse Act 2021*:

> (1) This section defines 'domestic abuse' for the purposes of this Act.
> (2) Behaviour of a person ('A') towards another person ('B') is 'domestic abuse' if—
>
>   (a) A and B are each aged 16 or over and are personally connected to each other, and
>   (b) the behaviour is abusive.

(3) Behaviour is 'abusive' if it consists of any of the following—

    (a) physical or sexual abuse;
    (b) violent or threatening behaviour;
    (c) controlling or coercive behaviour;
    (d) economic abuse (see subsection (4));
    (e) psychological, emotional or other abuse;

    and it does not matter whether the behaviour consists of a single incident or a course of conduct.

(4) 'Economic abuse' means any behaviour that has a substantial adverse effect on B's ability to—

    (a) acquire, use or maintain money or other property, or
    (b) obtain goods or services.

(5) For the purposes of this Act A's behaviour may be behaviour 'towards' B despite the fact that it consists of conduct directed at another person (for example, B's child).

(6) References in this Act to being abusive towards another person are to be read in accordance with this section.

(7) For the meaning of 'personally connected', see section 2.

Legislation

The following statutes and orders provide civil remedies for victims of abuse and impose criminal liability on perpetrators of abuse. The Crown Prosecution Service's (CPS) approach to prosecuting cases of domestic abuse includes identifying factors that determine the strength of the case to be presented at court without the need for the victim to attend. This means that police body camera footage and calls to 999 can be included in this evidence. The CPS also encourage the use of Independent Domestic Violence Advisors, who work with and support the individual experiencing domestic abuse and the multi-agency partners.

Domestic Abuse Act 2021

The *Domestic Abuse Act 2021* has provided a definition of domestic abuse (see above) and recognises children as victims in seeing, hearing and experiencing the effects of domestic abuse. It also provides for victims of domestic abuse, as listed in the box below.

The Act will:

- create a new offence of non-fatal strangulation;
- extend the controlling or coercive behaviour offence to cover post-separation abuse;

(Continued)

- extend the 'revenge porn' offence to cover the threat to disclose intimate images with the intention to cause distress;
- clarify the law to further deter claims of 'rough sex gone wrong' in cases involving death or serious injury;
- create a statutory presumption that victims of domestic abuse are eligible for special measures in the criminal, civil and family courts (for example, to enable them to give evidence via a video link);
- establish in law the Domestic Abuse Commissioner, to stand up for victims and survivors, raise public awareness, monitor the response of local authorities, the justice system and other statutory agencies and hold them to account in tackling domestic abuse;
- place a duty on local authorities in England to provide support to victims of domestic abuse and their children in refuges and other safe accommodation;
- provide that all eligible homeless victims of domestic abuse automatically have 'priority need' for homelessness assistance;
- place the guidance supporting the Domestic Violence Disclosure Scheme ('Clare's law') on a statutory footing;
- ensure that when local authorities rehouse victims of domestic abuse, they do not lose a secure lifetime or assured tenancy;
- provide that all eligible homeless victims of domestic abuse automatically have 'priority need' for homelessness assistance;
- stop vexatious family proceedings that can further traumatise victims by clarifying the circumstances in which a court may make a barring order under s.91(14) of the *Children Act 1989*;
- prohibit GPs and other health professionals from charging a victim of domestic abuse for a letter to support an application for legal aid.

Domestic Abuse Act: factsheet found at: https://homeofficemedia.blog.gov. uk/2021/04/29/domesticabuseactfactsheet/

Furthermore, the Act provides the following measures towards perpetrators of domestic abuse and important new protections for victims of domestic abuse.

The *Domestic Abuse Act* will:

- prohibit perpetrators of abuse from cross-examining their victims in person in family and civil courts in England and Wales;
- bring the case of *R* v *Brown* into legislation, invalidating any courtroom defence of consent where a victim suffers serious harm or is killed;
- enable domestic abuse offenders to be subject to polygraph testing as a condition of their licence following their release from custody;
- extend the extraterritorial jurisdiction of the criminal courts in England and Wales, Scotland and Northern Ireland to further violent and sexual offences;
- provide for a new Domestic Abuse Protection Notice and Domestic Abuse Protection Order, which will prevent perpetrators from contacting their victims,

as well as force them to take positive steps to change their behaviour, e.g. seeking mental health support;

- extend the extraterritorial jurisdiction of the criminal courts in England and Wales, Scotland and Northern Ireland to further violent and sexual offences;
- introduce a statutory duty on the Secretary of State to publish a domestic abuse perpetrator strategy (to be published as part of a holistic domestic abuse strategy).

See *R* v *Brown* [1993] 2 WLR 556, which involved whether a person could validly consent to sadomasochistic activity; the Court held that where the behaviour was sufficiently serious to constitute offences under the *Offences Against the Person Act 1861*, lawful consent could not be given.

Part IV *Family Law Act 1996* provides for occupation orders (ss.33–8) and non-molestation orders (ss.42–2A). These are private orders that need to be applied for by the person who is affected. Even though they are private orders, it is important for social workers to understand that they act as preventative measures in protecting a person experiencing domestic abuse.

Occupation orders regulate who can live in the family home and can also be used to restrict the abuser from entering the surrounding area. If a person does not feel safe continuing to live with their partner, or if they have left home because of violence, but want to return and exclude their abuser, they can apply for an occupation order. An occupation order is subject to two tests: 1) the 'balance of harm' test, whereby the court will balance the harm caused to the applicant, respondent and children if an order was not to be made; 2) the core criteria which takes into account housing needs, financial resources and the likely effect of the order and conduct of the parties. An example can be found in the case of *Banks* v *Banks (Occupation Order: Mental Health)* [1999] 1 FLR 726, where a court refused to grant an occupation order and non-molestation order to the husband of a woman who had been verbally and physical aggressive towards him; her behaviour was caused by her mental illness. The court also established that the behaviour did not cause the husband any significant harm to his health.

A non-molestation order is aimed at preventing a partner or ex-partner from using or threatening violence to their partner or child, or intimidating, harassing or pestering them. The definition is not restricted solely to acts of violence; it can include harassment and an action that causes distress to the applicant. The court has discretion when determining what constitutes 'molestation'. The order can be granted for a specified period or until a further order is made. Again, this is a private order available from the Family Court or County Court. A power of arrest can be attached which, if the order is breached, could result in a prosecution for a criminal offence.

Protection from the Harassment Act 1997

This Act can be used by individuals outside the family circle or who do not meet the cohabitation requirements required by the *Family Law Act 1996*. The Act provides for injunctions and damages for victims of harassment. A breach of an injunction is a criminal offence; cases are heard in the County or High Court.

The *Protection from Harassment Act 1997* was originally introduced to deal with the problem of stalking. However, it covers a much wider range of behaviour, including behaviour that alarms or distresses the victim.

The Act gives both criminal and civil remedies. There are two criminal offences:

- pursuing a course of conduct amounting to harassment;
- a more serious offence where the conduct puts the victim in fear of violence.

Harassing a person includes alarming the person or causing the person distress. According to the Briefing Paper, *The Protection from the Harassment Act 1997*:

A 'course of conduct', which can include speech, must normally involve conduct which has occurred on at least two occasions. There are special provisions covering harassment which targets two or more people in an attempt to persuade them to do something (for example, certain kinds of protest action against companies) and harassment of an individual carried out by two or more people.

In addition to the criminal offences, a civil court can impose civil injunctions in harassment cases as well as awarding damages to the victim for the harassment. Breach of an injunction is a criminal offence.
(Strickland, 2017)

Thought Box

Can silent phone calls constitute harassment?

Housing Act 1996

The local authority or social landlords can apply for a possession order where a tenant is violent to another tenant. A victim of domestic abuse may also be deemed homeless if they can no longer live safely in their home as:

- s.175(1) deems a person homeless if there is no accommodation which they are legally entitled to occupy;
- s.175(3) if they have accommodation, it must be reasonable for them to continue to occupy it;
- s.177(1) it is not reasonable for P to continue to occupy if it is probable that it will lead to 'domestic violence' or other violence.

See: *Yemshaw v London Borough of Hounslow* [2011] UKSC 3 and Chapter 19.

Chapter 21 of the *Homelessness Code of Guidance for Local Authorities* establishes the requirements placed on local authorities to provide homelessness services to people who have experienced or are at risk of domestic violence or abuse. See: www.gov.uk/guidance/homelessness-code-of-guidance-for-local-authorities/chapter-21-domestic-abuse

Human Rights Act 1998

Articles 2, Right to life, 3, Prohibition of torture and 8, The right to respect for private and family life can also be used to protect people from domestic abuse as the *Human Rights Act* places obligations on public bodies to ensure that people's human rights are not violated – e.g. the police and local authorities. See *Commissioner of Police of the Metropolis (Appellant)* v *DSD and another (Respondents)* (2018) UKSC11 where two victims of sexual abuse by a cab driver were granted damages for breach of Article 3 because the police had failed to investigate allegations made against him, which left them exposed to inhuman and degrading treatment.

However, suspected perpetrators of domestic abuse can also argue that their human rights have been breached if they are ordered (without just cause) to leave the family home as this could potentially be a breach of Article 8, or if they have not been given a fair trial in breach of Article 6 (see Chapter 2).

Criminal Law

The above has shown the significance of prevention orders that the social worker needs to be aware of when working with individuals experiencing domestic abuse. The criminal law also imposes liability on perpetrators of domestic abuse and the law has been developed to reflect increasing concerns about the problems that domestic abuse causes.

In *R v R (Rape B: Marital Exemption)* [1991] 1 FLR 217, the House of Lords abolished a husband's common law immunity from raping his wife. The definition of rape is found in section 1 of the *Sexual Offences Act 2003*.

---

1 Rape

(1) A person (A) commits an offence if—

    (a) he intentionally penetrates the vagina, anus or mouth of another person (B) with his penis,
    (b) B does not consent to the penetration, and
    (c) A does not reasonably believe that B consents.

A partial defence to murder was provocation, which if it was successful reduced the charge of murder to manslaughter. The case of *R v Ahluwalia* (1993) 96 Cr App R 133 highlights the use of the defence of provocation which involved a woman who had suffered years of abuse by her husband. One night, after he had threatened to attack her, she poured petrol on him while he was asleep and set him alight. The defence of provocation failed as her actions were judged a result of a well-thought out plan.

The defence was abolished by the *Coroners and Justice Act 2009*, and a new defence of 'loss of control' was created (see Parsons, 2015).

Domestic Violence, Crime and Victims Act 2004

This Act overhauled the legislation relating to domestic violence and introduced provisions for victims of domestic violence and created criminal liability for breaches of court orders. Under s.5, it also created a new offence of causing or allowing the death of a child or vulnerable adult. The Act made common assault an arrestable offence and enhanced the rights of victims. The *Domestic Violence, Crime and Victims (Amendment) Act 2012* extended s.5 to cover cases of 'causing or allowing serious physical harm to a child or vulnerable adult'.

Serious Crimes Act 2015

This Act introduced the new offence of controlling or coercive behaviour in an intimate or family relationship. 'Controlling or coercive behaviour' describes behaviour occurring within a current or former intimate or family relationship which causes someone to fear that violence will be used against them on more than one occasion or causes them serious alarm or distress that substantially affects their day-to-day activities. It involves a pattern of behaviour or incidents that enable a person to exert power or control over another, such as isolating a partner from their friends and family, taking control of their finances, everyday activities such as what they wear or who they see, or tracking their movements through the internet or mobile phone use.

According to the Crown Prosecution Service (n.d.), the definition of domestic abuse specifically states:

> Controlling behaviour is: a range of acts designed to make a person subordinate and/or dependent by isolating them from sources of support, exploiting their resources and capacities for personal gain, depriving them of the means needed for independence, resistance and escape, and regulating their everyday behaviour.

> Coercive behaviour is: an act or a pattern of acts of assaults, threats, humiliation and intimidation or other abuse that is used to harm, punish or frighten their victim.

> The offence carries a maximum custodial sentence of five years or is punishable by a fine.

Adoption and Children Act 2002

Section 31 of the *Children Act 1989* introduced significant harm as the threshold that justifies compulsory intervention in family life in the best interests of children. Physical abuse, sexual abuse, emotional abuse and neglect are all categories of significant harm. Harm is defined as the ill-treatment or impairment of health and development. Section

120 of the *Adoption and Children Act 2002* (implemented on 31 January 2005) amended s.31 definition of significant harm to include 'impairment suffered from seeing or hearing the ill treatment of another'.

Sections 38A and 44A of the *Children Act 1989* provide an exclusion requirement that the court may impose to remove a suspected abuser from their home. The courts must be satisfied that if the exclusion requirement is made, the child will stop suffering significant harm or be at risk of it, and that there is someone who can look after the child in the home and they give consent to the requirement (see Chapter 7).

Public Health England guidance on adverse childhood experiences reports that children exposed to four or more adverse experiences are more likely to have poorer health outcomes, show risk-taking behaviour and find it difficult to improve their outcomes (PHE, 2018).

The *Crime and Security Act 2010* provides for the following orders, which enable the police to apply to the magistrates' court for the protection of an individual following a domestic violence incident.

> 1.3 A DVPN is an emergency non-molestation and eviction notice which can be issued by the police, when attending to a domestic abuse incident, to a perpetrator. Because the DVPN is a police-issued notice, it is effective from the time of issue, thereby giving the victim the immediate support they require in such a situation. Within 48 hours of the DVPN being served on the perpetrator, an application by police to a magistrates' court for a DVPO must be heard. A DVPO can prevent the perpetrator from returning to a residence and from having contact with the victim for up to 28 days. This allows the victim a degree of breathing space to consider their options with the help of a support agency. Both the DVPN and DVPO contain a condition prohibiting the perpetrator from molesting the victim.
> (GOV.UK (2020) Domestic Violence Protection Notices (DVPNs) and Domestic Violence Protection Orders (DVPOs) Guidance)

The Domestic Violence Disclosure Scheme

This scheme is also known as 'Clare's Law' following the murder in 2009 of Clare Wood by her ex-partner who had a history of violence against women. The scheme sets out procedures by which the police may disclose information about potentially violent individuals that would prevent another being hurt. The scheme is not set out in legislation and must take account of an individual's human rights and data protection law.

> The Domestic Violence Disclosure Scheme recognises two procedures for disclosing information:
>
> - 'Right to ask' is triggered by a member of the public applying to the police for a disclosure.
>
> *(Continued)*

- 'Right to know' is triggered by the police making a proactive decision to disclose information to protect a potential victim.

12. The scheme provides the following benefits:

a. introduces recognised and consistent procedures for disclosing information that enables a partner (A) who is/was in an intimate relationship with a previously violent or abusive individual (B) to make informed choices about continuing in that relationship or about their personal safety if no longer in the relationship.

b. enhances the previous arrangements whereby disclosure occurred largely in a reactive way when agencies came into contact with information about an offender having a history of previous violence.

c. under 'right to ask', individual members of the public, whether the partner (A) or a third party (C), can now proactively seek information, with an expectation that the agencies responsible for safeguarding victims of domestic violence will check to see whether relevant information exists and, if it does, that consideration will be given to its disclosure where necessary to protect the victim.

d. under 'right to know', where a safeguarding agency comes into the possession of information about the previous violent and abusive behaviour of B that may cause harm to A, members of the public can now expect the safeguarding agency to consider whether any disclosure should be made and to disclose information if it is lawful – i.e. if it is necessary and proportionate to protect the potential victim from crime.

e. encourages individuals to take responsibility for safety of the potential victim.

(Home Office (2016) Domestic Violence
Disclosure Scheme (DVDS) Guidance)

Female Genital Mutilation

Female genital mutilation (FGM) includes procedures that intentionally alter or cause injury to the female genital organs for non-medical reasons. The procedure has no health benefits for girls and women, and can cause severe pain, mental health problems, problems with future sexual intercourse and childbirth. The practice is illegal in the UK but is a cultural and religious aspect of some families' lives in the UK. It is important for social workers to recognise that the harmful effects of this practice are severe and the names by which it is known. These include 'female circumcision or cutting' and other terms such as *sunna, gudniin, halalays, tahur, megrez* and *khitan* (NHS, *Overview: Female genital mutilation* (FGM), see: www.nhs/uk/conditions/female-genital-mutilation-fgm/). Health, social care professionals and teachers have a mandatory duty under the *Female Genital Mutilation Act 2003* ('the 2003 Act'), as amended by the *Serious Crime Act 2015*, to report known cases of FGM to the police.

Offences under the *Female Genital Mutilation Act 2003* include:
The primary offence of FGM: section 1

(1) A person is guilty of an offence if he excises, infibulates or otherwise mutilates the whole or any part of a girl's labia majora, labia minora or clitoris.

… unless the operation is necessary for the girl's physical or mental health, or

the girl is in any stage of labour, or has just given birth, for purposes connected with the labour or birth.

… assisting a girl to mutilate her own genitals: section 2;

… assisting a non-UK person to mutilate a girl's genitals overseas: section 3;

… failing to protect a girl from the risk of FGM: section 3A.

The above are criminal offences whether committed in or outside the UK. Civil law measures have also been implemented to protect victims of FGM. FGM Protection Orders (FGMPO) protect girls and women at risk of the offence or where the offence has already been committed. FGMPOs are applied for by a relevant third party for the victim through the family courts. The courts can make their own order without an application from another party due to its concerns following a criminal action or family law case.

The first prosecution in the UK for the practice of FGM was *R v N* [2019] 3 WLUK 161.

R v N [2019] 3 WLUK 161

The court was required to sentence a mother (N) who had been convicted of female genital mutilation (FGM) after trial.

N had called for an ambulance and said that her three-year-old daughter had been trying to get some biscuits and had fallen on metal which had ripped her private parts. N told hospital staff that the injuries had been accidental. The child lost a lot of blood and had surgery to repair three separate cuts which consultants believed had been deliberately inflicted with a sharp instrument. Under the World Health Organization's classification, it was a type 2 FGM involving the partial or total removal of the clitoris and labia minora. The wounds had healed, and the child was unlikely to suffer adverse obstetric outcomes or impairment of sexual enjoyment in the future. She was placed in foster care. It was not known whether N had cut the child or had held her down while another did so, or what instrument was used, or whether the child had been given local anaesthetic. N did not come from a culture in which FGM was practised and it was not known why the child had been mutilated. N maintained throughout her trial that the injuries had been accidental. She was convicted of an offence contrary to the *Female Genital Mutilation Act 2003*,

(Continued)

s.1(1). She did, however, plead guilty to four counts of possession and distribution of indecent images of children and extreme pornography which had been found on her phone following her arrest.

The court held:

The offence: FGM was a form of child abuse that involved deliberate physical mutilation. It was a barbaric practice and a serious crime. It was typically inflicted on young and vulnerable females. Whatever the physical consequences, the psychological effects were likely to remain with N's daughter. The true significance of what had occurred might not become apparent to her for years. She might only recognise the difference in her body in adulthood and might suffer embarrassment or inhibition in forming intimate relationships. That was a significant and lifelong burden to carry.

Sentencing guidelines: FGM was included within the definition of domestic abuse in the Overarching Principles on Domestic Abuse. The Assault Guideline was also relevant, and an analogy could be drawn with wounding with intent to cause grievous bodily harm under the *Offences Against the Person Act 1861*, s.18. If FGM was a s.18 offence, it would fall within the top category as the victim was particularly vulnerable, the offence was premeditated and it was committed with a bladed instrument akin to a weapon. That would require a starting point of 12 years with a range of 9 to 16 years. The maximum for a s.18 offence was life imprisonment, whereas the maximum for FGM was 14 years. The Child Cruelty Guideline was also relevant, and an analogy could be drawn with causing or allowing a child to suffer serious physical harm under the *Domestic Violence, Crime and Victims Act 2004*, s.5. If N had been charged with s.5, the offence would have fallen within category A2 given the use of the bladed instrument as a weapon, and the serious physical and emotional harm caused. The starting point would be seven years with a range of five to nine years. The maximum was ten years. That guideline also covered the lesser offence of failing to protect a girl from risk of FGM contrary to s.3A of the 2003 Act, which carried a maximum penalty of seven years, with a likely starting point of five years and a range of three to six years. The starting point in the instant case was in the region of ten years.

Aggravating and mitigating factors: The child had been particularly vulnerable due to her age. N had committed the offence at home where the child should have felt safe. N had betrayed the child's trust in her as her protector and had acted with another person to commit the crime. Those factors were serious. The court took account of the fact that N had sought medical treatment for the child and accepted that custody might be particularly difficult because the offending might evoke strong responses from other female prisoners. The mitigation was relatively slight and a term of 11 years' imprisonment was imposed.

Pornography offences: The most serious count involved images of children. A reduction of 15 per cent was applied for guilty pleas, and in the light of the totality principle, the sentence was two years' imprisonment, with concurrent terms of three months and two months on the remaining counts. The two-year sentence was to be served consecutively to the 11-year FGM sentence. N was made the subject of a sexual offences notification requirement for ten years.

Thought Box

How can social workers ensure that they are sensitive to the cultural and religious practices of families, and yet enforce the paramountcy principle of the child and protection of women?

Forced Marriage

It is important that social workers know the difference between a forced marriage and an arranged marriage. The latter is lawful if it is based on the couple involved both giving valid consent, whereas the former is not. Forced marriage is considered a form of domestic and child abuse as well as modern-day slavery. Furthermore, social workers need to be aware of people being forced to marry who lack capacity to give consent to the marriage.

The purpose of the *Forced Marriage (Civil Protection) Act 2007* was

> An Act to make provision for protecting individuals against being forced to enter into marriage without their free and full consent and for protecting individuals who have been forced to enter into marriage without such consent; and for connected purposes.

It introduced powers to make new civil orders requiring individuals to, among other things:

- hand over passports;
- stop intimidation and violence;
- reveal the whereabouts of a person;
- stop someone from being taken abroad.

Furthermore, s.120 of the *Anti-social Behaviour, Crime and Policing Act 2014* amends the *Family Law Act 1996* and makes a breach of a forced marriage protection order a criminal offence, which carries a maximum of five years in prison.

Data on forced marriage is collated by the Forced Marriage Unit (FMU), but it is very much an unreported crime and therefore difficult to produce true statistics of the victims.

Of the cases that FMU provided support to in 2019:

- 363 cases (27%) involved victims below 18 years of age.
- 485 cases (36%) involved victims aged 18–25.

(Continued)

- 137 cases (10%) involved victims with a learning disability.
- 1,080 cases (80%) involved female victims and 262 cases (19%) involved male victims. Gender in the remaining 13 cases was unknown. These proportions are broadly in line with previous years.
(https://assets.publishing.service.gov.uk/government/uploads/system/uploads/attachment_data/file/894428/Forced_Marriage_Unit_statistics_2019.pdf)

Honour-based Violence

The definition of honour-based violence as provided by the CPS is:

> an incident or crime involving violence, threats of violence, intimidation coercion or abuse (including psychological, physical, sexual, financial or emotional abuse) which has or may have been committed to protect or defend the honour of an individual, family and/or community for alleged or perceived breaches of the family and/or community's code of behaviour.

The offences include:

- attempted murder;
- manslaughter;
- procuring an abortion;
- encouraging or assisting suicide;
- conspiracy to murder;
- conspiracy to commit a variety of assaults.

See: www.cps.gov.uk/publication/honour-based-violence-and-forced-marriage

As with other forms of domestic abuse, honour-based violence is an abuse of an individual's human rights. The word 'honour' in this context can mean upholding the respect given towards a cultural belief and the obligations to fulfil it. Some families and communities regard a breach of these obligations as disrespectful and may impose a form of punishment to maintain the perceived respect. The practice is another form of controlling behaviour and mainly, but not exclusively, affects women. Because of the consequences feared by victims it is very difficult to establish the full extent of this offence in the UK.

As can be seen in all the various forms of domestic abuse, those affected by it need help and support both to report the abuse and seek help for themselves. The problems it causes have been given much higher profile in recent years and the law has recently been reformed as provided for in the *Domestic Abuse Act 2021*.

Chapter Summary

This chapter has:

- provided an overview of the legislation regarding domestic abuse;
- highlighted the many different forms that domestic abuse can take;
- considered the social work role when working with individuals affected by domestic abuse;
- highlighted the overlap between law and social work practice in relation to domestic abuse.

Exercises

1. Read the guidance on FGM for social workers and think about questions to consider when working with a family. See: www.basw.co.uk/resources/fgm-good-practice-guidance-and-assessment-tool-social-workers
2. What are the indicators of possible domestic violence and abuse a social worker may come across when working with a service user or family? See: www.gov.uk/guidance/domestic-abuse-how-to-get-help?gclsrc=aw.ds
3. Consider the questions a social worker would ask a service user they suspected was experiencing domestic abuse. See: basw.co.uk/media/news/2021/apr/basw-england-releases-new-domestic-abuse-guidance-social-workers

Answers can be found in the Appendix.

Further reading

Ellison, L. (2019) *Coercive and Controlling Men and the Women Who Kill Them*, available at: www.wlv.ac.uk/

Harne, L. and Radford, J. (2008) *Tackling Domestic Violence: Theories, Policies and Practice*. Oxford: Oxford University Press.

17

Substance Misuse

Introduction

Social workers need the skills to work with service users' issues around substance misuse. This includes being able to identify the substances being misused and which services are available to support the service user. This is a complex task with the increase of illicit drug use and the need to connect with other services, such as housing and mental health which the service user might require. The government regulates the possession, supply and distribution of harmful drugs in order to prevent drug misuse.

Government Statistics on Substance Misuse, 2019–20

Data between 2019 and 2020 shows:

- There were 270,705 adults in contact with drug and alcohol services between April 2019 and March 2020 – a slight increase from the previous year of 268,251.
- People being treated for opiates increased slightly from the previous year to 140,599.
- People being treated for alcohol declined slightly to 74,618 from 75,555 the previous year. This shows a continuous decline in treatment for alcohol misuse since 2013–14 when it was 91,651.
- There were 506,100 hospital admissions and 74,600 deaths attributable to smoking, the latter figure showing a decrease since 2018.

For the full discussions on the above data, see: www.gov.uk/government/statistics/substance-misuse-treatment-for-adults-statistics-2019-to-2020/adult-substance-misuse-treatment-statistics-2019-to-2020-report and https://digital.nhs.uk/data-and-information/publications/statistical/statistics-on-smoking/statistics-on-smoking-england-2020

Ethical Considerations

As with other areas in social work practice, substance misuse is one that the social worker must consider. The data above highlights the prevalence of substance misuse, which is known to have a negative impact on children's and adults' lives. The ethical issues to consider include the impact of substance misuse for individuals from different cultural and religious backgrounds, the terminology and the importance of self-determination. The same principles apply to those who misuse substances as to other service users, as provided by Principle 7 of the BASW *Code of Ethics* in that the service user should be empowered to make their own decisions while the social worker provides culturally sensitive services to the service user (see: www.basw.co.uk/about-basw/code-ethics).

Social Policy Considerations

Government drug strategy changed in 2017. The new strategy aims to reduce demand, restrict the supply of drugs, build on the treatment of substance misuse and ensure that global action is taken, which includes the sharing of best practice (HM Government, Drug Strategy report, 2017). In 2007, the Chair of the Advisory Council on the Misuse of Drugs (ACMD), David Nutt, criticised government policy on the classification of drugs as not being evidenced based, and that it did not properly regulate the harm caused by alcohol and tobacco. His research identified that tobacco and alcohol together amounted to 90 per cent of UK drug-related deaths and the pressure that accidents resulting from consuming them put on the health service (Nutt et al., 2007). However, the tobacco and alcohol industry bring in high tax revenues that may be seen to offset the cost put upon the health service and generate trade, and thus seemingly cause less concern.

Thought Box

From the current Government drug strategy, identify the reports that helped to develop policy around it (see: HM Government, Drug Strategy report 2017: https://assets.publishing.service.gov.uk/government/uploads/system/uploads/attachment_data/file/628148/Drug_strategy_2017.PDF)

Categories of Drugs

UK law determines the class of a drug in relation to the harm it can cause based on recommendations from the Advisory Council on the Misuse of Drugs (ACMD). This is a non-governmental department with expertise on drug-related issues that was set up under the *Misuse of Drugs Act 1971*. The ACMD provides reports that feed into policy decisions relating to drug issues affecting society. One of the ACMD's responsibilities is to classify dangerous and harmful drugs. A government table shows the different categories of drugs and the sanctions they hold based on the ACMD recommendations (see: www.gov.uk/penalties-drug-possession-dealing?cv=1).

In 2018, the government commissioned the ACMD to review the use of cannabis and cannabis-related products specifically, to consider whether 'cannabis-based medicinal products' should be removed from Schedule 1 of the Misuse of Drugs Regulations 2001. The recommendations from the ACMD review were:

- Recommendation 1: The Advisory Council on the Misuse of Drugs (ACMD) should be commissioned to conduct a further assessment of the impact of the rescheduling of cannabis-based products for medicinal use (CBPMs) in the two years following the publication of this report – as there is not yet sufficient evidence available to fully assess any and all of the consequences of the legislative change. Much of this evidence would not be expected to fully emerge for several years … ACMD report to be published in November 2022.
- Recommendation 2: The availability of a CBPM patient registry should be recognised as crucial for future assessments of the impact of the rescheduling of CBPMs in November 2018. The Government should continue to support the development of an official CBPM patient registry …

- Recommendation 3: Research should be commissioned:

  o to assess the impacts of the rescheduling of CBPMs in November 2018 on public knowledge and attitudes towards cannabis, unlicensed CBPMs, licensed CBPMs and licensed cannabis-based medicines; and to explore the safety, quality and efficacy of unlicensed CBPMs, licensed CBPMs and licensed cannabis-based medicines.

- Recommendation 4: Government departments should conduct a full review of international approaches to legislation facilitating the medicinal usage of cannabis-based medicines.

See: ACMD, Cannabis-based products for medicinal use (CBPMs) in humans, at: https://assets.publishing.service.gov.uk/government/uploads/system/uploads/attachment_data/file/939090/OFFICIAL__Published_version_-_ACMD_CBPMs_report_27_November_2020_FINAL.pdf

Legislation

Prior to the late nineteenth century, the drugs trade and use of drugs was unregulated, which helped economic growth in many European countries. Since then, much of the UK law on drugs is drawn from international law and regulations because the supply and use of drugs is a global issue. The *Pharmacy Act 1868* initiated the control of poisons and the dispensing of them by pharmacists in the UK. Control of drug use was tightened under the *Defence of the Realm Act 1914* when the First World War broke out, making possession of drugs illegal. The *Dangerous Drugs Act 1920* allowed medical professionals to dispense psychoactive drugs and the legislation was later amended to include a new offence of possession of cannabis. Between 1920 and 1968, the law increased the control of illegal drugs in the UK incorporating international law and providing greater police powers. The *Medicines Act 1968* provided for the control of drugs, the safety of prescribed drugs and consumer regulation.

Misuse of Drugs Act 1971

The MDA 1971 is the current legislation regulating the use of medicinal and non-medicinal drugs. The Act still controls the distribution of medicinal drugs as found under the *Medicines Act 1968* but categorises those that are not for medical use as controlled drugs. The Act determines the following as being unlawful: possession, unlawful supply; intent to supply, import or export; and unlawful production. If a person is found in possession of any controlled drugs, the person can be prosecuted. The Act provided for the three main classes of drugs as identified in the table below. Class A is the most harmful down to Class C. The temporary controlled drugs category gives the ACMD time to establish whether they need to be included in one of the categories A–C. There have been many amendments to the Act, specifically including new types of drugs to the categories. See the ACMD recommendations on cannabis-based products for medicinal use in humans (CBPMs): https://assets. publishing.service.gov.uk/government/uploads/system/uploads/attachment_data/ file/939090/OFFICIAL__Published_version_-_ACMD_CBPMs_report_27_ November_2020_FINAL.pdf

The Psychoactive Substances Act 2016

> With the increase in the availability of legal highs, the *Psychoactive Substances Act 2016* made it an offence: to produce, supply, offer to supply, possess with intent to supply, possess on custodial premises, import, or export psychoactive substances; that is, any substance intended for human consumption that is capable of producing a psychoactive effect. The maximum sentence is 7 years' imprisonment but excludes legitimate substances, such as food, alcohol, tobacco, nicotine, caffeine and medical products from the scope of the offence, as well as controlled drugs, which continue to be regulated by the Misuse of Drugs Act 1971.
>
> (GOV.UK (2016) *Psychoactive Substances Act*)

The definition of a psychoactive substance is one that is 'capable of producing a psychoactive effect in a person who consumes it'. This means 'things that cause hallucinations, drowsiness or changes in alertness, perception of time and space, mood or empathy with others'. For guidance, see: GOV.UK, *Psychoactive Substances Act 2016: guidance for researchers*, at: www.gov.uk/government/publications/ psychoactive-substances-act-2016-guidance-for-researchers/psychoactive-substances- act-2016-guidance-for-researchers

Currently, a major concern involving the misuse of a psychoactive substance is that of the potential harmful effects of nitrous oxide (known as laughing gas). These include, but are not exclusive to, a slowing down of the brain and the body's responses, hallucinations, severe headaches, dizziness and feelings of euphoria.

Under UK law, sanctions ranging from fines to incarceration can be used for making, carrying, supplying and taking drugs. The severity of the sanction depends on the class of drug and whether they are being produced and supplied.

Social Work Practice and the Impact of Substance Misuse

It is important for social workers to understand the different effects of drug and alcohol abuse to help make decisions in the best interests of the service user. The effect of substance misuse may be long or short term. There are organisations that provide help and support both locally and nationally that the service user can access with the help of their social worker. BASW have developed a useful pocket guide for social workers when working with service users and addiction.

> ## Thought Box
>
> Look up the recommended questions to be asked to help identify substance misuse issues with a service user from the BASW guidance: www.basw.co.uk/system/files/resources/AOD%20Pocket%20Guide%20REBRAND.pdf

Furthermore, the correct use of language and terminology when discussing service users' drug and alcohol-related issues should be considered. The BASW guidance above highlights this by using the wording 'in recovery', which does not necessarily mean abstinence when working with service users affected by substance misuse. As highlighted in previous chapters, it is important for social workers to use the correct terminology with service users to maintain the professional standards that underpin their practice.

Homelessness

Section 175 of the *Housing Act 1996* defines homelessness (see Chapter 19). In some parts of the UK drug dependency is often a bar to getting hostel accommodation for the homeless. Homeless accommodation organisations should, however, have policies in place to support homeless people dependent on drugs. The governmental strategy 2017 included a need to understand the circumstances of individuals affected by substance abuse and homelessness. As a result of this, the ACMD published a report in 2019 highlighting the difficulties for professionals treating individual's substance misuse if they were homeless.

A summary of the conclusions of the report includes the following.

> - Expert evidence concluded that drug-using homeless populations suffer a particular lack of social connectedness and their personal safety is at greater risk ... In addition, a high proportion of people who are homeless and who have drug use issues have experienced multiple adverse childhood experiences. The implementation of Universal Credit, the pursuit of localism and the lack of affordable housing add to the risk of homelessness among drug users.
> - People who are homeless, including those presenting as homeless to services and local authorities, those deemed statutorily homeless, and numbers who are rough sleeping have increased substantially with some variation across the UK since 2010. Whilst the problems are proportionally greater in inner city and urban areas it is also clear that the issue has become increasingly prevalent in rural areas.
> - The UK and devolved governments have statutory responsibilities regarding homelessness, although it is not entirely clear how this relates to drug users who are homeless. For all who present as homeless, a system of 'priority need' operates in England, Wales and Northern Ireland ...
>
> *(Continued)*

- The needs of people who are homeless, particularly rough sleepers, are not well met by mainstream benefit, health and social care and some drug services. Current regional and local initiatives to address rough sleeping have increased in number and capacity across the UK, but most policy initiatives require initiation or completion of formal evaluative measures.
- ... there is evidence that suggests a strong reciprocal association between being homeless and having an increased risk of problematic drug use.
- ... There is a higher rate of drug-related deaths among homeless populations compared with the general population. The number of drug-related deaths among homeless populations has increased in recent years. Mental ill-health is strongly associated with homelessness as both a cause and a consequence.
- There has been a rise in serious bacterial infections among injecting drug users and there is evidence that homeless populations are overrepresented in these infected groups ...
- There is strong evidence of high rates of multiple morbidities – i.e. severe mental illness and long-term physical health conditions among homeless people who use drugs and alcohol. There are many and varied subpopulations in the homeless sector who have drug use issues, including women, older people, young people, sex workers, offenders and ex-service personnel.
- ... Women who are homeless experience multiple oppressions and discriminations and many of them report domestic violence prior to being homeless. A substantial proportion of females who are sleeping rough have reported sexual, physical and verbal assaults while on the streets.
- The risk of being homeless and having a drug use problem is much greater for offenders than for the general population.
- Ex-service personnel who are homeless have increased risk of problematic substance use, although it appears that the greatest risks are related primarily to alcohol.
- An integrated health, social care and community care approach to the recovery and housing needs of people who are homeless would provide the optimal model of service delivery. This is particularly important for individuals with co-morbid disorders, including mental health and substance use and who are at the greatest risk of homelessness. In addition, safe, stable housing is essential for people who are homeless and who have problematic drug use and is associated with increased engagement with services.
- Harm reduction work within the homeless and drug use sectors in the UK utilises a holistic, pragmatic and supportive approach to encourage individuals to consider and reduce the harms related to their substance-using behaviour. Evidence-based Harm Reduction models in the UK include assertive outreach programmes, education, counselling, health promotion, peer support, user fora, needle exchange schemes, administration of Naloxone and opioid substitute prescribing. There is international evidence to support the effectiveness of 'safe injecting sites' to engage with and maintain contact with highly marginalised target populations and to prevent overdose deaths.
- Structurally, there must be an increase in the current support provided to the homeless population, including active drug users, with immediate and comprehensive assistance to reduce the risk of drug use and increase access to treatment.

- There is evidence to support the effectiveness of the 'Housing First' model in Europe and the US. The UK government is supporting the implementation of the model in several designated areas in England. An alternative model of abstinence-based housing has showed promising results which suggest that the abstinence-based approach has some success for some people where abstinence is the goal.
- Local statutory and non-statutory organisations must maintain an active awareness of the multiple stigma, oppressions and discriminations experienced by their service users. Professional values of respect and non-judgmentalism married with a warm empathic and compassionate approach were perceived as foundational to working with vulnerable people who are homeless and have drug use issues. Furthermore, service providers must endeavour to empower homeless people who experience harms related to drug use. One method of realistically achieving this goal would be to involve service users in the design and implementation of services.

(ACMD, 2019, available at: https://assets.publishing.service.gov.uk/government/uploads/system/uploads/attachment_data/file/810284/Drug-related_harms_in_homeless_populations.pdf)

The recommendations from the report include a multi-agency approach specifically between frontline professionals, local authorities and housing services using a 'Housing First' model, the concept being that an individual is housed first and then any other needs are provided for rather than an individual having to show that they are meeting other requirements of treatment before being housed. These could be mental health and drug-abuse issues. To summarise the above in relation to social work practice, the social worker needs to be well informed as to the causal factors associated with homelessness and substance misuse. With this information, the practitioner can empower the service user through an understanding of the multi-agency resources that can provide support to the service user affected by substance misuse and the consequences of it on their lives. For example, 'cuckooing' is also becoming an increasing concern among vulnerable adults and children. It involves people exploiting another for the use of their home for criminal activity. In relation to drug abuse, the individuals perpetrating this offence will use the home of another to store and supply drugs. Victims of this exploitation can be dependent on drugs or alcohol, have learning difficulties or mental health issues.

Impact on families

The following data provides the parental status of people starting treatment in 2019 to 2020:

- … 21% of people starting treatment were living with children, either their own or someone else's. A further 31% were parents who were not living with their children. This was highest among women in treatment for opiates, where 44% are parents who are not living with their children.

- Fifty-eight percent of females reported either living with a child or being a parent when they started treatment, compared to 49% of males.
- Eighty-one percent of the children of people starting treatment were receiving no early help. We also saw that 7% had a child protection plan, this figure was highest in the non-opiate group at 14%.

(PHE, 2020a)

The impact of substance abuse on families includes potential risks to children from pre-birth through to adulthood. The effects can be:

- physical maltreatment and neglect
- poor physical and mental health
- development of health harming behaviours in later life, for example using alcohol and drugs and at an early age, which predicts more entrenched future use
- poor school attendance due to inappropriate caring responsibilities
- low educational attainment
- involvement in anti-social or criminal behaviour.

(GOV.UK, 2018a)

Statutory guidance and recent legislation provide for the welfare of the child at risk of abuse and the measures needed to be taken. The *Working Together to Safeguard Children* 2018 (updated 2020) principles include:

- Safeguarding and promoting the welfare of children is everyone's business.
- The wide range of organisations and services that contribute to this agenda should have a child-centred approach.

The guidance includes the provision from the *Children and Social Work Act 2017* that local authorities should make 'locally determined multi-agency safeguarding arrangements'. Public Health England has developed a toolkit for professionals working with families affected by alcohol and drug abuse.

The guidance has been developed to support local authorities to:

- identify problematic parental alcohol and drug use as early as possible,
- ensure that the services they commission have sufficient capacity and resources to support parents and children affected by problem parental alcohol and drug use,
- identify and commission interventions to reduce harm and promote recovery for parents who misuse alcohol and drugs and also to reduce and prevent harm to their children,
- address the effects of adverse childhood experiences and to safeguard children.

(PHE, 2018a)

An example of an approach to supporting families where drug and alcohol problems affect the lives of children giving rise to safeguarding concerns is the development of Family Drug and Alcohol Courts (FDACs). These courts have been established since 2013 and are driven by the ethos of working with the parents affected by substance misuse to find an alternative to care proceedings for their children. The approach is a multidisciplinary one, involving different agencies and reviews of the parent's rehabilitation by a judge. They are initiated by the local authority who would be starting care proceedings. The different agencies are substance misuse specialists and social workers not linked to the childcare team who initiated the care proceedings. The approach places the parents on a trial for change with the underlying belief the parents can overcome their substance misuse and keep the children with the family. However, funding restrictions have meant that this approach is not a national one and is dependent on non-governmental funding sources.

Young People and Substance Misuse

GOV.UK statistics identify the following in relation to young people and substance misuse.

GOV.UK, National Statistics. Young people's substance misuse treatment statistics 2019 to 2020: report

Main findings:

1.1 Trends in young people's treatment numbers

There were 14,291 young people in contact with alcohol and drug services between April 2019 and March 2020. This is a 3% reduction on the number the previous year (14,777) and a 42% reduction on the number in treatment since 2008 to 2009 (24,494).

1.2 Trends in young people's substance use

Cannabis remains the most common substance (89%) that young people come to treatment for. Similar proportions of young people in treatment who use cannabis have been recorded in the last 3 years.

Around 4 in 10 young people in treatment (42%) said they had problems with alcohol (compared to 44% the previous year), 13% had problems with ecstasy and 10% reported powder cocaine problems.

There was a slight decrease in the number of young people seeking help for heroin (51 compared to 57 last year), which is less than 1% of those in treatment.

There was a 19% decrease from the previous year in young people reporting a problem with benzodiazepines. However, the number in the latest year was more than double the number in 2016 to 2017.

(Continued)

1.3 Vulnerabilities among young people in treatment

The most common vulnerability reported by young people starting treatment was early onset of substance use (76%), which means the young person started using substances before the age of 15. This was followed by poly-drug use (56%).

Proportionally, girls tended to report more vulnerabilities than boys, particularly self-harming behaviour (31% compared with 10%) and sexual exploitation (10% compared with 1%).

1.4 Mental health treatment need

More than a third (37%) of young people who started treatment this year said they had a mental health treatment need, which is higher than last year (32%). A higher proportion of girls reported a mental health treatment need than boys (49% compared to 30%).

Most young people (68%) who had a mental health treatment need received some form of treatment, usually from a community mental health team.

1.5 Treatment exits

Of the young people who left treatment, 82% left because they successfully completed their treatment programme, which is slightly higher than the proportion the previous year (81%). The next most common reason for leaving treatment (12%) was leaving early or dropping out, which was slightly lower than the previous year (13%).

Chapter 9 discusses the exploitation of children and young people affected by illegal drugs trade known as 'county lines'. The National Police Chief's Council definition of a county line is

> a term used to describe gangs and organised criminal networks involved in exporting illegal drugs into one or more importing areas [within the UK], using dedicated mobile phone lines or other form of 'deal line'. They are likely to exploit children and vulnerable adults to move [and store] the drugs and money and they will often use coercion, intimidation, violence (including sexual violence) and weapons.
>
> (National Crime Agency, County Lines)

Most of the children and young people involved in county lines are vulnerable with mental health and substance misuse problems. A multi-agency approach is used to enforce the law against the county lines trade and prevent children and young people becoming victims to it. The National Crime Agency, along with the police and other organisations, are working together to identify the perpetrators and safeguard the victims involved (see: nationalcrimeagency.gov/uk/what-we-do/crime-threats/drug-trafficking/county-lines).

The Government has provided guidance for frontline practitioners, which includes the following.

A young person who is involved in county lines activity might show some of these signs:

- persistently going missing from school or home, or being found out-of-area
- unexplained acquisition of money, clothes, or mobile phones
- excessive receipt of texts or phone calls
- relationships with controlling, older individuals, or gang association
- parental concerns, and leaving home or care without explanation
- suspicion of self-harm, physical assault, or unexplained injuries
- significant decline in school performance and changes in emotional well-being

See: GOV.UK (2018) County lines: criminal exploitation of children and vulnerable adults, at:
www.gov.uk/government/collections/county-lines-criminal-exploitation-of-children-and-vulnerable-adults

Substance Misuse Among Older People

Understanding and identifying substance misuse among older service users is an area gradually developing due to misconceptions such as older people are less likely to become addicts, long-term substance use resulted in premature death and illegal drug use was only found in small groups of adults such as older criminals (Badrakalimuthu et al., 2010).

Furthermore, alcohol misuse is increasing in the older generations and can lead to them having to leave their homes (Housing LIN, 2016).

Mental Health

The *Mental Health Act 1983* provides a definition of a mental health disorder (see Chapter 13). A total of 59% of people who were undergoing treatment for substance misuse in 2018–19 stated that they had a mental health need; 25% receiving treatment for substance misuse stated that they were not receiving treatment for their mental health need (GOV.UK, 2019).

BASW highlights the possible correlation between mental health needs and substance misuse as being, *inter alia*, a coping mechanism for the individual, which leads to substance misuse or vice versa, and the misuse leads to mental illness. The use of substances can resemble symptoms associated with psychiatric diagnosis, lead to self-medication and possibly the use of substances leading to self-harm (BASW, 2012).

A social work student going out into their first placement should understand the signs of substance abuse and the relationship this has with a service user's mental health needs in order to ensure that they receive the most appropriate help.

Chapter Summary

This chapter has:

- introduced the development of the law regarding the sale of and use of drugs in the UK;
- considered the policy approaches used in the UK to help improve the lives of those affected by substance misuse;
- discussed the impact on social work practice of service users misusing drugs and alcohol.

Exercise

Consider the following:

1. Why do people use drugs?
2. What might be the impact of being under the influence of drugs and the decisions an individual might make?
3. Identify any substance misuse issues in the following case study and what could be done to help the family.

Mandy is a single mother of three children. Faris is 15, Ahmed is 13 and Tanya is 6. Mandy's ex-partner Tariq is the father of Faris and Ahmed and is living abroad. Tanya's father Stuart is absent for the majority of the time but does see Tanya intermittently, although this is upsetting for Tanya and Mandy as he is short-tempered and has very bad mood swings. The family have been referred to social services by neighbours who have heard the arguments and noticed drug paraphernalia in the back garden. Mandy has also been self-medicating for her depression through alcohol, which has impacted on her ability to care for the children. She has been sent a housing caution, which means that the family could be evicted from their local authority housing.

Faris has been coming home with expensive new clothes and has been away from the home, sometimes for days. The neighbours have noticed he is mixing with strangers to the neighbourhood and that his character and demeanour has changed drastically.

Answers can be found in the Appendix.

Further Reading

Nutt, D. (2019) Drug policy in UK has regressed in past decade, says former chief adviser, available at: https://doi.org/10.1136/bmj.l6323

18

Refugees, Asylum and Immigration

Chapter Objectives

By the end of this chapter, readers will be able to:

- understand the legal rules that determine who has the right to enter, work and remain in the UK, including people seeking asylum, unaccompanied children, refugees and victims of human trafficking;
- identify the link between social policy and migration and the ethical principles relevant to social work practice;
- understand the consequences for people who, because of their immigration status, have 'no recourse to public funds';
- apply the legal rules and the social policy and ethical principles to social work practice.

Introduction

It is important for social workers to understand the legal rules governing a person's immigration status as it has important consequences for their right to access 'public funds' and affects the duties LAs owe to them. This chapter examines how a person's immigration status is determined and their right to access services provided by the welfare state.

This includes people seeking asylum, refugees, victims of human trafficking, nationals of countries in the European Economic Area (EEA) and those who are granted 'leave to enter' the UK (usually for a determinate length of time). The *Immigration Act 1971* provides the framework for immigration control; it has been amended on numerous occasions as successive governments have sought to restrict annual net migration into the UK. The rules have been widely criticised as 'long, complex, and difficult to use' and 'their drafting is poor'. The Law Commission: Simplification of the Immigration Rules: Report (January 2020) made 37 recommendations for the reform of the rules, including 'redrafting to enable non-expert users to understand them' and making them 'clear, more accessible and consistent'. The government has agreed that simplification 'is essential to the delivery of an effective migration system' (A response to the Law Commission's report and recommendations on Simplification of the Immigration Rules (Home Office, March 2020). No time frame has yet been set for this to be done.

In the year ending March 2020, net migration (that is the difference between people coming into the country for one year or more and those who have emigrated) was 363,000. Since 1998, net migration into the UK each year has been more than 100,000. The two most common reasons for immigration are formal study (36 per cent) and employment (32 per cent) (Migration Statistics, 6 March 2020, House of Commons Library). The impact of the pandemic on net migration is, at the time of publication, unclear, but from 'the best available data, it is clear that mobility and migration have changed significantly since March due to the impact of the coronavirus pandemic' (ONS, 2020).

Migration is not a new phenomenon. Between 1620 and 1914 (the beginning of the First World War) around 32 million people emigrated from Europe to the USA, mostly for economic reasons, and in each year between 1881 and 1915 approximately 900,000 people left Europe (Held et al., 1999). The *Aliens Act 1905* was the first UK legislation to limit immigration into the UK; it declared that 'undesirable immigrants' would be denied entry. The restrictions were, in practice, mostly imposed on Jewish and Eastern European immigrants. People immigrating from countries that the UK had colonised – e.g. India, parts of Africa and the West Indies – were not subject to any immigration control because they were regarded at that time as 'subjects of the British Empire' and had the right to free movement to and from the UK.

Ethical Principles

Farmer (2019) argues that the growing numbers of displaced people has resulted in the 'criminalisation of immigration'. It is also argued that 'little attempt has been initiated by social workers to fully comprehend the realities of how the profession may potentially be complicit within the immigration system' (Humphries, 2004). 'No Recourse to Public Funds' (NRPF) is a legal condition imposed on people subject to immigration control and means that their 'rights and entitlements to state support are severely restricted' (see below). Farmer argues that, in consequence, 'there are significant tensions between UK immigration legislation and social services' statutory duty to safeguard and promote the welfare of destitute NRPF families with children'. This has important ethical implications for social work practice (see BASW, 2016, Position Statement: Racism in Immigration), which challenges the inherent discrimination within immigration policy.

Thought Box

Do the restrictions placed on access to social service and welfare provision for certain groups compromise the ability of social workers to adhere to BASW social work values?

Social Policy and Immigration

Over the last decade, particularly, migration has become an important political issue in many European countries and North America (Seeleib-Kaiser, 2019). Since 2010, the UK government has pursued reform of the immigration system 'aimed at reducing net migration from hundreds of thousands to tens of thousands and limiting the rights of migrants in the UK' (Robinson, 2013). Immigration was one of the two most frequently cited reasons for voting 'leave' in the EU referendum; the other was 'sovereignty' (Nuffield College, 2017). In 2017, some 68.5 million people throughout the world were forcibly displaced due to persecution, conflict, violence or human rights violations (UNHCR, 2018) and sought refuge in other countries.

The 'Windrush scandal' (HMT *Empire Windrush* brought the first post-war migrants to the UK from the Caribbean in 1948) provides a stark account of how a generation of people who came to the UK from the Caribbean between 1948 and 1973 (and were almost all Black) were discriminated against. In 1948, there was no immigration control and the controls introduced in the *Immigration Act 1971* specifically gave these people an equal right to live, work and travel to and from the UK as people who were born here. However, because they had never been provided with the necessary documentation to reflect this, many subsequently suffered hardship and injustice. Some were wrongly deported, others refused re-entry to the UK, some lost their jobs and their homes. The *Windrush Lessons Learned Independent Review* (Williams, 2020) describes how changes to immigration law from the 1960s onwards, because of political pressure to restrict levels of immigration, created a 'hostile environment' for immigrants. The Windrush Compensation Scheme (Home Office, 2020a), which was reformed in December 2020, does not restrict compensation to people from the Caribbean, but includes anyone from a Commonwealth country who arrived in the UK before 1 January 1993 (the date the *Immigration Act 1991* came into force) and who were adversely affected by subsequent Home Office policies.

Thought Box

Read the *Windrush Lessons Learned Independent Review* (Williams, 2020) and consider what lessons should be learned from the Windrush scandal.

Immigration Law and EU and EEA Nationals

Section 1 of the *Immigration Act 1971* states that all people who have 'a right of abode' in the UK are free to live in and come into and go from the UK 'without let or hindrance'. People who do not have a right of abode can only live, work and settle in the UK by permission and are subject to rules that control their entry into, stay and departure from the UK. All British citizens have the right of abode in the UK. There are also other groups of people who, although they do not have 'a right of abode', have the right to live and work here and are exempt from immigration control. This includes both EEA (European Economic Area) nationals and people who have been granted 'Indefinite Leave to Remain' (ILR) in the UK. EEA nationals had freedom of movement under European Union (EU) law and were exempt from immigration control. The EEA includes nationals of EU member states and Norway, Iceland and Liechtenstein. Although Switzerland is not a member of the EEA, Swiss citizens also had freedom of movement into and from the UK.

As a result of the UK's decision to leave the EU, freedom of movement ended on 31 December 2020. All EU and EEA nationals and Swiss citizens living in the UK had to apply to the EU Settlement Scheme by 30 June 2021 for the right to continue living in the UK after that date (and the right to acquire indefinite leave to remain). If their application was successful, they acquired either 'settled' or 'pre-settled' status. Settled status applies to people who had lived in the UK (including the Channel Islands and Isle of Man) for a continuous five-year period by 31 December 2020 (subject to some exceptions; see: www.gov.uk/settled-status-eu-citizens-families/what-settled-and-pre-settled-status-means). They can also apply for British citizenship (if eligible; see: www.gov.uk/british-citizenship). If they did not have five years' continuous residence by 31 December 2020, they are allowed to stay in the UK and acquire ILR at the end of the five-year period (if the period is continuous).

In January 2021, a points-based immigration system was introduced for all migrants to the UK, except Irish nationals. The new system is designed to 'facilitate the entry of skilled workers while making it harder – often impossible – for employers to recruit from abroad for low-skilled or low-paid vacancies' (Chartered Institute of Personnel and Development, 2020).

Immigration Control

Immigration control is the mechanism for regulating who can enter the UK. Anyone without a right of abode (the right to live and work in the UK), must obtain either 'entry clearance' or 'leave to enter' – i.e. the requirement to obtain a visa before entry into the UK. This must be obtained from a British overseas mission. The different visas that can be granted include:

1.   standard visitor visas granted for a holiday, to visit family or friends and to attend business meetings (they usually last for between 6 and 12 months);

2. study visas allow people to come to the UK to study at a licensed college or university;
3. child student visas for children between the ages of 4 and 17 who want to study at an independent school;
4. work visas which are dependent on applicants' skills and qualifications and whether they have a job offer or sponsorship;
5. a spouse or family visa for a spouse, partner or family member of someone who has British citizenship or settlement in the UK; they are usually dependent on proof of appropriate financial support.

All visa applicants must submit biometric information as part of their application and pay a fee. People who come to the UK for one purpose cannot usually change their visa status while in the UK (para. 28 of the Immigration Rules).

'Leave to remain' in the UK has the same effect as leave to enter, but is granted inside the UK. The period for which leave is given and the conditions attached will depend on the basis for which the leave to enter/remain was granted. 'Indefinite leave to remain' is permission to stay permanently in the UK (the same as 'settled status' granted to EEA nationals) after a period of residence between two and ten years. Certain criminal convictions affect the right to be granted ILR (see 'General grounds for refusal', GOV.UK, 2014). ILR can also be revoked in certain circumstances (see s.76 of the *Nationality, Immigration and Asylum Act 2002* and Revocation of Indefinite Leave: Home Office, 2015).

Leave to enter and to remain are subject to certain conditions. Students in higher education (A4) are entitled to work a maximum of 20 hours per week in term time and cannot switch educational providers without reapplying. General visitors have no recourse to public funds; spouses/partners on a 'probationary period' – i.e. who do not qualify for indefinite leave as they have not lived in the UK for the minimum specified period – can work but have no recourse to public funds (see below); people on work visas (Tier 2) have no recourse to public funds and can work only in specified employment.

Illegal entry into the UK, deception, working illegally, entering the UK without the appropriate immigration documents and failing to co-operate with removal or deportation are all criminal offences under the *Immigration Act 1971* and *2004* and can result in deportation.

Domestic Abuse

A person with a spouse visa, or a person who has leave to enter or remain as the unmarried or same-sex partner of a person with indefinite leave or settled status, who becomes a victim of domestic abuse once they have come to the UK, can apply for indefinite leave to remain under the Domestic Violence Rules set out in Section E-DVILR: Eligibility for indefinite leave to remain as a victim of domestic abuse (Immigration Rules, February 2020, see: www.gov.uk/guidance/immigration-rules).

Refugees

The UN Convention Relating to the Status of Refugees 1951 was drawn up to provide retrospective help for people displaced after the Second World War. It defines who a refugee is and sets out the responsibilities of the nations who are party to it. It was amended by the Protocol to the Convention 1967, which removed the time limit and geographical restrictions contained in the original Convention. These two international instruments are called the Refugee Convention, but are often referred to as the Geneva Convention because the UN headquarters are there. The *Asylum and Immigration Appeals Act 1993* gave primacy to the Convention – that is, UK immigration rules must not contravene its provisions.

The UN Human Rights Commission was set up in 1950 to provide help to those who had fled or lost their homes because of the Second World War. Although the Commission was originally given three years to complete its work, events such as the Hungarian Revolution in 1956, which resulted in some 200,000 people seeking asylum in Austria who were defined as refugees, demonstrated the continuing need for refugee protection. The decolonisation of Africa from the 1950s to the mid-1970s often led to sudden and radical regime change, which was sometimes marred by violence and political upheaval. This also led to many people seeking asylum in other countries. Since 1950, the UN High Commissioner for Refugees (UNHCR) has provided help to over 50 million refugees.

Contrary to popular perception, Europe is not the primary destination of asylum seekers; Turkey has taken the largest number of refugees and asylum seekers (3.1 million), followed by Jordan (2.9 million) (UNHCR, 2017).

Who is a Refugee?

Article 1A(2) of the 1951 Convention states that a refugee is a person who:

> owing to a well-founded fear of being persecuted for reasons of race, religion, nationality, membership of a particular social group or political opinion, is outside the country of his nationality and is unable, or owing to such fear, is unwilling to avail himself of protection of that country; or who, not having a nationality and being outside the country of his former habitual residence is unable, or owing to such fear, is unwilling to return to it.

To be granted asylum – that is, to get refugee status – it is necessary for the applicant to show they have a *well-founded fear of persecution* for a reason set out in the Convention, that they are outside their country of origin or normal residence and cannot get protection from their own country. For a fear to be well founded, it must be fear of future harm if they return to their own country. Evidence of past persecution is not enough, although it may suggest a risk of future persecution.

There must be a real risk; the test is objective, not subjective – i.e. would a 'reasonable person' have a well-founded fear in the circumstances? In *R v Immigration Tribunal and another ex parte Shah* [1999] UKHL 20, persecution was held to be 'Serious Harm + The Failure of State Protection'. An act of persecution must be sufficiently serious to constitute a severe violation of a basic human right within the ECHR (Chapter 2) and may be physical or psychological violence, including sexual violence or prosecution or punishment which is disproportionate or discriminatory. It can be committed by the state or by groups or factions within a state (*Adan* v *Secretary of State for the Home Department* [1999] 1 A.C. 293). It must be committed for at least one of the Convention reasons set out in Article 1(A) for refugee status to be granted. These are:

Race: people who share the same identity, common descent and/or ethnic origin. The test is whether the group regards themselves and are regarded by others as having a historical identity. In *The Traveller Movement and Others* v *J D Wetherspoon Plc* [2015] 2CL01225, it was held that the definition of race included Irish Travellers and Romani Gypsies. The Equality Act 2010 defines race as being part of a group of people who are identified by their nationality, citizenship, colour, national or ethnic origins (Chapter 3).

Religion: systematic mistreatment of an individual or a group of individuals as a response to their *religious* beliefs or affiliations or their lack of any belief. This includes not only the world's major religions, such as Islam, Christianity, Judaism, Sikhism, Buddhism and Hinduism, but smaller religions and sects like Rastafarianism, Scientology or Paganism (Guidelines on International Protection: Religion-Based Refugee Claims under Article 1A(2) of the 1951 Convention and/ or the 1967 Protocol relating to the Status of Refugees, UNHCR, 2004).

Nationality: this is determined by birth, naturalisation (acquiring citizenship of another country after birth) or ties to a specific nation; this category is not contentious.

Membership of a particular social group: this is particularly difficult to define, but includes asylum claims by victims fleeing domestic abuse from countries that fail to protect them (Membership of a Particular Social Group: Analysis and Proposed Conclusions, UNHCR). The UNHCR has stated that women are a clear example of a social group 'defined by innate and immutable characteristics, and who are frequently treated differently than men' (UNHCR, 2002). The case of Rahaf Mohammed al-Qunun who fled from Saudi Arabia after disobeying her father and renouncing Islam is an example; she was subsequently granted asylum in Canada (see: www.unhcr.org/uk/news/press/2019/1/5c38e9134/unhcr-statement-canadas-resettlement-saudi-national-rahaf-al-qunun.html).

Political opinion: Holding political opinions different from those of a government is not in itself a ground for claiming refugee status; a claimant must show that they have a fear of persecution for holding those opinions. It presupposes both that the claimant holds opinions that are not tolerated, and the authorities know that the applicant holds those opinions. 'The relative importance or tenacity of the applicant's opinions – in so far as this can be established from all the circumstances of the case – will also be relevant' (UN Refugee Agency, 2019).

The burden of proof in asylum claims requires claimants to establish that there is a 'real risk' or 'reasonable degree of likelihood' or 'substantial grounds for believing' that they have a well-founded fear of persecution. It reflects the fact that asylum seekers will usually find it difficult to produce documentary evidence to support their claim.

In 2018, some 37,453 people applied for asylum in the UK. Around 15,000 people are granted refugee status each year. In March 2020, 44,244 asylum seekers were receiving government support (see: https://commonslibrary.parliament.uk/research-briefings/sn01403/).

Following the UK's departure from the EU, the immigration rules were amended on 1 January 2021; the amendments have important implications for new asylum claims (Changes to immigration rules, HC 1043, 10 December 2020).

> From 1 January 2021 the new rules . . . mean that the Home Office may not have to assess a person's asylum claim if they have travelled through, or have connection to, what is deemed a safe third country. The new rules also give the Home Office the power to remove people seeking asylum to a safe country that agrees to receive them, even if they have never been there or have any connections to it.
>
> (See: Changes to immigration rules will prevent people seeking asylum in the UK' (Refugee Council, 2021.)

Support for Asylum Seekers

Asylum seekers are entitled to housing and a weekly cash allowance while waiting for their claim to be considered. This is provided by the National Asylum Support Service (NASS), a division of the Home Office. They cannot choose where they want to live; the accommodation offered could be a house, flat, hostel or bed and breakfast accommodation. Mothers with young children under the age of 3 get an extra weekly sum, as do pregnant women. A one-off maternity allowance is also claimable. Failed asylum seekers receive an offer of accommodation and a smaller weekly allowance (www.gov.uk/asylum-support/what-youll-get). Asylum seekers have free access to the NHS and are entitled to free prescriptions, dental care, eyesight tests and help with paying for glasses. Children aged between 5 and 17 years must attend school and may qualify for free school meals. Appeals against the support provided can be made to a first-tier tribunal (asylum support).

Unaccompanied Children Seeking Asylum

An unaccompanied child seeking asylum is entitled to LA care and support (s.17 *Children Act 1989*), which includes accommodation (Chapter 6). However, many such children have difficulty establishing their age, as they often flee their own country without documents to prove this and are then denied support as a child in need under the CA 1989. In 2018, the Refugee Council helped over 3,000 children to challenge LA decisions that they were over 18 and thus did not qualify. In *AM* v *Wirrall MBC* (2021), where the Refugee Council acted as an advocate for AM, the upper tribunal immigration and asylum chamber held that the LA's assessment was 'fundamentally unfair' and had been conducted unlawfully. When assessing child applicants, they should be accompanied by an adult advocate (see: Assessing age for asylum applicants, Home Office, 2020, GOV.UK).

Humanitarian Protection and Human Rights Claims

People who do not meet the Convention criteria and therefore do not qualify for refugee status may, however, qualify for 'humanitarian protection' or be able to make a successful 'human rights' claim. Any such claims must be considered before the asylum seeker is removed from the UK. To be granted humanitarian protection, claimants must establish that they would face a real risk of serious harm if returned to their country of origin (Article 15 of the Qualification Directive; see Humanitarian Protection Home Office Guidance, 2017). It is not, however, necessary for them to establish that the risk posed is for a Convention reason (above). People fleeing from conflict zones – e.g. the wars in Iraq and Syria) are often granted such protection (see *AMM and others (conflict: humanitarian crisis: returnees; and FGM) Somalia CG* [2011] UKUT 445 (1AC). It is usually granted for three years in the first instance.

A human rights claim is based on the argument that removal from the UK (or a refusal of entry into the UK) would breach s.6(1) *Human Rights Act 1998*, which makes it unlawful for public bodies to act in way that is incompatible with the ECHR (Chapter 2). Article 3, which prohibits torture, inhuman and degrading treatment or punishment, applies where the person would, on return to their country, be subject to the death penalty or execution, or be at risk of being unlawfully killed, tortured or of suffering inhuman or degrading treatment, or 'be at serious risk of indiscriminate violence because of international or internal armed conflict'. It also applies to claimants excluded from Art.1F Convention protection because they are international terrorists. Article 8 (the right to a private and family life) may also be a relevant consideration (see Home Office (2019), Certification of protection and human rights claims under section 94 of the *Nationality, Immigration and Asylum Act 2002* (clearly unfounded claims)).

Appeals against the Home Office's refusal to grant asylum is only exercisable within the UK if it is based on a humanitarian protection or a human rights claim. *There is no* right of appeal from within the UK against a decision that the asylum claim is 'clearly unfounded' (s.94(1) of the *Nationality, Immigration and Asylum Act 2002;* this is aimed at deterring people from making unfounded claims). See: Certification of protection and human rights claims under s.94 of the *Nationality, Immigration and Asylum Act 2002* (clearly unfounded claims); Home Office, February 2019; and Domestic abuse: responding to reports of domestic abuse from asylum seekers (Home Office, 2019).

Refugees and people granted humanitarian protection are not subject to immigration control and therefore have access to the NHS and to welfare benefits and tax credits. They are exempted from having to satisfy the following tests:

- 'the habitual residence' test which applies to other applicants for means-tested benefits (Chapter 19);
- the requirement that claimants for Child Benefit and Child Tax Credit have to be living in the UK for the past three months (but they must satisfy the necessary requirements to be eligible for contribution-based benefits – e.g. state retirement pension and contribution-based job seeker's allowance);
- the 'past presence test' for disability and carers benefits which usually requires claimants to be present in the country for at least 104 weeks in the last 156 weeks.

The family reunion rules allow refugees and people with five years' humanitarian protection to be joined in the UK by their partners and children under 18 if they were part of a family before they were forced to leave their country. Proof of marriage or civil partnership or proof the couple have lived together for two years or more is needed, together with proof that they intend to live together in the UK. Application must be made outside the UK (see: Settlement: Refugee or Humanitarian Protection at: www. gov.uk/settlement-refugee-or-humanitarian-protection).

Human Trafficking and Modern Slavery

Human Trafficking is the recruitment, transportation, transfer, harbouring or receipt of people through force, fraud or deception, with the aim of exploiting them for profit. Men, women and children of all ages and from all backgrounds can become victims of this crime, which occurs in every region of the world. The traffickers often use violence or fraudulent employment agencies and fake promises of education and job opportunities to trick and coerce their victims.

(UN Office on Drugs and Crime, unodc.org)

Many victims in the UK work on construction sites, in agriculture, the sex industry, car washes and on cannabis farms. Because many are in the UK illegally, they are often reluctant to report their situation to the relevant authorities. Many come from Eastern Europe, Asia and Africa.

The Council of Europe Convention on Action Against Trafficking in Human Beings (2005; the 2005 Convention) applies to all forms of trafficking, both national and international, and whether or not it is linked to organised crime. The preamble defines trafficking in human beings 'as a violation of human rights and an offence to the dignity and integrity of the human being'. It provides certain rights for victims, which includes 'the right to be identified as a victim, to be protected and assisted, to be given a recovery and reflection period of at least 30 days, to be granted a renewable residence permit, and to receive compensation for the damages suffered'.

For a person to have been a victim of human trafficking there must have been:

- action (recruitment, transportation, transfer, harbouring or receipt, which can include either domestic or cross-border movement);
- means (threat or use of force, coercion, abduction, fraud, deception, abuse of power or vulnerability – however, there does not need to be a means used for children as they are not able to give informed consent);
- purpose of exploitation (e.g. sexual exploitation, forced labour or domestic servitude, slavery, removal of organs).

Under s.1 of the *Modern Slavery Act 2015*, a person commits an offence of slavery, servitude and forced or compulsory labour if:

1. (a) the person holds another person in slavery or servitude and the circumstances are such that the person knows or ought to know that the other person is held in slavery or servitude, or
2. (b) the person requires another person to perform forced or compulsory labour and the circumstances are such that the person knows or ought to know that the other person is being required to perform forced or compulsory labour. (National referral mechanism guidance: adult (England and Wales) Home Office, January 2020)

Article 4 of the ECHR prohibits slavery, servitude and forced labour and s.1 of the 2015 Act must be construed in accordance with the Article 4 provisions (see ECtHR factsheet 'Slavery, servitude, and forced labour, 2020, and Chapter 2). Businesses with an annual turnover of £36 million or more are required to publish a modern slavery statement setting out the steps they take to prevent modern slavery, both in their business and in their supply chains.

There were 5,144 modern slavery offences committed in the year ending March 2019 (an increase of 51 per cent over the previous year). There were 6,985 potential victims (a rise of 36 per cent) (ONS, 2020).

Modern slavery: how to identify and support victims (Home Office, 2020) describes the signs that victims of modern slavery may have, the support available to victims and the process for determining whether someone is a victim. There is also a National Referral Mechanism (NRM) (National referral mechanism guidance: adult (England and Wales) Home Office, January 2020). Referrals are made by first responders (this includes local authorities, the police, Gangmasters' Licensing Agency, the Salvation Army, Barnado's and the NSPCC) who are required to make a formal referral to the NRM (this is done online). The first responder should also explain to the victim that their case will be passed on to the police because they are a potential victim of crime.

The decision-maker is the Single Competent Authority (SCA) in the Home Office who must decide, usually within five days, whether it 'suspects but cannot prove' that the person is a victim. A person recognised as a potential victim of modern slavery will have access to specialist support (currently provided by the Salvation Army and other subcontractors); this may include access to legal advice, accommodation, protection, and emotional and practical help. The support is provided for up to 90 days while a 'conclusive grounds' decision is made by the SCA. If the decision is negative, it will be scrutinised by an independent panel.

Victims may be granted discretionary leave to remain in the UK (where this is relevant) if there are 'particularly compelling circumstances' which justify them being allowed to stay for a limited period. This could be to finish a course of medical treatment not available in their own country or to pursue a compensation claim under Article 15 of the 2005 Convention, and/or to 'assist the police in their enquiries'. Modern slavery victims who have not been trafficked are also required to meet the above criteria (the UK's obligations under EU Directive 2011/36 on preventing and combating trafficking and the 2005 Convention).

Decisions that find that a person has not been trafficked or is not a victim of modern slavery can be challenged by an action for judicial review (*R (AUJ)* v *Secretary of State for the Home Department* [2018] UKUT 00200 (IAC)). The SCA can also be asked to reconsider a decision, but this is not a formal right of appeal. The SCA will only reconsider their decision if they consider there are appropriate grounds.

Immigration Removal Centres

Immigration removal centres are used to detain people who are subject to immigration control and who are either waiting for permission to enter the UK or awaiting removal because they have, for example, entered the UK illegally, overstayed or breached their visa conditions. It is not a criminal procedure as decisions to detain a person are made by immigration officers, not the courts. 'The Government has a responsibility to use it sparingly, and for the shortest period possible' (House of Commons/House of Lords, 2020). Immigration detention bail is available in certain circumstances and subject to conditions – e.g. reporting regularly to an immigration official, having an electronic monitoring tag, restrictions on where they live (Immigration Detention Bail (Home Office)). In 2019, 24,400 people were held in immigration detention; over two-thirds were detained for less that 29 days and 44 per cent were deported (National Statistics, February 2020).

No Recourse to Public Funds

Section 115 of the *Immigration and Asylum Act 1999* provides that certain people 'subject to immigration control' will have 'no recourse to public funds' (NRPF). Examples include non-EEA nationals who:

- require, but do not have, leave to enter or remain in the UK;
- have leave to enter and remain but are subject to NRPF;

- have leave to enter or remain but this is subject to a maintenance undertaking – e.g. an adult dependant of a person with settled status.

For a comprehensive list of what does and does not constitute public funds, see: www.gov.uk/government/publications/public-funds--2/public-funds

Local Authority Care and Support for People with NRPF

Local authorities are required to provide people who have NRPF with housing and/or financial support to prevent homelessness or destitution in the following circumstances:

1. Where a child in a family is 'a child in need' under s.17 of the *Children Act 1989* – e.g. because of homelessness (Chapter 6).
2. Former looked after children under ss.23–4 of the *Children Act 1989* – e.g. unaccompanied asylum-seeking children who leave care (Chapter 7).
3. Adults requiring care and support – e.g. because of a physical disability or mental illness – under Part 1, *Care Act 2014*.

Schedule 3, *Nationality, Immigration and Asylum Act 2002* sets out the groups of people who are excluded from the LA support listed above. However, housing and/or financial support must be provided if it is necessary to prevent a breach of their human rights under ECHR. In these circumstances, LAs are required to undertake a human rights assessment: These groups are:

- EEA nationals who are not British citizens;
- people who are in the UK illegally – e.g. illegal entrants, visa overstayers and failed asylum seekers who did not claim at the port of entry;
- people with refugee status granted by an EEA country;
- refused asylum seekers who have failed to comply with removal directions;
- refused asylum seeking families who have been issued with a certificate by the Home Office confirming that they have failed to take steps to leave the UK voluntarily.

LAs have a legal obligation to check a person's immigration status and are obliged to inform the Home Office of people who are in the UK unlawfully; of refused asylum seekers who have not complied with their removal directions; and of refused asylum-seeking families who have been certified by the Home Office as having not taken steps to leave the UK. If the human rights assessment finds that the person or family can return freely to their country of origin, the local authority can offer assistance with travel to that country and can provide housing and financial support while this is being arranged (see also Chapter 19).

In a recent case which involved a 5-year-old boy born in the UK to a Zimbabwean mother with leave to remain but subject to an NRPF, it was argued that the Home Office's policy failed to safeguard the welfare of children and was indirectly discriminatory on the grounds of race. The High Court held that the instructions to caseworkers, as presently formulated, does not adequately give effect to the obligations which the Secretary of State accepts are imposed on her by Article 3 of the European Convention on Human Rights, as interpreted by long-standing case law of the UK courts. Our decision will not affect the ability of the Secretary of State to continue to make grants of leave to remain in the United Kingdom subject to a condition of 'no recourse to public funds' in the normal run of cases.

(ST (a child, by his Litigation Friend VW) & VW v Secretary of State for the Home Department [2021] EWHC 1085 (Admin))

Chapter Summary

This chapter has:

- provided an overview of the immigration system, the relevant legal rules, social policy and ethical issues, and how they impact on people who want to come into the UK which are relevant to social work practice;
- explained the rules applicable to claiming refugee status, human trafficking and modern slavery and the help available to these groups;
- highlighted the needs of unaccompanied children seeking asylum and difficulties establishing proof of age;
- explained the rules relating to no recourse to public funds and the duties owed by local authorities to some people who have NRPF and the implications for social work.

Exercises

1. Do the following claimants have recourse to public funds?

   a. asylum seekers;
   b. people on work visas;
   c. illegal immigrants;
   d. people who have overstayed their visa time limit;
   e. refugees;
   f. people granted indefinite leave to remain.

2. Explain what is 'humanitarian protection', why the safeguards it gives are needed and what protection it gives to successful claimants.

Answers can be found in the Appendix.

Further reading

Philmore, J. (2015) *Migration & Social Policy*. Cheltenham: Edward Elgar Publishing.

Whitt, M.S. (2014) The ethics of immigration. *Ethics & Global Politics*, 7(3): 137–41, DOI: 10.3402/egp.v7.24942.

19

Welfare Benefits and Homelessness

Chapter Objectives

By the end of this chapter, readers will be able to:

- identify the legal rules and the social policy and ethical considerations that determine eligibility to welfare benefits provided by the state;
- understand the scope of the benefits available and the eligibility rules;
- identify the legal rules determining local authorities' duties to homeless people;
- understand the implications of the rules for social work practice;
- apply the rules to case scenarios.

Introduction

The modern welfare state, established after the Second World War, focused on two 'giant evils': disease and want. Free universal healthcare should exist alongside a welfare system to protect people from poverty. The dual system of contributory and means-tested benefits that had developed from 1908 (when pensions for the poorest were first introduced) was maintained in the *National Assistance Act 1948*. All working-age people over 16 receive a National Insurance number and pay contributions (usually deducted from their wages), which give a 'contractual' right to certain benefits. However, contributory benefits are now only a tiny element of modern welfare, which is now dwarfed by the number of means-tested and non-means-tested non-contributory benefits. There is evidence that some people are reluctant to access the means-tested benefits they are entitled to claim. This is partly because of stigma, but also because of the suspicion that state help is taken by those who do not need it, 'which persists both at state level and in public consciousness' (Baumberg Geiger, 2017). A University of Kent study of public beliefs about the benefits system found that 20 per cent of respondents thought that most benefit claims were wrongly made and a further 14 per cent claimed that they were made fraudulently (Baumberg Geiger, 2017). The actual incidence of benefit fraud is difficult to determine, as the Department for Work and Pensions (DWP) compile yearly statistics of the overpayment and underpayment of benefits which combines fraud with claimant and official error. In the year 2019/20, there was a 2.4 per cent benefit overpayment and 1.1 per cent underpayment. A total of £191.7 billion was paid out in benefits, of which £2.8 billion was overpaid by fraud and error (1.9 per cent of benefit expenditure). Lack of knowledge about the benefits available is also a factor in underclaiming.

Thought Box

What other factors could deter people from claiming benefits to which they are entitled?

Welfare benefits theoretically provide a 'safety net' against destitution, yet in 2019 some 14.3 million people lived in poverty, of whom 8.3 million were working-age adults, 4.6 million were children and 1.3 million were pensioners (Social Metrics Commission, 2019). Shelter's 2019 survey found that 280,000 homeless people in England and a further 220,000 people were threatened with homelessness; under-reporting probably means that the statistics are much higher (see Chapter 20).

Ethical Implications

The availability of welfare benefits, the rules that determine entitlement and the amount payable have important ethical implications. Greater austerity results in more people falling into poverty (Joseph Rowntree Foundation (JRF) and Child Poverty Action Group (CPAG)) and this results in social workers having to find additional sources of support for many families, including food banks, charities and support for children in need. A 'two-child limit' was introduced in April 2017 to restrict tax credits, housing benefit and Universal Credit (see below) to the first two children born into a family (all children born before this date were unaffected). The rationale was to make the system 'fairer and more affordable' (House of Commons Work and Pensions Committee, 2019: The two-child limit).

Is limiting the number of children that claimants have (or can claim for) ethically justifiable, as it can adversely impact on people from ethnic minority backgrounds, families with disabled children and those who have large families for religious reasons? Similarly, is it ethically justifiable for the state to encourage single mothers to find work when their child(ren) will have to be looked after by others or to place a benefit cap on claimants (see below)?

BASW's document Understanding social work and poverty sets out what poverty is, its causes and impact, and explains why social workers should be concerned and how social work values apply (see: www.basw.co.uk/understanding-social-work-and-poverty). It also sets out the role that social workers can play though 'welfare advocacy and a rights-based approach to anti-poverty practice' and 'challenging unjust policies and practices' (see also Bywaters, 2020).

Social Policy and Reform of the Welfare System

The 2008 financial crisis heralded a new age of austerity, and welfare was seen as 'costly and wasteful'; it was targeted for reform. The *Welfare Reform Act 2012* introduced Universal Credit (UC) and Personal Independence Payments (PIPs), restricted the availability of Housing Benefit (HB), brought in the 'bedroom tax' (an 'underoccupancy charge') and the 'benefit cap' (which limits the amount of benefit that many working-age people can claim).

Since 2013, 'legacy benefits' – i.e. the benefits that existed before the introduction of UC – coexist with UC and PIP and until the transition period ends (estimated to be in 2024). The system is difficult for both managers to administer and claimants to understand. As a result, the different rules often lead to errors and over- and under-payments. In Keeping more of what you earn (Joseph Rowntree Foundation, 2017a), it is argued that 'whilst the rationale for UC in part was to ensure people are better off working the majority of people who experience poverty in fact live in working households'.

The policy underpinning the two-child limit was justified by the government on two grounds: 1) that benefit claimants should face the same financial choices as those people who work and whose pay does not increase because they have another child, and 2) the benefit system should provide a fair deal to the taxpayer (Machin, 2017). The child element, in 2019, was worth £2,780 per child per year and is subject to certain exceptions (see: www.gov.uk/guidance/child-tax-credit-exceptions-to-the-2-child-limit).

The complexity of the benefit system and the impact on service users who do not know about the benefits they are entitled to claim and/or know how to access them arguably places on social workers the need to have a basic understanding of the system (Little, 2013).

This chapter provides an explanation of the benefit system with the aim of ensuring that social workers can identify the benefits that their service users can claim, and either help service users negotiate the benefit system or direct them to organisations that can give more specialist help – e.g. the CPAG, money advice units and Citizens Advice (see also Chapter 20).

Welfare Benefits

Individuals or couples with savings of over £16,000 are ineligible for any means-tested benefit. For savings between £6,000 and £16,000, a notional income of £1 weekly for every £250 is deducted from benefit. The value of a home in which the claimant lives is disregarded. Claims for means-tested benefits can be refused or repayment required if someone is found to have deliberately 'deprived themselves of capital' – i.e. either spent or transferred money – in order to qualify for benefit. Current rates of all benefits and the eligibility criteria are available on GOV.UK. Entitlement to benefits can be checked using a benefits calculator: www.gov.uk/benefits-calculators

Relevant details of all the benefits referred to below can be obtained from GOV.UK. The following is a summary of the important benefits and a brief explanation of the eligibility rules.

Universal Credit (UC)

Since 2013, UC is available to everyone over 18 and under retirement age who is unemployed, self-employed, unable to work due to long-term health conditions or caring responsibilities, and people on low incomes with less than £16,000 in savings.

UC replaces six means-tested 'legacy benefits':

- child tax credit;
- working tax credit;
- income support;
- housing benefit;
- income-based job seeker's allowance (JSA);
- income-based employment support allowance (ESA).

UC aims to encourage more people into work by introducing 'better financial incentives, simpler processes, increasing requirements on claimants to search for jobs, reduce fraud, error and administration costs' (National Audit Office, 2018). Since December 2018, UC is the only means-tested benefit available for new applicants under pension age. It is the first 'digital' benefit and must be claimed online. The monthly entitlement is based on size and composition of the household and its housing costs (rent, not mortgage payments). Claimants' earnings are notified each month to the DWP by HM Revenue and Customs (HMRC) and relevant deductions made from the benefit entitlement. Self-employed claimants calculate and report net earnings each month. For every £1 earned above the work allowance, 63p is currently taken from benefit. The Social Security (Coronavirus) (Further Measures) Regulations 2020 increased UC and HB by £20 per week and relaxed the Minimum Income Floor for self-employed UC applicants, reduced work requirements for UC and Job Seekers Allowance (JSA) and updated index-linking to the Consumer Price Index of the Local Housing Allowance. Between March and November 2020, there were 2.8 million new UC claimants (House of Commons Briefing Paper (2021): Coronavirus: Universal Credit during the Crisis).

UC applicants unfit to work must attend a medical assessment to confirm whether they have 'limited capability' for work or 'work-related activities'. Work allowances (the tax credit element of UC allowing some earnings before reduction of benefit) are limited to disabled and sick claimants, and those with a child under one year old.

UC is paid monthly in arrears with an initial five-week wait. Advances of the first month's payment are now available to new claimants and repayment is by 12 monthly deductions. All new claimants are offered 'budgeting support' and must make a 'claimant commitment', which requires attending appointments with a work coach, searching for work where appropriate and disclosing any change of circumstances. Failure can result in a sanction and loss of all or part of the benefit, although hardship payments can be paid to sanctioned claimants.

Pensioner benefits

There are three benefits that can only be claimed by people who have reached state pension age (currently 66 years and then scheduled to rise to 67 between 2026 and 2028).

> *State retirement pension* (SRP) is a contribution-based benefit which is dependent on claimants having paid NI contributions for a minimum of ten 'qualifying years' – i.e. a tax year, which is 6 April to 5 April). A total of 35 qualifying years must be paid to receive the full rate of SRP.

> *Pension credit* is a means-tested (income-related) benefit payable to a single person or a couple (husband, wife, civil partner or cohabitee) if (since 15 May 2019) they have both reached state pension age, or one of the couple is receiving Housing Benefit. There are two elements: 'Guarantee credit', which ensures that a person (or couple) have a minimum weekly income (currently £177.10 for a single person and £270.30 for a couple); and 'Savings Credit', which is an additional weekly amount given as a 'reward' for saving money for retirement (currently, up to £13.97 per week for a single person and up to £15.62 for a couple). Attendance Allowance; the Christmas Bonus; Disability Living Allowance; Personal Independence Payment; Housing Benefit and Council Tax Reduction are not considered in assessing entitlement. In August 2020, there were 1,492,000 people in receipt of pension credit.

> *Attendance Allowance* is a disability benefit that is only claimable by people of state retirement age (see below).

> The *Winter Fuel Payment* is paid automatically to everyone in receipt of SRP irrespective of income. Cold Weather Payments are also paid to people on pension credit and other means-tested benefits, including UC (see: www.gov.uk/cold-weather-payment/how-to-claim).

Benefits and Unemployment

The following two benefits can be claimed by the unemployed under state retirement age.

Job Seeker's Allowance (JSA) is a benefit for people who work less than 16 hours per week, can work and are looking for work. There are two types:

Contribution-based ('new style') JSA is dependent on payment of Class 1 NI contributions in the last two to three years and is payable for the first six months of unemployment.

Income-based JSA is a means-tested benefit that can be claimed in addition to the new style JSA. It is dependent on the claimant's (and partner's) income and savings. The claimant must be available for work, be actively seeking work, be under pension age and, if working, this must be for less than 16 hours a week (if the claimant has a partner, together they must work fewer than 24 hours a week to qualify).

Employment Support Allowance (ESA) is paid to people too ill to work, either because of short-term sickness or whose illness either prevents them from working or limits the amount of work they can do. It is claimable by people who are employed, self-employed or unemployed. There are two types:

Contribution-based ('new style') ESA is claimable if two full years of NI contributions have been paid either from employment or self-employment. It is payable for one year.

Income-related ESA is a means-tested benefit claimable by people who have insufficient NI contributions to qualify for new-style ESA or have exhausted their new-style ESA entitlement. It can also be used to top up new-style ESA payments. The amount payable is dependent on age, income and savings.

ESA replaced Incapacity Benefit in 2011 (an NI contribution-based benefit), but there are still people receiving it, and this will continue until their circumstances change – e.g. in their work status or a partner leaves or joins the home – or they reach retirement age.

Statutory Sick Pay (SSP) is not a 'benefit' as it is paid by employers to employees who are off sick for four days or more. To be eligible for SSP, the employee must have an employment contract, earn an average of at least £120 per week and provide proof of their illness once they have been absent for more than seven days. It is paid for a maximum of 28 weeks. It cannot be paid if a person is in receipt of Statutory Maternity Pay or Maternity Allowance. New-style ESA cannot be claimed until entitlement to SSP has stopped. In January 2021 it was £95.85 per week (TUC, 2020).

Disability Benefits

A total of 7.9 million people in the UK aged between 16 and 64 years have a disability; 3.4 million are not in work and not looking for work (House of Commons Library

Briefing (2020) People with disabilities in employment). It is estimated that people living with a disability incur an average of £570 in extra costs a month, and because they cannot work, or can only work reduced hours, 'they are twice as likely as non-disabled people to live in poverty' (Scope (n.d.)).

In addition to ESA, the following benefits are paid to people with disabilities:

> *Disability or Severe Disability Premium (SDP)* is an amount included in the following means-tested benefits to help with the extra cost of disability: Income Support, income-based JSA, income-related ESA and Housing Benefit.

The following three benefits are tax-free, non-means-tested – i.e. income and savings are not taken into account – and can be claimed in addition to means-tested benefits, including ESA. The severe disability premium is not available to UC claimants (see: www.gov.uk/disability-premiums/eligibility). The benefits are to help with the extra costs associated with illness, disability and mental health problems.

> *Disability Living Allowance* (DLA) is a benefit available to both children and adults. It is payable for a child under 16 years who needs more care and supervision than a child of the same age who does not have a disability. It has two elements – care and mobility – and applies to children with a wide range of medical conditions – physical, behavioural and psychological – as well as children with learning disabilities. It includes children who have difficulty walking, need help with eating, washing and getting dressed, toileting, speaking, seeing and hearing. To qualify, the child must have been disabled or had the condition for at least three months, and the disability must be expected to last for six months or more. The residence requirement requires claimants to have lived in Great Britain for two of the last three years (if the child is over 3 years), be 'habitually resident' in the UK and not subject to immigration control (see Chapter 18).

> DLA for adults (see GOV.UK) has been replaced by *Personal Independence Payments* (PIP) for claimants born on or after 9 April 1948. PIP is paid to people who need help with mobility and/or care costs. The care component has three levels of benefit based on the level of care required; the mobility component has two levels. To qualify, claimants must have a health condition or disability that results in them having difficulty with activities of daily living – e.g. washing, dressing, preparing food, eating, communicating – and/or mobility. They must have suffered these difficulties for three months and it must be expected to last at least nine months. Almost all claimants are assessed. Psychiatric disorder is the most recorded disabling condition (36 per cent of claimants) and there is concern that such claimants are not being assessed appropriately and losing access to the Motability Scheme (see: www. disabilityrightsuk.org).

> *Attendance Allowance* (AA) is a benefit for people who are of state retirement age or over, have a disability and need someone to help look after them because of their care needs. It does not cover mobility needs and it is immaterial whether anyone is

providing the claimant with help or not. It covers any type of disability or illness, including sight or hearing impairments, and mental health issues such as dementia and depression. The claimant must have needed help with their care needs for at least six months to qualify (unless they are terminally ill). It is paid at two different rates dependent on the level of need. In February 2019, 2.1 million people were receiving PIP; 1.7 million were receiving DLA; 1.3 million were receiving carer's allowance; and 1.6 million were receiving AA.

Carer's Allowance is an income-replacement benefit paid to a person looking after someone with a 'qualifying disability benefit' (DLA middle or higher rate care, PIP Daily Living or AA (either level)). The carer must provide at least 35 hours care per week, be over 16 and not in full-time education nor, if employed, earning on average above £128 per week. The carer need not be related to nor live with the person to whom they are providing care. Care includes helping with washing, household tasks and taking people to hospital.

Other disability benefits exist for specific groups – e.g. Armed Forces Independent Payment and War Pensions for injured service personnel and Industrial Injuries Disablement Benefit (IIDB) for persons disabled following an industrial injury or who suffer from an industrial disease such as pneumoconiosis or deafness. For IIDB, there is no requirement to prove that the accident was a result of any fault on the employer's part.

Benefits for people in work but on low incomes

Since the introduction of the 'National Living Wage' (NLW) in 2016, the percentage of employees on low pay – i.e. those paid less than two-thirds of median hourly pay (which was £15.90 in 2020 for full-time employees) has fallen (although the pandemic will have affected these statistics). There were 4.7 million employees on low pay in 2019 (Joyce and Waters, 2019).

The following means-tested benefits are available to people in work (all have been subsumed into UC for new claimants or where legacy benefit claimants' circumstances have changed).

Housing Benefit (HB) is paid by local councils to help people on low incomes pay their rent. Approximately 73 per cent of HB claimants (2.6 million) are social housing tenants and 27 per cent rent privately (970,000). The *Welfare Reform Act 2012* introduced an under-occupation charge (colloquially called the 'bedroom tax'), which applies to people whose property has more bedrooms than are deemed to be needed. It is based on the following criteria: two people are expected to share one bedroom if two adults are in a couple; two children are under 10 years and two same-sex children are under 16. Exceptions to the rule apply if one of a couple has a disability and must sleep separately (the disabled partner must be in receipt of a disability benefit) and a disabled child if their disability means they cannot share a room.

Local authorities also operate a maximum housing allowance rate (see: https://lha-direct.voa.gov.uk/search.aspx). In May 2019, there were 3.6 million people in receipt of HB and 1.1 million with a housing element in their UC.

Discretionary Housing Payments (DHP) can be made by local councils to help claimants on HB (and UC if it contains a housing element) who have difficulty paying their rent and who cannot find anywhere cheaper to live. New claims for HB can now only be made by people of pension age, people whose benefits include a severe disability premium and people staying in a refuge, hostel or some types of supported or temporary housing. The DWP estimates that only eight out of ten families entitled to HB claim it.

Council Tax Support (or Council Tax Reduction) (means-tested help with Council Tax) continues to be administered by local councils and must be claimed separately by UC applicants.

Working Tax Credit is paid by HM Revenue and Customs (HMRC) to top up the earnings of low-paid workers. For claimants who have childcare costs, the 'childcare element' of Working Tax Credit can help with up to 70 per cent of those costs.

Child Tax Credit is also administered by HMRC and is paid to people on low incomes to help with the costs of bringing up a child. It is also available to people who are not working.

Income Support (which is being replaced by UC) is available for people on low incomes, but (unlike UC) it cannot be claimed by people working 16 hours or more a week (if a couple, the maximum number of hours is 24).

Support for Mortgage Interest (SMI) Owner-occupiers on means-tested benefits (including UC) can apply for SMI (which is a loan repayable when, for example, the house is sold). SMI pays the interest-only part of a mortgage (not the capital sum); it is paid directly to the lender, is payable on mortgages of up to £200,000 and only after 39 weeks from date of application (unless the claimant is on Pension Credit, when it is paid immediately). Claimants on income-based JSA can only get SMI for a maximum of two years.

Benefits for Children

The two-child limit (above) does not apply to help with childcare costs, passported benefits – i.e. entitlement as a result of eligibility for other benefits such as free school meals – or to any of the benefits/schemes discussed below.

Child Benefit is a non-means-tested benefit payable four-weekly for each child in the family under 16 years or under 20 if in full-time education. Where one parent earns £60,000 or more a year, the benefit is repaid via taxation. A parent earning between £50,000 and £60,000 will have to pay a proportion back in taxes.

Healthy Start food vouchers are available for pregnant women in receipt of: income support, income-based JSA and ESA, child tax credit, UC or pension credit. It is available until the child is aged 4. In addition, school-age children in low-income families can receive free school meals, the cost of transport to school and help with uniform costs, which are claimable from the LA. A total of 15 hours per week free childcare is available to all 3–4-year-old children; there are no earnings or work requirements; 30 hours per week is available to all children of working parent(s) unless one parent earns more than £100,000 per annum. Additional help with childcare costs is available through the government's tax-free childcare scheme (see: www.gov.uk/help-with-childcare-costs).

If a child is a 'child in need' under s.17 of the *Children Act 1989* (Chapter 6), local authority support – e.g. day-care facilities for children under 5 years of age and financial assistance – may be available.

Statutory Maternity Benefit (SMB) is paid by employers for up to 39 weeks at 90 per cent of average weekly earnings (before tax) for the first six weeks. For the remaining 33 weeks, £151.20 or 90 per cent of average weekly earnings (whichever is lower) is paid. *Maternity Allowance* (MA) is payable for 39 weeks to women who are not eligible for SMP and can be claimed by the self-employed and employees. Entitlement is dependent on relevant NI contributions. MA for 14 weeks may be payable to claimants who do not qualify for SMP or the higher rate MA.

Sure Start Maternity Grant (SSMG) is payable to all first-time mothers and those expecting a multiple birth or adopting a child under one year who receive a means-tested benefit, including UC. The non-repayable £500 grant can be claimed from 11 weeks before the birth and to up to 6 months afterwards.

Other benefits and support

Bereavement Support Payment is a non-means-tested benefit payable on the death of a spouse or civil partner where bereavement occurred on or after 6 April 2017. The claimant must be under state pension age and claim it within three months of the death.

Budgeting Loans are available to persons claiming income support, income-related JSA and ESA, PC or UC for at least six months. Money can be requested for items such as white goods, clothing, advance rent, costs of moving, maternity or funeral costs. Loans are interest-free and repaid by deduction from benefits over a two-year period.

Council or charitable help: some councils have crisis intervention schemes for people in extreme hardship to help with the cost of essentials – e.g. food, clothing and household items. Food banks (run by charities) also provide food for people in financial crises (Loopstra et al., 2018).

The 'benefit cap' is a limit on the total amount of benefit a claimant can get and was introduced in the *Welfare Reform Act 2012* to act as 'as an incentive to work'.

It does not apply where a person or a child with whom they live receives DLA or PIP, or where they work for 16 hours or more per week. It is also restricted to claimants below retirement age.

A person suspected of *benefit fraud* will usually have payment stopped and be interviewed under caution. If it is found that the benefit has been incorrectly paid – e.g. due to a deliberate failure to disclose or provision of false information – the over-payment is reclaimed. DWP/HMRC/local councils may also pursue a criminal prosecution.

Challenging DWP Eligibility Decisions

The DWP must inform claimants of their right to request a 'mandatory reconsideration' (MR) of their decision where this is available (the request must usually be made within a month of the original decision; see: www.gov.uk/mandatory-reconsideration).

If the MR is unsuccessful, applicants can apply to the first-tier tribunal (Social Security and Child Support; see: www.gov.uk/courts-tribunals/first-tier-tribunal-social-security-and-child-support).

Appeals (with permission) can be made to the Upper Tribunal (Administrative Appeals Chamber).

The same procedure applies to appeals to HMRC regarding Tax Credits (about eligibility or overpayment). For LA decisions about HB (eligibility, overpayment), there is a right to request a review by letter within one month and, if unsuccessful, a right of appeal to the First Tier Tribunal within one month.

Immigration and Access to Benefits

EU nationals

Following the UK's departure from the EU on 31 December 2019, EU citizens must have applied for 'settled' (resident for five years) or 'pre-settled' (resident for less than five years) status by 30 June 2021 if they wish to remain in the UK after that date (Chapter 18). To claim benefits, a person must have a right to reside; this is satisfied if a person has lived in the UK for five years. An EU national with pre-settled status who is not working and claims benefit must establish that the UK is their main residence and they have a 'settled intention to remain'. Evidence can include having children attending UK schools, a bank account, a tenancy agreement or owning property, and bills with name and UK address (see Chapter 18).

People who are subject to immigration control have 'no recourse to public funds' (NRPF) under s.115 of the *Immigration and Asylum Act 1999* (see Chapter 18).

Homelessness

The causes of homelessness are wide-ranging and include poverty, unemployment, lack of affordable housing because of a shrinking social housing sector, relationship breakdown, domestic abuse, and physical and mental health problems. Understanding the rules is important for social work practice as it helps determine whether an LA housing department has a statutory duty to provide accommodation and how service users might be helped to navigate the process (see: Homelessness code of guidance for local authorities (2018) at: www.gov.uk/guidance/homelessness-code-of-guidance-for-local-authorities).

For current homelessness statistics, see: www.gov.uk/government/collections/homelessness-statistics

Section 175 of the *Housing Act 1996* defines a person as homeless:

1. if they have no place in which they have a right to live in the UK or elsewhere. This includes accommodation such as a mobile home, vehicle or boat which they have nowhere to park or moor;
2. if it is not reasonable for them to continue to occupy accommodation – e.g. due to its condition, location, affordability, or because it is overcrowded, or they are at risk of violence (*Yemshaw* v *Hounslow LBC* [2011] UKSC 3);
3. if they are in 'crisis accommodation' (refuge/night shelter) or sleeping rough.

A person is threatened with homelessness if either 1) they are likely to become homeless in the next 56 days or 2) have been served with a valid s.21 notice (*Housing Act 1988*) asking them to leave their home and the notice expires within 56 days.

Excluded groups

People subject to immigration control (unless they are refugees or persons granted humanitarian protection) and some EEA nationals (those without a right to reside) are only owed an advisory duty.

LA requirement for a homelessness strategy

Since 2002, a local authority must regularly review current and future homelessness in its area and have a strategy to secure accommodation and provide support for those who are or may become homeless (*Homelessness Act 2002*).

Duty to advise

LAs must give housing advice to all homeless applicants. The prevention and relief duties under the *Homelessness Reduction Act 2017* stopped the LA practice of making applicants with an eviction notice (s.8 or s.21 of the *Housing Act 1977* notice) wait until they are issued an eviction (bailiff's) warrant. Both duties apply irrespective of whether an applicant is intentionally homeless.

Prevention duty

LAs must take reasonable steps to prevent any applicant (regardless of whether they qualify for a main housing duty) who is threatened with homelessness from becoming homeless. The LA must either help them to stay in their current accommodation or find a new place for them to live before they become homeless. The duty lasts for 56 days but will end earlier if accommodation is found or the person becomes homeless.

Relief duty

Where an LA is satisfied that a homeless applicant is eligible, it 'must take reasonable steps to help the applicant to secure that suitable accommodation becomes available' for at least six months (s.189B(2) of the *Housing Act 1996*, inserted by s.5(2) of the *Homelessness Reduction Act 2017*). The relief duty applies while the LA assesses the applicant's housing and support needs and draws up a personal housing plan; this should be jointly agreed with the applicant if possible. Alongside the relief duty, the LA must assess the applicant to see if a main housing duty is owed.

Main duty

Once temporary housing has been provided under the relief duty, an LA has an ongoing duty to secure suitable accommodation for an eligible applicant who is in priority need and not intentionally homeless. The duty ends if the applicant has turned down a suitable offer of accommodation or 'deliberately and unreasonably' refused to co-operate with their housing plan.

Eligibility enquiry

To be eligible for a main housing duty a homeless applicant must have the following.

A local connection: by normal residence, employment, family association, special circumstance or leaving care (on or after 3 April 2018). Exceptions apply to people discharged from hospital, released from prison or those wanting to return to an area where they were brought up or had lived for a long time. Where the applicant has a local connection with another LA, there is a duty to refer them. The Ministry of Housing, Communities and Local Government *Homelessness Code of Guidance for Local Authorities* on homelessness duties under the HRA 2017 advises LAs to consider each case individually on its own particular facts.

The following groups are deemed to be in priority need:

- pregnant women;
- those with dependent children;
- persons homeless due to fire or flood;
- care leavers aged 18–20;
- Victims fleeing domestic abuse;
- 16- and 17-year-olds (except those owed a duty under s.20 of the *Children Act 1989* – see Chapter 6).

The following people *may* be in priority need: the elderly, those with mental health problems or physical or learning disabilities, those who have spent time in the armed forces or prison, or care leavers under the age of 21. The LA will consider whether a person is vulnerable by ascertaining whether: they can cope with homelessness, whether their physical/mental condition affects their daily life, any support that is available to them from family/friends, and whether they are at greater risk of harm than other homeless applicants.

Service users may need help from social workers in providing evidence to support their claim.

An applicant who is 'intentionally homeless' under s.191(3) of the *Housing Act 1996* is excluded from LA help because they have deliberately done or failed to do anything that has caused them not to occupy accommodation which is still available to them and which it would be reasonable for them to continue to live in. Alternatively, they may have arranged with someone else whereby they are required to leave accommodation which it would have been reasonable for them to continue to occupy *and* this was done to enable them to access help under Part 7 of the *Housing Act 1996 and* no other good reason exists why they are homeless.

Acts or omissions done in good faith will not amount to intentional homelessness – e.g. leaving accommodation when they are not aware there was a right to stay; leaving accommodation due to bad advice; leaving because of actions of a third party. Non-payment of rent does not automatically constitute intentional homelessness (*Samuels* v *Birmingham City Council* [2019] UKSC 28). The *Homelessness Code of Guidance* advises that rent should not be seen as affordable if payment leaves the applicant without enough for food, clothing, heating, transport or other essentials. In assessing this, UC standard allowances can be used by LAs.

Referrals

Referrals to another English LA can be made at the relief duty stage and to any UK LA at the main duty stage, but only if the applicant does not have a local connection with the referring authority and is not at risk of violence.

Reviews

All LA decisions must be notified in writing with reasons and must include the right to request a review and any time limits. There are three ways to challenge an LA decision:

- Request an internal review (preferably in writing with reasons why the decision is considered wrong). If the matter is not resolved, complain to the Local Government and Social Care Ombudsman (www.lgo.org.uk) that the LA's decision was maladministrative and caused injustice.
- Appeal to the county court (legal advice is advisable).
- Apply for a judicial review of the decision (legal advice is essential to bring a High Court challenge).

Chapter Summary

The chapter has:

- identified the legal rules and social policy and ethical considerations that determine eligibility to welfare benefits provided by the state;
- explained the benefits available and the eligibility criteria;
- set out the legal rules that determine local authorities' duties to homeless people;
- explained the implications of the rules for social work practice.

Case study – Welfare benefits and protection from homelessness

A and B have three children, aged 8, 5 and 1. The 1-year-old suffers from spina bifida and the 5-year-old is autistic. A, who was employed as a porter at the local hospital, was diagnosed with motor neurone disease ten months ago and has had to stop work. Now he has no income and they have £500 left in their bank account. They live in a three-bedroomed house rented from a housing association, which is in poor repair. The rent is £300 per week. They are currently in six months' rent and Council Tax arrears. The housing association has served on them a notice to quit because of the rent arrears. B does not have paid work. A and B seek your help. What help can they claim?

Answers can be found in the Appendix.

Further Reading

Lund, B. (2017) *Understanding Housing Policy* (3rd edn). Understanding Welfare: Social Issues, Policy and Practice series. University of Bristol: Policy Press.

20

Social policy and ethical considerations relevant to the relief of poverty

Chapter Objectives

By the end of this chapter, readers will be able to:

- understand the importance of social policy considerations in relieving poverty;
- analyse the impact of poverty on individuals and groups in our society;
- analyse the ethics and values relevant to working with service users impacted by poverty;
- understand their application to social work practice.

Introduction

This chapter examines poverty, the social policy measures aimed at reducing poverty and the impact that poverty has on individuals and families who live in poverty. It then discusses why poverty is a key issue for social work in general, but more particularly because of the unfair discrimination that people living in poverty face, which impacts on their ability to access the necessary resources. The chapter also explores how individuals and certain groups try to cope with poverty, the disadvantages they experience, and how social work values frame social work responses to such issues at both personal practice and agency levels.

Poverty in the UK is measured by reference to the median UK household's disposable income, which was £29,400 in the financial year ending 2019 (UK Office for National Statistics (ONS) (2020): Average household income, UK). People are deemed to be living in poverty if their income is 60 per cent or less than the median disposable income – i.e. £17,640 or less per annum in 2019. Disposable income is the money left after deduction of taxes and social security, which is available to a household to spend (and/or save). Housing costs play an important part in household budgets and push 3.1 million people into poverty. Income includes earnings from employment as well as benefits.

Social Policy

Social policy in this area is concerned with the measures that the state takes to relieve poverty and improve people's lives. Means-tested benefits provide a minimum income 'safety net' below which people's incomes should not fall. However, determining what the minimum income should be is clearly influenced by the government's view of what is affordable and public support for the policies that determine it. Furthermore, people's perception of the reasons why people live in poverty is also an important factor, as is understanding the causes of poverty. Lifestyle, inadequacy and 'fecklessness' are seen by some people as a justification for distinguishing between the 'deserving' and 'undeserving' poor: 'There are fundamental problems with attempting to draw a line between the 'deserving' and 'undeserving' poor. We need to ask ourselves what price, both financially and ethically, we are willing to pay as a society in the service of this paternalistic view of the poor' (Barker, 2016). Barker provides as illustration of the 'contradictory and inconsistent ways' that the current system uses to separate the deserving and undeserving poor by citing JSA statistics in 2015/16 which demonstrated that 93 per cent of JSA (Job Seeker's Allowance) sanctions that were reviewed were overturned.

There are also structural explanations to explain poverty, including social class, the failure of public services and inequality (Spicker, 2021). Disability (both mental and physical) is a well-recognised causal factor. The Social Metrics Commission report, A new measure of poverty for the UK (2018), found that nearly half of the 14.2 million people living in poverty are in families with a disabled person which is caused by the increased costs of living with a disability and the value of disability benefits (see Chapter 19). See also Child Poverty Action Group (n.d.).

One of the key questions that is particularly relevant is whether the minimum income 'safety net', embraced by the Beveridge reforms after the Second World War, is now failing to protect the most vulnerable in society. The House of Commons Work and Pensions Select Committee's Welfare Safety Net Committee conducted an inquiry into the current state of the UK's safety net, prompted by evidence of 'debt, hunger and homelessness and considered the effectiveness of our welfare system in protecting against hardship and chronic deprivation'. Their report in July 2019 states the following:

> The Government has shown that it can make target-busting savings through devastating, cumulative cuts to the incomes of the poor, by capping and freezing benefits ... likewise there is now no effective strategy to increase the life chances of poorer children. It has failed to recognise the bleak picture emerging as it shreds our social safety net because it doesn't really want to look.

The Committee also noted in July 2019 that 'on the Government's own measure, of the 14 million people who live in poverty (20% of the UK population) 4 million are more than 50% below the poverty line and 1.5 million are destitute'. Joseph Rowntree's definition of destitution is:

> going without the bare essentials we all need. That's a home, food, heating, lighting, clothing, shoes and basic toiletries. We define destitution as when people have lacked two or more of these essentials over the past month because they couldn't afford them; or if their income is extremely low – less than £70 a week for a single adult.
>
> (Fitzpatrick et al., 2020)

Following the Safety Net Committee's report, the Government announced, in November 2019, an increase of 1.7% Universal Credit (the first increase since 2015) and 3.9% in state pension from April 2020. As a result of the Covid-19 pandemic, the government in 2020 increased UC (and the appropriate legacy benefits – see Chapter 19) by approximately £80 per month until September 2021 because of the potential economic consequences of the pandemic.

The Impact of Poverty on People's Lives

Living in poverty is known to impact on a person's cognitive, social and behavioural development, as well as their mental and physical health, and their ability to participate in mainstream society. Levitas et al. (2007) define social exclusion as the lack of, or denial of resources, rights, goods and services, and the inability to participate in the normal relationships and activities, available to most people in society, whether in economic, social, cultural and political arenas. It affects both the quality of life of individuals and the equity and cohesion of society as a whole.

The impact on people's health is evidenced by the life expectancy statistics which indicate that men living in more affluent areas of England in 2016–18 could expect to live nearly ten years longer than those living in the 10 per cent most deprived areas (83.4 years and 73.9 years) and women living in the most affluent areas could expect to live to 86.3 years, compared with 78.6 years for women in the most deprived areas. Heart, respiratory disease and lung cancer are more prevalent in deprived areas than affluent ones (see also The King's Fund, 2019).

Poverty also 'increases the risk of mental health problems and can be both a causal factor and a consequence of mental ill health' (Mental Health Foundation, 2016). The review recognised 'the corrosive impact of stigma and discrimination on people experiencing mental health problems and those living in poverty'.

Breakdown Britain (Centre for Social Justice, 2006) examined the extent of family breakdown in the UK and its impact on poverty. It found that 'family breakdown was widespread in our poorest areas' and that the UK has 'some of the highest levels of breakdown anywhere in the world'. It also said that 'if you're a poor child in the UK today you're overwhelmingly more likely to see your parents separate and your family break apart than the middle-class child down the road'.

While poverty levels among pensioners have fallen in the last two years, 2 million pensioners live in poverty in the UK. Groups of older people at particular risk of poverty are private tenants (35 per cent) and social housing tenants (29 per cent) compared with owner occupiers with no mortgage (13 per cent). 'Poverty rates are highest for people in households where the head of the household is from the Pakistani or Bangladeshi ethnic groups and lowest for those from White ethnic groups' (House of Commons Library (2021) Poverty in the UK: Statistics).

Poverty and Ethnicity in the Labour Market (Joseph Rowntree Foundation, 2017b) identified the following drivers:

- higher unemployment;
- higher rates of economic inactivity;
- higher likelihood of lower pay;
- geographic location;
- migration status;
- educational attainment.

The report discusses strategies that could be adopted to help mitigate this problem.

The Budget Group and Runnymede Trust's report, Intersecting inequalities: The impact of austerity on Black and Minority Ethnic women in the UK (2017), provides an assessment of the effect of the changes in public spending since 2010 on Black,

Asian and Minority Ethnic (BAME) women, and concluded that the poorest families had suffered around a 70 per cent drop in their living standards by 2020.

A report by the DfE and DWP, 2010 to 2015 government policy: poverty and social justice (DfE and DWP, 2015) stated that 'Poverty, as measured by a household's income relative to the national average, is often a symptom of deeper, more complex problems. Many of these problems are passed on from one generation to the next.' The report states that there are 'almost 300,000 households in the UK where none of the adults has ever worked, and 300,000 children have parents with serious drug problems'. As a result, the children 'have reduced chances of success in their own lives'. Government strategy to deal with this problem includes action to:

- help troubled families turn their lives around;
- improve mental health;
- reduce child poverty and make sure that children are properly supported so that they complete their education;
- make work pay, and help people to find and stay in work;
- help people recover and become independent if things have gone wrong;
- work with the voluntary, public and private sectors to deal more effectively with complex problems.

Thought Box

What strategies have been adopted by Government to address the problems identified?

JRF's Child Welfare Inequalities Project (2016) analysed data of 35,000 children in the care system who were either looked after by the LA or on a child protection plan. It found that roughly 1 in every 60 children in the most deprived communities was in care compared to 1 in every 660 children in the least deprived communities. It noted that early intervention support in children's lives had 'decreased significantly' in the past five years and estimated that the cost of late intervention was around £17 billion a year in England and Wales (see: House of Commons Library Briefing Paper No. 7647 (2019) Early intervention. See also: DWP (2019) *Households Below Average Income (HBAI): An analysis of the UK income distribution:1994/95-2017/18*).

Poverty and Lack of Affordable Housing

The main forms of tenure (the basis on which a person has a right to occupy property) are:

- owner-occupation;
- local authority housing;

- registered social landlords (including housing associations);
- private rented housing.

Since the beginning of the twentieth century, owner-occupation has risen from 10 per cent to 63 per cent, private rentals have fallen from 90 per cent to 20 per cent, and the social housing sector (both council and social housing) has fallen from around 33 per cent to around 18 per cent. People on low incomes are concentrated in the social housing sector. The average income of council and housing association tenants is just over a quarter of the income of people who are buying houses with a mortgage (Department for Communities and Local Government, 2020).

Council house building (originally designated for the 'working class') began after the First World War and, by 1981, over 6 million such homes had been built, many because of slum clearance (particularly in the 1960s) which saw a mass building programme, often of high-rise blocks. From 1970, the Conservative government withdrew its support for council housing and the subsidies for council house rents, and introduced housing benefit for tenants on low incomes. From 1980, both council and registered social housing tenants were given the 'right to buy' their homes at a 'generous' discount, dependent on the length of the tenancy. Between 1980 and 2018, over 2 million social rented homes were sold and the role of council housing has been reduced considerably. Housing associations have largely taken over any opportunities for development that exist.

Owner-occupation increased, not just because of the right to buy policy, but also because tax advantages were given to owner-occupiers buying their homes with a 'mortgage' from a bank or building society in the 1960s to the 1990s. These advantages no longer exist.

Private rented housing declined from 1919 because of the growth of owner-occupation and the provision of LA housing. However, since the 1980s when the availability of social housing declined, the private rented sector has overtaken social housing as the UK's second largest tenure. The proportion of children living in the private sector has increased and private renters spend a greater proportion of their income on housing costs than social renters (see House of Commons, 2017). See also House of Commons, 2019.

The pandemic has further impacted on housing insecurity because of both social and private tenants falling into rent arrears. For a discussion of the issues, see, for example, CPAG and the Church of England, 2020, and House of Commons, 2021.

Benefit Reform and its Impact on Poverty

The review by the Institute for Fiscal Studies (IFS) (2019), *Universal credit and its impact on household incomes: the long and the short of it*, found that 'as an overall cut to benefits, universal credit hits the persistently poor harder than those with higher longer-term incomes'. For a further analysis of the impact of the reforms introduced by the *Welfare Reform Act 2012*, see Chapter 19.

Ethical Issues and Poverty

This section looks further at the issues of poverty for individuals and groups of people as set out above. It considers why poverty is important to social work in general, but particularly in relation to social work with individuals and groups subject to unfair discrimination and lack of access to resources in society. It looks in detail at certain groups of people living in poverty who, it can be argued, suffer disadvantage to a greater extent than others, such as those from certain ethnic minority groups. It then examines how social work values frame social work responses to such issues at personal practice, agency and, potentially, wider campaigning levels in attempting to remedy this.

Intersectionality, 'a tool for analysing how different forms of oppression (e.g. ageism, racism, sexism, ableism, heterosexism, classism) interact and intersect to influence lived experiences' (Bernard, 2020), is seen as a key to understanding how discrimination and disempowerment compound the ability of some service users to access the resources they need. Intersectionality has also come to be recognised as an influential feminist approach for making sense of how inequalities manifest for individuals and groups. Crenshaw (1989) explained intersectional feminism as 'a prism for seeing the way in which various forms of inequality often operate together and exacerbate each other' (UN Women, 2020).

Building on the issues in the analysis of policy examined above, evidence of the barriers to participation and access to resources are identified. It examines how this relates to the social work values of Social Work England (2019a, 2019b) and the British Association of Social Workers (BASW) set out in the document it produced jointly with service user organisations on poverty and social work (British Association of Social Workers/Child Welfare Inequalities Group (CWIG), 2019).

The Effects of Poverty and its Relationship to Social Work

As can be seen from the policy and research review in this chapter, poverty and inequality are still major features of our society and have been since the end of the nineteenth century (Boyd, 1982). The effects of poverty are both psychological and physical. People can be viewed negatively if they live in poverty and are subject to potentially discriminatory responses. Dealing with these issues is at the core of the ethical and value base of the profession (BASW/CWIG, 2019).

Austerity policies in the early twenty-first century, linked to the individualisation of social problems in policies and practice, has meant that social work in England is now less focused on work with communities and challenging structural inequalities, but more with work with individuals, families and formal organisations, with an emphasis on resource management and risk rather than preventive or emancipatory practice. From the 1950s, social work methods have included casework based on psychodynamic counselling and psychotherapy, which operated alongside Marxist and emancipatory theories that became influential and informed radical social work approaches from the 1960s to the 1980s in the UK (Jones, 2015; Lavalette, 2011; Payne, 2021). The emphasis on social work that empowers communities living with poverty has diminished, while individualistic and marketised ideas have come to the forefront of government policies and funding mechanisms, and government-influenced sectors. This means that forms of individually focused task-centred work are in the ascendancy at the expense of community and radically based approaches. It is now more difficult for social workers to use community-based approaches, particularly if they are employed within local authority agencies (Littlechild, 2019; Jones, 2015; Lavalette, 2011).

How do professional social work values and ethics attempt to influence and change such views? The place of advocacy and challenging unfair discrimination experienced by individuals and groups living with higher rates of poverty are examined, particularly in relation to those in poverty who are even more vulnerable because of added pressures – e.g. living with/escaping from domestic violence (Siddiqui et al., 2013). Social workers engage with their service users' personal stresses, distress and loss on a very personal level, while at the same time engaging with the family, community and other agency networks to help strengthen and improve their lives. Social workers must also engage with the wider environment to ensure that professional support is made available to help provide effective responses to lack of resources. This requires social workers to use their skills and knowledge to help service users advocate for themselves in relation to the various issues affecting them, but also to advocate for them with relevant agencies and organisations when necessary. Social Work England's *Professional Standards* (2019), s.1.6 requires social workers to 'Promote social justice, helping to confront and resolve issues of inequality and inclusion' and s.3.13, to 'Provide, or support people to access advice and services tailored to meet their needs, based on evidence, negotiating and challenging other professionals and organisations, as required'.

A 2019 report from across six countries, led by ATD Fourth World and the University of Oxford (ATD, 2019: 4) produced in part by people with lived experience of poverty, identified the key dimensions of poverty as:

- disempowerment;
- suffering in mind, body and heart;
- struggle and resistance;
- institutional maltreatment;
- social maltreatment;
- unrecognised contributions;
- lack of decent work;
- insufficient and insecure income;
- material and social deprivation.

Social Work Values and Poverty

BASW/CWIG's *Anti-Poverty Practice Guide* (2019) draws on the 'Values and ethical principles' and 'Social justice' domains of the BASW *Code of Ethics*, emphasising:

- Social workers believe that poverty is not a character flaw. Instead, it is the denial of resources and opportunities to others and, consequently, social workers have a role to play in fair redistribution. In practice, this can be achieved through welfare advocacy and a rights-based approach to anti-poverty practice.
- Challenging unjust policies and practices, as a response to the ongoing period of austerity which can be argued to lead to unjust welfare benefit cuts and cuts to services.

(Webb and Bywaters, 2019)

BASW's *Code of Ethics for Social Work* (BASW, 2014) states that human rights and social justice serve as the motivation and justification for social work action, and sets out how BASW members (and all social workers) should advocate for social justice for people living in poverty and to work against all inequalities, which can result from uneven access to material resources and civic participation. In their *Anti-Poverty Practice Guide* (2019), BASW/CWIG argue that poverty causes harm to children, adults and families with care and support needs. Austerity exacerbated existing social inequalities and led to increasing poverty, which is associated with rising numbers of children in the care system, increased mental distress and illness, homelessness and addiction. This has made it necessary for social workers to adopt a multidimensional approach that addresses the need for equal rights to participation in society. BASW states that the profession strives to alleviate poverty and to work with vulnerable and oppressed people, taking account of intersectionality issues in order to promote social inclusion, drawing on the International Federation of Social Workers' Definition of Social Work (2014), which states: 'Principles of social justice, human rights, collective responsibility and respect for diversities are central to social work.' These are important issues in relation to social work values and practice, and are reflected in Social Work England's *Professional Standards*, 2019 (see: www.socialworkengland.org.uk/standards/professional-standards-guidance).

Rights and Advocacy in Relation to Social Justice for Those in Poverty

According to SWE's *Professional Standards* (2019), under s.1(2), a social worker must 'Respect and promote the human rights, views, wishes and feelings of the people I work with, balancing rights and risks and enabling access to advice, advocacy, support and services'. Under s.1(6), a social worker must 'Promote social justice, helping to confront and resolve issues of inequality and inclusion' – e.g. by aiding and supporting service users' and carers' self-help and self-advocacy groups, campaigning with service users' groups on health and childcare provision in local areas, making representations to managers and councillors in local authorities, and managers and Board members of other providers, and supporting them in accessing complaint procedures. Whistleblowing may also be a relevant to this (see Chapter 15).

With particular regard to advocacy, s.3(13) highlights the duty to 'Provide, or support people to access advice and services tailored to meet their needs, based on evidence, negotiating and challenging other professionals and organisations, as required' through, for example, Child Poverty Action Group, MIND, Shelter, Age Concern, welfare rights advice organisations, Citizens Advice, housing associations/local authorities, etc.

Anti-oppressive Practice and Black, Asian and Minority Ethnic (BAME) Groups

A key area for social work in many countries is that of anti-oppressive practice. In England, people from Black, Asian and Minority Ethnic groups are more likely to live in deprived areas and be poorer (Child Poverty Action Group, 2017); health benefits and social care systems can then amplify and compound these inequalities. Such groups are also subjected to a greater degree to the control elements of, for example, mental health work, in being detained under the *Mental Health Act 1983* (see also Chapter 15), in child safeguarding and youth justice, and in the looked after children system where there exists a disproportionate number of children and young people from ethnic minorities, particularly certain groups of BAME children (GOV.UK, 2017 (Lammy Review); Lankelly Chase Foundation, 2014; Littlechild, 2012; see also Chapter 10). In addition, in order to fully understand different BAME communities' experiences of mental health problems and of the services provided, it is necessary to consider the 'intersectionality' of other aspects of identity and shared social circumstance such as gender, age, religion, disability, health and location (Lankelly Chase Foundation, 2014) and LGBTQ+ issues. The International Federation of Social Workers' (IFSW) statement (2014) relating to intersectionality informs on this:

> Structural barriers contribute to the perpetuation of inequalities, discrimination, exploitation and oppression. … reflecting on structural sources of oppression and/or privilege, on the basis of criteria such as race, class, language, religion, gender, disability, culture and sexual orientation, and developing action strategies towards addressing structural and personal barriers are central to emancipatory practice …

In addition to advocacy and making representations individually with and for service users and carers, social workers need to make efforts to get to know local communities in order to reduce disempowerment and lack of access to support by enabling better inclusion for them there.

The Child Welfare Inequalities Project (CWIP) Final Report examined the links between socioeconomic circumstances and state interventions, and found that social workers and their managers had difficulties accessing and using data about their local communities (Bywaters, 2020). Furthermore, some social workers had exhibited stigmatising narratives about their local areas and lacked understanding about their areas' strengths, which does not reflect social work's core values. BASW sets out how agencies and teams need to give more credence and value to knowledge about how to maximise local income-support services, work with anti-poverty organisations, relief services and community informal support, to include third-sector providers, religious organisations and others that people draw on for support. What social workers can do is to consider how they can support this in their agencies, teams and in their personal practice, including in the ways suggested by BASW.

The BASW/CWIG *Anti-Poverty Practice Guide* (2019) has examples of co-location of income maximisation personnel in duty teams and social workers working in collaboration with local food banks. However, it also points out how the relative lack of partnerships with housing, employment and poverty relief agencies is in contrast to the attention more frequently paid to collaboration with health, education and therapeutic services, although poverty is so often the common experience of those needing services.

The guide sets out how social workers can more readily recognise themselves as part of the communities they serve and to get to know the area better, and appreciate and liaise with the resources available there. It states that it is 'evident that established individual casework models can only achieve specific impact when people's needs are driven by wider systematic patterns of poverty and socioeconomic hardships' (BASW/CWIG, 2019: 18).

Chapter Summary

This chapter has:

- examined the importance of social policy considerations on the relief of poverty and the impact on individuals and groups in society;
- analysed the ethics and values relevant to working with service users impacted by poverty;
- examined how intersectionality and discrimination against service users can compound disadvantage;
- examined how social workers can best represent services users' rights and interests and the application to social work practice.

Exercises

1. What reforms do you consider necessary to reduce poverty in the UK and why?

2. Consider how thinking on social work values, ethics, skills and methods for working with people in poverty and disadvantage in the following situations can aid a social worker intervene most effectively where:

   a) a BAME older person who is finding it hard to make ends meet living on the benefits that they receive, and finding it difficult to access the hospital treatment may need due to appointments being cancelled, and not being able to use transport to get to the hospitals;

   b) a young person who is leaving care, who is concerned or worried that they have nowhere to go to, little prospects of employment and concerns about not being able to live on the benefits they will receive;

   c) a woman from a BAME community who has been suffering domestic violence, who is being controlled by her partner, so has no friends and no financial resources of her own, and who is worried where she will be able to live with her two young children, where they would go to school;

   d) a young person from a BAME community in a disadvantaged area who says he was unfairly treated by the police when being stopped on suspicion the previous night.

   List the ways the social worker might go about helping service users/carers to be assertive with relevant agencies and/or the social worker doing this on their behalf and advising on/using complaints procedures.

   List what you would want from a social worker if you were one of these four service users in terms of their skills/attitudes ...

   Answers can be found in the Appendix.

Further Reading

Dermott, E. and Main, G. (2018) *Poverty and Social Exclusion in the UK: Vol. 1: The Nature and Extent of the Problem.* Bristol: Policy Press.

Part 5

Report Writing and Court Skills

21

Report Writing for Social Workers

Chapter Objectives

By the end of this chapter, readers will be able to:

- understand the importance for social workers of developing good report-writing skills;
- identify the different types of reports that social workers can be required to write;
- understand the benchmarks for good report-writing skills and their importance for social work practice.

Introduction

Report writing is an essential part of a social worker's role and the need to develop good report-writing skills is critical for effective practice. This chapter examines the reasons why it is crucial for social workers to learn these skills, examines the benchmarks for good report writing, the information that must be included in the different types of reports that social workers may have to write and the reasons why. Social work reports are often written for the courts and, over the years, courts have sometimes criticised them for being poorly written, failing to address the relevant issues required and failing to provide sufficient evidence to justify the recommendations made. Badly drafted reports can also lead the courts to question whether poor communication skills have adversely impacted on the relationship between the social worker and service user. Courts will, however, compliment well-drafted reports that provide them with the information they need, in the form they need it, and their value in the court's decision-making process. Extracts from a report, which will usually name the social worker providing it, will be included in the court's judgment.

It is important to remember that the reports that social workers write may be read by a wide range of different people and organisations, including lawyers, magistrates, judges, service users, line managers, other professionals providing evidence to the courts, as well as inspectorates such as the Audit Commission and Ofsted. They may also be read by complaints managers and the Local Government and Social Care Ombudsman (LGSCO) and by safeguarding review panels (Chapter 7). It is imperative to keep the potential audience in mind when drafting reports.

The Importance of Good Record Keeping

Report writing is dependent on good case recording. Record keeping is a legal requirement and essential, as it is not only a record of the relationship between the service user and social worker, but it is necessary for accountability and should provide evidence of the interaction with other agencies. Social workers must ensure that their records are robust, are made contemporaneously (*M and N (Children: Local authority gathering, preserving, and disclosing evidence)* [2018] EWFC B74) and include an analysis of what was done and why. The information contained in the case records also provides evidence, not just for the courts, but for managers, complaint handlers, inspectors, serious case reviews and as evidence in public inquiries. Research has shown that the quality of case records will impact on outcomes and decision-making (Preston-Shoot, 2003; Cumming et al., 2007).

Social Work England's *Professional Standards Guidance* (April 2020) states, in relation to record keeping:

> Maintaining accurate, clear, objective, and up-to-date records is an essential part of social work. Documenting decisions and actions provides a clear record of work with people. These records are open to scrutiny and help to provide a continuity of support if people are transferred between social workers. They can help to protect people and social workers.

Note that the SWE's *Professional Standards* are accurate at the time of publication, but are subject to periodic review and their website should be checked for any changes. See also: BASW (2020) The Right Side of Regulation: Recording with Care.

Remember that the Data Protection principles apply to both the content and access to them (Chapter 4).

Thought Box

Who has the right of access to a service user's case records?

Good record keeping is dependent on the following requirements. They must:

- be clearly written and 'jargon free';
- contain only relevant information;
- be accurate;
- make a distinction between facts and opinion;
- record the wishes, feelings and views of service users;
- contain an analysis of what was done and why.

Thought Box

How do you distinguish between fact and opinion, and why is it important to make this distinction?

It was noted in the Victoria Climbié Inquiry: Report of an Inquiry by Lord Laming (GOV.UK, 2003) that Victoria's wishes and feelings were almost entirely absent from her own file.

What Reports are Social Workers Required to Write?

This will be determined by the area of social work practice. Social workers in children and family services can be expected to have to write the following reports, all of which require knowledge and application of the provisions in s.1 of the *Children Act 1989* as all family courts in cases involving children must apply them.

Section 7 of the *Children Act 1989* gives the family courts the power to request a local authority to provide a 'welfare report' to help inform decision-making in private law actions under s.8 of the CA 1989. Section 8 cases (private law cases) involve disputes about where and with whom children should live, have contact with and about aspects of their upbringing which are the subject of dispute (Chapter 6). The court can decide whether the report should be made orally or in writing, and will set out the matters it wants addressed. It is important to note that research by CAFCASS and Women's Aid in

2017 (CAFCASS, 2017) estimated that 62 per cent of private law cases involved domestic abuse allegations. The Family Procedure Rules (PD 12J) sets out the rules that the court must follow in such cases and these rules must be adhered to by social workers too (see: www.justice.gov.uk/courts/procedure-rules/family/practice_directions/pd_part_12j).

The Family Procedure Rules (FPR) 2012 (PD16A, Part 6, updated January 2017) set out the following duties that social workers (called 'officers') writing s.7 reports owe the court (see: justice.gov.uk/courts/procedure-rules/family/practice_directions/pd_pt_16a).

9.2

The officer must make such investigations as may be necessary to perform the officer's powers and duties and must, in particular –

(a) contact or seek to interview such persons as appear appropriate or as the court directs; and

(b) obtain such professional assistance as is available which the children and family reporter thinks appropriate or which the court directs be obtained.

9.3

The officer must –

(a) notify the child of such contents of the report (if any) as the officer considers appropriate to the age and understanding of the child, including any reference to the child's own views on the application and the recommendation; and

(b) if the child is notified of any contents of the report, explain them to the child in a manner appropriate to the child's age and understanding.

9.4

The officer must –

(a) attend hearings as directed by the court,

(b) advise the court of the child's wishes and feelings,

(c) advise the court if the officer considers that the joining of a person as a party to the proceedings would be likely to safeguard the interests of the child,

(d) consider whether it is in the best interests of the child to be made a party to the proceedings, and if so, notify the court of that opinion together with the reasons for that opinion; and

(e) where the court has directed that a written report be made –

    (i) file the report; and

    (ii) serve a copy on the other parties and on any children's guardian, in accordance with the timetable set by the court.

The social worker preparing the report is obliged by rule 16.33 FPR to consider the principle that delay is prejudicial to the child's welfare (s.1(2); CA, 1989) and the provisions in the welfare checklist (s.1(3); CA, 1989). All reports in family proceedings must be cross-referenced to other relevant reports, such as carer assessments, and reports from professionals who know the child and/or family, etc.

Section 37 of the *Children Act 1989* states that in family proceedings concerning the welfare of a child where it appears to the court that it 'may be appropriate for a care or supervision order to be made', the court can order the local authority to investigate the child's circumstances. This requires the LA to provide a report for the court that considers whether they should apply for a care or supervision order, or provide appropriate help to the child and family, or take any other action. If a decision is taken not to apply for a care or supervision order, the LA must inform the court why they have reached that decision, what, if any, help they will provide, or other action they have taken or propose to take.

Under s.37(4), the information must be provided to the court 'before the end of the period of eight weeks beginning with the date of the direction unless the court otherwise directs'. See: Court Orders and pre-proceedings for Local Authorities (DfE, 2014).

Child and Family Assessment Reports

The purpose of Common Assessment Framework (CAF) assessments is to gather sufficient information about the child and family to inform decisions about whether a child is a 'child in need' (s.17, *Children Act 1989*) and what, if any, help and support is required. A copy of the CAF assessment report must be provided to parents/carers and shared with children where this is appropriate. The child's and family's needs must be identified, and the improvements that are needed to bring about change and how this can be achieved. It must also have clear recommendations and conclusions; any disagreements should be recorded. The family must also be told that they have a right to complain and how this can be done. See: Chapter 1, Assessing need and providing help, in *Working Together to Safeguard Children: A guide to inter-agency working to safeguard and promote the welfare of children* (2018, updated 2020); available at: https://assets.publishing.service.gov.uk/government/uploads/system/uploads/attachment_data/file/779401/Working_Together_to_Safeguard-Children.pdf

Adoption Reports

The requirements for the structure and content of adoption reports (see Chapter 8) are set out in detail in Practice Direction 14C: Reports by the Adoption Agency or Local Authority (which supplements Part 14, rule 14.11(3) of the *Family Procedure Rules 2010* (Practice Directions set out the rules for how the court works). They can be accessed from: www.justice.gov.uk/courts/procedure-rules/family/practice_directions/pd_part_14c

Reports for Care and Supervision Orders Applications

When a local authority is concerned that a child may no longer be safe if they continue to live with their family, a legal planning meeting will be convened with the social worker, their manager and the LA's solicitor. The solicitor will give legal advice as to whether the threshold criteria in s.31 of the *Children Act 1989* is met (see Chapter 7) before making an application to the court for a care or supervision order. If the local authority decides that the parents should be given further time to demonstrate that they can improve the care they are giving their child(ren), a *letter before proceedings* will be sent to the parents warning them that if the care does not improve, care proceedings will be initiated. It will set out the LA's concerns about the child's care, summarise the support that is provided, what the parents need to do, the help they will receive and the timescale for improvement. A *letter of issue* is sent to parents when the local authority decides that the threshold criteria has been met, it is in the child's best interests to be removed and placed into the care of the LA and they intend to initiate care proceedings (Court orders and pre-proceedings for Local Authorities (DfE, 2014)). Parents are advised to seek legal advice; free legal aid is available which is not means tested.

In care and supervision cases, the Public Law Outline applies (see Chapter 7). This is the legal framework that sets out how care and supervision cases should be managed. The key aims are to reduce delay by:

- strengthening judicial management of cases;
- ensuring that cases are better assessed before going to Court through the introduction of a pre-proceedings framework;
- narrowing the issues in dispute and to try to resolve these at an earlier stage;
- reducing the amount of written material and oral evidence in proceedings.

See: Practice Direction 12A – Care, Supervision and other Part 4 Proceedings: Guide to Case Management at: www.justice.gov.uk/courts/procedurerules/family/practice_directions/pd_part_12a.

In LA applications for care and supervision orders, the social worker must write an initial statement setting out the evidence explaining why the LA wants the court to make an order. Parents must be given the opportunity to respond and can provide relevant witness statements in support of their opposition to the LA's case. All papers are filed with the court and served on the parties to the proceedings. An initial court hearing, called a *case management hearing*, will be held which could result in the judge granting in Interim Care Order (s.38). An Interim Care Plan will set out where the child should live (e.g. foster care) and other arrangements that should apply for the duration of the order (e.g. contact).

The court can require assessments to be completed – e.g. parenting assessments, psychiatric assessments, drug and alcohol work – and will set a time frame for the proceedings to be managed. Once completed, the assessments must be filed with the court. The LA will then start the 'parallel planning process', which requires the social worker to assess and plan different options for the care of the child in parallel with each other – i.e. returning the child to the family; placing the child with other family members, whether special guardianship is relevant, and exploring the need for adoption or other long-term care such as fostering. This will require assessments of the parents and relevant family members. A family group conference will be held (see, for example, Action for Children: family group conferencing) and a viability assessment made up of any family members put forward as potential carers for the children. If this is a possibility, a full special guardianship assessment (also known as connected persons or kinship care assessment) will be made. If there are no viable family members, the LA will explore alternative options such as long-term foster care or adoption.

The social worker will write the *Final Evidence Statement*, based on the assessments that have been undertaken. When this has been filed, the children's guardian (CAFCASS; see Chapter 6) will file their report, and the parents will also submit their statements. An *Issues Resolution Hearing* will then take place to narrow any 'matters in dispute' and for the parties to try to see if an agreement can be reached that avoids the need for a full *Final Hearing*. Oral evidence may be heard at this hearing. If agreement is not reached, the final hearing will hear oral evidence from the parents, the social worker, the children's guardian and expert witnesses (e.g. psychiatrists, paediatricians, etc.). At the end of the hearing, the judge will decide whether to make a placement order, a full care order, a supervision order, a special guardianship order, or no order.

Practice Direction 12A (see above) requires the following documents to be annexed in an application for a care or supervision order filed with the court.

Social Work Chronology

A chronology (in both child and adult safeguarding cases) is a factual record (*not* opinion) of what happened and when. It includes key dates in the person's life in date order – e.g. date of birth, important life events and changes – key interventions, e.g. assessments, reviews, hearings, investigations (e.g. under s.41 of the *Children Act 1989* and s.42 of the *Care Act 2014*), and any medical interventions. It also includes the views of other professionals and work undertaken with the child or adult.

In *Re E and Others (Minors), Care proceedings* [2000] 2 FLR 254 FD 20, Bracewell J stressed that every social work file should contain a running chronology of significant events, which should be kept up to date so that 'serious and deep-rooted problems' can be identified. This judgment has important implications for social work record keeping.

Social Work Statements and Genograms

Social works statements should include the following:

- an analysis of risk and protective factors;
- a child impact analysis;

- an analysis of parenting capability;
- an analysis of wider family and friends' capability (the SWET genogram, which is mandatory, although the format may be adapted).

See: PSPD – Resources and Tools: Drawing a genogram at: https://practice-supervisors. rip.org.uk/wp-content/uploads/2019/11/Drawing-a-genogram.pdf

Care Plans

Section 31A of the *Children Act 1989* provides that when a court is deciding whether to make a care order, the court is required to consider the following permanence provisions of the plan.

(a) such of the plan's provisions setting out the long-term plan for the upbringing of the child concerned as provide for any of the following—

    (i) the child to live with any parent of the child's or with any other member of, or any friend of, the child's family;

    (ii) adoption;

    (iii) long-term care not within sub-paragraph (i) or (ii);

(b) such of the plan's provisions as set out any of the following—

    (i) the impact on the child concerned of any harm that he or she suffered or was likely to suffer;

    (ii) the current and future needs of the child (including needs arising out of that impact);

    (iii) the way in which the long-term plan for the upbringing of the child would meet those current and future needs.

The SWET template includes a section entitled: 'The proposed s.31A care plan – the realistic options analysis'.

Reports for Adult Social Care

Social workers working in adult social care may be required to provide evidence to the Court of Protection under the *Mental Capacity Act 2004* (Chapter 13).

If the LA is making an application to the Court of Protection, the evidence that needs to be included can be accessed from the following documents, which are available from the COP website (the LA lawyers will advise on what needs to be included):

- evidence for the application (COP1; COP1A or COP1B);
- a witness statement (COP24);
- a mental capacity assessment (COP3).

An assessment report to accompany the information provided on the relevant forms is also required. See: Making a personal welfare application to the Court of Protection: Court of Protection guidance leaflet, which states:

> This leaflet will provide you with help about making a personal welfare application to the Court of Protection (the 'court'). It also explains what the Court does, what decisions it can make, the powers it holds and how it appoints a deputy to make personal welfare decisions on behalf of someone who lacks capacity.

(https://assets.publishing.service.gov.uk/government/uploads/system/uploads/attachment_data/file/714384/cop-gn4-eng.pdf)

An example of a COP witness statement can be accessed from: Form COP24: Give a witness statement about a person who lacks capacity:

www.gov.uk/government/publications/give-a-witness-statement-about-a-person-who-lacks-capacity-form-cop24

Reports for Mental Health Tribunals

Mental health social workers can be required to provide Social Circumstances Reports (SCR) for Mental Health Tribunals when they are considering requests to discharge patients from detention under the *Mental Health Act 1983*. Social workers can also be required, as can probation officers, to provide pre-sentence reports. A SCR is a statutory report that must be provided to a mental health tribunal, or a hospital manager's hearing by either a community-based (not a hospital-based) social worker, or a community psychiatric nurse when a person challenges their detention under one of the following provisions in the MHA 1983:

- detention for assessment under s.2; or
- detention for treatment under s.3; or
- subject to a Community Treatment Order under s.17A; or
- subject to a conditional discharge (ss.72–3);
- subject to guardianship under s.7.

The main purpose of the report is to advise the Tribunal on the level of support that could be provided in the community and whether such support would be adequate for the person concerned. Support includes family and medical support, financial support, accommodation, employment, etc.

The Tribunal Judiciary Practice Direction, Statements and Reports in Mental Health Cases sets out the *specific* requirements for all statutory tribunal reports. It must include the background and history, the proposed plan, an analysis of the risks, how they will be managed and who was consulted. A professional recommendation must be made about whether or not the application for discharge is supported. See the following website for more details: www.judiciary.uk/wp-content/uploads/JCO/Documents/Practice+Directions/Tribunals/statements-in-mental-health-cases-hesc-28102013.pdf

Unless instructed otherwise, the completed and signed report must be submitted to the mental health administrator at least three weeks before the date of the tribunal or hearing. If the person is detained under s.2 (a 28-day order), it must be provided 'as soon as practicable'. Forensic mental health social workers can also be required to prepare and present reports for tribunals, legal hearings and parole boards. See: *Best Practice Guidance* (DH, 2016) at: https://assets.publishing.service.gov.uk/government/uploads/system/uploads/attachment_data/file/569389/Forensic_SW_Capabilities.pdf

Youth Offending Teams (YOT) Pre-sentencing Reports

YOT pre-sentencing reports are required by officers of the YOT to provide the courts with information about the sentencing options available to them when they are sentencing a person who has pleaded guilty to an offence. The reports play an important part in the court's decision. The person will either be interviewed at home, at the YOT office or, if in custody, visited there. The parents/carers will be contacted to allow them to express their views. Information can also be obtained from a school or college, social worker (if there is one), doctor or youth worker where this is necessary. The report will include the following information:

- The person's attitude to the offence committed, the consequences and their risk of reoffending.
- Their personal circumstances.
- The sentencing options available to the court.

If the child is under 16 or the court requests this, the report must contain an assessment of the parents/carers. The report will be shown to the person, their parents/carers, their lawyers, the judge or magistrate (dependent on the court in which the person is tried), the court legal adviser, the CPS, YOT staff and the social worker if there is one. If a custodial sentence results, the unit where the person is sent will be provided with a copy of the report. The accuracy of the report can be challenged by the person or their lawyer at the court hearing (see Chapter 22).

What is the Role of the Social Worker in the Court Process?

The role of the social worker in the court process is as a witness – that is, to provide factual evidence. This will be set out in the report's chronology (see above).

The social worker's role is as an expert – that is, to provide opinion based on the facts. This requires an analysis of what the facts mean – e.g. the harm that has been suffered (fact) and an opinion of future risk of harm to the person/s involved. It will also require an opinion of the ability of the family or others to provide care, the needs of the child or adult at risk, and a care plan that sets out the best way of meeting those needs (including contact provisions). An analysis of the other options that have been explored must also be included. Sir James Munby, President of the Family Division for England and Wales, speaking at an Expert Witness Conference in 2013, said that, in his view, 'social workers are experts … they may not be experts for the purpose of Part 25 FPR (which sets out the duties of experts in civil proceedings), but that does not mean that they are not experts in every other sense of the word'.

The social worker's role is also as an advocate for the child or adult at risk, which includes setting out their wishes and feelings (if these can be ascertained), their life experiences and what help, if any, they need to be able to participate in the process – e.g. arranging a translator.

Report Writing: The Essential Requirements

All reports, for whatever purpose they are written, must be prepared using the relevant template where this is applicable. Writing a report can be a daunting task, especially in the early stages of a social worker's career. The following reference list should help:

- Check what criteria the report is required to meet – e.g. from relevant Practice Directions (see above).
- Always draw up a plan, a first draft and then edit it.
- Consult line managers and lawyers if this is appropriate.
- Identify the potential audience – i.e. who is going to read the report.
- Make sure it is up to date and not copied and pasted from another report.
- Consider each relevant person separately – e.g. child(ren) or adult(s) at risk.
- Be clear and concise (avoid writing over-lengthy reports as they may be criticised – see below) and do not use complicated terminology. Plain English is needed!
- Ensure that it is well structured, contains numbered paragraphs and relevant headings.
- It must be prepared specifically for the relevant court/tribunal or hearing.
- Make sure that it is relevant and addresses the questions that need to be answered.
- Do not include irrelevant or inappropriate information.
- Make sure it contains fact-based information.
- Ensure that it is evidence based and includes the sources used (attached to the report if relevant).
- Provide a rationale for the recommendation(s) made.
- Ensure that the rationale and recommendations are clear.
- Summarise the recommendations and findings you are making near the beginning of the document to ensure that the judge reads them.
- Get it checked by a line manager and/or the LA lawyer (if relevant).
- Proofread it before its submitted.
- Sign and date it, and file it with the court within the timescale required.

Remember: a report is not an academic essay, but presentation and analysis are crucial in both forms of written work. A well-structured report makes it easier to refer to in cross-examination (see Chapter 22).

If a previous report has been written addressing the same issues – e.g. an application for discharge from detention under the *Mental Health Act 1983* or a previous application for a care order – establish what has changed since it was written. If relevant, that information can be referred to in the current report, but that report should not be resubmitted, or attached to the new report, or parts of it cut and pasted into the new report.

Learning from Case Law

The following cases demonstrate the importance of good report writing to the outcome of cases.

Derbyshire County Council v *SH* [2015] EWFC B102

In *Derbyshire County Council* v *SH* the judge emphasised that expert reports are not written solely for the benefit of other professionals, lawyers and judges, but 'parents and other litigants need to understand what is being said and why'. He criticised the social work report as 'its meaning was obscured by the language used' and 'might just as well have been written in a foreign language'. He doubted that the litigant in the case would have understood it (the social worker was named in the report and his criticisms reported in the national press).

Another judge criticised a social worker's report as containing 'incorrect and inaccurate' evidence and, in concluding that a care order should not be granted, said that the social worker's evidence tended only to look at the negative aspects of the parents' behaviour and wrongly inferred that something was 'a concern' when it was not.

M and N (Children: Local authority gathering, preserving and disclosing evidence (2018) EWFC B74

In *M and N (Children: Local authority gathering, preserving and disclosing evidence)* the social worker's notes were not contemporaneous and their reliability was called into question. The judge said that it was 'difficult to overstate how unprofessionally prepared these notes were' and the LA had to withdraw their application for a care order.

A Local Authority v *M & Ors* [2017] EWFC B66

In *A Local Authority* v *M & Ors* the judge described the social work report as 'balanced and fair' because it identified both the positive and negative aspects of the mother's parenting skills and was 'focused, thoughtful and reflective'.

Re R (Children) [2013] EWCA Civ 1018

In *Re R (Children)* [2013], which involved an application for a care and placement order, the Court of Appeal said that the local authority and children's guardian must, in their reports, address all the options realistically possible and provide an analysis of the arguments for and against each option which 'is sufficient to drive the court to the conclusion that nothing short of adoption is appropriate for the child'.

Re J (A Child) [2015] EWCA Civ 22

In *Re J (A Child)* the judge said:

> It is vital that LAs, and, even more importantly, judges, bear in mind that nearly all parents will be imperfect in some way or other. The State will not take away the children of 'those who commit crimes, abuse alcohol or drugs or suffer from physical or mental illness or disability, or who espouse antisocial, political or religious beliefs' simply because those facts are established. It must be demonstrated by the LA, in the first place, that by reason of one or more of those facts, the child has suffered or is at risk of suffering significant harm. Even if that is demonstrated, adoption will not be ordered unless it is demonstrated by the LA that 'nothing else will do' when having regard to the overriding requirements of the child's welfare. The court must guard against 'social engineering'.

Thought Box

What do you understand by 'social engineering' and why is this term relevant to decision-making in child protection cases?

How legal decisions influence social work practice (de Silva, 2018) highlights some of the important decisions made by Sir James Munby, who was President of the Family Division from 2013 to 2018, which have made more rigorous demands on social workers in child protection and have implications for both social work practice and report writing.

Re B-S (Children) (2013) EWCA 1146

Re B-S (Children) provided guidance for local authorities on permanency planning which led to the issue of an updated SWET template in 2014.

Re D (A Child) (No.2) [2015] EWFC 2

Re D (A Child) (No.2) involved consideration of whether Child D should live with his parents or, if they were unable to care for him, whether he should live with another family member or be placed for adoption. A delay of ten months took place between Child D being removed from his parents and the final hearing because of the difficulty in arranging legal aid funding. It was described as 'unconscionable' that the parents, both of whom had learning disabilities, should have had to face an application for the placement of their child for adoption without the benefit of legal aid.

Re A (Child A) (2015) EWFC 11

In *Re A (Child A)* the court was very critical of both the social worker(s) and children's guardian. A's mother was in prison and A's father wanted A to live with him. The LA concluded that it was not in A's best interests to live with his father and made an application for a care and placement order. The court found that a proper assessment of the father had not been made, nor a robust analysis of the facts which underpinned the LA's case. Sir James Munby concluded that although the father 'may not be the best of parents' and 'less than a suitable role model', that was not sufficient grounds to justify making a care order 'let alone adoption'. A was placed in the care of his father. The judgment is a reminder of the fundamental principles which, he said, were increasingly overlooked by LAs.

1. *Fact-finding and proof.* The LA must prove, on the balance of probabilities, the facts on which it seeks to rely. Findings of fact must be based on evidence and not on suspicion or speculation. Sir James Munby said that allegations such as 'X appears to have' lied, that people have 'stated' or 'reported' things, and that 'there is an allegation' should not be used. If there is evidence to support the allegation, it must be stated that 'X lied' or 'he did Y'.
2. *Establishing the link between facts and the conclusion that the child has suffered, or is at risk of suffering, significant harm.* Sir James Munby reminded judges and practitioners of the judgment in *Re L (Care: Threshold Criteria)* [2007] 1 FLR 2050, para. 50:

Society must be willing to tolerate very diverse standards of parenting, including the eccentric, the barely adequate and the inconsistent. It follows too that children will inevitably have both very different experiences of parenting and very unequal consequences flowing from it. It means that some children will experience disadvantage and harm, while others flourish in atmospheres of loving security and emotional stability. These are the consequences of our fallible humanity and it is not the provenance of the state to spare children all the consequences of defective parenting. In any event, it simply could not be done.

Thought Box

Do you agree with the sentiment expressed?

GM v *Carmarthenshire CC* (2018) EWFC 36

In *GM* v *Carmarthenshire CC* the mother applied to the court to discharge a care order (under s.39 of the CA 1989) made in favour of her son (L) in 2015. The LA opposed the application, and the grounds were set out in a witness statement from the LA social worker which were described by the judge as 'extremely long' (44 pages) and 'long on rhetoric and generalised criticism but very short indeed on any concrete examples of where and how the mother's parenting had been deficient. Indeed, it was very hard to pin down within the swathes of text what exactly was being said against the mother.' The court also heard evidence provided by an independent social worker which concluded 'that the risks to L of a return home at this stage are too high and that he should have the opportunity to consolidate the evident progress he is making in his settled foster placement'. To support her conclusion, she made detailed reference to attachment theory: 'Attachment refers to the specific dynamic relationship that develops between an infant and their primary carer. During the first year or two of life children develop certain attachment patterns in response to the quality of caregiving they receive ... '

In his judgment, Mostyn J stated:

> A number of points may be made about this description of the theory. First, the theory, which I suppose is an aspect of psychology, is not stated in the report to be the subject of any specific recognised body of expertise governed by recognised standards and rules of conduct.

> Second, the theory is only a theory. It might be regarded as a statement of the obvious, namely that primate infants develop attachments to familiar caregivers as a result of evolutionary pressures, since attachment behaviour would facilitate the infant's survival in the face of dangers such as predation or exposure to the elements.

> For my part I would say with all due respect that I do not need a social worker to give me evidence based on this theory to help me form a judgment about L's attachments.

Thought Box

What lessons can be learned from these decisions? Do you agree with Mostyn J's criticism of attachment theory (see Shemmings, 2018 in the Further Reading section)?

Chapter Summary

This chapter has:

- provided an overview of the different types of reports that social workers are required to write and the important information they should contain;
- provided a checklist of the essential requirements of good report writing;
- examined some important court decisions relevant to social work practice in this area.

Exercise

Read the judgment in *GM* v *Carmarthenshire CC* (2018) EWFC 36 and consider its implications for report writing.

Answers can be found in the Appendix.

Further Reading

Shemmings, D. (2018) Why social workers shouldn't use 'attachment' in their records and reports. *Community Care*, 28 June.

Stevenson, L. (2018) Attachment theory evidence not admissible in care order case, judge rules. *Community Care*, 28 June.

22

Giving Evidence in Court

Chapter Objectives

By the end of this chapter, readers will be able to:

- understand the procedural rules that govern the court process and the obligations owed to the court by witnesses giving evidence in court;
- understand the importance of examination and cross-examination of witnesses in court decision-making;
- apply the skills necessary for social workers to be effective witnesses in the court process.

Introduction

Giving evidence in a court or tribunal for the first time can be an intimidating experience for many people, whatever capacity they are appearing in. For newly qualified social workers giving evidence in their professional capacity this is no exception. This chapter examines how an understanding of the court process, the obligations that witnesses owe to the court, the relevant rules that apply and knowledge of the skills that are required to be an effective witness can help allay the understandable fears that many have. Social work courses, including placement experience, should provide students with the opportunity to develop the necessary skills, whatever their future area of practice.

Preparation

Good preparation is vital. Many of the preparatory steps that witnesses should take before attending court are common sense but worth spelling out to avoid unwanted distractions and heightening anxiety on the day. Pre-court preparation includes reading and re-reading (several times if necessary) the report that will have been submitted to the court and that the judge, the lawyers and children's guardian involved in the case will already have seen (see Chapter 21). That report will form the basis of examination and cross-examination by the relevant lawyers and should be drafted to pre-empt critical questioning.

Good preparation also includes the following:

- check the date, time and place of the hearing;
- check how to get there and establish the journey time (allowing for potential delays);
- arrive in good time and check the list to establish in which courtroom the case is being heard;
- dress appropriately – i.e. professionally, smartly and comfortably;
- wear comfortable shoes as witnesses normally have to stand while giving evidence;
- switch mobile phones off;
- check the required etiquette for addressing a judge, magistrate or tribunal chair (ask your lawyer if necessary).

Addressing Judges, Magistrates and Tribunal Chairs

The accepted forms of address for the different categories of judges are:

> High Court judges should be addressed as My Lord or My Lady.
>
> Circuit judges should be addressed as Your Honour.
>
> District judges, magistrates and tribunal chairs should be addressed as Sir or Madam (or your worship).
>
> (www.judiciary.uk/you-and-the-judiciary/what-do-i-call-judge/)

Taking an Oath or Affirmation

Remember that all witnesses must take an oath or affirm that the evidence they are providing is the truth:

The Witness Oath is:

'I swear by ... (according to religious belief) that the evidence I shall give shall be the truth, the whole truth and nothing but the truth.'

The Witness Affirmation is:

'I do solemnly, sincerely and truly declare and affirm that the evidence I shall give shall be the truth, the whole truth and nothing but the truth.'

Remember, at the end of the court report there must be a signed 'statement of truth' (the SWET template states: 'The facts in this application are true to the best of my knowledge and belief and the opinions set out are my own').

Criminal Liability

Intentionally lying under oath is perjury (*Perjury Act 1911*), a criminal offence that carries a maximum prison sentence of seven years. The legal test requires proof that the lies had a direct impact on the trial (prosecutions are, however, rare).

Perverting the course of justice is an offence at common law. It involves the following types of behaviour: doing something deliberately to cover up a crime – e.g. destroying evidence; interfering with witnesses and/or jurors and intimidating judges. It carries a maximum sentence of life imprisonment. 'A large number of offences cover conduct, which hinders or frustrates the administration of justice, the work of the police, prosecutors and courts' (cps.gov.uk). (See Norman, 2015, which recounts a case where a 'bullying manager told a newly qualified social worker to lie on oath in child protection proceedings'.)

Contempt of court, which carries a maximum prison sentence of two years, 'happens when someone risks unfairly influencing a court case' (see: Contempt of Court: gov. uk) and *London Borough of Wandsworth* v *Lennard (Application for Committal)* [2019] EWHC 1552 (Fam).

Court Rules and Procedures

Social workers may be required to give witness evidence in a number of different courts or tribunals, including youth courts, magistrates' courts and the Crown Court for social workers working in youth offending teams; family courts for social workers working with children and families; the Court of Protection for social workers in adult social care; and Mental Health Tribunals for social workers in mental health services (see Chapter 21). Each has their own rules. One universal rule that applies in all cases is that it is the overriding objective of the court or tribunal to ensure that cases are dealt with 'justly and fairly'. Most courts do not sit with a jury. One important exception is the Crown Court. Coroners' courts can also sit with juries and social workers may be required to give evidence at an inquest following the death of a service user (see: www.cps.gov.uk/legal-guidance/coroners).

Youth Courts

The relevant rules and procedure are set out in Chapter 9. See also paras. 3D, 3E and 3G of the Criminal Practice Directions [2013] EWCA Crim 1631), The Advocates Gateway – Effective Participation of Young Defendants, Toolkit 8, 21 October 2013. In all criminal trials (which includes trials in the youth court) the defendant is presumed innocent until proved guilty; the prosecution has the burden of proving guilt. The standard of proof in all criminal cases is 'beyond reasonable doubt'.

> 1.1(1) Criminal Procedure Rules (2015) states:
>
> The overriding objective of this procedural code is that criminal cases be dealt with justly.
>
> Dealing with a criminal case justly includes—
>
> (a) acquitting the innocent and convicting the guilty;
> (b) dealing with the prosecution and the defence fairly;
> (c) recognising the rights of a defendant, particularly those under Article 6 of the European Convention on Human Rights [Chapter 2];
> (d) respecting the interests of witnesses, victims and jurors and keeping them informed of the progress of the case;
> (e) dealing with the case efficiently and expeditiously;
> (f) ensuring that appropriate information is available to the court when bail and sentence are considered; and
> (g) dealing with the case in ways that take into account –
>
> > (i) the gravity of the offence alleged;
> > (ii) the complexity of what is in issue;
> > (iii) the severity of the consequences for the defendant and others affected; and
> > (iv) the needs of other cases.

Conduct of the trial

The Judicial College *Youth Court Bench Book* (2017) sets out the procedural rules that apply to the conduct of cases in the youth court (available from: www.judiciaryuk). At the start of the trial, defendants are asked to confirm whether they plead guilty or not guilty. If they plead guilty, the court should, if possible, pass sentence on the same day. The sentence will take into account the YOT's report (either oral or written).

If a defendant pleads not guilty, the trial then proceeds. If the prosecution wishes to use evidence in the trial of the defendant's past bad behaviour, permission must be obtained from the judge. Section 101 of the *Criminal Justice Act 2003* sets out the grounds on which permission will be granted (see: Bad Character Evidence at: www.cps.gov.uk).

The prosecution lawyer will make an opening speech, setting out the allegations and a summary of the evidence against the defendant, including any areas of dispute and matters of law. The judge or magistrates will then invite the defendant's lawyer to set out their defence and identify the issues that will include a record of the police interview (this will have been sound or video recorded, but will usually be presented as a written summary). The prosecution will then set out to prove their case by producing relevant evidence, calling witnesses, reading statements of witnesses, and agreeing the relevant evidence with the defence.

When a prosecution witness is called to give evidence, they will be questioned by the prosecution lawyer and asked to give their account of what happened; this is called 'evidence in chief'. Once completed, the witness will then be cross-examined by the defence lawyer whose questioning will aim to discredit the prosecution's case by putting the defendant's version of events. However, any attempt to bully or harass witnesses should be stopped by the judge or magistrates. The prosecution will then (if appropriate) re-examine the witness to help clear up any inconsistencies arising from the cross-examination. Once completed, the prosecution will close their case. If it appears to the defence that the prosecution case is very weak, they can ask the court to agree that 'there is no case to answer'. If successful, this stops the need for the defence to put their case. However, it is rare for this to happen.

The Criminal Procedure Rules, 2015, Part 25.9(2)(f), states that:

at the end of the prosecution evidence, the court must ask whether the defendant intends to give evidence in person and, if the answer is 'no', then the court must satisfy itself that there has been explained to the defendant, in terms the defendant can understand (with help, if necessary) — (i) the right to give evidence in person, and (ii) that if the defendant does not give evidence in person, or refuses to answer a question while giving evidence, the court may draw such inferences as seem proper.

See: Adverse inferences (Crown Prosecution Service, 2018).

The defendant's lawyer will also call witnesses to provide evidence in support of the not guilty plea. Witnesses for the defence will give evidence in chief, be subject to cross-examination by the prosecution lawyer and re-examination by the defence lawyer. If the defendant agrees to give evidence, they will be subject to the same examination and cross-examination process as other witnesses. The prosecution will try to exploit any inconsistencies in their evidence. The judge or magistrates determine guilt or innocence and, if guilty, sentence. The procedure in the Crown Court follows the same order, but a jury determines guilt or innocence, and the judge passes sentence if the defendant is found guilty, taking into consideration any social work or other professionals' reports.

Family Courts

Cases that fall under the *Children Act 1989* cases are heard in the family courts which are situated in different locations around the country. Cases may be heard by magistrates, district and circuit judges or High Court judges depending on their level of complexity. The burden of proof is 'on the balance of probabilities' – that is, it is more probable than not. Most hearings are heard in private, but the press can usually attend; there are restrictions on what journalists can reports (see: www.gov.uk/government/publications/media-attendance-at-family-court-hearings-ex711#page=3). The judgments are usually published with the initials of the child/family. In January 2014, two sets of practice guidance were issued (Transparency in the Family Courts, Publication of Judgements and Transparency in the Court of Protection) which presume that expert witnesses (which includes social workers) will be named in the judgments 'unless there are compelling reasons not to'.

Procedure in the family court

The applicant's lawyer (in care order cases that is the LA or NSPCC) will make an opening statement and then call witnesses to give evidence in support of their case. This will include the social worker's evidence based on the written report submitted to the court and any expert witnesses – e.g. paediatricians, general practitioners, clinical psychologists, etc. The other parties to the case (which includes parents, the child through their guardian and, where relevant, grandparents) will cross-examine the applicant's witnesses (usually through their lawyers, although a party who is unrepresented can question witnesses too) and the applicant's lawyer will then re-examine if necessary.

Oral evidence will be heard from parents, social workers, the children's guardian and expert witnesses. Each of the parties in turn can make an opening statement and call witnesses who can be cross-examined by the applicant's lawyer. The applicant and the other parties can all make closing statements. The judge or magistrates decide whether any order should be made and, if so, which order – e.g. placement order, care order or supervision order.

The legal system recognises that children (under 18) and vulnerable adults need help and therefore special measures are put in place to help protect them. This includes 1) screening a witness from the accused, 2) giving evidence via a live link or 3) evidence in chief being video recorded and played to the court.

Layout of the family court
Judge/magistrates
Witness box

	Clerk of the court	
LA solicitor	Children's solicitor	Parents' solicitor
Social worker and manager	Children's guardian	Parents

The court room is 'a place where discipline is maintained with rules, procedures and codes of conduct which have to be followed' (Foster, 2017).

Reforms in the administration and practice of family justice are currently taking place (see: www.gov.uk/guidance/the-hmcts-reform-programme). This involves the provision for evidence to be submitted and shared electronically so that cases can be 'managed much more securely and effectively'. The first phase of a new digital system was introduced in January 2019 to allow LAs to submit C110a applications for care and supervision orders online and there has also been a change in the 'content and structure of the application to make it simpler and quicker for LAs to provide the right information to assist the gatekeeper (HMCTS legal adviser) in making their decision and reduce unnecessary delay'. See also the Family Justice Board's statement 'Priorities for the family justice system' (www.judiciary.uk/announcements/family-justice-board-statement-priorities-for-the-family-justice-system, December 2020) which reported the following initiatives to deal with the increasing number of delays in the family court:

> HMCTS has recruited approximately 900 additional support staff across all jurisdictions, with currently around 700 further appointments sought. Approximately £3.5m additional funding has helped Cafcass increase staffing levels to respond to record levels of open cases and a programme of recruitment to increase judicial capacity is ongoing.

For a discussion on the Family, Drug and Alcohol Courts (FDACs), see Chapter 17. Research by Brunel and Lancaster Universities (Harwin et al., 2011) found that they are 'more successful than ordinary proceedings in helping parents achieve abstinence from drugs and alcohol and have thus enabled more children to be reunified with their parents'.

The Court of Protection Rules and Procedure

The Court of Protection is an office of the High Court. Since 2017, cases are usually held in public but are subject to reporting restrictions and the names of the parties anonymised (see Chapter 14). The applicable rules are set out in the following Statutory Instrument:

The Court of Protection Rules 2017 No. 1035 (L. 16) Mental Capacity, England and Wales:

> Rule 1.1.(1) states: 'These Rules have the overriding objective of enabling the court to deal with a case justly and at proportionate cost, having regard to the principles contained in the Act.'

Rule 1.4.(1) 'The parties are required to help the court to further the overriding objective. (2) Without prejudice to the generality of paragraph (1), each party is required to—

(a) ask the court to take steps to manage the case if (i) an order or direction of the court appears not to deal with an issue; or (ii) if a matter including any new circumstances, issue or dispute arises of which the court is unaware.
(b) identify before issue if the case is within the scope of one of the case pathways and comply with the requirements of the applicable case pathway.
(c) co-operate with the other parties and with the court in identifying and narrowing the issues that need to be determined by the court, and the timetable for that determination.
(d) adhere to the timetable set by these Rules and by the court.
(e) comply with all directions and orders of the court.
(f) be full and frank in the disclosure of information and evidence to the court (including any disclosure ordered under Part 16).'

Rule 14.2 sets out the power of court to control evidence:

'The court may—

1. (a) control the evidence by giving directions as to—

     (i) the issues on which it requires evidence,
    (ii) the nature of the evidence which it requires to decide those issues; and
   (iii) the way in which the evidence is to be placed before the court,

2. (b) use its power under this rule to exclude evidence that would otherwise be admissible,
3. (c) allow or limit cross-examination,
4. (d) admit such evidence, whether written or oral, as it thinks fit, and
5. (e) admit, accept and act upon such information, whether oral or written, from P, any protected party or any person who lacks competence to give evidence, as the court considers sufficient, although not given on oath and whether or not it would be admissible in a court of law apart from this rule.'

See: *A Court of Protection Handbook* at: https://courtofprotectionhandbook.com/legislation-codes-of-practice-forms-and-guidance/ and 'Making a personal welfare application to the Court of Protection', COP Guidance leaflet.

8.3 of the Mental Capacity Act *Code of Practice* states that:

'An application to the Court of Protection may be necessary for:

• particularly difficult decisions
• disagreements that cannot be resolved in any other way, or
• situations where ongoing decisions may need to be made about the personal welfare of a person who lacks capacity to make decisions for themselves.'

Mental Health Tribunals

Mental Health Tribunals are governed by the Tribunal Procedure (First-tier Tribunal) (Health, Education and Social Care Chamber) Rules 2008 No. 2699 (L.16) Tribunals and Inquiries, England and Wales) available at: legislation.gov.uk. The rules specifically applicable to mental health cases are contained in Chapter 4 of the Rules. The patient (applicant) is entitled to attend the hearing (but the hearing can take place in their absence if they do not attend, and the tribunal is satisfied that they had the necessary notice). The patient is also entitled to be legally represented (legal aid is available without a means test) and to have a relative accompany them. Hearings are usually heard in the hospital where the applicant is a patient. Rule 38 (1) provides that 'all hearings must be held in private unless the Tribunal considers that it is in the interests of justice for the hearing to be held in public'.

A panel is made up of the tribunal chair (judge), who is normally a qualified solicitor or barrister specialising in *mental health* law, or a full-time *judge,* together with a medical member who is a psychiatrist but not employed by the hospital where the patient is being cared for, and a specialist lay member who has relevant professional experience in mental health (see the *Guide to Mental Health Tribunals* which is written for patients by the Royal College of Psychiatrists (2015) and is available on their website at: rcpsych. ac.uk). It includes a plan of the layout of the room where the hearing is held.

Witnesses and experts can be ordered to attend, but a person cannot be compelled to give any evidence or produce any document that the person could not be compelled to give or produce in a trial in a court of law. Although mental health tribunal hearings are usually heard in hospital rooms, they are, nonetheless, courts of law and part of the judicial process. The same rules apply to attendance, dress and behaviour as in all other courtrooms. Patients should be given a break during the hearing if it is requested. The procedure is more inquisitorial in nature (as opposed to adversarial); the medical member of the panel – i.e. a decision-maker) must undertake a medical examination of the patient. The social worker who has compiled the social circumstances report should arrange to see the patient before the hearing to provide the tribunal with any relevant up-to-date information which is not contained in the report that has been submitted.

> Para. 12.33 of the *Mental Health Act, Code of Practice* (2015) provides:
>
> It is important that other people who prepare reports submitted by the responsible authority attend the hearing to provide further up-to-date information about the patient, including (where relevant) their home circumstances and the aftercare available in the event of a decision to discharge the patient.

> Para. 12.41 provides:
>
> The Tribunal will normally communicate its decision to all parties orally at the end of the hearing. Provided it is feasible to do so, and the patient wishes it, the Tribunal will speak to them personally. Otherwise, the decision will be given to the patient's representative (if they have one). If the patient is unrepresented, and it is not feasible

to discuss matters with them after the hearing, the hospital managers or local authority should ensure that they are told the decision as soon as possible. All parties to the hearing should receive a written copy of the reasons for the decision.

For further discussion, see Chapter 13.

Giving Evidence in Court

> If you are called to give evidence in court, you must expect to go through rigorous questioning from the defence and, in some instances, your integrity may be questioned. Complex or hostile questioning from the defence or allegations of impropriety (improper behaviour) can make you feel that either you or the organisation is on trial rather than the defendant. If you do not prepare your case correctly or detail the facts properly you can do a disservice to yourself, the organisation and to the cause of justice.
>
> (Home Office, 2020)

The most important characteristics that witnesses need to display in the witness box are honesty, credibility, confidence, competence and the ability to remain composed. Credible witnesses are well-prepared, have good powers of recall, their report will stand up to scrutiny and they will not attempt to answer questions that go beyond their knowledge.

Note the following:

- Look at the lawyer/person asking the questions, but direct answers to the judge or magistrates (they are the 'decision-makers').
- Listen carefully to each question and think before answering.
- Ask the court for guidance if this is necessary.
- If seeking clarification of a question, ask the decision-maker if it can be repeated or rephrased.
- Decision-makers, not witnesses or lawyers asking the questions, decide whether a question has to be answered or not.
- If you don't know the answer to a question, say so.
- Do not assume the report you submitted has been read thoroughly.
- Speak clearly and slowly so everyone in the courtroom can hear (there are no microphones). Do not use jargon or technical terms. The proceedings are not recorded and therefore the decision-makers and the lawyers make notes (in long-hand!) when witnesses are giving evidence.
- Decision-makers are entitled to ask witnesses questions at any time during the proceedings.

Giving 'evidence in chief' should be straightforward, as the lawyer asking the questions will be representing the party the witness has been called to give evidence for.

However, do not be lulled into a false sense of security as cross-examination may not be so easy!

Surviving Cross-examination

The ability of the other party's lawyer to cross-examine witnesses, in both criminal and civil cases, is an important part of the adversarial process as it can expose weaknesses and untruths in a witness's evidence, as well as any flaws in the investigation. This may have important implications for the outcome of the case. It is regarded as necessary to ensure a fair trial. However, it is demanding and can appear to be intimidating as it can be used to try to discredit a witness's expertise. Although the LA's lawyers can object to questions they consider unfair, decision-makers have the final say about what questions can be properly asked and therefore require answering as discussed above.

Techniques used in cross-examination include the following types of questions (these techniques are not used when giving in evidence in chief):

- closed questions – i.e. those that can be answered with a simple yes or no – rather than open (those that require more than a one word answer) – e.g. the care plan is not carefully thought through, is it?;
- hypothetical questions – i.e. 'what if' questions – which are based on assumptions rather than facts, and are used to elicit an opinion;
- leading questions – i.e. ones that aim to manipulate, prompt or encourage a given answer – e.g. what would you do if . . . ?).

Do not be trapped into giving an answer to these types of question without considering the implications.

Interrupting witnesses when they are responding to questions is also a technique used. If this happens, look to the decision-maker for help.

Thought Box

Think of relevant examples of the different types of questions that can be asked and why they are considered a useful tool in the cross-examination process.

It is part of the core function and responsibility of family courts and lawyers to scrutinize and challenge the social work that underpins the removal of children from their families. . . . It is vital to protect families from poor social work, to protect children from poor parenting and to formally approve good protective social work and sanction local authority intervention. (Reed, 2012)

Knowing what to expect and knowing the contents of the report inside out and where to find the relevant part that is needed to answer a question are crucial. A copy of the report can be taken into the witness box, but additional notes cannot unless they were made around the time the events took place – i.e. they are deemed to be reliable evidence. However, the cross-examining lawyer is entitled to see a copy and if the note is contained in a file (which will usually be the case), the whole file must be given to the other side's lawyers, which may lead to further questioning. Ensure, therefore, that all the facts in the file have been accurately recorded. In any event, the children's guardian, who will also be represented, will probably have seen the file and taken copies before compiling their report.

The following are some important dos and don'ts when being cross-examined:

- Avoid taking lawyers' adverse comments personally. If an attack is made on professional expertise – e.g. the suggestion that a newly qualified social worker does not have sufficient expertise – a response should be given calmly and politely – e.g. by stating that the decisions were taken after detailed discussions with managers and the legal department, where appropriate.
- Take time to answer any questions and consider how detailed the response should be.
- If necessary, ask for time to think or, if relevant, to find the information in the report.
- Seek the help of the decision-maker (judge/magistrates) if necessary.
- Stick to the point that needs to be made.
- Avoid giving long and/or complex answers.
- Don't use jargon.
- Don't be defensive, aggressive or emotional.

Victims of Domestic Abuse

Section 65 of the *Domestic Abuse Act 2021* provides the following prohibition on cross-examination in person of victims of offences in:

- (a) proceedings in the family court,
  (b) proceedings in the Family Division of the High Court which are business assigned, by or under section 61 of (and Schedule 1 to) the Senior Courts Act 1981, to that Division of the High Court and no other, and
  (c) proceedings in the civil division of the Court of Appeal arising out of proceedings within paragraph (a) or (b);
- witness, in relation to any proceedings, includes a party to the proceedings.

See: www.legislation.gov.uk/ukpga/2021/17/section/65/enacted. See also: An adversarial court system that requires proof is a hard place to be for those who believe themselves to be, or who actually are victims of abuse (Phillimore, 2019).

'Winning or Losing' a Case

If the court decides not to make the order sought – e.g. does not grant the care order applied for, or order a patient to be discharged contrary to the advice given, or determines that a service user has capacity when the social worker's assessment found that they had not – this should not be taken as a criticism of the social worker's professional competence or integrity. The judge/magistrate is the ultimate determiner; it is not appropriate to regard the outcome as 'winning or losing'.

While the outcome of a court/tribunal decision may be the subject of an appeal, it is very rare for witnesses to have to attend an appeal hearing.

Chapter Summary

This chapter has:

- identified the procedural rules that govern the court process and the obligations owed to the court by witnesses giving evidence in court;
- explained the importance of examination and cross-examination of witnesses in court decision-making;
- examined the skills necessary for social workers to be effective witnesses in the court process.

Exercise

A is aged 44 years and was brain damaged in a road traffic accident when he was 14. He is also quadriplegic. He needs 24-hour care which until recently was partly provided for by his mother and father and the remainder by a care agency. A attends a day-care centre three days a week. The compensation he received from the accident is administered by the Court of Protection; his brother B is his deputy. C, his mother, suffers from Alzheimer's disease and can no longer provide the care that he needs. D, his father, has recently been diagnosed with Parkinson's disease and now struggles to provide the help that A needs. B has recently moved back to the family home and is trying to persuade D to transfer the house into his name.

The day-care centre recently complained that A was often dirty and hungry when he arrived at the centre, and bruising had been noted. The care agency reported to adult care services (ACS) that B often refuses to allow the carers entry to the home and they are concerned that he is abusing A. B denies this. There is also concern that B, who spends much of the day in the betting shop, is misusing A's money. C and D's daughter, E, lives 5 miles

(Continued)

away and visits frequently but cannot provide care regularly as she has three young children. She has expressed concern about A's care.

As a result of the concerns expressed, ACS undertook a safeguarding investigation and concluded that B should be replaced as A's deputy and either B should leave the family home and a 24-hour domiciliary care package put in place, or A should be cared for in an appropriate residential facility. B refuses to leave the home and denies that he has misused A's money. The family do not want A to live in a residential care home. They are seeking legal advice.

ACS are considering an application to the Court of Protection.

1. What information is it necessary to consider before making an application?
2. What assessments are required to be completed and by whom?
3. What should be included in the witness statement?
4. What should be done about the allegation that B is misusing A's money?
5. If an application is made to the COP and a hearing takes place, consider how you would answer the following questions put to you by the family's lawyer:

   a) What steps have you taken to try to resolve this dispute before making an application to the Court of Protection?
   b) You say that A lacks capacity to decide about his future care. What evidence do you have to support this?
   c) You say that B refuses to leave the family home. What steps should be considered to achieve this?

Answers can be found in the Appendix.

Further Reading

Davis, L. (2015) *See You in Court: A Social Worker's Guide to Presenting Evidence in Care Proceedings* (2nd edn). London: Jessica Kingsley.

Seymour, C. and Seymour, R. (2011) *Courtroom and Report Writing Skills for Social Workers* (Post-Qualifying Social Work Practice Guides). Exeter: Learning Matters.

Appendix

Suggested Answers to Exercises and Case Studies

Chapter 1: Exercises

1. What is judicial precedent and statute?
   Judicial precedent means that the judges in the courts stand by the previous decision of a case with similar facts. Statute is a formal legal document that has been passed by Parliament and becomes part of UK law.

2. What is the relevance of judicial precedent in relation to the hierarchy of the court system?
   The relevance of judicial precedence to the hierarchy of the court is to ensure consistency in the decision-making of cases brought before the courts. For example, the high court will follow a decision made by the appeal court or the Supreme Court.

3. What is a tribunal and how does it differ from a court?
   Tribunals are a less formal body of legal decision-making, but do decide cases before them as they include a panel of experts dealing in the area they are required. For example, a mental health tribunal will hear cases whereby a patient wishes to be discharged from their detention and treatment, apply to change a community treatment order or the conditions placed on the patient such as a 'conditional discharge' from hospital.

4. What is a judicial review?
   A judicial review is the process by which the administrative court checks the process by which the decision made by a public body is lawful. This is in relation to the process by which the decision was made. The court cannot alter the decision but can identify any errors in the decision-making process and ask the public body.

Chapter 2: Case study – Human rights

Consider the potential violation of human rights in this scenario. Are there any restrictions on those rights?

The following articles have potentially been breached against J and her family:

- *Article 6: by not informing J's parents that they could make an application to the Court of Protection for a decision on J's best interests and by not carrying out a thorough investigation into J's bruising. This right is absolute.*
- *Article 8: by restricting and limiting contact between J and her family. This is a qualified right.*
- *Article 5: deprivation of J's liberty based on the fact that she was not able to make the decision to go home. This is a limited right.*
- *Article 14: safeguarding decisions made on disability and not on best interests. These are qualified when used with the articles above.*

Chapter 3: Case study – Anti-discrimination

Identify what equality rights are being breached in the case of Yousef and Simon and in what form. Who is liable and what can be done, if anything?

Yousef is experiencing harassment based on his race from T. Yousef should discuss how T's comments are affecting him in his role with T. Carmel needs to speak to T and explain how she cannot have her employees subjected to any form of discrimination.

Carmel should then provide Yousef with any support he may need to continue his work.

S is potentially being directly and indirectly discriminated against based on the protected characteristic of gender reassignment. The gym management would have to show that their policy did not disadvantage transgender members and that it was a proportionate measure.

Chapter 4: Exercises

1. Does English law include a law of confidentiality and/or privacy?
   The law of confidentiality has been established through English common law. A law of privacy is not enacted in common law, but the UK has provided for a right to private life through the Human Rights Act 1998.

2. What changes has the *Data Protection Act 2018* brought and how does it impact on social work practice?
   Discuss the information provided in the chapter. For example:

   - *The introduction of the DPA was to ensure personal information stored about individuals was not misused.*
   - *Lord Laming's inquiry into the death of Victoria Climbié identified the potential for the free exchange of information being inhibited by the* Data Protection Act 1998.
   - *The 2018 government guidance states: 'the … Data Protection Act 2018, practitioners need to balance the common law duty of confidence, and the rights within the* Human Rights Act 1998, *against the effect on children or individuals at risk, if they do not share the information'.*

3. Consider the key points whether to share information against someone's wishes from the scenario.

There are two factors to consider here. Delia does have rights to privacy, but there is a safe-guarding issue here and the GP should explain to Delia the concerns regarding the violence and that he may need to share confidential information in order to protect her.

Second, regarding the contraceptive advice, the GP would need to follow the Fraser guide-lines and consider a Gillick competency test.

Chapter 5: Case study – Ethical principles

As the social worker involved in this case study, what ethical considerations might you use to reflect on whether you should be completely honest with the service user who is in mental distress that may help you to put in operation the apparently conflicting SWE requirements set out here?

Consider responsibility; how might the average person in the street view M – as responsible for his problems and therefore 'unworthy' of support, or otherwise?

Consider any interventions to help M. Do these support M's best interests and rights?

Are there utilitarian principles to consider concerning the rights of others? It may be that the social worker judges there are no risks to others; does this mean this consideration is irrelevant?

With regard to M's suicidal thoughts, at what point and how might the social worker try to agree with M about liaising with his GP about his concerns? Can the social worker argue that this is acceptable within utilitarian approaches 'for his own good' as applied to the law and SWE Standards?

What if M does not want the social worker to do this? Is it acceptable for the social worker and, if so, on what legal and SWE Standards grounds, should they contact the GP without M's knowledge? Virtue ethics would, within SWE Standards honesty requirements, say that the social worker would have to let M know if they were to do any of these things, even if he did not agree. If the social worker still decided to do this, should they tell him they were doing it? If so, why? If not, why not?

Might the social worker try to persuade M to accept them making a referral to other professionals – e.g. mental health agencies to provide appropriate support?

Utilitarianism might provide a perspective that if M does not do more to take responsibil-ity for his own condition, the social worker should concentrate time and effort on other people who are making more of an 'effort'. This can happen in the NHS where someone will not be offered an operation if they do not lose weight or stop smoking. What might the social worker's thoughts be on such a position?

The ethical issues and SWE Standards that are appropriate to evidence in this situation in assessing and responding to M's needs are:

1.2 Respect and promote the human rights, views, wishes and feelings of the people I work with, balancing rights and risks and enabling access to advice, advocacy, support and services.

The social worker needs to explore their concerns about the risks and fears that M is facing as openly and honestly as possible.

Other key issues relate to being 'open, honest, reliable and fair', and in how social workers will sensitively and respectfully engage with him to agree what these areas are:

> *1.3 work(ing) in partnership with people to promote their wellbeing and achieve best outcomes, recognising them as experts in their own lives*

and how they both might move forward together, in what ways and how, bearing in mind the social worker's duty to

> *2.3 Maintain professional relationships with people and ensure that they understand the role of a social worker in their lives.*

In having a high caseload, a social worker might need to determine how much time they can spend with him, how often they should do this, what to do if they see no changes, and determine how they can best raise and review these issues jointly with him.

The social worker needs to try to appreciate the concerns or even fears that M may feel about their involvement and how to address them, in terms of explaining their role and their concerns for him in a spirit of openness and shared decision-making, as required by the SWE Standards.

Chapter 6: Exercises

1. What changes have there been to the construct of a family in recent years?

   Examples of how families have changed include, for example, children parented by same-sex couples; children who have been born as a result of surrogacy; children living in one-parent families and some who have no knowledge or contact with their other parent; families with step-children/step-parents, etc.

2. In what ways do children live 'increasingly complex lives' and what policies are needed to give recognition to this?

   The impact of parental breakdown may result in children moving between two separate families, which may provide tensions. The impact of social media has resulted in the greater susceptibility to exploitation and bullying, etc. Children's voices need to be heard so that policy-makers can a) understand the problems and b) involve children in decisions about how they can be better protected – e.g. by regulating social media. The role of the Children's Commissioner is important here, too.

3. Identify the circumstances where the determination of whether a person has PR for a child is relevant to social work practice.

   Sections 2–4 of the Children Act 1989 *set out who has PR and what PR means in terms of the responsibilities that they owe to the children they have responsibility for. This includes well-being, safety, ensuring that they are educated, etc. They also have an important part to play in making decisions about medical treatment, etc. Section 3 states: 'parental responsibility' means all the rights, duties, powers, responsibilities and authority which by law a parent of a child has in relation to the child and his property.*

If the LA are involved with a child – e.g. because the child is a 'child in need' or because of safeguarding concerns, those with PR have a right to be involved in decision-making and are entitled to be legally represented in care proceedings.

4. Read the *R (on the application of G) v Southwark London Borough Council* [2009] UKHL 26 case report and explain why the court came to that decision.

   The court recognised that the Homelessness (Priority Need for Accommodation) (England) Order 2002 provided that children aged 16–17 without appropriate accommodation should be deemed in 'priority need' and, provided the other criteria were met, were entitled to assistance from a local authority housing department (see Chapter 19). However, an LA could not avoid their duty to accommodate under s.20 CA (as in this case) if the child fell within the relevant provisions in s.20, even if the housing department had an obligation to house them (a child accommodated under s.20 becomes a looked-after child and is therefore entitled to help when leaving care).

5. What is the 'no delay' principle?

   b)   The 'no delay' principle means any delay in making an order is likely to be detrimental to the child.

6. When working with safeguarding children, who is the primary client for the social worker?

   a)   The child(ren)

7. Who is the 'no order' principle aimed at?

   b)   The courts

8. How many principles are there in s.1 of the *Children Act 1989*?

   c)   3

9. Are all children with severe learning difficulties children in need under s.17, CA 1989?

   a)   Yes

10. Can parents who have a child aged 6 who falls within the definition of a child in need in s.17, CA 1989 refuse to allow their child to be assessed under the CAF?

    a)   Yes

11. Consider whether the following children are 'children in need' and, if so, which category in s.17(10) applies:

    1.   A: s.17(a)
    2.   B: s.17(c)
    3.   C: s.17(b)

Chapter 7: Exercises

1. Consider whether the harm is significant in the following scenarios and justify your decision by reference to the legal rules/decided cases:

   a)   A child aged 4 months is found with a broken wrist.

Yes, as it is unlikely to have been caused by any action other than abuse.

b) A child aged 6 months has bruising around the mouth.

Yes, as it is likely to be force feeding.

c) A child aged 2 has 20 random bruises of different ages around the knees and lower leg.

No, as it is likely to be random accidental falls.

d) A child aged 3 has serious burns on her face.

Yes, as it is more likely to be neglect rather than commonplace human failure.

e) A child aged 4 found wandering alone along a busy road.

Yes, as again it is more likely to be neglect.

Note: even if this satisfies the threshold criteria, the courts must still determine whether it is in child's best interests to be made the subject of a care or supervision order.

2. Read the decision in *A Local Authority* v *R–B* [2019] EWCA Civ 1560 and answer the following questions:

1. In what court was the case heard?
    The Court of Appeal.

2. What orders did the local authority ask the court to make?
    Care and placement orders.

3. If the court granted those orders, what would be the outcome for baby J?
    J would be subject to a care order and placed for adoption.

4. What decision did the court make?
    It ordered a new hearing of the case.

5. Why did the court reach the decision it did?
    The decision by the judge in the lower court was flawed as the judge had not given a full and reasoned judgment to support the decision.

Chapter 7 – Case study – Child protection

1. Identify the key legislation (including the specific sections) relevant to this scenario.

Refer to s.17: are the children considered to be children in need and known to the Social Services Department?

Can the children be supported at home? If so, what support would they need?

Does a s.47 investigation need to be initiated?

Convene a Child Protection Conference and agree any necessary action (refer to the Statutory Guidance). Draw up a child protection plan to safeguard the children.

Consider the need for emergency protection order (s.44) and prepare for the test period.

Explain an interim care order (s.38).

Consider a child assessment order if M and F refuse to cooperate.

Discuss s.31 care and supervision orders. Consider the two-stage test: 1) the threshold criteria (suffering or likely to suffer significant harm) and 2) what is in the child's best interests.

Consider the seriousness of the allegations made against F. Is there any relevant past history? Has there been any abuse or neglect? Are there signs of physical harm and the child being hungry? What is the concept of a 'reasonable parent' and how does it apply?

Consider any relevant family support that can be given.

In what ways are M and F not meeting E's needs? Consider whether more support is necessary.

Consider any possible criminal offence(s).

2. What do you think the LA should do and why?

In order to answer the question 'What do you think the LA should do and why' you need to consider the following:

Consider each child separately and in what ways, if at all, M and F are failing to meet the children's needs.

Discuss school's safeguarding duty and consider if the children are CiN under s 17 Children Act 1989 and whether they are known to Children's Services. Consider whether the children could be supported at home and the support that they would need to achieve this (S17 and Schedule 2 Children Act 1989). Consider whether any relevant support can be given by other family members.

Consider whether a S47 investigation needs to be initiated, what the criteria are and the possible outcomes. If so, make reference to the role of Child protection conferences and the (Statutory guidance). Explain the significance of Child protection plans. Consider whether there is a need for emergency protection (s44) and set out the test. Explain the criteria for courts making an Interim care order (s38).

Consider whether a Child assessment order is necessary if M and F refuse to cooperate with Children's Services.

Discuss S31 care and supervision orders, including the 2-stage test (i) the threshold criteria (suffering or likely to suffer significant harm and (ii) the child's best interests.

Consider the seriousness of the allegations made against F, any relevant past history involving abuse and neglect. Also consider the concept of the 'reasonable parent" (under 31). Consider whether any criminal offence/s have been committed and identify which.

Conclusion which addresses the questions asked.

Chapter 8: Case study – Achieving permanence for children in care

Identify the relevant law, ethics and social policy of this case study and explain how it applies to the facts. What human rights considerations are relevant here?

Outline the important sections of the ACA, s.1 paramountcy principle.

Explain what adoption is (permanency) and the possible alternatives to adoption – e.g. SGO and fostering.

Who has parental rights for the children? E does (ss.2–4 CA 1989), but it is unclear whether F and G do. The LA has PR for all four children as they are subject to a care order (s.31, CA 1989). Discuss the relevance of whether parental consent is needed or could be dispensed with. Explain placement orders. Consider continued contact with the family (the possibility of post-adoption contact, s.51A ACA).

Consider whether E can continue caring for A and B. What support might she be entitled to and what would be the legal status of the arrangement? Would a special guardianship order be applicable?

What is the relevance of C and D being of mixed race but foster being carers white? How much influence might this have on any possible adoption decision? Is there an alternative to adoption for them? Consider the relevance of how much contact parents have with the children and G being in prison.

What ethical issues should be considered? Refer to the BASW Code of Ethics and relevant provisions, and Social Work England's standards. Discuss the enquiry's findings on ethics and human rights considerations in the adoption process: adoption is a permanent transfer of PR to the adoptive parents. It is a 'draconian interference' with family life (refer to art. 8 of the ECHR). When can adoption be justified? Consider the importance that government policy places on permanency if it is in the child's best interests.

Chapter 9: Exercises

Look at the sentencing guidelines and decide what sentence you would give for the scenario described.

1.   *G and C have two children: P, who is 12 years old, and T, who is 16. They both live at home. YOT would work with both boys as P could be exploited under county lines and T may need to get away from the gang using a s.20 under the* Children Act 1989.

Chapter 10: Case study – Ethical issues for safeguarding child interventions

How should the rights of M and A be balanced against the rights and needs of their children described in this case study?

As a guide, use Figure 10.1 to consider the key issues that need to be taken into account for each person.

   Look at respecting and valuing each person involved in this situation, while protecting the interests and rights of the most vulnerable. This means communicating with each person involved as openly and honestly as possible, considering this within a hierarchy of needs where the rights of each may be in competition. Demonstrate how the three key ethical ideas set out in Chapter 3 might be relevant.

   The best interests, safety and well-being of the children are of paramount importance, working with parents as far as possible, where this does not conflict with the children's safety and well-being to help improve their and the children's situation.

   Look at M's rights given that we know she is subjected to domestic violence, is disempowered and finds it difficult/impossible to be open with professionals, particularly because of fear that the children will be taken away from her and she may be held accountable for the abuse, particularly when she is vulnerable because of her mental health problems.

   Finally, this means ensuring that the work taking place does not put M and/or the children at greater risk by any actions of the social worker and how they approach the work with her and A, and who has what information, at what point, to ensure the plans immediately and in the longer term are put into place to meet primarily the needs of the children.

Chapter 11 – Exercise

In *R (on the application of Cornwall Council (Respondent))* v *Secretary of State for Health* [2015] UKSC 46, which Council had to pay PH's care costs when he reached 18 and why?

   Wiltshire, because that is where he was living when he became 18.

Chapter 11: Case study – Adult social care: working with families: the legal, ethical and social policy considerations

Consider the legal, ethical and social policy of the people involved in this case study.

Identify the relevant provisions in the Care Act 2014 *which include well-being and the right to refuse an assessment. Discuss the relevance of C's short-term memory loss and whether a* Mental Capacity Act *assessment should be conducted.*

Consider the possibility of whether an advocate is needed.

Consider the need for the daughter to be assessed because of the impact on her.

Consider whether other people could be involved.

Examine the right of carers under the Care Act.

Consider whether there are any safeguarding concerns and whether a s.42 Care Act *investigation might be appropriate.*

Discuss the rules about who pays for social care.

What is the relevance of the son's refusal to help when the law does not impose on him a legal obligation?

Discuss the ethical issues with reference to SWE and BASW principles and relevant social policy issues discussed in the chapter, including the right to self-determination, the cultural issues and family conflict.

Chapter 12: Case studies – Safeguarding adults at risk of harm

Identify the legal rules relevant to the scenarios in the case studies and discuss how they might be used (if at all) to safeguard the people involved.

Mr A: *Discuss the concept of self-neglect; the right to make decisions (including unwise decisions) if that person has capacity. Consider whether A needs safeguarding with reference to the relevant legislation and guidance. Consider the rules that apply to gaining entry if A refuses access to his property.*

Ms B: *this scenario requires a discussion about safeguarding and whether s.42 CA 2014 is triggered. Consideration must be given to the extent of B's learning disability and whether she can be involved in decision-making. A discussion of the role of the COP in decisions about future care should also be included.*

Mr C: *discuss the law in relation to forced marriage and relevant case law described in the chapter. Consider whether C has the capacity to make decisions (and the test relevant to determine this). Consider whether social workers have a duty to safeguard Mr C by reference to the rules set out.*

Mrs D: *consider who owns the care home and why this is relevant (discuss whether the care home is a 'public body' within the definitions in the* Human Rights Act *and* Care Act*).*

Consider the relevance of whether Mrs D is funded (in part or fully) by the LA.

Consider what constitutes abuse and whether it includes giving people medication unnecessarily. Identify the circumstances when (or if) medication can be administered covertly. Consider the human rights issues that are involved. Identify whether the care home has a complaints procedure and make reference to the role of the Care Quality Commission's home complaints procedure.

Mr E: *Discuss the concept of financial abuse and whether this abuse should trigger a safeguarding enquiry. Consider holding a discussion with care agency and ask how they vet staff? Question whether DBS checks been made and whether this abuse should be reported with reference to the Safeguarding Vulnerable Groups Act 2006. Consider whether this should be reported to the police.*

Ms F: *discuss Ms F's right to choose with reference to the relevant legal rules and ethics capacity as she jointly owns the home and the right to have her voice heard.*

Consider whether to discuss the implications of this with Ms G and whether Ms G and Ms F are willing to discuss this together, either with a social worker or specialist mediator.

Consider whether Ms G has a legal obligation to provide care for Ms F (she does not).

Consider whether there are alternative solutions available with reference to their finances given that they jointly own the home – e.g. buying in night care.

Chapter 13: Case study – Mental Health Act 1983 provisions study

1. What specific legislative provisions in the *Mental Health Act 1983* are relevant to this scenario relating to assessment, detention and treatment?

s.1: is S suffering from a mental disorder? Define, giving details of the nature and degree of the disorder.

Who applies for admission to hospital – the nearest relative or the AMHP?

The decision should be supported by two relevant doctors.

Consider voluntary admission.

s.2 as the patient is not known to MH services.

s.3 may follow detention for treatment.

s.4 for emergency detention.

ss.135–6.

CTO, s.117, if following s.3.

The County Court can appoint someone as the nearest relative (NR) if the patient does not have one. The patient can nominate someone they would like to be the NR. However, it will be up to the court to decide who the most suitable person is.

   The approved mental health professional (AMHP) should try to identify who the nearest relative (NR) is during a mental health assessment.

2.   Briefly explain what the terms below mean and their possible relevance to the facts in the scenario:

   a)   approved mental health professional;
   b)   community treatment order;
   c)   responsible clinician.

Approved Mental Health Professional

An AMHP can be a social worker, a psychiatric nurse, an occupational therapist or a clinical psychologist. A doctor cannot be an AMHP. The AMHP is acting as an autonomous professional rather than as an agent of their employees, whether this is a local authority or an NHS Trust. An AMHP cannot be told by a manager to 'go out and section' someone. All they can be asked to do is to conduct an assessment under the MHA and reach their own conclusion based on all the evidence.

Community Treatment Order

A CTO is an order made by the responsible clinician. It sets out the terms under which a person must accept medication and therapy, counselling, management, rehabilitation and other services while living in the community. It is implemented by a mental health facility that has developed an appropriate treatment plan for the individual person. A CTO authorises compulsory care for a person living in the community.

Responsible Clinician

The Responsible Clinician has overall responsibility for care and treatment for service users being assessed and treated under the Mental Health Act 1983.

Chapter 14: Exercises

1.   Identify whether the following scenarios constitute a deprivation of liberty:

   a)   P lives in a residential care home and is physically unable to leave his room without the help of staff, family or friends who come to visit him. He can make a call to staff when he wants to leave his room as they only check in on him when making their routine rounds throughout the day.
   b)   P is in a private room and is checked continuously throughout the day, due to his physical and mental condition.

Use the definition from the Cheshire West case described above and it will show that in the first scenario P is not DoL but in the second P is.

2. Shirley is known to the local mental health team as she suffers from depression; she is also a diabetic and is refusing to take her medication, which leaves her delirious. Should Shirley be treated under the *Mental Health Act 1983* or the *Mental Capacity Act 2005*?

Following the guidance found in AM *v* SLAM, *the least restrictive method is required in order to establish whether a DoL under the MCA or detention under the MHA is applicable.*

3. How is Article 5 of the *Human Rights Act 1998* relevant to the *Mental Capacity Act 2005*?

Art. 5 determines the patient's right to liberty and this can be breached under the MCA without correct decision-making of assessment.

4. What is the impact of the Cheshire West case in relation to the *Mental Capacity Act 2005*?

The Cheshire West case provides the precedent for what a DoL is.

Chapter 15: Exercises

1. A social worker working with a person suffering from dementia who wishes to remain at home. They are living with other members of their family, but the family members' health and well-being are being severely undermined by caring for the person. Is it right to plan for the person to go to a residential unit, even though they cannot really fully consent to this, because the social worker thinks it may be in their overall best interests, and in the best interests of the rest of the family?

In order to do this, you need to:

a) *Consider what key policies, legislation and ethical issues apply as a social worker involved in the situations you have looked at, why and how.*
b) *Plan your intervention in terms of who you will speak to and when, considering which points you will discuss with each of the people involved in a planned sequence, in order to be as open and honest as far as possible about possible plans, taking into account the interests of each person, and the possible vulnerability in terms of being able to agree to plans from the point of view of the person with dementia. With whom and in what ways should this discussion take place, taking into account the legal and ethical perspectives?*

c)   *Consider looking into any possible MCA issues for the person with dementia, if you have a concern that they do not have the capacity to consent fully to any possible plans.*

Think about how you would go about gaining such an assessment if you thought it was necessary.

2.   You are the social worker for a person in a care home. Assume this is a resident at Sweet Pea Care Home under a Care Plan. You receive concerns from their relatives that they have found them dishevelled and seemingly neglected and fearful on some visits. The managers say that the person's mental/physical state is a function of the disabilities the person has and, despite raising concerns, no safeguarding process has been enacted. If you make known your concerns within your agency, but there is no response from managers apart from you being told off and a decision that they will not pursue the matter, what can you do?

What ethically should the social worker do and what protection does the law give?

Consider the relevant ethical principles in Kant, Bentham and virtue ethics described in Chapter 5.

Consider the relevant ethical value contained in SWE's Professional Standards *and BASW's* Code of Ethics.

Section 1(14g) of the Care and Support Statutory Guidance (2020) states: 'The need to protect people from abuse and neglect.'

Sections 6.2–6.5 of Social Work England's Professional Standards *relating to whistleblowing states: 'The BASW Code of Ethics (2014b) s.3(9) concerns "Being prepared to whistleblow" in that "Social workers should be prepared to report bad practice using all available channels and discuss the protection given in the Public Interest Disclosure Act 1998".'*

Chapter 16: Exercises

1.   Read the guidance on FGM for social workers and think about the questions to consider when working with a family.

From the BASW guidance list (2018), identify questions that you would ask when working with a family affected by FGM – for example:

- *Consider the principles of confidentiality and information sharing if the girl has disclosed information about FGM.*
- *Consider the feelings and wishes of the girl(s) and their understanding of risk the procedure involves.*
- *Are the girls and their families aware of the protection they have in the UK and the options they have for support?*
- *See: National FGM Centre, 2016.*

2. What are the indicators of possible domestic violence and abuse a social worker may come across when working with a service user or family?

From the GOV.UK guidance list (2018), identify indicators of possible domestic violence and abuse.

   For example:

- *being withdrawn, or being isolated from your family and friends;*
- *having bruises, burns or bite marks on you;*
- *having your finances controlled, or not being given enough to buy food, medication or pay bills.*

See: GOV.UK (2018) Domestic abuse: how to get help.

3. Consider the questions a social worker would ask a service user they suspected was experiencing domestic abuse.

From the BASW guidance (BASW, 2021), identify the questions that a social worker would ask a service user potentially affected by domestic abuse – for example:

- *Who do you trust and who makes you feel safe?*
- *When do you spend time away from perpetrator?*
- *Tell me about a challenging day that you've had and what helped you to get through it?*
  See: BASW, 2021.

Chapter 17: Exercises

1. Why do people use drugs?

Peer pressure, ability to self-medicate and experimentation.

2. What might be the impact of being under the influence of drugs on the decisions an individual might make?

Consider capacity under the MCA and the dangerous situations an individual can get into when they are under the influence of alcohol and drugs. This will have an impact on the children in the family and their welfare.

3. Identify any substance misuse issues in the case study of Mandy and her children, and what could be done to help the family.

The welfare of the children is paramount, which means sections of the Children Act 1989 *would come into consideration regarding potential significant harm (see Chapters 6 and 7).*

- *Under the housing first principle, the housing needs of the family should be addressed first.*
- *Using a multi-agency approach consider the needs of Mandy and Stuart to help them treat their possible drug and alcohol misuse.*

- *Faris could be involved in and a victim of county lines, which would again require taking action to protect him, involving a multi-agency approach and contacting his father once parental responsibility has been established. Consider the mental health implications.*

Chapter 18: Exercises

1. Do the following claimants have recourse to public funds?
   a) Asylum seekers
      No
   b) People on work visas
      No
   c) Illegal immigrants
      No
   d) People who have overstayed their visa time limit.
      No
   e) Refugees
      Yes
   f) People granted indefinite leave to remain?
      Yes

2. Explain what 'humanitarian protection' is, why the safeguards it gives are needed and what protection it gives to successful claimants.
   According to the Home Office's document on Humanitarian Protection (2017), 'HP is designed to provide international protection where it is needed, to individuals who do not qualify for protection under the Refugee Convention' – e.g. where someone might be at risk of serious harm if they returned to their country of origin. It is needed because the reasons are not covered by the Refugee Convention (1951) and in order for the UK to meet its international obligations.

   People who qualify for HP are normally granted limited leave to remain in the UK for five years. Any children who are dependent on the claimant(s) will be granted the same leave. In exceptional circumstances, a longer period of leave can be granted.

Chapter 19: Case study – Welfare benefits and protection from homelessness

A and B have three children, aged 8, 5 and 1. The 1-year-old suffers from spina bifida and the 5-year-old is autistic. A, who was employed as a porter at the local hospital, was diagnosed with motor neurone disease ten months ago and has had to stop work. Now he has no income and they have £500 left in their bank account. They live in a three-bedroomed house owned by a private rented accommodation which is in poor repair. The rent is £300 per week. They are currently in six months' rent and Council Tax arrears. The housing association has served on them a notice to quit because of the rent arrears. B does not have paid work. A and B seek your help. What help can they claim?

The answer should discuss the following points:

UC is the most obvious benefit and is means tested. With savings below the threshold of £16,000 there will be no reduction.

ESA and PIP, which are not means-tested, will be applicable for A. The daily living and mobility allowance can be paid in addition to means-tested benefits as A has been disabled for more than three months.

Under s.17 of the CA, DLA is applicable for the two children in need, with the rent element paid.

Is B entitled to carer's allowance?

Discretionary housing payment is applicable for the rent arrears.

Council Tax reductions will help with arrears.

Free school meals etc. for children in school.

Consider whether the two-child limit applies.

Explain the LA's homelessness duty. They have been threatened with homelessness and served with a s.21 notice. They are therefore in priority need. Are they intentionally homeless because of rent arrears? Note: the non-payment of rent does not automatically constitute intentional homelessness: Samuels v Birmingham City Council [2019] UKSC 28.

Obtain the help of Social Services regarding the children's disabilities and A's illness.

Chapter 20: Exercises

1. What reforms do you consider necessary to reduce poverty in the UK and why?

Answers should discuss the following:

The 'safety net' and whether the basic level needs to be improved.

The need for more affordable housing and an uplift in benefits.

Whether the benefits cap and the 'bedroom tax' should be abolished.

Whether people in work and in receipt of UC should keep more of their earnings.

Whether there is a need for better help with child care and the possible funding implications.

2. Consider how thinking about social work values, ethics, skills and methods for working with people in poverty and disadvantage in the following situations can aid a social worker intervene most effectively in relation to:

a) The BAME older person.
b) The young person who is leaving care.
c) The woman from a BAME community who has been suffering domestic violence.
d) A young person from a BAME community in a disadvantaged area who says he was unfairly treated by the police when he was stopped on suspicion the previous night.

The methods a social worker might use in these different situations include:

- *shared decision-making;*
- *task-centred work;*
- *strength-focused approaches;*
- *motivational interviewing;*
- *problem-solving approaches;*

Advocacy approaches are key. Relevant organisations for advice and/or with help advocating with/for might include:

- *local law centres;*
- *Child Poverty Action Group (CPAG);*
- *Department for Work and Pensions (DWP);*
- *GOV.UK (www.gov.uk);*
- *Citizens Advice, which offers independent advice about benefits, work, debt, housing and many areas of legal rights;*
- *National Domestic Violence Helpline, which is available seven days a week.*
- *The Independent Office of Police Conduct to make a complaint about police conduct.*

The following organisations can also be contacted for help for people living in poverty:

- *Local food banks.*
- *Local NHS Trust drivers' scheme to help people get to appointments.*

Chapter 21: Exercise

Read the judgment in *GM* v *Carmarthenshire CC* (2018) EWFC 36 and consider the implications for report writing.

Ensure that, in a care order application (or in this case, the discharge of a care order) the criteria for justifying the grant or continuation of the care order is referenced to the threshold criteria and the child's best interests (see Chapter 7). What is the evidence to support the argument that the child is suffering or likely to suffer significant harm? This must be supported with the requisite evidence, as courts make it plain that severing the link between children and their natural parents should only be done in exceptional circumstances. Explain what these are.

'*Since well before the CA came into force, the courts have recognised that there is a line to be drawn between parents whose personal characteristics mean that they may be less than perfect parents and parents who may cause harm to their children.*' *Lord Templeman put the point this way in his well-known words in* Re KD (A Minor) (Ward: Termination of Access) [1988] AC 806, 812:

The requirement that the court must consider the child's best interests starts from the pre-sumption that the 'welfare will be best served if s/he is raised by his natural parent unless it can be positively shown that his physical or moral health would thereby be endangered'. Provide the evidence that is needed to support this.

Reports that fail to address these issues sufficiently robustly could face uncomfortable cross-examination (see Chapter 22).

Chapter 22: Exercise

Having read the case study, answer the following questions:

1. What information is it necessary to consider before making an application?
    Follow COP guidance in 'Making a personal welfare application to the Court of Protection'.

2. What assessments are required to be completed and by whom?
    The social worker should carry out Care Act assessments for both A and C (see Chapter 11). A mental capacity assessment should be made for A and C (see Chapter 14 – either or both social worker and doctor).

3. What should be included in the witness statement?
    See COP24.

4. What should be done about the allegation that B is misusing A's money?
    Report to the Office of the Public Guardian and request that B is replaced. Establish who could undertake this role – someone trustworthy, such as E or another relative, or a family friend (see Chapter 12).

5. If an application is made to the COP and a hearing takes place, consider how you would answer the following questions put to you by the family's lawyer:

    a   What steps have you taken to try and resolve this dispute before making an application to the Court of Protection?

    Informal and/or formal dispute resolution involving ASC and possibly a lawyer/mediator.

    b   You say that A lacks capacity to decide about his future care. What evidence do you have to support this?

Obtain the evidence that capacity assessment has been undertaken and outline who is involved.

    c   You say that B refuses to leave the family home. What steps should be considered to achieve this?

Look up the decision of the court in DL *v* A Local Authority *[2012] EWCA Civ 253 DL (Chapter 12) which deals with the protection of vulnerable adults and the test for the grant of an Occupation Order in Chapter 16. (Note that the family are taking legal advice.)*

References

Advisory Council on the Misuse of Drugs (ACMD) (n.d.) Cannabis-based products for medicinal use (CBPMs) in humans. Available at: www.gov.uk/government/organisations/advisory-council-on-the-misuse-of-drugs

Advisory Council on the Misuse of Drugs (ACMD) (2019) ACMD Report – Drug-related harms in homeless populations and how they can be reduced. Available at: www.gov.uk/government/publications/acmd-report-drug-related-harms-in-homeless-populations

Age UK Paying for Care and Support at Home: Factsheet 46. Available at: www.ageuk.org.uk/documents/factsheets/

António Guterres (UN Secretary-General) at launch of Policy Brief on Persons with Disabilities and COVID-19. Available at: http://webtv.un.org/watch/watch/ant%C3%B3nio-guterres-un-secretary-general-at-launch-of-policy-brief-on-persons-with-disabilities-and-covid-19/6154362529001/?term=&lan=kiswahili

Arthur, R. (2010) *Young Offenders and the Law: How the Law Responds to Youth Offending*. Abingdon: Routledge.

Association of Directors of Adult Social Services (ADASS) (n.d.) *Applications to the Court of Protection: A Guide for Council Staff*. Available at: adass.org.uk

ATD Fourth World (2019) *Understanding Poverty in All its Forms*. A participatory research study into poverty in the UK. London: ATD Fourth World.

Aynsley-Green, A. (2019) Children's Commissioner for England 2005–09. Thirty years on, has the Children Act changed family life for the better? *The Guardian*, 13 November.

Badrakalimuthu, V., Rumball, D. and Wagle, A. (2010) Drug misuse in older people: old problems and new challenges. *Advances in Psychiatric Treatment*, 16 (6), 421–9. doi:10.1192/apt.bp.108.006221

Banks, S. (2012) *Ethics and Values in Social Work* (4th edn). Basingstoke: Palgrave.

Barker, K. (2016) Is poverty in the UK in 2016 caused by employment, habit or circumstance? New Policy Institute.

Barksy, A. (2019) *Ethics and Values in Social Work*. Oxford: Oxford University Press.

Bateman, T. and Hazel, N. (2014) Beyond Youth Custody: Youth Justice Timeline. Available at: beyondyouthcustody.net/wp-content/uploads/youth-justice-timeline.pdf

Bateman, T., Day, A.-M. and Pitts, J. (2018) Looked after children and custody: a brief review of the relationship between care status and child incarceration and the implications for service provision. University of Bedfordshire, Nuffield Foundation. Available at: www.beds.ac.uk/dta/assets/pdf_file/0007/592882/Nuffield-Literature-review

Baumberg Geiger, B. (2017) *Benefit 'Myths'? The Accuracy and Inaccuracy of Public Beliefs about the Benefits System Benefits Stigma in Britain*. Wiley Online Library (17 September).

Beckett, C., Maynard, A. and Jordan, P. (2017) *Values and Ethics in Social Work* (3rd edn). London: SAGE.

Bernard, C. (2020) Why intersectionality matters for social work practice in adult services – social work with adults (blog.gov.uk). London: Department for Health and Social Care.

Biehal, N., Sinclair, I. and Wade, J. (2014) Reunifying abused or neglected children: decision-making and outcomes. York: University of York.

Biestek, F. (1961) *The Casework Relationship*. London: George Allen & Unwin.

Blakemore, S.J. (2008) Development of the social brain during adolescence. *The Quarterly Journal of Experimental Psychology*, 61 (1): 40–9.

Bogg, D. (2016) *Report Writing for Social Workers*. Social Work Pocketbooks (UK Higher Education). London: Open University Press.

Bottery, S. (2020) How Covid-19 has magnified some of social care's key problems. The King's Fund. Available at: www.kingsfund.org.uk/

Boyd, N. (1982) *Josephine Butler, Octavia Hill, Florence Nightingale: Three Victorian Women Who Changed Their World*. London: Macmillan.

Brandon, M., Sidebotham, P., Belderson, P., Cleaver, H., Dickens, J., Garstang, J., Harris, J., Sorensen, P. and Wate, R. (2020) Complexity and challenge: a triennial analysis of SCRs 2014–2017. Final report. Department for Education. Available at: Complexity and challenge: a triennial analysis of SCRs 2014–2017 (publishing.service.gov.uk).

Braye, S., Orr, D. and Preston-Shoot, M. (2017) Autonomy and protection in selfneglect work: the ethical complexity of decision-making. *Ethics and Social Welfare*, 11 (4): 320–35.

Brigden, G. (2014) Safeguarding is everyone's responsibility. *Community Care*. Available at: www.communitycare.co.uk

British Association of Social Workers (BASW) (n.d.) The right side of regulation: recording with care. Available at: www.basw.co.uk/events/right-side-regulation-recording-care

British Association of Social Workers (BASW) (2012) *Mental Health and Substance Use: Essential Information for Social Workers*. A BASW Pocket Guide. Available at: www.basw.co.uk/resources/mental-health-and-substance-use-essential-information-social-workers

British Association of Social Workers (BASW) (2014a) Whistleblowing policy. Available at: basw.co.uk/resources/basw-whistleblowing-policy

British Association of Social Workers (BASW) (2014b) *Code of Ethics for Social Work*. Available at: www.basw.co.uk/about-basw/code-ethics

British Association of Social Workers (BASW) (2016) Position statement: racism in immigration. Available at: basw.co.uk/resources/basw-position-statement-racism-immigration

British Association of Social Workers (BASW) (2016) The role of the social worker in adoption – ethics and human rights: an enquiry. Available at: basw.co.uk/resources/role-social-worker-adoption-ethics-and-human-rights-enquiry

British Association of Social Workers (BASW) (2017) Guidance on social media. Available at: www.basw.co.uk/resources/guidance-social-medias

British Association of Social Workers (BASW) (2018) Professional capabilities framework (PCP): readiness for direct practice. Available at: basw.co.uk/professional-development/professional-capabilities-framework-pcf/the-pcf

British Association of Social Workers (BASW) (2018) The context, roles and tasks of the child and family social worker. Available at: basw.co.uk/system/files/resources/basw_england_-_children_and_families_practice_policy_and_education_group_role_of_a_child_and_family_social_worker_v2_September_2020_pdf

Britsh Association of Social Workers (BASW) (2018) FGM Good practice guidance and assessment tool for social workers. Available at: basw.co.uk/resources/fgm/good-practice-guidance-and-assessment-tool-social-workers

British Association of Social Workers (BASW) (2019) Capabilities statement for social workers working with adults with learning disability. Available at: basw.co.uk/resources/capabili-ties-statement-social-workers-working-adults-learning-disability

British Association of Social Workers (BASW) (2019) Work with No Recourse to Public Fund 'NRPF' challenges and dilemmas. Available at: basw/co.uk/resources/social-work-no-re-course-public-fund-'nrpf'-challenges-and-dilemmas

British Association of Social Workers (BASW/CWIG) (2019) *Anti-Poverty Practice Guide for Social Work*. British Association of Social Workers: Birmingham.

British Association of Social Workers (BASW) (2020) BASW statement: George Floyd. BASW wholly condemns the murder of George Floyd and the frightening circumstances that led to it.

British Association of Social Workers (BASW) (2020) NRPF: Statement and guidance. Birmingham.

British Association of Social Workers (BASW) (2020) *Coronavirus Act 2020 and Social Work Practice* – A Briefing.

British Association of Social Workers (BASW) (2020) The right side of regulation: recording with care. Available at: www.base.co.uk/events/right-side-regulation-recording-care

British Association of Social Workers (BASW) (2021) Social work during the Covid-19 pan-demic: initial findings.

British Association of Social Workers (BASW) (2021) *Domestic Abuse Practice Guidance: For Children and Family Social Workers*. Birmingham. BASW.

British Geriatrics Society (n.d.) Coronavirus: advice to older people, families, friends and carers. Available at: bgs.org.uk/

Budget Group and Runnymede Trust (2017) *Intersecting Inequalities: The Impact of Austerity on Black and Minority Ethnic Women in the UK*. Available at: https://wbg.org.uk/wp-content/uploads/2018/08/Intersecting-Inequalities-October-2017-Full-Report.pdf

Bywaters, P. (2020) *The Child Welfare Inequalities Project: Final Report*. University of Huddersfield. Nuffield Foundation.

Bywaters, P., Bunting, L., Davidson, G., Hanratty, J., Mason, W., McCartan, S. and Steils, N. (2016) The relationship between poverty, child abuse and neglect: A rapid evidence review. London: Joseph Rowntree Foundation.

Bywaters, P., Scourfield, J., Webb, C., Morris, K., Featherstone, B., Brady, G, Jones, C. and Sparks, T. (2019) Paradoxical evidence on ethnic inequities in child welfare: towards a research agenda. *Children and Youth Services Review*, 96: 145–54.

Cabinet Archives (n.d.) Protection of children: adoption and foster care. *National Archives*. Available at: nationalarchives.gov.uk/cabinetpapers/default.htm

CAFCASS (2017) Allegations of domestic abuse in child contact cases. Available at: www.caf-cass.gov.uk/2017/07/25/cafcass-womens-aid-collaborate-domestic-abuse-research/

Cantwell, N. (2014) *The Best Interests of the Child in Intercountry Adoption*. UNICEF.

Cardiff University (n.d.) Children's social care law in Wales. Cardiff University.

Care Quality Commission (CQC) (n.d.) Regulation 13: Safeguarding service users from abuse and improper treatment.

Care Quality Commission (CQC) (2018) Guidance on accessing medical and care records using powers under the Health and Social Care Act 2008.

Care Quality Commission (CQC) (2018) Protect people's privacy when you use surveillance, available at: cqc.org.uk

Carter, R. (2016) Self-neglect: the tension between human rights and duty of care. *Community Care.*

Castles, S., de Haas, H. and Miller, M.J. (2019) *The Age of Migration: International Population Movements in the Modern World.* London: Red Globe Press.

Centre for Social Justice (2006) Breakdown Britain: interim report on the state of the nation. Available at: www.centreforsocialjustice.org.uk

Chartered Institute of Housing (n.d.) Housing rights information for new arrivals.

Chartered Institute of Personnel and Development (2020) Employers' legal guide to post-Brexit immigration. London.

Child Poverty Action Group (CPAG) (n.d.) The causes of poverty. Available at: https://cpag.org.uk/child-poverty/causes-poverty

Child Poverty Action Group (CPAG) (2017) *Poverty: The Facts* (6th edn). CPAG: London.

Child Poverty Action Group (CPAG) and the Church of England (2020) Poverty in the pandemic: the impact of coronavirus on low-income families and children.

Children's Commissioner (2019) Bleak houses: tackling the crisis of family homelessness in England. Available at: www.children'scommissioner.gov.uk/report/bleak-houses

Children's Commissioner (2020) *Report of the Children's Commissioners of the United Kingdom of Great Britain and Northern Ireland to the United Nations Committee on the Rights of the Child.* Available at: www.childrenscommissioner.gov.uk/wp-content/uploads/2020/12/cco-un-crc-report.pdf

Children's Commissioner (2020) Fact checking claims about child poverty.

Church of England (2018) *Promoting a Safer Church, Parish Safeguarding Handbook.* London: Church House Publishing.

Community Care (2020) Staff abused women at learning disability unit. Available at: www.communitycare.co.uk

Coward, S. (2015) *The Emotional Well-being of Black and Dual Heritage Looked After Young People.* Buckinghamshire: New University.

Crenshaw, K. (1989) Demarginalizing the intersection of race and sex: a black feminist critique of antidiscrimination doctrine, feminist theory and antiracist politics. University of Chicago Legal Forum: Vol. 1989, Article 8.

CRIN (n.d.) Minimum ages of criminal responsibility in Europe. Available at: https://archive.crin.org/en/home/ages/europe.html

Crown Prosecution Service (CPS) (n.d.) Domestic abuse. Available at: www.cps.gov.uk/domestic-abuse

Crown Prosecution Service (CPS) (n.d.) Honour based violence and forced marriage. *Health and Social Care Act* 2008.

Crown Prosecution Service (CPS) (2018) Adverse inferences. Available at: cps.gov.uk/legal-guidance/adverse-inferences

Crown Prosecution Service (CPS) (2021) Drug offences. Available at: cps.gov.uk/legal-guidance/drug-offences

Cullen, D. (2021) The Adoption and Children Act 2002. *Family Law Week*, 15 January.

Cumming, S., Fitzpatrick, E., McAuliffe, D. and McCain, S. (2007) Raising the Titanic: rescuing social work documentation from the sea of ethical risk. *Australian Social Work*, 60 (2).

Day, M.R., Leahy-Warren, P. and McCarthy, G. (2016) Self-neglect: ethical considerations. *Annual Review of Nursing Research*, 34 (1).

de Silva, N. (2018) How legal decisions influence social work practice: Local Government Lawyer.

Department for Children, Schools and Families (DCSF) (2009) Lord Laming. The protection of children in England: a progress report.

Department for Communities and Local Government (DCLG) (2020) English Housing Survey: housing costs and affordability 2018 to 2019. London: Ministry of Housing, Communities and Local Government.

Department for Digital, Culture, Media and Sport (DCMS) (2018) Data Protection Act 2018. Factsheet – Overview.

Department for Education (DfE) (2006) Statutory guidance for local authority children's services on representations and complaints procedures.

Department for Education (DfE) (2011) Munro review of child protection: a child-centred system.

Department for Education (DfE) (2011) Fostering services: national minimum standards DfE-00029-2011.

Department for Education (DfE) (2013) Statutory guidance on adoption: for local authorities, voluntary adoption agencies and adoption support agencies.

Department for Education (DfE) (2014) Adoption: national minimum standards.

Department for Education (DfE) (2014) Statutory guidance: Vol. 1. Court orders and pre-proceedings, para. 22, April.

Department for Education (DfE) (2015) The Children Act 1989. Guidance and regulations. Volume 2: care planning, placement and case review.

Department for Education (DfE) (2016) Putting children first.

Department for Education (DfE) (2016) Adoption: A vision for change.

Department for Education (DfE) (2017) Children looked after in England (including adoption), year ending 31 March 2017.

Department for Education (DfE) (2018) Foster care in England: a review for the Department of Education. Sir Martin Narey and Mark Owers.

Department for Education (DfE) (2018) Outcomes for children looked after by local authorities in England.

Department for Education (DfE) (2018) Information sharing advice for safeguarding practitioners: guidance on information sharing for people who provide safeguarding services to children, young people, parents and carers.

Department for Education (DfE) (2018) Working together to safeguard children: statutory guidance on inter-agency working to safeguard and promote the welfare of children.

Department for Education (DfE) (2020) A guide to looked after children statistics in England.

Department for Education (DfE) (2021) A wide-ranging, independent review to address poor outcomes for children in care as well as strengthening families to improve vulnerable children's lives. Available at: www.gov.uk/government/news/education-secretary-launches-review-of-childrens-social-care

Department for Education (DfE) (2021) *Early Years Foundation Stage Profile Handbook*.

Department for Education (DfE) and Department of Health and Social Care (DHSC) (2014) *Special Educational Needs – Code of Practice: 0–25 years*.

Department for Education (DfE) and Department of Health and Social Care (DWP) (2015) 2010 to 2015 government policy: poverty and social justice. Available at: www.gov.uk/government/publications/2010-to-2015-government-policy-poverty-and-social-justice

Department for Work and Pensions (DWP) (n.d.) Households below average income (HBAI): an analysis of the UK income distribution: 1994/95–2017/18. Available at: https://assets.publishing.service.gov.uk/government/uploads/system/uploads/attachment_data/file/789997/households-below-average-income-1994-1995-2017-2018.pdf

Department for Work and Pensions (DWP) (2021) Family resources survey: financial year 2019 to 2020.

Department of Health (DoH) (2011) Statement of government policy on adult safeguarding. Gateway reference: 16072.

Department of Health (DoH) (2011) Commission on funding of care and support (The Dilnot Commission Report).

Department of Health (DoH) (2012) Reforming the law on adult social care and support: the government's response to the Law Commission Report 326 on Adult Social Care.

Department of Health (DoH) (2013) *Information: To Share or Not to Share? The Information Governance Review*. London: The Stationery Office.

Department of Health (DoH) (2013) *Statement of Government Policy on Adult Safeguarding*. Available at: www.gov.uk/dh

Department of Health (DoH) (2018) *Care and Support Statutory Guidance*.

Department of Health (DoH) (2000) *Adoption: A New Approach*. DH Cm. 5017.

Department of Health (DoH) (2000) No secrets: guidance on developing and implementing multi-agency policies and procedures to protect vulnerable adults from abuse.

Department for Health and Social Care (DHSC) (2013) Adult safeguarding: updated statement of government policy.

Department for Health and Social Care (DHSC) (2016) Forensic mental health social work: capabilities framework.

Department of Health and Social Care (DHSC) (2018) *Modernising the Mental Health Act – Final Report from the Independent Review*. London: DHSC.

Department of Health and Social Care (DHSC) (2019) *Strengths-based Approach: Practice Framework and Practice Handbook*.

Department of Health and Social Care (DHSC) (2020) *Care and Support Statutory Guidance*.

Department of Health and Social Care (DHSC) (2021) Reforming the Mental Health Act.

Department of Health and Social Care (DHSC) (2021) Liberty protection safeguards: overview of the process.

Dicey, A. (1885) *Introduction to the Study of the Law of the Constitution* (8th edn). London: Macmillan.

Dickens, J., Masson, J. Gardside, L., Young, J. and Bader, K. (2019) Courts, care proceedings and outcomes uncertainty: the challenges of achieving and assessing 'good outcomes' for children after care proceedings. Wiley Online Library.

Dingwall, D., Eekelaar, J. and Murray, T. (1983) *The Protection of Children: State Intervention and Family Life*. Oxford: Basil Blackwell.

Dingwall, D., Eekelaar, J. and Murray, T. (2014) *The Protection of Children: State Intervention and Family Life*. New Orleans, LA: Quid Pro Books.

Disability Rights UK. Greaves, I. (ed.) (2020) *Disability Rights Handbook*. London: Disability Rights.

Disclosure and Barring Service (DBS) (n.d.) *Barring Referrals: Your Guide to How and When to Make One*. Available at: https://assets.publishing.service.gov.uk/government/uploads/system/uploads/attachment_data/file/782483/CCS0119367774-001_Barring_Referrals_Document__Flowchart_A5_Booklet_V3_DG-2.pdf

Donelan, M. (MP) (2020) Adoption as a permanence option: Children's Minister's letter to Directors of Children's Services.

Dyke, C. (2019) *Writing Analytical Assessments in Social Work (Critical Skills for Social Work)* (2nd edn). St Alban's: Critical Publishing.

Economic and Social Research Council (ESRC) (2017) *CSI Brexit 2: Ending Free Movement as a Priority in the Brexit Negotiations*. Centre for Social Investigation, Nuffield College.

Elliott, M., Featherstone, B., Mason, W., McCartan, C., Morris, K., Scourfield, J. and Webb, C. (2020) *Identifying and Understanding Inequalities in Child Welfare Intervention Rates: Comparative Studies in the Four UK Countries*. Available at: www.nuffieldfoundation.org

Ellison, L. (2019) Coercive and controlling men and the women who kill them. *Wolverhampton Law Journal*, 3. Available at: www.wlv.ac.uk/

Equality and Human Rights Commission (EqHRC) (2011) *The Equality Act 2010. Employment Code of Practice*. London: The Stationery Office.

EU legislation and UK law. Available at: www.legislation.gov.uk/eu-legislation-and-uk-law

European Court of Human Rights (ECtHR) (2020) Guide on Article 4 of the European Convention on Human Rights: Prohibition of slavery and forced labour.

European Court of Human Rights (ECtHR) (2020) Factsheet: Slavery, servitude, and forced labour, July 2005–June 2020. Available at: www.echr.coe.int/Documents/FS_Forced_labour_ENF.pdf

European Court of Human Rights (ECtHR) (2021) Slavery, servitude and forced labour, available at: www.echr.coe.int/Documents/FS_Forced_labour_ENG.pdf

European Data Protection Supervisor (n.d.) The History of the General Data Protection Regulation. Available at: https://edps.europa.eu/data-protection/data-protection/legislation/history-general-data-protection-regulation_en

Family Rights Group (2014) How important is the Human Rights Act for vulnerable children and families? Briefing, May. Available at: frg.org.uk

Farmer, N. (2017) No recourse to public funds insecure immigration status and destitution: the role of social work?' BASW.

Farmer, N. (2019) Social worker or border guard? Ethics and values in the 'hostile environment' of UK immigration policy.

Farrington, D.P. and Welsh, B.C. (2007) *Saving Children from a Life of Crime: Early Risk Factors and Effective Interventions*. Oxford: Oxford University Press.

Fauth B., Jelicic, H., Hart, D. and Burton, S. (2010) *Effective Practice to Protect Children Living in 'Highly Resistant' Families*. Centre for Excellence and Outcomes in Children and Young People's Services. Available at: www.c4eo.org.uk/evidence/default.aspx

Featherstone, B., Gupta, A. and Mills, S. (2018) The role of the social worker in adoption – ethics and human rights: an enquiry. BASW, the University of Huddersfield and Royal Holloway, University of London.

Fitzpatrick, S., Bramley, G., Blenkinsopp. J., Wood, J., Sosenko, F., Littlewood, M., Johnsen, S., Watts, B., Treanor, M. and McIntyre, J. (2020) Destitution in the UK 2020. Joseph Rowntree Foundation. Available at: jrf.org.uk/report/destitution-uk-2020

Foreign and Commonwealth Office (2010) Forced marriage and learning disability: new guidelines to help prevent abuse.

Forrester, D., McCambridge J., Waissbein C. et al. (2008) How do child and family social workers talk to parents about child welfare concerns? *Child Abuse Review*, 17 (1): 23–35.

Foster, J. (2017) If social workers feel uneasy in court, that should be reassuring: cross examination and court processes are vital to ensuring family justice is fair and transparent. *Community Care*.

Garraway, E. (2015) How can social workers tackle unconscious bias? *Community Care*.

GOV.UK (n.d.) Youth offending teams. Available at: www.gov.uk/youth-offending-team

GOV.UK (n.d.) Adoption records.

GOV.UK (n.d.) Adoption pay and leave.

GOV.UK (n.d.) Disability premiums.

GOV.UK (n.d.) Drug penalties.

GOV.UK (n.d.) Equality Act 2010 guidance. Available at: www.gov.uk/guidance/equality-act-2010-guidance#overview

GOV. UK (n.d.) Marriages and civil partnerships in England and Wales. Available at: www.gov.uk/marriages-civil-partnerships

GOV.UK (n.d.) Form COP24: give a witness statement about a person who lacks capacity.

GOV.UK (n.d.) Office of the Public Guardian. Available at: www.gov.uk/government/organisations/office-of-the-public-guardian

GOV.UK (n.d.) Immigration Detention Bail.

GOV.UK (n.d.) Report a concern about an attorney, deputy or guardian.

GOV.UK (2003) *The Victoria Climbié Inquiry: Report of an Inquiry by Lord Laming*. CM5730.

GOV.UK (2010) Equality Act 2010: What do I need to know? Quick start guide to discrimination by association and perception for voluntary and community organisations. Available at: https://assets.publishing.service.gov.uk/government/uploads/system/uploads/attachment_data/file/85022/vcs-association-perception.pdf

GOV.UK (2014) General grounds for refusal (immigration staff guidance). Available at: www.gov.uk/government/collections/general-grounds-for-refusal-modernised-guidance

GOV.UK (2015) Keeping children safe in education. Available at: www.gov.uk/government/publications/keeping-children-safe-in-education—2

GOV.UK (2015) Disability and domestic abuse risk, impacts and response.

GOV.UK (2016) Psychoactive Substances Act 2016: guidance for researchers.

GOV.UK (2017) Competition and markets authority care homes market study report.

GOV.UK (2017) Lammy Review.

GOV.UK (2018) County lines: criminal exploitation of children and vulnerable adults.

GOV.UK (2018) Safeguarding and promoting the welfare of children affected by parental alcohol and drug use: a guide for local authorities.

GOV.UK (2018) Independent review of the Mental Health Act.

GOV.UK (2018) Guidance – Domestic abuse: how to get help. Available at: www.gov.uk/guidance/domestic-abuse-how-to-get-help

GOV.UK (2018) Working together to safeguard children. Available at: www.gov.uk/government/publications/working-together-to-safeguard-children—2

GOV.UK (2018) NHS continuing healthcare fast-track pathway tool.

GOV.UK (2019) Adult substance misuse treatment statistics 2019 to 2020: report.

GOV.UK (2019) Adult social care: quality matters. Available at: www.gov.uk/government/collections/adult-social-care-quality-matters

GOV.UK (2020) Disagreeing with a qualifying determination about fostering, adopting, or protected adoption information.

GOV.UK (2020) Domestic Violence Protection Notices (DVPNs) and Domestic Violence Protection Orders (DVPOs) Guidance.

GOV.UK (2020) National Statistics. Young people's substance misuse treatment statistics 2019 to 2020: report.

GOV.UK (2020) Homelessness guidance for local authorities.

GOV.UK (2020) Independent Human Rights Act review. Available at: www.gov.uk/guidance/independt-human-rights-act-review

GOV.UK (2021) Detentions under the Mental Health Act.

GOV.UK (2021) Landmark Domestic Abuse Bill receives Royal Assent.

GOV.UK (2021) Average household income. *Office for National Statistics*. Available at: www.ons/gov.uk/incomeandwealth/bulletins/financialyear2020

Gray, M. and Webb, S. (2010) *Ethics and Value Perspectives in Social Work*. London: Macmillan Education UK.

Griffith, R. and Tengnah, C. (2006) Protecting vulnerable adults from sexual abuse. *British Journal of Community Nursing*, 11 (2): 72–7.

Haines, K.R. and Case, S.P. (2015) *Positive Youth Justice: Children First, Offenders Second*. Bristol: Policy Press.

Hansard (1957) Mental illness and mental deficiency (Report). HC Deb, vol. 573, cc35–103, 8 July.

Hansard (2000) Lord Whitty, Local Government Act 1988: Section 28 HL Deb, 3 February, vol. 609, cc347–50.

Hansard (2011) Lord Greaves. Col 1404, vol. 728, 23 June.

Hardy, R. (2017) Tips for social workers on case recording and record keeping. *Community Care*.

Hardy, R. (2018) Social workers can see producing a chronology as an administrative 'chore' – but they are a vital foundation for analysis. *Community Care*.

Harms-Smith, L. et al. (2019) *Social Work and Human Rights: A Practice Guide*. BASW.

Harris, D. et al. (n.d.) Immigration, asylum and special interest group. BASW.

Harris, D., Mansuri, N. and Stringer, A. (2019) *Social Work with no Recourse to Public Fund 'NRPF': Challenges and Dilemmas*. BASW, Immigration, Asylum and Special Interest Group.

Harris, J. (2003) Consent and end of life decisions. *Journal of Medical Ethics*, 29 (1).

Harwin, J. et al. (2011) The Family Drug and Alcohol Court (FDAC) evaluation project final report. Research Team, Brunel University, March.

Health Foundation (2019) What should be done to fix the crisis in social care? 30 August.

Health Foundation (2020) *Understanding the Needs of Those Most Clinically Vulnerable to Covid-19*. London: Health Foundation.

Held, D., McGrew, A., Goldblatt, D. and Perraton, J. (1999) *Global Transformations*. Stanford, CA: Stanford University Press.

HM Courts and tribunals (2014) Media attendance at family court hearings EX711.

HM Courts and tribunals (2019) HMCTS reform update – family.

HM Government (2018) Advice for practitioners providing safeguarding services to children young people, parents and carers.

HMICFRS (2019) Gangmasters and Labour Abuse Authority: An inspection of the use of investigative powers by the Gangmasters and Labour Abuse Authority. Available at: www.justiceinspectorate.gov.uk/hmicfrs

Hoffman, D. and Rowe, J. (2003) *Human Rights in the UK: A General Introduction to the Human Rights Act 1998*. London: Pearson Longman.

Hollins, S., Lodge, K.M. and Lomax, P. (2019) The case for removing intellectual disability and autism from the Mental Health Act. Published online by Cambridge University Press. *British Journal of Psychiatry*, 215 (5): 633–5.

Home, A. and Maer, L. (2010) From the Human Rights Act to a Bill of Rights? Key issues for the new parliament. House of Commons Library Research. Available at: www.parliament.uk/globalassets/documents/commons/lib/research/key_issues/key-issues-from-the-human-rights-act-to-a-bill-of-rights.pdf

Home Office (n.d.) Home Office Guidance: Immigration Detention Bail.

Home Office (2015) *Revocation of Indefinite Leave*. Available at: https://assets.publishing.service.gov.uk/government/uploads/system/uploads/attachment_data/file/926380/revocation-of-indefinite-leave-v4.0.pdf

Home Office (2016) Domestic Violence Disclosure Scheme (DVDS) Guidance.

Home Office (2017) Drug strategy.

Home Office (2017) Humanitarian Protection.

Home Office (2018) Domestic abuse: get help during the coronavirus (COVID-19) pandemic.

Home Office (2019) Domestic abuse: responding to reports of domestic abuse from asylum seekers.

Home Office (2019) Assessing age for asylum applicants.

Home Office (2019) Certification of protection and human rights claims under section 94 of the Nationality, Immigration and Asylum Act 2002.

Home Office (2019) Criminality guidance in article 8 ECHR cases.

Home Office (2019) Assessing Age. Available at: www.gov.uk/government/publications/assessing-age-instruction.

Home Office (2020) Windrush Compensation Scheme Rules.

Home Office (2020) UK annual report on modern slavery.

Home Office (2020) National referral mechanism guidance: adult (England and Wales).

Home Office (2020) Giving evidence in court.

Home Office (2020) Simplifying the immigration rules: a response.

Home Office (2020) Forced Marriage Unit Statistics 2019.

Home Office (2020) Assessing Age (Guidance for Home Office Staff).

Home Office (2021) Blog: Domestic Abuse Act: Factsheet.

House of Commons (2004) Mental Capacity Bill, HC Deb, vol. 422, cc67–70WS, 18 June.

House of Commons (2017) Housing: Changes in the Private Rented Sector. House of Commons Library.

House of Commons (2019) Early intervention. House of Commons Library Briefing Paper No. 7647.

House of Commons (2019) Immigration detention: government response to the Committee's Fourteenth Report of Session 2017–2019. HC 2602.

House of Commons (2019) Housing: changes in the private rented sector. Available at: https://commonslibrary.parliament.uk/social-policy/housing/rented-housing/housing-changes-in-the-private-rented-sector-podcast/

House of Commons/House of Lords Joint Committee on Human Rights (2020) Immigration detention: government response to the committee's sixteenth report of session 2017–19: Second Special Report of Session 2019–2020.

House of Commons Work and Pensions Committee (2019) Two-child limit. Available at: https://publications.parliament.uk/pa/cm201919/cmselect/cmworpen/51/51.pdf

House of Commons (2020) Migration statistics, 6 March. House of Commons Library.

House of Commons (2020) Changes to immigration rules. HC 1043, 10 December.

House of Commons (2021) Briefing paper: Coronavirus: support for landlords and tenants. House of Commons Library.

House of Commons (2021) Poverty in the UK: statistics. House of Commons Library.

House of Commons (2021) Briefing paper: Coronavirus: Universal Credit during the crisis. Available at: https://commonslibrary.parliament.uk/research-briefings/cbp8999

House of Commons/House of Lords (2020) House of Commons/House of Lords Joint Committee on Human Rights Immigration detention: government response to the committee's sixteenth report of session 2017–19: second special report of session 2019–20.

House of Lords (2000) Research Paper 00/47: The Local Government Bill [HL]: the 'Section 28' debate Bill 87 of 1999–2000.

House of Lords/House of Commons Joint Committee on Human Rights (2003) The UN Convention on the Rights of the Child Tenth Report of Session 2002–03. HL Paper 117 HC 81.

Housing Learning and Improvement Network (LIN) (2016) Older people and alcohol misuse: helping people stay in their homes.

Hughes, R. (1998) Children Act 1948 and 1989: similarities, differences, continuities. *Child & Family Social Work*, 3: 149–51.

Humphreys, C. and Bradbury-Jones, C. (2015) Editorial: Domestic abuse and safeguarding children: focus, response and intervention. *Child Abuse Review*, 24 (4).

Humphries, B. (2004) An unacceptable role for social work: implementing immigration policy. *British Journal of Social Work*, 34: 93–107.

Information Commissioners Office (ICO) (n.d.) Guide to Freedom of Act.

Information Commissioners Office (ICO) (n.d.) Guide-to-data-protection/guide-to-the-general-data-protection-regulation-gdpr/exemptions.

Information Commissioners Office (ICO) (n.d.) Personal data breaches.

Institute for Fiscal Studies (IFS) (2019) Universal credit and its impact on household incomes: the long and the short of it.

Interim report into the Independent Inquiry into Child Sexual Abuse (April 2018): HC954-1 Available from government publications (GOV.UK).

International Federation of Social Workers (IFSW) (2014) Global social work statement of ethical principles. Available at: www.ifsw.org/global-social-work-statement-of-ethical-principles/

International Labour Organization (n.d.) Trafficking in children.

Jay, A. (2018) *Independent Inquiry into Child Sexual Exploitation in Rotherham, 1997–2013.* Rotherham Metropolitan Borough Council.

Jay, M. and McGrath-Lone, L. (2019) Education outcomes of children in contact with social care in England: a systematic review. *Systematic Reviews*, 8 (155), 28 June.

Johnson, K. and Boland, B. (2019) Adult safeguarding under the Care Act 2014. *British Journal of Psychiatry Bulletin*, 43 (1): 38–42. Available at: https://doi.org/10.1192/bjb.2018.71

Jolly, A. (2018) No recourse to social work? Statutory neglect, social exclusion and undocumented migrant families in the UK. BASW.

Jones, R. (2015) The marketisation and privatisation of children's social work and child protection. Integration or fragmentation? *Journal of Integrated Care*, 23 (6): 364–75.

Joseph Rowntree Foundation (JRF) (2017a) Keeping more of what you earn. Available at: jrf.org.uk/keeping-more-what-you-earn

Joseph Rowntree Foundation (JRF) (2017b) Poverty and ethnicity in the labour market. Available at: www.jrf.org.uk/poverty-enthnicity-labour-market

Joyce, R. and Waters, T. (2019) Reducing in-work poverty: the role of minimum wages and benefits: Institute of Fiscal Studies briefing note.

Judicial College (2017) *Youth Court Bench Book*. Available at: www.sentencingcouncil.org.uk/wp-content/uploads/youth-court-bench-book-august-2017.pdf

Judiciary UK (2020) Family Justice Board statement: 'Priorities for the family justice system'.

Justice (n.d.) Practice Direction 12A – Care, supervision and other Part 4 proceedings: guide to case management.

Keene, A., Kane, N., Owen, G. and Kim, S. (2019) Taking capacity seriously? Ten years of mental capacity disputes before England's Court of Protection. *International Journal of Law and Psychiatry*, 62: 56–76, January–February.

Kelly, D. (2020) *Slapper and Kelly's the English Legal System*. Milton Park: Taylor & Francis Group.

Kent, S. (2015) 10 top tips for report writing: local authority social work evidence template (SWET) – guidance notes. BASW.

Killapsy, H. (2006) From the asylum to community care: learning from experience. *British Medical Bulletin*, 79–80 (1): 245–58, June.

King's Fund, The (2015) Devolution: what it means for health and social care in England.

King's Fund, The (2019) What is happening to life expectancy in the UK? Available at: www.kingsfund.org.uk/publications

King's Fund, The (2021) The social care system is failing the people who rely on it and urgently needs reform.

Lankelly Chase Foundation report (2014) *Ethnic Inequalities in Mental Health: Promoting Lasting Positive Change. Report of Findings to Lankelly Chase Foundation*. Mind. The Afiya Trust and Centre for Mental Health.

Lavalette, M. (ed.) (2011) *Radical Social Work Today: Social Work at the Crossroads*. Bristol: Policy Press.

Law Commission (1988) *Review of Child Law, Guardianship and Custody* (1988) HC594.

Law Commission (2011) *Adult Social Care*. Law Com. No. 326.

Law Commission (2011) *Reform of Adult Social Care*. Law Com. No. 326.

Law Commission (2017) *Mental Capacity and Deprivation of Liberty*, HC 1079. Law Com. No. 372.

Law Commission (2020) *Simplification of the Immigration Rules: Report*.

Levitas R., Pantazis C., Fahmy E., Gordon D., Lloyd E. and Patsios, D. (2007) *The Multi-Dimensional Analysis of Social Exclusion*. Bristol: University of Bristol.

Little, M. (2013) Social worker or benefits adviser? Examining the impact of welfare reforms. *Community Care*.

Littlechild, B. (2012) Values and cultural issues in social work. *European Research Institute for Social Work Web Journal* (pp. 62–76) Available at: http://eris.osu.eu/index.php?kategorie=35170

Littlechild, B. (2019) Social work and social policy in England. In Chytil, O. and Keller, J. (eds) *The European Dimension in Social Work Education and Practice*. Sociologique Nakladadatelstvi (Slon).

Littlechild, B. and Bourke, C. (2006) Men's use of violence and intimidation against family members and child protection workers. In Humphreys, C. and Stanley, N. (eds), *Domestic Violence and Child Protection: Directions for Good Practice*. London: Jessica Kingsley.

Littlechild, B. and Hawley, C. (2010) Risk assessments for mental health service users: ethical, valid and reliable? *Journal of Social Work*, first published online on 4 August 2009 as doi:10.1177/1468017309342191, then in print April 2010, 10 (2).

Littlechild, B., Hunt, S., Goddard, C., Cooper, J., Raynes, B. and Wild, J. (2016) The effects of violence and aggression from parents on child protection workers' personal, family and professional lives. *Sage Open*, DOI: 10.1177/2158244015624951, 31 January.

Littlechild, B. with Mills, K. and Parkes R. (2020) *Working with Conflict in Social Work Practice*. London: Open University Press/McGraw-Hill Education.

Lloyd, L. and Sullivan, M.P. (2018) Ageing, ethics and social welfare: contemporary social work and social care practices with older people. *Ethics and Social Welfare*, 12 (3): 201–3.

Local Government Association (n.d.) Return to Social Work.

Local Government Association (2009) Transforming adult social care: access to information advice and advocacy.

Local Government Association (2017) Volunteering and social action and the Care Act: an opportunity for local government.

Local Government Association (2018) Meeting the health and wellbeing needs of young carers. Available at: www.local.gov.uk/sites/default/files/documents/LGA_Meeting%20the%20 health%20and%20wellbeing%20of%20young%20carers_22%2019_January%202018.pdf

Local Government and Social Care Ombudsman (LGSCO, updated 2021) Guidance on Good Practice: Remedies. Available at: file:///C:/Users/ms14adk/Downloads/Remedies%20guidance%20v10%20Jan%2021.pdf

London Safeguarding Children's Board (2015) Best practice for the implementation of child protection plans.

Lonne, B., Harries, M., Featherstone, B. and Gray, M. (2015) *Working Ethically in Child Protection*. Abingdon: Taylor & Francis.

Loopstra, R., Fledderjohann, J., Reeves, A. and Stuckler, D. (2018) Impact of welfare benefit sanctioning on food insecurity: a dynamic cross-area study of food bank usage UK. *Journal of Social Policy*, 24 January.

Lord Laming (2003) *The Victoria Climbié Inquiry: Report of an Inquiry by Lord Laming*. UK Government.

Lucy, R. (2016) Guidance on the use of voluntary accommodation ('section 20'). February 24: The Transparency Project.

Machin, R. (2017) Professional and ethical dilemmas of the two-child limit for child tax credit and universal credit. *Ethics and Social Welfare*, 11: 404–11.

Manthorpe, J. and Stevens, M. (2014) Adult safeguarding policy and law: a thematic chronology relevant to care homes and hospitals. *Social Policy and Society*.

Marczak, J., Wistow, G. and Fernández, J.-L. (2019) Evaluating social care prevention in England: challenges and opportunities. *Journal of Long-Term Care*, pp. 206–17.

Matthey, J. and McGrath-Lone, L. (2019) Educational outcomes of children in contact with social care in England: a systematic review. *Systematic Reviews*, 8 (155).

McCarthy, M., Clawson, R., Patterson, A., Fyson, R. and Khan, L. (2020) Risk of forced marriage amongst people with learning disabilities in the UK: perspectives of South Asian carers. JARID.

McNicoll, A. (2017) Service users give mixed verdict on Care Act's impact. *Community Care*.

Mental Health Foundation (2016) *Poverty and Mental Health: A Review to Inform the Joseph Rowntree Foundation's Anti-Poverty Strategy*. Available at: mentalhealth.org.uk/ Poverty and Mental Health.pdf

Ministry of Housing, Communities and Local Government (MHCLG) (2021) Homelessness code of guidance for local authorities.

Ministry of Justice (MOJ) (2010) *Green Paper Evidence Report Breaking the Cycle: Effective Punishment, Rehabilitation and Sentencing of Offenders*.

Ministry of Justice (MOJ) (2013) *Youth Out-of-Court Disposals: Guide for Police and Youth Offending Services*.

Ministry of Justice (MOJ) (2016) *Review of the Youth Justice System in England and Wales*.

Ministry of Justice (MOJ) (2018) *Referral Order Guidance*.

Ministry of Justice (MOJ) (2018) *Our Secure Schools Vision*. GOV.UK.

Ministry of Justice (MOJ) (2019) *Standards for Children in the Youth Justice System*.

Ministry of Justice (MOJ) (2020) *Assessing Risk of Harm to Children and Parents in Private Law Children Cases*.

Morris, K., Mason, W., Bywaters, P., Featherstone, B., Daniel, B., Brady, G., Bunting, L., Hooper, J., Mirza, N. Scourfield, J. and Webb, C. (2018) Social work, poverty, and child welfare interventions. *Child and Family Social Work*, 23 (3), 364–72.

National Audit Office (2017) Rolling out Universal Credit.

National FGM Centre (2016) The FGM assessment tool for social workers. Available at: nationalfgmcentre.org.uk/

National Health Service (NHS England) (2015) *Safeguarding Policy*. Available at: www.england.nhs.uk/publication/safeguarding-policy/

National Health Service (NHS) (2017) Next Steps on the NHS Five Year Forward View.

National Health Service (NHS) (2018) Overview – Learning disabilities.

National Health Service (NHS) (2018) Abuse and neglect of vulnerable adults.

National Health Service (NHS) (Digital) (2019) *Safeguarding Adults, England, 2019–2020*. Available at: www.digital.nhs.uk

National Health Service (NHS) (Digital) (2020) *Statistics on Smoking, England 2020*.

National Health Service (NHS) (2021) *Mental Capacity Act*.

National Health Service (NHS) (2021) Abuse and neglect of vulnerable adults. Available at: www.nhs.co.uk/social-care-support-guide/help-from-social-services-and-chrities/abuse-neglect-vulnerable-adults

National Institute for Health and Care Excellence (NICE) (2014) Managing medicines in care homes. Social care guideline (SC1).

National Society for Prevention of Cruelty to Children (NSPCC) (2014) Culture and faith: learning from case reviews: summary of risk factors and learning for improved practice around culture and faith.

National Statistics (2020) Characteristics of children in need.

Neil, E. (2013) The contact after adoption study: A longitudinal study of adoptive and birth parents (from 1996–2013). UEA/CRCF.

Norman, A. (2015) Concerns for a child's welfare can never justify illegal practice. *Community Care*.

Nuffield Family Justice Observatory (2019) Special guardianship: a review of the evidence.

Nuffield Trust (2019) Are patients benefitting from better integrated care?

Nuffield Trust (2020) Delayed transfers of care. May.

Nutt, D., King, L.A., Saulsbury, W. and Blakemore, C. (2007) Development of a rational scale to assess the harm of drugs of potential misuse. *The Lancet*, 369 (9566): 1047–53.

Office for National Statistics (ONS) (2016) Families and Households in the UK. Office for National Statistics.

Office for National Statistics (ONS) (2020) Domestic abuse prevalence and trends, England and Wales: year ending March 2020.

Office for National Statistics (ONS) (2020) Modern slavery in the UK. Available at: www.ons.gov.uk/articles/modernslaveryintheuk/march2020/pdf

Office for National Statistics (ONS) (2020) International migration and mobility: what's changed since the coronavirus (COVID-19) pandemic (November). Available at: ons.gov.uk/peoplepopulationandcommunity

Office of the Public Guardian (OPG) (n.d.) Making decisions: the Independent Mental Capacity Advocate (IMCA) service. OPG66.

Office of the Public Guardian (OPG) (2019) Guidance: how we deal with safeguarding concerns.

Ofsted (2019) Children's social care in England: Official Statistics.

Parsons, S. (2015) The loss of control defence – fit for purpose? *The Journal of Criminal Law*, 79 (2): 94–101.

Parton, N. (2014) *The Politics of Child Protection: Contemporary Developments and Future Directions*. Basingstoke: Macmillan Palgrave.

Payne, M. (2021) *Modern Social Work Theory* (5th edn). Oxford: Oxford University Press.

Penton-Glynne, (2016) Adoption without consent. European Parliament Directorate for Public Affairs, Policy Department C.

Phillimore, J. (ed.) (2015) *Migration and Social Policy*. London: Edward Elgar Publishing.

Phillimore, S. (2019) The government's family court's review will achieve nothing. *Community Care*, 24 May.

Preston-Shoot, M. (2003) A matter of record? *Social Work Action*, 15 (3).

Public Health England (PHE) (2018) Introduction to adverse childhood experiences.

Public Health England (PHE) (2018) Problem parental drug and alcohol use: a toolkit for local authorities.

Public Health England (PHE) (2020) Adult substance misuse treatment statistics 2019 to 2020: report.

Public Health England (PHE) (2020) Disparities in the risk of outcomes of COVID-19.

Reed, L. (2012) How to avoid humiliation when you're cross examined in court. *Community Care*.

Refugee Council (2021) Changes to immigration rules will prevent people seeking asylum in the UK.

Restorative Justice Council (RJC) (2015) Restorative justice in youth offending teams – information pack.

Ridge, T. (2015) *Children and Social Policy*. Oxford Bibliographies.

Robinson, D. (2013) Migration policy under the coalition government. *People, Place and Policy*, 7 (2): 73–81.

Royal College of Psychiatrists (2015) *Guide to Mental Health Tribunals*. Available at: rcpsych. ac.uk/mental-health/treatments-and-wellbeing/guide-to-mental-health-tribunals

Sabbagh, M. (2016) A lack of parental responsibility for young offenders? A developmental approach to the adolescent risk-taking stage. Ph.D. thesis.

Sabbagh, M. (2017) Restorative justice and black, Asian and minority ethnic children in the youth justice system: a restorative Justice Council research report. Restorative Justice Council.

Scobie, S. (2019) Are patients benefitting from better integrated care? Nuffield Trust.

Scobie, S. (2021) Covid-19 and the deaths of care home residents. London: Nuffield Trust.

Scope (n.d.) Disability facts and figures. Available at: scope.org.uk/media/disability-facts-figures

Scott, P.D. (1975) The tragedy of Maria Colwell. *The British Journal of Criminology*, 15 (1): 88–90, January.

Section E-DVILR (2020) Eligibility for indefinite leave to remain as a victim of domestic abuse immigration rules.

Seeleib-Kaiser, M. (2019) Migration, social policy, and power in historical perspective. *Global Social Policy*, 19 (3): 266–74.

Sentencing Council (2017) Sentencing children and young people. Available at: www. sentencingcouncil.org.uk/overarching-guides/magistrates-court/item/sentencing-children-and-young-people

Shelter (2019) This is England: A picture of homelessness in 2019. Available at: www.england. shelter.org.uk

Siddiqui, H.M., Kelly, L. and Rehman, Y. (2013) *Moving in the Shadows: Violence in the Lives of Minority Women and Children*. Farnham: Ashgate Publishing.

Smithson, R., Richardson, E., Roberts, J., Walshe, K., Wenzel, L., Robertson, R., Boyd, A., Allen, T. and Proudlove, N. (2018) *Impact of the Care Quality Commission on Provider Performance: Room for Improvement?* London: The King's Fund.

Social Metrics Commission (2018) A new measure of poverty for the UK.

Social Metrics Commission (2019) *Measuring Poverty*. A report of the Social Metrics Commission.

Social Work England (SWE) (2019a) *Professional Standards*. Available at: www.socialworkengland.org.uk/standards/professional-standards/

Social Work England (SWE) (2019b) *Professional Standards Guidance*. Available at: www.social-workengland.org.uk/standards/guidance-documents/professional-standards-guidance/

Spicker, P. (2021) *Poverty: An Introduction to Social Policy* (3rd edn). Bristol: Policy Press.

Stevenson, L. (2017) Special guardianship orders: are they being used safely? *Community Care*.

Stevenson, L. (2018) Attachment theory evidence not admissible in care order, judge rules. *Community Care*.

Stothart, C. (2014) Southern Cross-style collapse in care home market cannot be ruled out, warns study. 28 June. *Community Care*.

Strickland, P. (2017) *The Protection from the Harassment Act 1997*. Briefing paper no. 6648, 6 June. House of Commons Library.

Supreme Court (n.d.) The The Supreme Court and Europe. Available at: www.supremecourt. uk/about/the-supreme-court-and-europe.html

Szawarski, P. and Kakar, V. (2012) Classic cases revisited: Anthony Bland and withdrawal of artificial nutrition and hydration in the UK. *Journal of the Intensive Care Society*.

Szerletics, A. (2011) Vulnerable Adults and the Inherent Jurisdiction of the High Court: Essex Autonomy Project.

Timmins, N. (2017) The problems with Universal Credit. Institute for Government.

Trades Union Congress (TUC) (2020) Sick pay for all: how the Coronavirus has shown we need urgent reform of the sick pay system.

UK Parliament (1942) Beveridge Report. Available at: www.parliament.uk/about/living-heritage/transformingsociety/livinglearning/coll-9-health1/coll-9-health/

UK Parliament (2013) The Francis Report (Report of the Mid-Staffordshire NHS Foundation Trust public inquiry) and the Government's response.

UK Parliament (2019) How might Brexit affect human rights in the UK? Available at: https://commonslibrary.parliament.uk/how-might-brexit-affect-human-rights-in-the-uk/

UK Parliament (2021) Children's social care services in England. House of Commons Briefing Paper.

UK Parliament (2021) Coronavirus: Universal Credit during the Crisis (House of Commons Briefing Paper (January). UN Convention on the Rights of a Child (CRC) (2016) Concluding observations on the fifth periodic report of the United Kingdom of Great Britain and Northern Ireland.

UN Convention on the Rights of a Child (CRC) (2016) Concluding observations on the fifth periodic report of the United Kingdom of Great Britain and Northern Ireland. Available at: www.unicef.org.uk

UN Women (2020) Intersectional feminism: what it means and why it matters right now. New York: UN Women.

UNHCR (2002) Guidelines on International Protection No. 1: Gender-related persecution within the context of Article 1A(2) of the 1951 Convention and/or its 1967 Protocol relating to the Status of Refugees (HCR/GIP/02/01). Available at: unhcr.org.uk/publications/legal/3d58ddef4/guidelines-international-protection-1-gender-related-persecution-html

UNHCR (2004) Global refugee trends.

UNHCR (2017) Global trends: forced displacement in 2017.

UNHCR Refugee Agency (2004) Guidelines on International Protection: Religion-Based Refugee Claims under Article 1A(2) of the 1951 Convention and/or the 1967 Protocol relating to the Status of Refugees.

UNHCR Refugee Agency (2018) Global trends study. Available at: unhcr.org/uk/news-stories/2018/6/5b222c494/forced-displacement-record-685-million-html

UNHCR Refugee Agency (2019) *Handbook on Procedures and Criteria for Determining Refugee Status under the 1951 Convention and the 1967 Protocol relating to the Status of Refugees* (HCR/IP/4/Eng/REV.1. Re-edited Geneva, January 1992, UNHCR 1979, para. 80.

United Nations (n.d.) Department of Economic and Social Affairs: UN's Programme on Ageing. Available at: http://social.un.org/ageing/

University of Leeds (n.d.) Young people who refuse life sustaining treatment: a briefing paper on current law and the need for reform: School of Law.

Walker, A. (2018) A social policy on ageing to reduce the costs of old age, we must improve the entire life course. LSE blogs.

Walker, R. (n.d.) The English law of privacy – an evolving human right (supremecourt.uk/docs/speech_100825.pdf)

Ward, H., Brown, R. and Hyde-Dryden, G. (2014) Assessing parental capacity to change when children are on the edge of care: an overview of current research evidence. Research Report Centre for Child and Family Research. Loughborough University.

Watt, J. (2012) *Report Writing for Social Workers* (Post-Qualifying Social Work Practice Guides). London: Learning Matters.

Webb, C. and Bywaters, P. (2018) Austerity, rationing and inequity: trends in children's and young peoples' services expenditure in England between 2010 and 2015. Local Government Studies.

Wesseley, S. (2019) Modernising the Mental Health Act: increasing choice, reducing compulsion.

Which? (2019) Later Life Care: Deferred payment agreements and the property disregard (19 December).

Wilkins, D. (2017) Writing court reports: Community Care Practice Guidance.

Williams W. (2020) The Windrush lessons learned independent review (HC 93).

Wilson, K., Ruch, G., Lymbery, M. and Cooper, A. (eds) (2011) *Social Work: An Introduction to Contemporary Practice* (2nd edn). London: Pearson Education.

Women's Budget Group and Runnymede Trust (2017) Intersecting Inequalities: the impact of austerity on Black and Minority Ethnic Women in the UK. Available at: www.wbg.org.uk/wp-content/uploads/2018/08/intersecting-inequalities-October-2017-Full-Report.pdf

Wood, M. and Selwyn, J. (2015) *Children and Young People's Views of Being in Care*. Bristol: University of Bristol.

World Health Organization (WHO) (2021) Elder abuse. Available at: www.who.int/news-room/fact-sheets/detail/elder-abuse

Youth Justice Board (2015) Keeping children in care out of trouble: an independent review chaired by Lord Laming: response by the Youth Justice Board for England and Wales to the call for views and evidence.

Youth Justice Board (2020) Youth Justice Statistics 2019/20.

Youth Justice Board for England and Wales (2019) How to use out of court disposals. Available at: www.gov.uk/government/publications/how-to-use-out-of-court-disposals

Index